# HONORED
## —AND—
# BETRAYED

## IRANGATE, COVERT AFFAIRS, AND THE SECRET WAR IN LAOS

## Richard Secord
### with Jay Wurts

**John Wiley & Sons, Inc.**
New York • Chichester • Brisbane • Toronto • Singapore

In recognition of preserving what has been written, it is a policy of John Wiley & Sons, Inc., to have books of enduring value printed on acid-free paper, and we exert our best efforts to that end.

**Library of Congress Cataloging-in-Publication Data:**

Secord, Richard V.
  Honored and betrayed : Irangate, covert affairs, and the secret war in Laos / Richard Secord with Jay Wurts.
    p.    cm.
  Includes index.
  ISBN 0-471-57328-0
  1. Iran-Contra Affair, 1985–1990. 2. Vietnamese War, 1961–1975—Campaigns—Laos. 3. Intelligence service—United States—History—20th century. 4. Secord, Richard V. I. Wurts, Jay. II. title.
E876.S4 1992
973.927—dc20                                                    92-18436

Printed in the United States of America

10  9  8  7  6  5  4  3  2  1

The Tribunes brought up the old charges ... which were based more on suspicions than on evidence. They accused him of peculation; they alleged that ... he had been a dictator rather than a subordinate ... that his nod was the equivalent of senatorial decrees and the decisions of the popular assembly. Thus they assailed with spiteful calumny a man untouched by any ill repute.

—Livy, On the Trial of Scipio Africanus

To my 22 comrades of the 1st Air Commando Wing killed in action during *Operation Farmgate*, Southeast Asia, 1962–64.

# — Preface —

Memory is a poor soldier until it's trained. At West Point, I was taught the difference between useful information and mental clutter. As a fledgling Air Force pilot, and later in combat, I learned pretty fast that ignorance kills more quickly than anything else, including the enemy. Detailed to the CIA, I learned, too, that knowledge is power and without it, the game is over before it starts. As Bill Casey used to say, "If you have to write things down, you don't belong in this business." But only in Washington did I discover the bureaucratic art of "forgetting," and I have to admit, I never developed a taste or aptitude for it.

This book is the product of what I believe to be a reasonably disciplined mind kept sharp from a lifetime of constant drill. Like many people who've had to depend on accurate recollections for survival, I use a variety of memory-aiding tricks: from military-style mnemonics to keywords and images that release torrents of detail. But people aren't computers and my memory is far from photographic. Just before the Iran-Contra Congressional hearings in 1987, I put a lot of my recollections onto tapes so that whatever I knew about that strangest of episodes—and other important but unreported bits of contemporary American history I've been privy to—wouldn't be lost. Documentation for much of what you'll find in this book exists in my personal files or in records kept by the principals involved. Some of what I have to say has been made public, although much of it has been confused and distorted by the press. A lot has never before been divulged. The truth isn't fussy about how she gets to the party, but she always shows up eventually.

When documentation exists for an important new fact, I'll tell you where you can find it. If an assertion pits my word against another's, I'll tell you that, too, and let you decide who you want to believe. In some cases, I've had to give real people pseudonyms; a cheap price to pay when you consider the alternative: deleting an important part of his story.

If I remember a particular event in vivid detail, it's because whatever happened made a big impression on me. If I couldn't recall exactly what was said or how things happened, I'll give you the gist of the conversation and my best estimate of how things went down. Seldom do I rely on second- or third-hand information or controversial information from single sources. I've never been in a business where that was a good idea, and writing this book was no exception.

# — Contents —

Prologue: Mission to Tehran     1

**I   The Making of a Hot-War Warrior**     **7**

1   Duty, Honor, Country     9
2   To Fly and Fight     17
3   Vietnam Before the Crowd     29
4   Winning the War Nobody Heard Of     44
5   CIA Station Laos     52
6   Disaster at Site 85     74

**II   Crusades in the Puzzle Palace**     **93**

7   Merry Christmas, Uncle Ho     95
8   Iran Before the Fall     112
9   The Raid That Never Happened     142
10   Where No GI Has Gone Before     166

**III   High Noon in the Cold War**     **181**

11   CBS Strikes Back     183
12   "Hello Dick, This Is Ollie . . ."     198
13   Iran Redux     218
14   Bear Any Burden . . .     265
15   . . . Oppose Any Foe     287
16   No Good Deed Goes Unpunished     318

Epilogue     353
Appendixes     361
Acknowledgments     393
Index     395

# HONORED
## — AND —
# BETRAYED

# — Prologue —

# Mission to Tehran

For over a year, the United States and Israel had been secretly courting a small group of Iranian revolutionaries to arrange a high-level, government-to-government meeting. We'd traded missile parts and promises for one last chance to recoup our influence in this vital strategic region. Now, after a dismal record of fits and starts, a date for the meeting had been set. At midnight, May 25, 1986, President Reagan's personal envoy, Robert (Bud) McFarlane, and his party would depart Tel Aviv secretly for their proverbial "dance with the devil."

Unfortunately, we had two problems. One was small, like the other snafus and annoyances that had made President Reagan's Iran Initiative one long headache since its inception in 1985. The other was big enough to blow the entire operation sky-high: the meeting was to be held in Tehran.

In the middle of its long and bloody war with Iraq, with "Death to America" still echoing through its streets and the specter of our embassy hostages still fresh in everyone's mind, Tehran was no place for an ex–National Security Advisor or anyone else with a Yankee passport. I had led and planned many covert operations in my time, from Laos and Vietnam to the Middle East, but this one felt all wrong. It was a disaster waiting to happen.

By comparison, our "small problem" seemed like child's play. Shortly after Manucher Ghorbanifar (code named "Gorba"), our slippery Iranian middleman, made a $15 million mid-May deposit to finance the next shipment of antiaircraft missile spare parts to Iran, he told Israeli Counter-Terrorism Chief Amiram Nir (the "Israeli Oliver North") that the Iranian government now demanded two additional I-HAWK radars. It seemed like more welshing on a done deal, but that had become standard procedure for Gorba and his Iranian contacts. With McFarlane's secret trip looming like a squall on the horizon, Gorba's greed was the last of my worries. I had promised

1

Ollie North I would be the President's "operations officer" on this most secret of covert programs. Now, come hell or high water, I was the guy who had to make it happen.

On May 22nd and 23rd, Southern Air Transport, Inc., or SAT, cargo planes arrived in Tel Aviv from Texas with the I-HAWK spares and 508 replacement TOWs—wire-guided antitank missiles—we owed Israel from an earlier transaction. I arrived in Tel Aviv from Geneva late on the 23rd, as did the two elite SAT crews I'd picked to fly our chartered, unmarked, and "sanitized" Israeli 707s to Tehran.

These pilots test-flew our aircraft the next day, astounding even the battle-hardened Israeli instructors with their airmanship. If anybody could nurse a commercial jet over a demanding 10-hour flight plan, avoiding Arab airspace while evading numerous air defense systems and Iraqi fighters, it was Paul Gilcrist, captain of McFarlane's flight, and Lyn Toodle, pilot of the backup plane. These guys weren't just the best special ops pilots in the business; they were magicians in the air.

Bud, Ollie North, George Cave (our suave CIA advisor), and Howard Teicher (like North, a National Security Council staffer), plus two CIA communications men and their gear, arrived from Germany on the 25th via CIA aircraft. I took them straight to the Carlton Hotel near the beach, where they prepared for a midnight departure.

McFarlane, whose face had appeared almost nightly on worldwide television as Reagan's National Security Advisor, was my biggest security problem. Though he had been out of the public eye for five months, I felt I had to keep him under wraps at all times. Howard Teicher was almost as well known in Israel, so the first thing I did when he checked into the Carlton was to politely remind him to keep his hands off the phone. With a possible one-way ticket to Tehran, Howard's temptation to say goodbye to local friends just might prove to be too great.

Amiram Nir, the ruggedly handsome Israeli agent, posed a different problem. The public knew him not only as a campaign staffer for Shimon Peres, but also through his past career as a television journalist. Fortunately, Ami was a pro and knew that Israel had as much to gain from the Iran Initiative as the United States. He voluntarily dyed his hair grey—enough to discourage curious glances—and kept his profile low. There were a thousand ways the McFarlane mission could go wrong, but a mistake by Ami Nir just wasn't one of them.

At about 9 P.M., I alerted our Israeli security detail and took Bud's delegation for a "last supper" at a nearby seafood restaurant, where we dined on crab, fresh-fried "whitebait," and chilled Israeli wine. The group was talkative but reflective. When the nervous chatter died down, we just watched the Mediterranean waves lap quietly on the moonlit beach. Most of our guys had seen combat before. They knew about that time of silence before a battle when one can focus one's energy and relax his grip on the outside world of wives, children, and tomorrow.

I, however, had other reasons for enjoying the full moon.

On past covert missions to Iran, improper Israeli maintenance had caused problems with our aircraft's radar and OMEGA electronic navigation over the Red Sea. Tonight's full moon would help Paul keep his plane over international waters visually. He'd have enough to worry about once he got to Iran—the last thing we needed was an international incident along the way. I prayed the weather, like our good luck with security, would continue to hold.

After dinner, I chatted with Ollie in his room while he got ready to move out. The boyish, jug-eared Marine had a bag full of gifts for their Iranian hosts, including five trophy-style .357 Magnum Blackhawk revolvers in presentation cases purchased by a member of my staff.

"You didn't bring ammo for these cannons, did you?" I asked, hefting a weapon.

Ollie gave me one of his patented gap-toothed grins. "Hell, no!"

The delegation's chance of facing the business end of an Iranian firing squad was bad enough without our bringing along the bullets.

Ollie mentioned he'd bought a cake from the Israelis. I guessed it was for the junior Iranian officials not worthy of ceremonial weapons. Since I never saw it, I can't say if it was shaped like a key (as later reported) or a cake or the Statue of Liberty. But I did know how aircrews liked to snack on long missions. Without saying it, I gave the cake about as much chance as the delegation of surviving the flight unscathed.

Despite my many years in covert operations and dealing with international security matters at the highest level, I was the operations man, not a policymaker. That was my biggest frustration. I had already put in my two cents and told Bud, Ollie, and John Poindexter, McFarlane's replacement at the White House, that I thought the trip was a mistake. But until the mission was actually under way, the decision to scrub it just wasn't mine to make.

A second Israeli security squad arrived at 11:15 P.M. to take us to the airport. Before we left, I briefed Bud's party on the security arrangements I'd made—what would happen if any of a dozen misfortunes befell the mission en route or after its arrival in Tehran. I then went through their personal effects, confiscating U.S. passports, billfolds, and any other "pocket litter" (key chains, coins, documents) that might reveal the owner's place of origin. It was an old ritual in covert operations, but one that always tightened my throat. The only papers I let them keep were Bud's "talking points" he'd need at the high-level meeting, assuming the mission got that far, and the Irish passports Ghorbanifar insisted they carry—as if those would fool anyone but the most credulous customs official.

If anybody had CIA-issued cyanide pills on that flight, as has been reported, I never saw them. You don't carry stuff like that in your suitcase, and I patted them down pretty good. I suppose that's one of those apocryphal stories that blooms after fertilizer gets applied to the facts. Everyone from President Reagan on down would take a lot of heat if someone with a headful of secrets like Bud McFarlane fell into enemy hands. I was surprised the "armchair commandos" in the press never made much hay about that, but it sure bothered me that night.

The security detachment took us directly to the 707, sitting on the ramp like a giant bird of prey—cockpit lights blazing like the eyes of an eagle, auxiliary power unit screeching defiantly into the night. Paul and his crew had already gone over the plane, looking for sabotage, malfunctions, and stray Israeli markings, and were checking things again. Satellite photos confirmed the weather en route was excellent. Given their long detour south of Israel—over the Red Sea and around the Arabian peninsula, stretching the 707's range to the limit—they'd need all the help they could get.

Before Paul and his copilot strapped in, I wished them all good luck, took a last glance around the cabin, and then stepped back into the warm Israeli night. Descending the stairs, I heard the pressure door seal behind me like the lid to a crypt.

As the aircraft taxied out, I felt the same sense of helplessness and foreboding I'd felt when I sent my aircrews—USAF, Air America, and allied—into combat over Laos some 20 years before. Then, I was a young staff officer—an Air Force major and combat veteran detailed to the CIA to fight a war my country wouldn't acknowledge. Now, I was a retired two-star general with a hell of a lot more flying time, battles, and crises behind me—but that gut-wrenching question was always the same: Had I done all that *could* be done to give our guys the best possible chance of coming back? Had I complained loudly enough, banged on the right desks in Washington, to make my worries known?

Then, as now, there was no clear answer. Our guarantee for the delegation's safety came mainly from our middleman, Ghorbanifar, whom Bud himself described as "the most despicable man I've ever met." Because of Tehran's remoteness and the country's wartime footing, even the 82nd Airborne Division—assuming it had been ready—wouldn't be able to get them out. In fact, ever since our original plan to hold the meeting on Kish Island, in the lap of our own Indian Ocean fleet, had been scrapped, no contingency plans for a rescue had been authorized, nor were any practical. In my view, that was potentially the biggest blunder of the whole Iran Initiative. It was the thought that tormented me as the 707 lined up for takeoff.

The mission was finally under way. As Operations Chief, I could abort it if I wanted to. Nothing Bud, Ollie, or Ami could say would override my decision. And I was a gnat's eyelash away from doing just that.

Instead, I just gritted my teeth and watched the big jet surge down the runway, engines roaring.

*There is a tide in the affairs of men*, Shakespeare's Brutus said, *which, taken at the flood, leads on to fortune.* Sadly, I remembered what happened to Brutus.

Just before the sweep second hand on my watch passed 2400 hours, the nosewheel lifted off. Seconds later, the main gear followed and retracted into the big ship's belly. The great roar became a rumble, and the four glowing red specks that bore my friends and the hopes of two great nations disappeared into the night.

# —I—

# The Making of a Hot-War Warrior

# — 1 —

# Duty, Honor, Country

Laura Secord was a spy. A nineteenth-century French-Canadian relative, she managed to slip through American lines during the War of 1812 and warn the British of an impending Yankee attack, becoming a Canadian national heroine in the process. Since then, my family's allegiance has slipped south of the 49th parallel, but that sense of obligation to one's country seems to persist as a family trait.

My grandfather, Vernon, a second-generation American who gave me my middle name, was an artist in brick and stone, making masterwork fireplaces, hearths, and chimneys. As it is with many endeavors, his artistry lay hidden in the details. I learned an early appreciation for this, carrying hod for him as a kid during World War II. His once-thriving business was wrecked by the Great Depression, so his only real legacy to my father, Lowell Secord, and me was a strong sense of craftsmanship: a conviction that whatever we did should be the best that we could make it. My father carried that principle into the trucking business he started, and I suppose I made it a religion in my career.

I was born just after Independence Day, on July 6, 1932, in the little town of LaRue, Ohio. Two and a half years later, my sister Sandra was born, and a couple of years after that, my brother Jim. Our mother, Wahneta, was a Quaker orphan. By tradition and conviction, her family always came first. As the oldest child, my job was to help her keep things together, no matter what was going on around us. It's the kind of training—sense of responsibility—you get only in a close-knit family.

By the time I was old enough to notice things like toys, clothes, and furniture, the local bank had already failed. The whole community was suffering from the Crash of 1929, so my family's poverty was nothing unusual. Because my dad usually found work, we always had enough to eat, but cash was scarce. He introduced me to guns at an early age, and we'd hunt rabbits and game birds to help put food on the table. People usually find a way to take care of themselves as long as they're given a free hand to do it.

On these outings, my father talked constantly about how important it was for me to make something of myself. The Depression had robbed him of his own chance to go to college, and he was determined that the same thing wouldn't happen to me—although we both knew it would be just about impossible for a part-time teamster to put a son through school. That's when he started talking about the service academies, which were (and still are) the only first-class colleges that pay *you* to go to school. One of our neighbors, a fellow about my father's age, had been appointed to West Point and was a legend in our little town. My dad liked the way the military rewarded merit and could think of no higher calling—or honor—for his son.

"If you're smart enough and persistent enough and have some guts," he used to say, "you'll get in."

He never pressured me, but encouraged me to the point that, by the time I was 12 or 13 and old enough to really think about such things, I swore I would get there no matter what.

When World War II started, we moved to Marion, Ohio, where my dad took a job as a welder at a defense plant. My main escape from class and after-school jobs was going to the movies. I liked war pictures but for completely different reasons than most boys my age. I didn't watch them so much for the blood-and-guts violence, but for the details of military life and human struggles they portrayed.

After VJ Day in 1945, economic pressures and the effects of an often-disrupted family life finally took their toll, and my parents were divorced. All of us kids were shocked, but I probably felt it worst, being the oldest and a kind of "corporal" to my mom's Top Sergeant. Our goal had been to keep the family together all through the Great Depression, and I viewed their breakup as personal failure. I suppose every kid feels a little responsible when his or her parents divorce, and I was no exception.

In 1947 we relocated to Columbus, Ohio, because my mom believed big-city high schools would prepare me better for college. She never warmed to the idea of my attending a service academy. Whether she just didn't understand military life or disapproved of it because of her Quaker convictions, I never knew. Whatever her reasons, she never held the armed services in quite as high a regard as my father did, who continued to "preach the gospel" whenever I saw him, which was as often as I could. He even managed to get a private pilot's license from the CAA—the old Civil Aviation Administration—and gave me my first ride in an airplane, an old Aeronca. He couldn't afford to fly much, but he loved it, and that early enthusiasm for a military career and the joy of flying contributed a lot to my later success.

The postwar economy made life a little better, but we never quite made it to Easy Street. I worked part-time as an usher in the local Loew's theater and pulled in the then-princely sum of 40 cents an hour, which I put away toward college. There were no student loans in those days, so if you didn't have a nest egg, well-to-do parents, or a good part-time job, even state universities were out of reach.

After an early graduation from high school, I wrote to our congressman, Republican James Vorys, for information about an appointment to West Point. He responded with a schedule for competitive Civil Service exams, which I took, scoring high enough to be tagged third alternate for a place in the class beginning in July 1950. Both of the guys ahead of me flunked the screening physical, which I passed with flying colors. To my surprise and delight—and my dad's great pride—I was named the primary candidate from our district.

Unfortunately, a congressional appointment and physical qualification are only the first steps on a very steep and slippery road to a bunk at any service academy. In 1950, candidates for West Point had to pass the academic entrance exams, and that big trip to New York—my first ever out of Ohio—left me so bug-eyed with excitement that I could hardly read the questions. That lack of sophistication affected my performance; after passing everything else, I narrowly flunked the math exam.

After my big send-off, I was crushed; but I was also mad as hell. I wanted to please my dad, who looked to me to fulfill that part of the American dream that had passed him by. But after flunking the test, I discovered how much I was also doing this for myself. I didn't like losing—*at all.*

I vowed that West Point would hear from me again.

I went back to Columbus and parlayed my minor celebrity and high school diploma into a job as assistant manager at my old theater. I could now work full-time, and, owing to the golden age of cinema, the postwar vaudeville revival, and the big-name big bands that came to town—Harry James, Benny Goodman, Tommy Dorsey—I made more money than I thought existed. Loew's was a particularly successful chain, and I was quickly promoted to "roving" relief assistant manager, entrusted with disbursing cash advances to some of the road-show performers who couldn't wait for their portion of the gate to pay their bills. To my friends I was a real high roller, and I was impressed with myself, although I remained, in fact, a kid of 18 with no college and a growing grudge against math—a secret score that, one day, I was bound to settle.

A year later, in March 1951, the Korean War had broken out, and I wrote to Congressman Vorys about reapplying to West Point. He replied that I could stand on my earlier Civil Service scores, which were pretty strong, so I decided to focus all my energy on blitzing the Academy's math test. The big risk, of course, was that somebody among the new crop of candidates would beat me on the Civil Service exam, but that was a chance I had to take—the first of many in a career filled with calculated risks. As it turned out, that first big gamble paid off.

On July 3, 1951, to my great satisfaction, I entered West Point as a plebe with the class of 1955.

I arrived at the Point with over 800 aspiring brother officers and was shown at once to the "Beast Barracks," traditional home to new cadets, and some of the most intense hazing servicemen can see this side of a POW camp. Two recent events had conspired to make our experience at the Academy even more grueling than usual. First was the infamous "cribbing" scandal that erupted the month we arrived. Ninety cadets had been expelled for cheating, including most of the football team and its quarterback.

Someone in authority at the Academy decided that the failure hadn't been due to overaggressiveness, but rather to some fault of character; and nothing (in the military mind, at least) builds character like a little hardship— so a lot of hardship must be better. Boy, did we build character over the next four years!

The second event had been the virtual annihilation of "Black '50"—the class of 1950, which had taken enormous losses in Korea. Although armies often glamorize costly disasters as heroic, they're less apt to do so when it's labeled a scandal by *Life* magazine and politicians start clamoring for a congressional investigation.

What actually happened to Black '50 was simple and, in retrospect, easily foreseen. After World War II, "Give 'em Hell" Harry Truman had allowed an unconscionable RIF (reduction in force) in which the veteran officer corps that had achieved historic victories in Germany and the Pacific was allowed to dwindle to near prewar levels—this at a time when we were playing a much larger role in world affairs than in the 1930s. When the balloon went up in Korea, second lieutenants from the class of 1950 were whisked out to take charge of undermanned, underequipped frontline platoons in actions that would have tested even hardened combat commanders. The problem wasn't so much that the new graduates were unprepared, it was just that platoon leadership is universally recognized as about the most dangerous job in warfare, with inordinately high casualties even when the odds are in your favor. Predictably, the class of 1950 was nearly wiped out.

Predictable, too, was the Army's reaction: Ignore the real lesson (keeping an adequate supply of veteran officers at hand) and instead make every cadet combat-ready by the day of graduation. This meant not just competency with infantry weapons and tactics, but inculcation of a "killer's mentality."

Because of these two factors, 1951–52 was by far the worst year of my life. Unofficial polls of later graduating classes show that these Lacedaemonian reforms eventually went the way of most military overreactions and faded away. But we who had to live with them at the time went through hell.

Beast Barracks traditions were aimed at breaking down a plebe's civilian sense of self-worth. These included such stressful indignities as the "shower formation" (an intimidating, buck naked, open-ranks inspection), the "fourth classman meal" (breakfast, lunch, and dinner eaten strictly by the book, including the way we swallowed), and taking "plebe routes" (following the walls, making square corners when we turned, and double-timing it everywhere). Our only respite was the classroom—our lifeline to the rational world—and most of us took advantage of it by really applying ourselves to the hard-core engineering curriculum demanded of every cadet.

The goal of all this was to train officers who could perform under great pressure, act precisely, and realize that even little mistakes can have grave consequences. They also cultivated the reflex of making small privileges (like walking, instead of marching, to class) or symbolic gestures (like ribbons and decorations) seem like big rewards, which is a trait the Army shares with most big organizations that need to discipline and motivate people in large numbers.

We lost almost half our class in the first year, which is how the system is supposed to work. Unlike civilian schools that have a vested interest in milking tuition as a source of income, the service academies want to pare an entering class down as soon as possible to those who have an iron will to succeed.

On the plus side, we had some of the best instructors of any school, anywhere in the world. Our academic and Tactical (TAC) instructors nearly all saw action in World War II or Korea, and there was nothing hypothetical about their courses. We learned combat engineering from a man who helped to build the pontoon assault bridge at Remagen. We learned tank warfare from a staff officer who helped plan Patton's counteroffensive at the Battle of the Bulge. These were guys who had been down "in the mud and the blood and the beer," and you could hear a pin drop during their lectures. Their experience made the postwar era a real golden age at West Point, which paid dividends in every conflict from Vietnam to Desert Storm. In a very real way, our class and the classes of the next decade were the recipients of the most important "data dump" in history, learning hard-won lessons from both the last big conventional war and the first hot conflict of the new nuclear age.

Everybody knows that the Point (like most good schools) is very competitive, but most people don't realize how unrelenting, widespread, deeply ingrained, and intense that competition really is. Class rankings didn't appear just at graduation, but were posted every 30 days, and included not just academics, but points for "military bearing," "athletic prowess," and a dozen other subjective factors assessed by your TAC officer and peers. If you think television networks are obsessed with their ratings, you should see how some of our cadets reacted to dropping a notch or two in the monthly rankings.

It made some of us reach inside ourselves for resources we didn't know we had (which was the whole point); but it taught others simply to play the system, to focus on what was evaluated like politicians playing to the polls. That was a career skill, too, but most of us wouldn't know it until we got to the Pentagon.

Because of the legacy of "Black '50," we got more than our share of combat training—vastly more than many commissioned officers receive in a career. We didn't just go out to the local weapons range and monkey around with mortars. We went to the places where the real business was done: to Fort Knox to drive tanks; to Fort Sill to fire cannon; to Forts Bragg and Benning to learn how to lead and survive on a battlefield and parachute out of aircraft and land, fully armed, ready for battle. We went to Little Creek, Virginia, to make amphibious landings with the Marines, ending in a full-scale beachhead assault under the proud (but undoubtedly still-smarting) eyes of our commander in chief, President Truman. When it came to combat demolition, we didn't just study with experts; we built the damn bridges ourselves, and then blew them up. By the time we graduated, I believe we could've taken on a regiment of regular troops from any army in the world.

One place that tests this combat spirit regularly is corps athletics. Because of the cribbing scandal, most of Army's 1951 football team were freshmen, which didn't stop us from beating a powerhouse squad from Cal in Yankee Stadium during a blinding snowstorm. We called our intramural sports the "intramurder" program because the accent was on dealing out and absorbing punishment as much as putting points on the board.

At five foot eight, I was too short to compete in most team sports, so I wound up going out for boxing, which I already knew something about. I was no "Rocky," but guts counted as much as footwork, and Coach Harold "Punchy" Creighton groomed me for the varsity squad, where I fought for three years. Looking back, I should've been suspicious of any boxing coach named Punchy. I fought in one of the lighter weight classes (below 138 pounds), which was fine for my height but all wrong for my metabolism, which always liked to store a few extra pounds for survival purposes, and still does. Consequently, I was often matched against guys with a longer reach, which works in boxing about as well as it does with bombers and battleships. I finished my last fight with half an eyelid hanging over my cheek, and the first thing the Army surgeon asked when he saw me was, "What assignment do you want when you graduate?"

I answered, "Air Force flight school, if they'll take me," because that's how the just-established USAF got most of its regular officers in those days— volunteers from the other services. A recent ride in a jet trainer during a field trip to Eglin AFB, Florida, as well as those hours spent droning around in my dad's Aeronca, had convinced me that was the way to go. It's not that I disliked soldiering; I just liked flying better.

"Okay," he said, stitching my face back together, "then you'll have to hang up the gloves. You can't take any chances with a pilot's best asset: a good pair of eyes."

I took his advice and have never regretted it.

The high point of our four years at West Point was marching in President Eisenhower's inaugural parade in 1953. We all felt enormously proud passing in review before the leader of the Normandy Invasion—the Supreme Commander of all Allied forces in the biggest war, and the biggest victory, ever conducted on the planet—and only the second West Pointer to be elected president. Believe me, we looked and marched our best and didn't need any upperclassmen to tell us to do it.

Eisenhower returned the favor on June 3, 1955 by coming up to West Point to speak at our graduation and hand out our diplomas. Our graduation was also the occasion for a reunion of Ike's class, and the parade ground literally sprouted general's flags. They called his class of 1915 "the class the stars fell on" because so many graduates became general officers, including Omar Bradley—who, like Ike, became a five-star general. Every one of us who shook Ike's hand that day hoped a little of that stardust would rub off on him; and for a few of us, it did.

I graduated 163rd out of a class of 490—in the top third by virtue of a little luck and a lot of math tutoring. This was fortunate because operational assignments were parceled out each March according to class standing. Cadets wore dress greys and gathered in the auditorium (so that there was room for spectators) and, beginning with the top-ranked cadet, stood and shouted, "Sir, I choose . . ." and named whatever branch of the service they had selected from the allocations remaining on the blackboard. A lot of America's military history began this way, and everyone in my class felt the significance of the moment.

In 1955, many of the top cadets went into infantry, especially airborne, but armor was deemed more desirable because of the glamour of "cavalry"— cutting through the enemy with bold strokes, which is what tank warfare was supposed to be about. Either armor or infantry could give you the career boost you needed, because most West Pointers dream about commanding large numbers of troops in battle, and those branches were where you found the big battalions. The more intellectual cadets often chose the signal corps or combat engineers because Uncle Sam sent them straight on to graduate school. My academics weren't bad, and I toyed with this option myself but couldn't really envision spending five or six years—let alone a whole career— tending to the nation's canals and waterways.

When my turn came to call out my branch, I, along with four others from my company, chose Air Force. This brought us to the immediate attention of our company TAC Officer, then Captain Alexander Haig, Jr., who "invited" us into his office individually for a very private pep talk.

"What the *hell* do you think you're doing?" this lecture went in my case. "You think we gave you the best damned combat training any soldier anywhere in the history of the world has ever received just to go fly around like the birds? I just don't understand it!"

Al Haig—the future commander of NATO, Secretary of State, and man briefly "in charge" of the country following President Reagan's trip to the trauma ward—had been a company commander in Korea and an aide to a general in charge of a corps. The top brass chose only the cream of the crop for West Point assignments, so everyone knew he was on a fast-track career. He was also a man who, although being extremely tough, had always been fair with us, so I had no complaints. If the Point makes you good at one thing, it's getting chewed out. He just couldn't accept pilot-officers as real warriors—leaders of men in battle. He wasn't biased against the Air Force, I think, just baffled by us.

But West Point also makes you pretty good at standing up for what you believe in and going ahead with what's right.

Captain Haig administered the officer's oath to our company's new graduates and pinned on my second lieutenant's bars—the heaviest gold ingots any young soldier can wear—and, still shaking his head, shook my hand and wished me good luck.

As things turned out, I would need every bit of it.

# —2—

# To Fly and Fight

For a bunch of would-be screaming eagles, USAF's Pilot Class 56 Tango—the 20th class of fledgling fliers to be trained in 1956—started off low and slow.

In those days, Air Force pilots began their careers in Piper Cubs, the little civilian tail-draggers you can still see in the sunny skies over most of the United States. We were so green, we weren't even deemed ready to try the patience of military flight instructors, so (as is still the case today) primary training was conducted by civilians on contract to the government.

Our school was located at Marianna, Florida. Its main purpose was to teach basic airmanship skills while eliminating those students who were prone to airsickness, claustrophobia, spatial disorientation, and a dozen other maladies you just can't detect until you fly—and don't want to discover in bigger, more demanding airplanes.

Of the 80 or so student pilots in '56-T, half were officers, like me, from the service academies or ROTC. The other half were "aviation cadets"—uncommissioned candidates who were undergoing basic officer training while in flight school, standard procedure for the old Army Air Corps during World War II. Having just finished a much rougher stint as a cadet at the Point, my heart went out to those poor guys who had to put up with military orientation and physical conditioning while they were trying to accustom themselves to the equally unfamiliar and often intimidating environment of the cockpit.

After 40 hours in Cubs (with about the same airmanship training that civilians got for a private pilot's license), we moved on to basic flight training in the Air Force T-6G "Texan": the sturdy, conventional gear, radial engine aircraft with the "birdhouse" canopy used since the early 1940s to introduce student pilots to true military flying, including formation. This was also our first exposure to "complex" aircraft—those with variable pitch props and

17

retractable landing gear. We lost a few more students at this stage who had trouble "rubbing their bellies and patting their heads" at the same time.

The Air Force likes to think that college kids make better pilots, especially in high-performance aircraft where intelligence and judgment count as much as good coordination, sharp eyes, and a killer instinct—and maybe they're right. My experience, though, has shown that a lot of truly *great* pilots have come from the ranks of the "partially educated." There's more to flying a jet than the data in the flight manual, and, for every college grad I've seen washed out of flight school with a surprised look on his face, I've seen a so-called mustang (officer commissioned on merit or after Officer Candidate School) graduate and go on to become a superior combat flier and even commander. No group has a monopoly on talent. Motivation to fly and fight can make up for a lot of courses in accounting and French literature.

In the winter of 1956, half our remaining class went on to multiengine training in venerable B-25s. These pilots were slated for SAC, the Strategic Air Command, which had entered its glory days and was consuming pilots with a voracious appetite; or MATS, the Military Air Transport Service, now the Military Airlift Command, the Air Force's not-so-mini airline that hauls personnel and equipment to our military installations around the world.

Thank God, I wasn't with this group.

Military pilots have always tended to divide themselves (foolishly, perhaps) into two camps—the hot sticks who fly fighters, and everybody else: an argument you can hear at any officer's club bar. I never really subscribed to the underlying premise of these arguments, though, that the airplane makes the pilot. Some airplanes are harder to fly than others, but all are equally difficult to fly really well. Good pilots know that, and you can find them in any sort of cockpit.

The main issue to me was really one of self-reliance and personal initiative rather than skill. Big bombers and tactical transports can fly harrowing combat missions, and I'm the first to admire the skill and courage of their crews. But the pilot in command doesn't work alone. He's got anywhere from a few to a dozen warm bodies to worry about as well as his own. And big airplanes in flight are a lot like ships at sea—with lots of power and control systems to worry about—and, let's face it, a speedboat is just more fun to skipper than an oil tanker. In a fighter, your decisions are your own. You succeed or bust your butt because of personal resourcefulness, skill, self-discipline, and daring, and to me that's what flying is all about, particularly military flying and *especially* flying in combat.

At any rate, that part of my class escaping the gentlemanly world of multiengines went to a variety of single-engine jet bases for advanced flight training. After another 40 hours in the T-28 (the last big reciprocating, fighter-type trainer the military built), I was assigned to fly Lockheed T-33s at Greenville AFB in Mississippi.

In those days, turbine engines weren't too reliable, and it was something of an accomplishment just to finish the jet program with an equal number of takeoffs and landings. What made engine failure so dangerous in those early jets was the airplane's relatively high wings-level stalling speed—the airspeed at which the airplane simply quits flying and becomes uncontrollable—especially in an emergency landing.

Making a forced landing in a Piper Cub, for example, is like taking your foot off the gas pedal and letting your car run off the road onto a soft shoulder—a little scary, perhaps, but at 40 or 50 knots, no big deal if you pick the right spot. Even the old T-6, with a stalling speed of 60 or 70 knots, wasn't much worse. The T-33, however, stalled straight and level at 95 to 110 knots, and a dead-stick landing even on a concrete runway could really pucker your seat cushion. The casualty rate at Greenville was so high, in fact, that our commanding officer (CO) let the whole wing stand down for beer call one day because we had actually gone a whole month without a fatality. Not a month without an accident, mind you, but a *fatality!*

Unfortunately, internal failure of that first-generation, centrifugal flow turbine wasn't the only way you could flame out. Those big burner cans drank so much gas that it seemed like your fuel low-level warning light came on just about the time you raised the gear after takeoff. This drawback was partially offset with the addition of a 230-gallon tip tank, or extra, bomb-shaped fuel vessel at the end of each wing, but these were seldom fully serviced due to the added weight and maneuvering penalties exacted on an already underpowered airplane. Consequently, with only an hour or so endurance down low and just double that at altitude, you had to keep one eye on the fuel gauge while the other scanned for birds (the feathered as well as the sheet-metal kind), since sucking a duck or seagull into the intakes, or taking one through your windscreen, was another common way to find yourself walking home.

With so many ways to get into trouble, and only one way to fly right—your instructor pilot's way—we quickly began to think of ourselves as the Air Force's pilot elite, which, indeed, we were. By the time we survivors won our wings in the summer of 1956, we considered ourselves pretty hot sticks, with brass for balls and ice water in our veins. The only reasonable place for the Air Force to send us was into the cockpits of first-line tactical or air-defense fighters, and that's what I drew as my first operational assignment: the F-86 Sabre, the famous "MiG-killer" of the Korean War, at Williams Field, Arizona. Not only was the Sabre the hottest thing around in fighters, but its axial flow J-47, a second-generation turbine, was also a lot more reliable than the T-Bird's J-33. Jousting with the enemy's aerial knights is a lot more practical when you don't have to worry about your war horse falling out from under you.

Unfortunately, because of the country's increasing emphasis on SAC, with its growing bomber and tanker fleet, the Air Force's tactical air arm, so instrumental to success in both World War II and Korea, was being allowed to wither. Whole wings of tactical fighters, including my new assignment, were mothballed in favor of the bigger "aluminum overcast"—more B-47s and B-52s—needed for massive nuclear retaliation.

Along with others, I was yanked out of a fighter cockpit and reassigned to Craig AFB, Selma, Alabama. Instead of becoming America's next Chuck Yeager, I was consigned to the role of "plow-back": an instructor in the Air Training Command's old faithful, the T-33.

Despite my firm belief that I belonged in fighters and would be wasted in ATC, I have to admit that going through the three-month flight instructor course at Craig was a humbling and healthy experience. More than any other training to date, it turned me into the kind of pilot I really wanted to be—a *good* one. The old saw that "you never know a subject better than when you have to teach it" is doubly true in flying. I also learned the value of precise instrument flying, which most multiengine pilots master early on and most fighter pilots used to eschew, mainly due to lack of practice. I came to realize that good instrument flying makes a good contact pilot even better.

Looking on the bright side, I was still flying single-engine, fighter-type aircraft, and that was, to me, a damned sight better than B-47s, where some of my fighter-bound classmates wound up. In those days, once you fell into the black hole of SAC, there was no way out except retirement.

After qualifying as an IP—instructor pilot—I was transferred to Laredo AFB in extreme south Texas. The very day I arrived, a midair collision between two T-33s over an auxiliary field had claimed four lives. One ship on initial approach (flying upwind over the runway before "pitching out"—banking sharply to the downwind leg of the traffic pattern) had been hit by another descending from "high key," the first reference point on a simulated dead-stick landing.

*Jeeze!* I thought, processing my paperwork through the endless stream of long faces, *this place is gonna be worse than Greenville!* Happily, I was mistaken.

Flying turned out to be pretty good at Laredo, mostly because of an ample supply of planes, student pilots, and good weather. I also rediscovered the pleasures of flying light airplanes, too, and joined the local aero club, which became a fixture in my flying career, no matter where I was stationed. Most of the other pilots thought I was nuts.

"Who wants to putt around the sky in a little bug smasher when you can be out playing Steve Canyon in jets?" they would ask, but flying of any kind was in my blood. If I wasn't up with a student or on a cross-country building time in a T-Bird, I'd be out touring the local area, sightseeing and buzzing cattle in the communal Piper Cubs and Aeroncas we aero clubbers maintained with our dues.

My two worst days came toward the end of my three-year tour, which at least found me fortified with enough experience to survive them—mentally and physically.

The first was the loss of a buddy, "Wee Willy" Shelton, an IP who made first lieutenant about the same time I did. He was departing Laredo on a hot day in a T-Bird with fully loaded tip tanks and lost his engine just after takeoff. He was high enough to contemplate a dead-stick landing on a nearby diagonal runway, which would have worked for a normally loaded bird. With the extra weight in the tip tanks, though, he just couldn't make it. He committed the pilot's cardinal sin by trying to "stretch" his glide with too much back pressure on the stick during the final turn. The result was a classic stall-spin accident—one we both had trained a hundred students to watch out for and avoid. Poor Willy ended his career in a big smoking hole in the ground. He would not be the last of my friends to do so.

Not long after that, a student and I were taking off on the same runway (we could still see the scorch marks from Willy's explosion at the departure end) on an almost identical day but with partially loaded tip tanks when I heard a disturbing *pop* and *zing* from the back of the airplane. The engine RPM began to fluctuate.

I knew from prior bad experience exactly what had happened. My engine had thrown a turbine blade, one of the hundreds of tiny airfoils that make the paddlewheel-like turbine rotors spin in the superhot exhaust flow of the engine. The turbine wheels, in turn, rotate the compressor at the front of the engine, which feeds cold air to the fuel burner cans, providing the continuous ignition that keeps the engine running. Turbine failures happened periodically, and almost every IP could count on having one or a few of them during his tour. The effect could be as small as a clean, bulletlike puncture through the aircraft's skin or as bad as a burst turbine disk: disintegration of the massive turbine wheel that, as the engine becomes more imbalanced, shatters and flies off in chunks, usually in seconds, sometimes taking the tail of the aircraft with it. Needless to say, it was not the kind of malfunction you wanted low and slow after takeoff.

According to the flight manual, the first thing to do in case of turbine blade failure is retard the throttle and minimize vibration. But I had Willy's experience, not just the pilot's handbook, fresh in my mind. I left power on and reached up and jettisoned the tip tanks, which fell away immediately, plowing two deep furrows in a drive-in movie theater just outside the base. (Fortunately, drive-ins don't show matinees and the tip tanks didn't explode.)

We gained some much-needed altitude, but by now the engine was really rattling—tearing itself apart and shaking the aircraft like hell. The fire-warning light blinked red in the cockpit.

In as calm a voice as I could muster, I told the student in the front cockpit to pull the throttle to idle, then, a second or two later, into the cutoff detent, shutting down the engine. I then said the magic words every student longs to hear in such situations, "I have the airplane," and waggled the stick to let him know I was on the controls. I eased the still-shuddering bird around toward the same diagonal runway where Willy Shelton had been killed a week or two before.

Fortunately, without the tip tanks, our stalling speed was a little lower than Willy's. I squeaked through the turn successfully, "riding the nibble"—the light wing buffet that signals an impending stall—all the way. In my peripheral vision, I saw the cloud of black smoke we were trailing but put it out of my mind. What counted now was our airspeed and rate of descent, and the rapidly flattening angle of the runway ahead of us.

The concrete flashed by and I eased the wings level. We bounced once or twice, then stayed put and I climbed on the brakes and started the canopy up so that our exit, if undignified, could at least be quick.

We stopped straight ahead on the runway, flung off our seat belts, shoulder harnesses, and parachutes, and hit the concrete just as fire trucks arrived, spraying foam. It was a lousy way to end what was otherwise a pretty good tour, but I think Wee Willy—wherever he was—would've been happy to know that his costly example hadn't been wasted on a friend.

Shortly after this memorable ride, my career took another unexpected turn.

In late 1958, I received an order out of the blue to report to the University of Oklahoma in Norman (near Oklahoma City) to study for a master of arts degree in English literature.

*Say again?*

It seems the Air Force was busy staffing its brand-new air academy at Colorado Springs, Colorado, and decided that a certain number of service academy graduates must be laid on to teach academy cadets. This was probably a good idea, except for the way they went about it. I couldn't imagine any shortage of Annapolis or West Point graduates who would've given their eyeteeth for such an opportunity. Unfortunately, I wasn't one of them. I hadn't spent all those years at West Point—on bayonet courses and in tank turrets—and later in airplane cockpits, just to teach fuzz-cheeked college kids about T.S. Eliot.

But the Air Force wasn't joking. Shortly thereafter, First Lieutenant Secord reported as ordered to the University of Oklahoma, a huge campus from the West Point perspective and one with one of the nation's leading English programs. My new boss, the English department chairman, had been a light colonel in G-2 (Army intelligence) in World War II. He gave me an initial writing evaluation and declared, "Lieutenant Secord, you write just like a damned Army field manual!" which, although derogatory to him, pleased me to no end. I didn't have the heart to tell him I couldn't write even *that* well before I got to the Point.

Naturally, he was shocked at my lack of prerequisites for an English degree, which nobody, including the Air Force, seemed to take into consideration. Calculus and civil engineering didn't cut much ice on the liberal arts side of the campus, but my courses in German (fluency in at least one foreign language was a graduation requirement at West Point) showed I had at least some verbal skills. He later let me cobble together a thesis subject ("The Impact of the Napoleonic Wars on Nineteenth-Century Literature") that paid lip service to my military education.

My personnel folder went to nearby Tinker AFB, which was home to the Oklahoma City Air Materiel Area—one of the largest warehousing and overhaul centers in the Air Force's sprawling logistics system and site for depot-level repairs for a variety of aircraft systems, many of which needed flight testing before they could be returned to operational units. Needless to say, my eyes lit up when I heard about all those aircraft waiting to be flown, and my department chairman was more than generous in giving me time off to visit Tinker and maintain my flying status. In addition to giving me a chance to gain my first hours in (and a new respect for) big multiengine airplanes like the C-54 and C-97, Tinker also kept a number of T-33s for chase aircraft and pilot proficiency missions, so I wound up putting in a lot of flight hours as instructor and chase pilot, too. It was a much-needed oasis from what for me was a pointless and arid classroom assignment, and I soon discovered the area had other attractions as well.

I hadn't been on a coed campus since high school, and Oklahoma had 25,000 students, half of them female. As an older guy with jet pilot's wings (this was well before the Vietnam era; a uniform was considered a plus) and access to light planes at the Tinker aero club for joyrides, I was probably more popular with the coeds than I should've been; especially in the English department, where the other male students tended to wear wire-rimmed glasses and goatees, and affect consumptive coughs.

After a year and a half I'd battled my way through enough course work to be within a semester or two of graduating. I'm not sure all that effort made me a better officer, but it didn't make me any worse, and it sure opened my eyes to human vistas I never would've seen at even 30,000 feet.

One of those gorgeous vistas was Jo Ann, the woman I would marry.

I met Jo Ann toward the end of my stay in Oklahoma. I had moved from the town of Norman to Midwest City, just outside of Oke City, to be a little closer to Tinker, and shared a house with another lieutenant named David Finney, a young lawyer on the judge advocate's staff. Jo Ann, who was dating Dave, worked as a secretary on the base. An only child who had attended Oklahoma State for two years, she had a serious side that appealed to me and that Dave didn't seem to appreciate.

When he told me there was nothing special between them, I asked her out myself and count that idea as one of my better life decisions. The more time I spent with her, the more I began to wonder why I razzed my married buddies so much at Laredo. Before long, being with Jo Ann was less like a date and more like real life—something I just didn't want to do without, like flying.

About this time I was promoted to captain and had to get serious about passing the master's orals. While the rest of the country worried about Russian cosmonauts circling the globe, Freedom Riders in Alabama, and the newly erected Berlin Wall, a coed friend of mine named Tressie set up a "murder board"—three or four inquisitors to simulate the panel of professors who would grill me on the exam—and got me so pumped up and well prepared that the test itself was anticlimactic. If it hadn't been for Tressie I'd still be locked up in the university library with Lord Byron and Walt Whitman— and even *those* guys wouldn't have wanted that.

By late summer 1961, I had completed everything I needed for my degree except the master's thesis, which for me was like removing my appendix orally. Part of my problem was lack of focus; I had never really bought into the program and knew I never would. Part of it was practical—a complete disinterest in writing anything longer than a love note to Jo Ann.

One hot August day after wringing out an F-86 on a maintenance test hop at Tinker, I was snagged by the duty officer on my way through Base Operations.

"Captain Secord, you're to report to General Mundell's office—ASAP."

My first thought was that some civilian had complained about Captain "Mick" Jones, my chase pilot in a second aircraft, and me rat-racing through the test area southeast of the field. Normally, that wouldn't involve a general, let alone the boss of the whole Air Materiel Area. After leaving West Point, I'd never even *met* a general officer. Something very big, or very strange, must be going on.

I quickly changed out of my flight suit and into summer tans—regulation 1505s—and reported to Major General Mundell. He sat stoically in his wood-paneled office bracketed by Old Glory and his two-star general's flag.

"Have a seat, Captain. This won't take long." The general put on his glasses and read from a TWIX (a military telegram) that, even from upside down, I could see had been stamped *Top Secret*. It came from the Air Staff at the Pentagon direct to all major commands.

"To the attention, Commander, etcetera, etcetera," he began, "from the Chief of Staff, USAF. You will request volunteers from the list of active duty officers, appended this notice, for assignment to Project Jungle Jim, temporary duty which—" General Mundell peered at me over his glasses, "may include combat."

He flashed the TWIX in my direction before putting it face down on his desk. The list attached to Tinker's copy was short. It contained only one name.

Mine.

Project Jungle Jim, whatever it was, was obviously high priority, and there didn't seem to be too many combat-qualified, high-time fighter jocks available in my pay grade to call upon, at least at the Oke City area. Calling it to the attention of a general officer was the Pentagon's way of casting the widest possible net for volunteers while ensuring maximum security.

Actually, I thought I had a pretty good idea of what Jungle Jim was about. President Kennedy's abortive Bay of Pigs invasion, using anti-Castro Cuban exiles and virtually no air support, had self-destructed in April, and I felt certain that the order meant the Air Force was collecting a new squadron of attack pilots to go back and do the job right.

"General," I grinned, "I'll be happy to volun—"

"This is a very serious matter, Captain Secord," General Mundell interrupted. "You don't have to answer right away. You should think about what you're getting into." The general took off his glasses. "I don't know the details of this so-called Jungle Jim, but I've seen these special assignments come through before. They're not for just anyone."

"What do you think they're looking for?"

The general shrugged. "A good man who can keep his mouth shut—put up with a lot of grief and do things that won't show up on his record. You've got a good career going for yourself, Captain." He glanced at my personnel folder, which I just now noticed was open on his desk. "West Point graduate, lots of time in fighter-type aircraft, instructor pilot, tagged for the faculty at the new Air Academy—hell, you might just be sitting in a major general's slot yourself one day. This cloak-and-dagger stuff, it's not for everybody, especially a regular officer on a fast-track, conventional career."

"I understand, sir," I said, not comprehending a damn thing he'd said after *may include combat.* "I'm still ready to go."

"Okay, Captain. I'll start your paperwork. If you're chosen, you'll hear from my office. In the meantime, keep this to yourself. Don't discuss it with anyone."

I saluted and went back to town, bursting with excitement I couldn't share, even with Jo Ann, who worked in the Air Force depot across the field. Unfortunately, nothing happened for the next two months, and my enthusiasm had begun to flag, when orders came for me to report for several days of psychological screening, to determine my suitability for special operations, at Lackland AFB, San Antonio, Texas.

I arrived to find several hundred fliers like myself, some of whom were to become my lifelong friends both in and out of special ops. We took a battery of written exams and had interviews with staff psychiatrists at the base's big medical center. They told us all tests were aimed at helping the Air Force select the men who would be most trustworthy and reliable under the pressures of a sensitive assignment, but we pilots had our own explanation: *They were only accepting the crazy guys!*

Apparently my form of dementia matched their profile and I was in. I returned to Oklahoma ready to pack my bags.

Without revealing the details (we *still* didn't know what Jungle Jim was), I gave Jo Ann the news. It was already late in October, and I had orders to leave Tinker at the end of the month. We had been engaged for a while and had set the wedding for December. Now, we had to fish or cut bait. I told Jo Ann that the wedding would have to be "next Saturday" or not at all. As cold consolation, I added that such short-notice fire drills was what military life was all about, and if she agreed to marry me, it was something she'd have to get used to. Uncle Sam would always come first.

To Jo Ann, becoming an Air Force wife was like jumping headfirst, eyes closed, into a cold pond; she didn't know how deep it was or whether anyone would be around later to fish her out if she got into trouble. Nonetheless, she took the plunge. We were married on November 18, 1961.

Our honeymoon was spent driving to Stead AFB outside Reno, Nevada, where I had been ordered to attend a special 22-day survival course in the high Sierras along with about 30 pilots and a third as many navigators. November 23 was Jo Ann's 22nd birthday, as well as Thanksgiving, which I had to spend in class. Three days later, I put her on an airplane to return to live with her parents in Oklahoma.

That was her introduction to military life. It was the pattern our marriage would take, on and off, for the next 30 years.

Our group spent the next couple of weeks in survival school trudging through the chest-high snow and 40-below-zero temperatures of the high Sierras, trying to evade our mock captors, stay warm, and find anything we could to eat. The Air Force, like the Army at West Point's Beast Barracks, used the ordeal to winnow out the weak. After living off the land awhile, we were rounded up and herded into a mock POW camp, where we were incarcerated and put through simulated interrogation. Compared to our hazing at the Point, the camp was pretty tame, but it was enough to make some in our group realize that wartime risks simply weren't for them.

Afterward, we were shipped to Hurlburt Field, Florida, which only confirmed the now-rampant rumor that we were on our way to Havana. Jo Ann and I rendezvoused in Oklahoma for the long drive south. We rented a small, two-bedroom house near the intracoastal waterway that flowed peacefully by the base—a picture-perfect hideaway for newlyweds. Predictably, we wouldn't enjoy it for long.

Hurlburt Field in the early 1960s was home to the 4400th Combat Crew Training Squadron, which at the time was a veritable air museum of vintage aircraft. One section of about 30 pilots, including me, was designated "strike" and flew World War II–era A-26s (the North American B-26, not the old Martin Marauder); AT-28Bs, which were similar to the T-28As I had flown briefly in advanced flight school in Greenville. These, however, were Navy birds, hung with guns and other ordnance, and boasted a bigger, 1,425-horse-power engine.

The second section of about 40 pilots and navigators was called "airlift." They operated C-47 "Gooney Birds"—the military analogue to the venerable DC-3 airliner. It also had a few planes I had never seen before—utility category aircraft with leading-edge as well as trailing-edge flaps that could take off and land on a dime.

The aircraft in both sections had one thing in common, though: They were painted dull grey and carried few markings, highly unusual in an era when the rest of the Air Force inventory wore Day-Glo anticollision panels and other "war paint," such as colorful squadron emblems, on the wings, tail, and fuselage. If we were bound for glory, it was obvious that few people were going to know about it.

Our commander was Colonel Ben King, a famous fighter pilot from World War II and Korea who had handpicked us for the cadre. His deputy commander was Colonel Chet Jack, a good man who later retired and finished his life near Hurlburt, like an old sailor who couldn't get away from the sea. Led by these two icons and a number of highly qualified instructors (mostly World War II and Korean War veterans) we practiced air-to-ground gunnery and a variety of low-level tactics over the Florida and Alabama swamps. Unlike in our previous tactical training, night was no barrier to special ops, and we got as proficient dropping our ordnance and laying our rounds on target under flares as we did during daylight.

Finally, our superiors judged us competent to handle our aircraft in battle. A small advanced party was collected and disappeared one day to begin deployment preparations; the rest of us would follow in sections to some soon-to-be disclosed secret location. I could almost taste those Cuban cigars when my group was ordered to report to our intelligence officer for a short theater briefing.

The intelligence officer told us that not later than March 1, 1962, under the code name of Detachment Two Alpha, we'd be deployed to a place called Bien Hoa, Republic of Vietnam, to assist the South Vietnamese Air Force— or VNAF—and the indigenous army in the suppression of a North Vietnam-ese–sponsored insurgency. The enemy, he said, identified itself as the Viet Cong. The American objective was to assist the South in putting down the pro-Communist insurrection, drive the NVA (North Vietnamese) Army forces back across the border, and restore law and order to the countryside.

It sounded like a job for Superman—but that's not what was on our minds. Like most of the guys, the first thing that popped into my head was, *where the hell is Vietnam?*

# —3—

# Vietnam Before the Crowd

When I stepped onto the ramp at Bien Hoa, a little French-built airstrip covered with PSP—pierced-steel planking landing mats—Project Jungle Jim became Operation Farmgate, perhaps the biggest little war that "never happened."

I left Jo Ann in Florida in a state of terminal puzzlement. We gave our wives a dummy APO mailing address in the Philippines to match our dummy orders, so at first she didn't have the foggiest idea of where we actually were, except it probably *wasn't* Cuba or the Philippines. The nation's eyes in those days were focused elsewhere: on John Glenn's first orbital flight, or the return from Russia of U-2 pilot Francis Gary Powers in exchange for a Soviet spy. The only people who knew the truth about our assignment besides the 4400th commanders and the deployed troops themselves were the Joint Chiefs and President Kennedy, and they weren't talking either.

Farmgate was a secret and significant Air Force program that basically meant attacking and destroying the VC whenever we could find them. We Americans were involved because the VNAF, Vietnamese Air Force, was still being born, and midwifing it was part of our job. We had one squadron of AT-28s while the VNAF contingent (virtually their whole air force at the time; President Nguyen Cao Ky, whom I met when he was a lieutenant colonel, commanded a C-47 transport squadron at Tan Son Nhut) consisted of one squadron of ADs, or Douglas Skyraiders. The big, single-prop attack plane was built for the Navy after World War II and carried 7,000 pounds of ordnance low and slow over enemy positions—a real aerial "Howitzer" ideally suited to this environment. Later designated A-1s and nicknamed "Spads" by their American crews, the Skyraider could absorb a lot of punishment, more than its pilot was ever likely to stick around and take, and

29

was popular because of it. I took it up a few times—it flew like a barn door and was honest as most straight-wing airplanes are—but I preferred the smaller AT-28s I had trained with at Hurlburt. The "Trojan," as it was called, was easy to fly because it had originated as a trainer, and the visibility from its big bubble canopy was spectacular—a big asset not only for putting our ordnance on target but also for avoiding high terrain and low-level obstacles, like trees.

The 4400th was an exceptional unit, but Detachment Two Alpha was even more elite—the pick of America's tactical pilots. Even though I was a captain with 2,000 hours of stick time, I was *the* junior officer in our detachment by experience as well as rank.

Major Robert Allison, our first ops officer, was one helluva flier and such a mean cuss we used to call him "Sweet Old Bob" (a euphemism for SOB). Captain Tom Temple was one of the most expert dive-bombers anybody had seen or heard of, and that included a lot of World War II vets. In the era before smart bombs, he amazed us once by calling his shot in advance—putting a napalm canister through the front door of an old French plantation house being used by the VC—then proceeding to do just that. Both Temple and Allison had flown P-51s over Hitler's Europe, and their experience with prop-driven attack planes showed. Don Gephardt and Gene Connally, both captains senior to me, were also great fliers, deadly gunners, and, just as important, truly exceptional leaders. Closest to me personally and in flying experience was Captain Bill "Willy" Cox, who would become a real contender, if not titleholder, for most hours flown in Southeast Asia.

Officially, we weren't stationed anywhere *near* Vietnam. Our cover, should we be rooted out by reporters, was that we were "instructors" for VNAF pilots, although the first and most important lesson we ever gave our "students" was to keep their hands off the controls while we flew the airplane. Actually, about a quarter of our time was allocated to combat training, but the Vietnamese didn't fly at night, which was when a third of the war was fought, so we never really thought of them as true combat pilots. In fact, since our standing orders were to always fly with a Vietnamese national in the backseat, and VNAF pilots weren't always available, our "copilot" was often a crew chief or maintenance man or some poor soldier who happened to be standing around while we were getting ready to take off.

We Americans wore no name tags or unit patches or even rank on our flight suits; just dog tags so that our bodies could be identified by friendly forces in a wreck. We also cleansed ourselves of all "pocket litter," wallets or religious tokens or photos of our dogs, kids, wives, or sweethearts, anything that would help the enemy prove Americans were participating in the war. We even gave up our Geneva Convention cards, which every serviceman carries to show he's entitled to humane treatment as a POW.

Our VNAF counterparts, however—the actual Vietnamese pilots—usually flew in resplendent uniforms with all the ropes and whistles of a Lord Mountbatten or Idi Amin. One standard phrase of the war was "all dressed up like a Vietnamese second lieutenant"; junior VNAF officers had more pips to denote their rank than our Chairman of the Joint Chiefs of Staff.

Once, early in my first tour, General Curtis LeMay, Air Force Chief of Staff, came out to inspect our installation. Since I was the outfit's junior officer, my VNAF backseater and I got the dubious honor of turning out for a ceremonial inspection in front of our fully loaded fighter bomber. I showed up in a faded green cotton flight suit with my captain's bars on my cap. The VNAF lieutenant, however (a guy we called "Flash" Vuy because he dressed so spiffily and moved so slowly), appeared in an Australian bush hat with a zebra-skin band, black leather gloves, and a holstered German Luger.

LeMay stopped in front of us and his chin fell down to his low quarters. I gave him a crisp, West Point salute, which he returned like a man in shock.

"How many missions have you flown, son?" he asked, possibly suspecting battle fatigue.

"I don't know, sir," I replied, which was the truth. Because our assignment was secret, we kept no records of our missions; the flight hours normally logged on our Air Force Form 5, the airman's "bible" from which flight currency, flight pay, pilot seniority, and a host of other career-related goodies were derived, just didn't exist.

My answer seemed to confirm his hypothesis. "What do you mean you don't know? Did you just report for duty?"

"No, sir. I've been here two months. It's just that we're not permitted to log our missions. They all kind of run together after awhile—sir."

The staff officers from Saigon accompanying LeMay drilled holes in my head with their dirty looks, but hell—I hadn't been briefed on what to say to the Chief of Staff, so why not tell him the truth?

General LeMay didn't answer and went on with the inspection. A few days later we received an order to start logging all combat missions. The ops clerks even had us go back and try to reconstruct the missions we had flown to date, but I saw no reason to remember anything but the life-and-death lessons every new combat pilot picks up in his first 10 or 20 sorties. When you're sweating out those early missions, a minute under fire seems like an eternity—and they want *us* to guess how many hours we logged? That's why, to this day, my officially documented 285 combat missions in Southeast Asia are probably in error and could be over 300. As I said, in those days nobody kept score.

In February 1961, the Defense Department announced the creation of the U.S. Military Command in South Vietnam (called MACV) under General Paul Harkins and gave U.S. troops in that country permission to return hostile fire if necessary to protect themselves. By May, the pro-Communist Pathet

Lao had driven Royal Laotian troops from neighboring Northern Laos in violation of a recent cease-fire, causing President Kennedy to dispatch another 4,000 U.S. troops to Thailand, joining the 1,000 already there. For a war that wasn't happening, things were beginning to get pretty hot for us Americans.

Most combat pilots will tell you the first few missions are scary as hell until you actually saddle up and get the wheels in the well; then you are so totally focused on doing your job and achieving your objective that you don't have time to be nervous until you're back on the ground. If you survive the first dozen missions or so, you know basically what will get you killed and what won't, and your odds of surviving go way up—at least until you hit that next plateau of danger when, because nothing too bad has happened to you yet, you begin to feel bulletproof. A lot of guys don't survive that phase either, because it takes a real close call to let you know that it's even arrived.

Ordinarily, we'd fly several sorties a day (I once flew as many as 10) and rest when we got the chance or began seeing double because of fatigue. There was no such thing as a "duty day" or mandatory "crew rest" in those days, which made the air war a lot more like ground combat. Standing orders were to fly no matter what the weather was like, and I once got in trouble—tagged as a smartass—for suggesting to the CO that we send our base weather briefer home for eating our food and drinking our whiskey and not contributing a thing to the war effort.

After a short time, I was promoted to flight commander and allowed to lead strikes on my own.

Our job was to provide "aerial artillery" for the infantry, and each mission was usually carefully choreographed by forward air controllers (FACs) or by the flight leader on the scene. On a typical mission, we'd receive a request for support from a ground unit currently engaging the enemy, or receive preplanned strike ("frag") orders from Saigon against targets identified by G–2. Depending on weather and terrain, we would typically attack along a variety of axes using a weaving, curvilinear flight path to confound the defenders. We always wanted to minimize our time in the "dead man's zone" that ran from a few hundred to 3,000 feet above ground level. Higher than this, we were out of range for most antiaircraft weapons. Lower was generally better because we could hide behind trees and hills until the last second. In war, surprise is everything; even if the enemy knows you're there, he doesn't know where you'll pop up next. During the dry season, I once "stuck it in the weeds" by flying an attack course *below* the rim of a canal and came back with gravel pits and stone strikes all over my wings. Ground crews sometimes complained about pulling foliage out of our wing roots, cowling, and weapons pylons, but that was a lot better than the alternative—repairing holes from enemy slugs—or not coming back at all.

Contrary to popular belief, the rainy monsoon was not a particularly big problem for us because the clouds tended to move through quickly and in waves. We would attack in the bands of clear air following the troughs of bad weather, often several times during the course of one mission. Night missions, though, were a real double-edged sword. In those days, we had no self-steering or remotely guide bombs or terrain-avoidance radar, so low-level nighttime attacks were always a dicey affair, even in good weather. However, we were harder to see at night, and when you had both darkness and clouds for cover, you were statistically a little safer—at least from enemy fire.

The VC and NVA had some pretty good antiaircraft defenses and we never regarded *any* enemy positions as sitting ducks. Aside from small-arms fire (AK-47s and even pistols), we were most often opposed by ZPU-2s and -4s, the standard 12 mm and 14.5 mm Soviet triple-A cannon; and later 23 mm ZPU-23s, whose exploding shells could reach up to 20,000 feet, making them, for me, the most dangerous defensive weapon of the war. The only reason the enemy didn't get more of us was because both model ZPUs lacked an effective fire control system and the VC, at least, didn't operate them particularly well.

In bad weather and at night, the enemy's ground defense problems became even worse, since our engine noise echoed all over the place, and they seldom knew where to train their guns. When our C-47 Gooney Birds dropped their white phosphorous parachute flares, the VC gunners had to look up into what was essentially a high-intensity arc-welding flame. These flares bothered us as well, particularly when we completed a pass and had to pull up into the blackest black imaginable. But the VC had to stare constantly at these things and were, for all intents and purposes, blind as bats. More than one VC night attack was broken up simply by our flare ship arriving on the scene and dispensing its wares. No VC who had been conditioned by our nighttime tactics wanted to stick around for what was bound to happen next.

All this is not to say that we didn't take our lumps. We picked up ground fire constantly, even on dead-head ferry flights between bases, and every ship in the squadron was eventually a crazy quilt of aluminum scab patches and heavy adhesive tape (what we called "Japanese sheet metal") placed over non-load-bearing parts of the air frame until more permanent repairs could be made. The NVA also installed "spoofer" stations on the Cambodian and Laotian borders to deceive our electronic navigation systems and give false bearings to our targets and airfields.

Landing after a mission was sometimes as exciting as the mission itself. In those days only a few Vietnamese airports had what we would today consider modern (asphalt or concrete), multiple (parallel or diagonal) runways. Tan Son Nhut at Saigon, and Danang and Nha Trang were fine facilities, and a few other places—mostly emergency fields built by the Japanese and French in the 1940s—had short but hard-surfaced runways. Elsewhere the runways were surfaced with either laterite (packed red clay) or PSP, which was slicker than ice when it rained—like landing on an aircraft carrier with no arresting hook. Because of this, our airplanes always flew with "balloon" tires for soft-field operations. Even when we staged strikes from a modern runway like Da Nang, we never knew where we'd be landing, so we had to be mentally prepared for anything.

One airport diversion taught me this lesson fast. My two-ship formation had been flying cover for Army helicopters near the Plain of Reeds on the Cambodian border, and we ran low on fuel. I radioed that we would be returning to base and the chopper commander replied, "Hell, we've got some avgas [aviation gasoline—higher octane than gas used by surface vehicles and completely different from the kerosene fuel jets burn]. You can refuel with us."

My wingman, Bill Cox, and I landed on a dirt strip called Muc Hoa that was used by Army choppers. It was pretty crowded and we had to be very careful not to ding a wingtip taxiing to the makeshift POL (petroleum, oil, and lubricants) dump. The helos were being refueled by hand from 50-gallon drums and it was taking forever. When it was our turn, I pumped an hour or so's worth of flying time into my tanks and turned the pump over to Bill. Standing on my wing, I could see across the strip into the fields and, as they say in the movies, it was quiet—too quiet. But not for long. Gunfire erupted around the perimeter and a bunch of guys in black pajamas began running toward the strip. All of a sudden, we were watermelon at a picnic.

"Let's get the hell out of here!" I yelled at Bill, and I jumped into the cockpit. Our VNAF backseaters hadn't gotten out and, although startled like us, were ready to go. I fired up the engine and pulled onto the runway blasting everybody and everything around the fuel dump with propwash. The choppers had already cranked up and departed, and dust and debris flew everywhere. Without even closing the canopy, I lowered some flaps and firewalled the throttle.

I was airborne in seconds. Bill was right behind me.

I climbed out as steeply as I dared to avoid the small-arms fire, then banked sharply to observe the attack. As I did, I tried to close the canopy and noticed I wasn't quite ready to fly. The railing of the big Plexiglas bubble was jammed by my shoulder harness. *Jesus Christ—I hadn't even strapped in!*

Now it was time for my adrenaline to give way to a little basic airmanship. I leveled off, unjammed the canopy rail, hooked up my parachute, strapped in, and sorted things out in the cockpit, checking switch positions and warning lights and a half-dozen other really useful things. When I was pretty sure I hadn't done anything else too stupid, I got on the radio to find out about the battle.

The ground commander said he was having a hard time keeping Charlie off the strip; could we come back and put some ordnance on them? We had expended nearly all our load in earlier attacks and had only enough rounds for a few strafing passes, but that would be better than nothing. Bill was tucked up tight on my wing, so I bobbed my plane's nose a couple of times—the leader's signal for his wingman to "go trail," or drop directly behind and just below the lead aircraft—and racked it over into a steep, descending dive back toward the base and all of a sudden found a dozen choppers in my face, scattering like ducks from a blind.

Somehow Bill stayed with me while I zigzagged through the cloud of helicopters, and we laid down some pretty convincing fire on the attackers. Fortunately, it was enough to slow the assault and gave the ground guys a chance to regroup. But it was a closer call than it had to be, and I promised myself right then never to get caught with my pants down—out of gas and unarmed—on an unfamiliar strip again.

The first mission where I really thought I'd bought the farm was on a two-ship strike against VC positions on a rugged ridge southwest of Da Nang in central Vietnam. My wingman, Bill Cox again, carried guns and rockets, and I had two pods of 2.75-inch rockets, two napalm canisters, and guns—the 50-caliber Browning machine guns the AT-28 mounted in each wing. The name of the game that day was to lay our ordnance along the ridgeline despite heavy enemy fire, so each of us took turns keeping the enemy's head down so that the other could fly along the ridge and drop his ordnance. The only way I could do this for Bill was to come in at a very steep dive angle (to avoid being zapped myself), unload a whole pod of rockets (which usually quieted things down fast), and give Bill the few seconds he needed to make his run.

I had just "whifferdilled" (maneuvered to set myself up at altitude), dropped the nose, and "climbed into the gunsight" (focused all my attention on the attack) when the stick flew out of my hand and jerked back toward me as if I'd just run over a pothole in the sky.

*Holy shit—am I hit?* I cobbed the throttle and racked the plane around, aborting the pass, and looked to see if I was trailing smoke and flames or had any damage to the empennage—about the only thing that could've given the stick such a romp. I asked my Vietnamese backseater if he noticed anything wrong, but he didn't answer, which wasn't unusual. Half of them didn't speak English and most were too scared in combat to say anything, even in Vietnamese. I couldn't see any damage and the instruments read fine. We were still in good shape. It was probably just turbulence.

I grabbed some altitude, fell off on one wing, and lined up again, this time gripping the stick a little tighter. (You normally fly high-performance aircraft with your fingertips, not your fist. Except for takeoff and landing, you seldom have to move the stick more than an inch or two in any direction.)

At about the same place in the run, the damned stick jerked back again—but this time there was no mistaking it: That was a *human* hand on the controls! The nose popped up and the airplane buffeted a bit, signaling airflow separation on the wing and an impending high-speed stall. I grabbed the stick with both hands and broke off the attack, easing us back to altitude. All this time, Bill was out there boring holes in the sky, waiting to do his thing. I'm sure he wondered what the hell I was up to.

"Red Two, Red Lead—I've got a small problem up here. Stand by one."

I turned in my seat and glared at my so-called copilot.

"Don't touch the stick!" I yelled on the intercom, which was always hot between the front and back seats. "Leave the fucking stick alone!"

The crew chiefs usually cinched the backseater's inertia-reel shoulder harness up tight and locked it so that the passenger couldn't reach the controls even if he had to, but this guy must've learned how to release it. Again, the Vietnamese troop didn't answer. He just looked scared out of his mind.

I reefed the plane back into the attack pattern, putting on plenty of Gs so my backseater would stay glued to the backrest, and barrel-rolled into a dive. I squared the wings and was ready to pickle the rockets when he did it again!

This time I was ready.

I locked both hands around the control grip, but he wouldn't let go. Worse, he was applying forward pressure to the stick, which only increased our dive angle and made us both float out of our seats. My boots stabbed the air above the rudder pedals.

Fortunately, I overpowered the guy and pulled about four Gs, clawing for altitude with an accelerated stall nibbling at our wings. All I could see outside was a lot of green and enemy muzzle flashes. The ridge vanished under our belly and the canopy filled with blue. I pulled out my side arm, a Smith & Wesson 38-Special that I never expected to unholster, twisted around, and pointed it at the Vietnamese soldier's head.

I was so angry and scared that I couldn't speak and was only a microsecond away from blowing that bastard's head off when the whole problem became academic.

Previously white as a sheet, the guy now turned green as the jungle and puked all over the cockpit.

Well, hell—you can't shoot a guy when he's airsick, so I put my gun away and aborted the mission. No friendlies were being threatened, and I really didn't feel like continuing the fray with the stench of this guy's breakfast all over the airplane.

Bill joined up on our wing and followed us home. I radioed Da Nang to have a security team meet us on the ramp. We landed without incident, and as soon as the big canopy slid back, the poor bastard jumped out and took off toward the runway. He got nabbed instantly and was brought before the Vietnamese base commander. After hearing what happened, they were convinced he was VC, but I never really believed it. Charlie or not, I've seen guys paralyzed with fear, and his face belonged in a textbook.

During a joint-force operation, near the end of my tour, I thought my number had come up again.

In many ways, we at Detachment Two Alpha helped to write the book on joint fixed- and rotary-wing operations—lessons future MACV planners would inherit as standard operating procedures. We invented such tactics as the elliptical racetrack pattern used to provide CAP—combat air patrol—for heliborne assault forces. We were the first to "troll" for ground fire with a plane sent out low and slow ahead of the choppers, and then cream the enemy with a ship held high and out of sight when they stuck their heads up to shoot. The problems coordinating flexible helicopter gunnery with fixed, forward-firing (and free-fall) weapons on airplanes were enormous, and we were among the first to have solved them, sometimes on the spot and with the enemy shooting back at us. When we had the chance, we rehearsed our new ideas before we tried them. But our cardinal rule was to *keep it simple*, because even straightforward plans have a way of getting complicated when they're viewed through the fog of battle.

The closest call of my tour came during one of these joint helicopter/ fixed-wing missions. A Marine Corps advisor was supervising a heliborne insertion of some ARVN troops in H-34 helicopters into a VC-controlled village on the northernmost branch of the Mekong River. The Marine Corps FAC had spotted some VC sampans hiding under overhanging trees on the south side of the river and called us in to attack. I was leading a three-ship formation with two inexperienced wingmen who had just arrived as replacements. In order to even *see* the vessels, we had to skim the wavetops, which radically multiplied the problem of attacking them properly.

Because rockets fired from above tended to detonate in the trees, I finally elected to make a few strafing runs along the river, literally kicking up foam with the tips of my propeller. This meant I had to push the left rudder pedal with my foot and add a little right aileron and fire in a forward slip so that my flight path would stay over the river while my bullets went under the trees—a tricky maneuver usually forbidden by the handbooks.

The first pass was a little hairy. It was hard to aim the guns and keep one eye on the water. Toward the end of the pass the plane felt like she wanted to snap roll because I had cross-controlled so badly to keep the tracers on target.

But I did manage to sink a boat, and I got another on the next pass and yet another on the third. They were way overloaded and went down like anvils or just broke apart like they were made of toothpicks.

On the third pass, though, the VC really opened up on me—not just with small arms, which I could hear rattling over the airframe like hail on a tin roof, but ganged antiaircraft weapons, including what had to be ZPUs.

On my fourth or fifth pass the whole airplane shuddered; a burst of automatic-weapons fire hit me on the starboard cowling and completely blew away the exhaust collector ring that surrounds the engine.

The cockpit lit up like a Christmas tree—filled with red and amber warning lights—I could almost hear that aircraft *groan* like a wounded warhorse as she wallowed out of the mud and tried to keep a foothold in the air.

Instinctively I pulled up, to gain altitude to bail out if the damage was really bad, or to think things through and save the airplane if it wasn't. I cobbed the throttle, but without an exhaust manifold, superheated fumes belched out of the engine directly against the firewall, turning the cockpit into a furnace.

As I zoomed up, my novice wingmen tried to rejoin and advise me of my condition. Their excited chatter didn't help.

"Jesus Christ, Red Lead—you're on fire! You're trailing smoke!" one cried in a squeaky soprano.

"You're hit bad—" the other said, his transmission breaking up because the FAC was trying to talk on the same frequency at the same time, "—trailing smoke and flame! Eject! Eject!"

These were stimulating but not especially helpful comments as I tried to figure out what the hell I was going to do. As my airspeed bled off, the heat seemed less intense, so I concluded it would be a good idea to keep my speed as slow as possible and give myself as much time as I could to assess my options.

I advanced the throttle to continue the climb, but the room got hot and I was forced to back off. I finally found a manifold pressure setting that would let me hang on the prop without scorching my eyebrows, although the heat on the rudder pedals was now almost beyond endurance—the original hotfoot. If I reduced the throttle further I would fall from the sky, and adding power for a climb to a proper bailout altitude was positively out of the question. Besides, the people downstairs shooting at me seemed really angry. A forced landing or "nylon letdown" anywhere near the target would probably be my last.

"This is Red Lead," I finally called to my wingmen, "I'm gonna try to make Soc Trang. Stick with me and fly cover."

My plan was to nurse the burning plane another 15 or 20 miles to a little airstrip built by the Japanese during World War II and recently reconditioned by the U.S. Marines. It had about 3,000 feet of concrete runway—more than enough to get me down in one piece—and a fire truck, which seemed to be in order. The only problem was staying airborne long enough to make the landing, which would be a straight-in approach on my current heading. I wanted my wingmen with me all the way to spot and protect me in case I crash-landed and survived. At this early date in the war, we had no air-rescue service. If I was to get picked up in the boondocks, it would have to be by a chopper pulled from another mission—not very likely, and another reason it would be nice to set down on a real runway long enough to accommodate a rescue ship.

It took about 10 minutes to cover the distance from the river to Soc Trang, the longest 10 minutes of my life. I had plenty of time to shop for real estate on the proverbial farm—prime land in the middle of "Indian country," as we called the territory occupied by the Viet Cong. The right rudder pedal was now so hot that I had to keep putting my foot on and off, making the airplane fishtail and the horizon undulate dizzily over the nose. Each time I put a boot down, the sweat squished between my toes.

I called ahead to the Soc Trang "tower" (really a little trailer parked by the runway) and told them a flight of one was coming in with "one burning and one turning" as the old bomber pilots used to say.

When the field was in sight and the landing almost assured, I pulled the mechanical emergency landing gear release handle (it didn't seem wise to pump combustible hydraulic fluid from possibly ruptured lines into an engine fire) and waggled the rudder with tender toes until gravity locked the mains.

With all this new drag, going down was no problem. I began to sink like a stone and cranked down the flaps. The wheels shaved the trees and the runway appeared beneath me. I chopped the throttle and plopped down in front of a bunch of gawking Marines. I gingerly pumped the brakes—the pedals were a bit cooler—and stopped as soon as I could on the short strip without blowing the tires.

The fire truck met me and hosed down the engine, and my feet felt like I landed on broken glass when they hit the ground. A second later my wingmen roared over, waggling their wings. I gave them a thumbs-up and hopped, weak-kneed, into a jeep for a ride to the runway supervisory unit where my CO was waiting for me on the phone. I figured he'd congratulate me for saving at least part of his airplane, but that was not the case. Instead, the maintenance officer got pissed because he now had to send a Gooney Bird, parts, and repair crew into the bush to fix and pick up the plane. Sometimes, I guess, it's just smarter to let the jungle have them.

But not today.

Life at Bien Hoa was probably easier for me than some other pilots because I had learned to put up with a lot of physical discomfort at the Point. Everyone lived in tents set up on planks with screens between the canvas roof and waist-high wall. At some of the deployment bases and alternates out in the bush, we slept with the rats on rice sacks amid our own munitions and spare parts.

We never went to town on weekends. After all, we weren't even supposed to be in Vietnam, so keeping a low profile and staying on base was the easy way to maintain security. Periodically one of us had to don civilian clothes and go to Tan Son Nhut air base near Saigon to pick up groceries (and buy liquor at the Class VI store), but everyone tried to evade "the duty." Strangely, we didn't miss what was to become one of the more bizarre fixtures of the war: fighting during the day and going to town at night, as if war was a regular job. Back then, we were fighting or we were sleeping and there wasn't much in between. All told, we had a few hundred Americans to socialize with on base, so we never felt too alone.

Toward the end of my first tour, the war began taking an ominous direction. We were called on more and more often to pull the fat out of the fire for ground commanders who got in over their heads due to overzealousness or plain bad planning, something that would also become a fixture in later years.

A classic case of this occurred in 1962 when a colonel named Archie Clapp, commander of the U.S. Marine H-34 helicopter group at Soc Trang in the Delta, arrived in country. Now, you'd think that a guy with a name like that would have his own press agent, and he did: a famed woman reporter for *National Geographic* named Dickie Chappel, who admired Archie and published a big spread on his outfit—all this while the rest of us were trying to keep things quiet. Archie was a mean hombre—pure Marine—and worked hard to let everyone know it. Because my flight escorted his helicopter task force off the helo carrier when it arrived in the spring, he adopted me as his unit's guardian angel (at least for a while), and seldom took his men into harm's way, which was about 10 times more often than necessary, without me and my flight of AT-28s flying cover.

Gene Connally and I had escorted the Marine choppers in from the boat on the South China Sea and were refueling at Can Tho, I noticed that my plane had been gulping an abnormal amount of oil. Gene told me to set down at Soc Trang and stand ground alert in case I was needed while he continued to orbit the area.

As usual, it was miserably hot, and that day was hotter than normal. I climbed out of the cockpit in my unmarked fatigues, drenched in sweat. My backseater, good old Flash, followed me with his bush hat, black gloves, and German Luger. My feet had barely hit the ramp when Colonel Clapp and a two-star Marine Corps general pulled up in a jeep. Naturally, I saluted smartly.

"Good morning, sir, I'm Captain Secord."

Archie looked me up and down, undoubtedly noticing my lack of a name tape, insignia, unit patch, or any other militaria, and said, "Captain? Captain of what?"

"Captain, U.S. Air Force—sir."

Archie looked over at Flash (now there's a *real* officer, he must've thought) as if for confirmation. The general and the colonel stepped aside and huddled; I'm sure they concluded I was a mercenary; there was just no other explanation.

That was when I began to realize that maybe we were headed down the wrong pike if we planned to win this war. Nobody had briefed these guys (a two-star general, for Christ's sake) on the nature of the air support, the *only* air support, his men were going to get. When they finished their caucus and walked back to me, I explained as best I could that a bona fide tactical air control system did, in fact, exist. We had our own brigadier general in Saigon with the 7th Air Division directing classified air operations for the entire country—and had been doing so for some time. For the Marines, though, it just didn't seem to compute. Each service had its own war going, and theirs was the one that mattered.

This gap in joint forces command and control was becoming all too common in Vietnam, and I got into some of the worst shoot-'em-ups of my career because of it. The worst by far was a 25-helicopter assault, led by Colonel Clapp, into a very dicey combat situation. By sunset, almost half his choppers were down and I'd been forced to call in most of our available fixed-wing support—A-26s, ADs, and half our AT-28s—just to keep the VC from picking off the survivors of the various crashes sprinkled all over the countryside.

I have nothing against aggressive ground commanders and I'm the first to concede that the tide of battle can swing both ways. Sometimes you must improvise to achieve your objectives. But in a guerrilla war, some victories lay in simply avoiding defeat—staying out of those situations where the deck is stacked against you. Too often in this rapidly expanding war, U.S. or American-led troops would blunder into a situation, guns blazing, and hope that sheer firepower or our air advantage would bail them out. A wild-West shootout where all your firepower is directed at rescue—saving your butt and not knocking the "dreaded enemy" (as we referred to Communist forces) onto his—is not what any war, let alone a successful counterinsurgency, is supposed to be about.

As far as I'm concerned, this was where the Vietnam War began to go wrong, and it only got worse. The American presence began not just as "advisors," as textbooks claim, but as a handpicked band of highly qualified combat volunteers who got the job done, even if that required some unconventional thinking. We did not use state-of-the-art equipment. We used third-world equipment because that was what (according to the 1954 treaty) our hosts used, and it became part of our cover. We went in as stiffeners for the local troops and routed the enemy virtually every time we encountered him.

But it was clearly *not* our war.

We engaged the enemy directly only because the VNAF and ARVN lacked the capability, at that time, to do it effectively themselves; we had no intention of carrying on the battle indefinitely. We could've sustained that kind of low-intensity conflict for 30 years if we had to—which, as we now know, was the Communist plan all along, and it was a good one. If we had done that, our involvement would never have raised the hue and cry it eventually did in Congress, in the media, or among the American public that the alternative approach made inevitable.

Where we went wrong was to turn an unconventional situation—covert gap-filling and stiffening—over to conventional military thinkers. It's not so much that the commanders of our big Army and Marine units and tactical Air Wings went in to fight this war like we did the last one—a classical prelude to defeat; it was that we went in using those kinds of numbers and commanders at all. After things reached a certain size, the scope got so big that *nobody* could manage it using the conventional mind-sets, interservice rivalries, and technical methods that existed at the time. We eventually had MACV, 7th Air Force, CINCPAC, Telstar, Walter Cronkite, and three television networks, and we still never got the message. The North Vietnamese didn't win the war; they just hung on until we defaulted, smothered ourselves with too many players and would-be quarterbacks. If a little is good, we thought, a lot more must be better. If high tech gives you an edge, base your whole battle plan on gizmos instead of people. It was crazy.

When it became obvious that these "doctrines" would never work, we clung to what we knew and committed ourselves to even more conventional thinking. That didn't work for gas-guzzlers with big tail fins in Detroit and it sure didn't work in Southeast Asia.

My first tour in Vietnam ended in September 1962, and I returned to Hurlburt Field, Florida, for a little R&R and reassignment. I won three Air Medals and a DFC (Distinguished Flying Cross) during my seven months in country, presented, in true military fashion, for actions that were neither the most harrowing nor significant of my assignment.

My replacement, a Captain Simpson, was a very nice guy with a lot less fighter time than I had when I first reported to Bien Hoa. But the war was expanding fast, and even Detachment Two Alpha was growing by leaps and bounds. Before I left, I told Simpson to take things easy at first: "Be cautious, learn the terrain, and master the tricks of the trade before you get too aggressive."

By the time the MATS transports got me back to Florida four days later, word had been received at Hurlburt that Simpson had already been killed in action.

Simpson's quick demise was a great shock and a foretaste of things to come. By 1964, our "strike section" would lose over 22 aircrewmen killed in action, about the same number of "air commandos" we started out with in 1961. We survivors from that original group would forever after feel more than a little charmed—and because of that, a little guilty as well. These feelings may be common for combat veterans anywhere, but that doesn't make them any easier to bear.

# —4—

# Winning the War
# Nobody Heard Of

My B-4 bag was barely unpacked from Bien Hoa, and Jo Ann and I had just settled in for some much-anticipated family planning when the phone rang from Hurlburt operations. All leaves were being canceled. All pilots from the 6th Fighter Squadron (as my unit had been renamed) were being recalled to the base.

It was October 1962. Soviet intermediate-range ballistic missiles (IRBMs) had been discovered in Cuba—not by U-2 overflights, which was a cover story, but by CIA assets on the ground, who were never mentioned to the media in order to preserve their usefulness, if not their lives. Even then, presidents didn't go to war based on a single source of information, including high-tech information—*especially* high-tech information in those barely transistorized days. The resulting operation, called "Cuba II" in deference to Cuba I, the Bay of Pigs fiasco, brought the nation to the brink of war.

President Kennedy and the Joint Chiefs had given the Air Force primary responsibility for knocking out the IRBMs before they became operational, should an attack prove necessary. As is customary in such institutions at such times, the Air Staff's first impulse was to showcase its newest and shiniest toy. In those days, that was the F-100 Super Sabre, supersonic follow-on to the Korean War–vintage F-86. This plan would have been fine, except that the parallel trend in tactical air power at the time had been preparing for nuclear war. In TAC, the Tactical Air Command, this meant using low-yield nukes to offset the overwhelming infantry and armor advantage of the Warsaw Pact.

The result was an almost total absence of F-100 pilots who were up to speed on delivering conventional ordnance. All their effort had gone into esoteric maneuvers, like the famous vertical "over-the-shoulder toss" to deliver battlefield nuclear weapons and live to tell about it. Obviously, this advanced "Sabre" rattling was setting up the Air Force for a major embarrassment. TAC commanders knew that if they went into battle with F-100s, unnecessary losses and poor results were inevitable, possibly a botched raid, and maybe Armageddon.

Fortunately, discretion got the better part of valor. Somebody at Air Staff was wise enough to realize that this was not the time to screw around with half-trained crews and unproven equipment. The consensus grew that the job should go to guys who were experienced in conventional warfare, even if they weren't flying the latest aircraft. As it turned out, the only pilots in TAC that had current combat experience were we pilots in the 6th—and we flew AT-28s, hardly the most glamorous plane in the inventory. Even worse, the '28 was similar to the airplanes that had supported Cuba I, and nobody wanted to evoke comparisons with *that* disaster.

What the Air Force decided to do was this. Ten AT-28s from the 6th would fly a pathfinder, or FAC, mission to mark the targets for the F-100s. Our ordnance, in theory, would not be flares or smoke bombs, but napalm.

Now, anyone familiar with tactical air operations could see through this ploy instantly. Marking a target with napalm was like an usher showing you to your seat with a searchlight. If you could get ordnance that heavy close enough to "mark" the target, you could destroy it just as easily with the same load, which was what they had in mind. Without question, the supersonic Sabres would roar in on cue and make the rubble bounce, but if everything went right, the World War II–era prop planes would have done the job first, and nobody but the Cubans would know. As far as Congress, the headline-hungry press, and the justifiably anxious taxpayers were concerned, it would be just another triumph of the high-tech Air Force. Appropriations would go up, and the Cold War could grind on. Of course, as one of the '28 drivers who would be doing the heavy lifting, that was fine with me.

What we hadn't counted on was the possibility that World War III might start as a consequence of our little raid—an important concern to the Joint Chiefs of Staff (or JCS), and rightfully so. As a result, Florida almost sank under the weight of all the troops, support personnel, materiel, and tactical and air-defense firepower deployed in case a good plan went wrong.

Our main problem would be fuel. AT-28s had no in-flight refueling capabilities, and preliminary computations showed that unless winds were light or extremely favorable going out, we would land in the drink on our way back from the target. Our contingency plan was to ditch alongside any of the numerous Naval vessels that swarmed through the Florida strait enforcing the blockade, but that wasn't a pleasant prospect. The AT-28 didn't have good ditching characteristics, and if there was any chop at all, our most famous mission would likely be our last. As a result, some of us decided that if push came to shove, we'd try at least to make landfall, trim up the airplane, and bail out.

To tell the truth, I took the whole thing as a kind of exercise until the sun went down on the last day before the planned attack. I just didn't associate CONUS (continental United States) operations with a shooting war. That attitude changed when the last daylight "recce" (reconnaissance) photos came in "dripping wet." They showed the missiles, trucks, buildings—hell, even some of the *people*—we would be incinerating in 24 hours. That's when the knot formed in my stomach. I didn't feel much better when several B-47s landed at Hurlburt, fully armed and fueled for nuclear strikes on Soviet targets if even *one* atomic-tipped missile was launched from Cuba. I thought about Jo Ann and the millions of civilians who could die as a result of tomorrow's raid. That was the first time, I think, that the true dimensions and dynamics of the Cold War really sank in, and it was a deeply sobering experience.

Around midnight, our commander, Colonel King, was awakened by a priority TWIX. The message was short and sweet: *Stand down.*

Eleven hours before the first wave's scheduled takeoff time, the attack was canceled. Khrushchev and Kennedy had struck a secret bargain. Soviet ships in the eastern Caribbean had already turned around and were steaming back to port. Castro had begun dismantling his launchers. The Air Commandos' alert was terminated. After a decent interval, American Jupiter missiles would come home from Turkey—the other half of the bargain.

The politicians had averted Armageddon, at least for the time being.

As Cuba II "slid off the scope," my annual leave was reinstated. Jo Ann and I wanted to start a family and, as I recalled, you needed a mother *and* a father for that. Although my remaining leave didn't last long, we made the most of it. In September 1963, our first child, Julia, was born, although I would barely make it back from my next assignment in time to see it. In February 1963, I was on my way to yet another remote corner of the world: the rugged mountains of northwest Iran, home of the Kurdish people and site of a top-secret war that, to my knowledge, few, if any, Americans have read about.

The Kurds are an independent-minded people with a warrior tradition going back to antiquity. Their ancestral homeland, Kurdistan, is an amorphous area the size of several U.S. states, encompassing a small part of southeast Turkey and a sliver of what once was the Soviet Union and big chunks of northern Iraq and northwest Iran. Similar in culture to the Afghans but anthropologically grouped with Aryans, the Kurds' light skins and blue eyes made them very appealing to Western television cameras covering Desert Storm and its aftermath. Those same traits, conversely, have made them objects of scorn and distrust to the more numerous Arab and Persian peoples that surround them. Consequently, the Kurds' independent spirit has had few opportunities for expression—and none of them peaceful.

One attempt at Kurdish independence was instigated, oddly enough, by the Soviets. After World War II, a short-lived, Communist-backed state called the Mahabad Republic was carved out of the Soviets' Iranian occupation zone. The republic was a veiled attempt to expand Communist influence into Iran's ethnic bouillabaisse, which was at least as heterogeneous and potentially troublesome to central authorities as the Soviets' own.

Understandably, creation of this new socialist state did not sit well with the American and Iranian governments. In 1946–47 President Truman helped the youthful Shah obliterate this young republic and keep the Russians at bay with a promise to "use the bomb," which, in those days, was a threat only Americans could make.

This caused the focus of Kurdish independence to shift to Iraq. After the militant Baathists came to power in 1959, Baghdad began supporting Kurdish insurgents under the "Great General" (as he was known to his people), Ben Bella Mustafa Barzani. Their objective was to help the Kurds drive across the Iranian border to harass and destabilize the local Persian authorities. By 1962, the Iranian police, despite the assistance of army units, had lost control in many of the rural and mountainous areas. The Soviets had jumped in, covertly joining hands with Iraq to help the Kurds against their "common and ancient enemy," Iran. By 1963, this well-orchestrated war, prosecuted by several hundred thousand Kurdish irregulars from Iraqi sanctuaries, had alarmed the Shah enough that he was forced again to appeal for U.S. help.

This pattern of Soviet-sponsored insurrection against authoritarian U.S. allies was common in that era, and was repeated in Southeast Asia (Vietnam, Cambodia, Laos), Africa (Ethiopia, Egypt, Libya, Angola, Mozambique), and Central America (Cuba and later El Salvador and Nicaragua). When you chart these and other cases on a map, as we did, you get not so much a case of falling dominoes as the outbreak of measles: one red blotch following another—all driven by a well-known vector, a heads-up COMINTERN establishing congenial socialist governments. World communism may not have been monolithic, but it was certainly well coordinated, chiefly by the Soviet Union.

Not that our own skirts in this area were too clean. The West had been doing something similar since the dawn of European colonialism, pitting friendly against unfriendly factions in colonized countries to preserve the status quo. Shortly after I left Vietnam, a Buddhist priest, Ngo Quang Duc, immolated himself in protest over President Diem's repressive regime in South Vietnam, a watershed event many people consider our first warning that we were backing a fatally unpopular government. (Diem would, in fact, be overthrown and killed in a U.S.-backed coup in early November 1963, shortly before Kennedy himself was assassinated. The junta would fall in 1964, as did the next three South Vietnamese governments in as many years.)

In a tactical sense, that's what the Cold War was about: the two major powers fencing, and taking their lumps, through proxies, with the local people picking up the tab, at least in terms of bloodshed. Defending American interests in such spots once again became my end of the log.

Our team consisted of an 80-man Army "SF" (or "Special Forces") contingent and two Air Force officers: me and my immediate supervisor, Major Arnie Tillman. Tillman had more SF experience than I did, but I had seen more recent combat, which was why I was selected. Arnie had been shot down in a B-17 over Russia in World War II and was repatriated through Tehran. He was a very knowledgeable and demanding officer who deserves credit for what we accomplished—a lot with very little.

Our overall commander was an SF lieutenant colonel named Bill Simpson, a great officer—thoughtful and intelligent, one of the best bosses I've ever had. He would gain some notoriety during a later tour in Vietnam when he retired in disgust after the attempted court-martial of a Colonel Rheault, another special-forces officer unjustly accused of torturing and killing VC prisoners. (All charges against Rheault were subsequently dropped, but the damage to his reputation had already been done.)

We arrived in Iran in March 1963—the dead of winter. I had expected something like the Arizona desert, chilly at night but pleasant during the day, and was totally surprised to find a scene out of *Doctor Zhivago*: ice and snow everywhere, alpine mountains, and villagers who were occasionally eaten by wolves. We hadn't even been issued heavy winter clothing. We slept in the basement of the MAAG (Military Assistance Advisory Group) compound, which was a palace compared to our pup tents on the ice ledges in the field.

When we got to "the front" (actually a series of camps, each more remote and ill-maintained than the last), we found four heavy-infantry divisions under Iranian General Azhari bogged down not only by the bad weather and worse terrain, but by lack of discipline, disorganization, poor communications, poor logistics, poor training, and totally inappropriate tactics. Other than that, the Shah had fielded a crackerjack team.

Our MAAG detachment was based at Kermanshah, a town on the Tehran-Baghdad highway in extreme southeastern Kurdistan, a few kilometers from the Iraqi border. It was far enough from the fighting to let us get our act together without excessive threats but close enough to gauge results before they became ancient history. Our first strategic goal was to seal the Kurdish border between Iran and Iraq and prevent rebel troops and supplies from moving freely between the two. To do this, we'd need a vastly more effective fighting force and the logistics to keep it in the field.

The ground advisors started with the basics: field hygiene, weapons proficiency, small-unit tactics, and aggressiveness training for Iranian junior officers and NCOs who would then disseminate that training throughout the force. The Iranian *sarboz*—the private soldier—was typically a compliant conscript who, owing to the harsh civilian life, made a pretty tough trooper, especially when it came to suffering privations in the field. Our biggest complaint was with the Iranian leadership. Iranian officers too often held their men in contempt and administered corporal punishments, including beatings, for the smallest infractions. Strong discipline is fine. But in the absence of good commanders, it just turns army camps into prisons.

After administering this indoctrination and training, our advisors went into the field with Iranians in the role of stiffeners. We didn't fight their battles for them, as we did too often in Vietnam, but coached the Iranians in combat, observed their performance, and critiqued them afterward. The advisors also brought back information for analysis by U.S. and Iranian intelligence. Unlike Vietnam, too, we had no rules of engagement. As far as the outside world was concerned, this war wasn't happening, so we had no interference from foreign governments, the press, or international agencies. Also, because of the bare, mountainous terrain and sparse population, we knew pretty well who and where the enemy was, so civilian casualties were low. It was a textbook anti-insurgency war, and we were determined to make a casebook success of it.

Any successful unconventional strategy includes a strong dose of "civic action" initiatives—building schools, digging water wells, constructing aid stations—aimed at winning the hearts and minds of the population and leaving them disenchanted with the rebels. The absurd overkill by both sides made such programs an eventual laughingstock in Vietnam (destroying villages in order to save them and VC shooting villagers to ensure their loyalty), but in Iran we got it right from the beginning. Everywhere we went, the locals invited us to sit down and have tea, and it was hard to refuse, even though the frequently unboiled water was sometimes more dangerous than the enemy. In Vietnam, we seemed to forget that war is about *people*, not technology. We would not make this mistake in Iran.

Those of us in the air contingent had a different—and in some ways, more challenging—task. Although the Kurdish insurrection was a genuine threat to the Shah (if they managed to set up even a de facto independent state in the northwest, the patchwork of ethnic minorities in the rest of Iran could unravel), the whole theater was treated like a leper colony by the Iranian air establishment. Fighting mountain rebels isn't the most glorious task, and the powers-that-be wanted to support us without getting much mud on their boots. As a result, our junkyard air force of a dozen C-47s and 15 T-6Gs (World War II trainers with zero-launch hard points on the wings for light ordnance) at our only air base, a narrow gravel strip, was manned mostly by misfits and malcontents from the Iranian air force: an "F Troop" of the skies. The real Iranian air force operated F-86Fs at Hamadan and other major airfields just beyond a comfortable combat radius from the scene of action. We used them whenever we could, which was seldom and mostly for show.

However, we did have a couple of things going for us, and we made them the foundation of our "air campaign." First, our local pilots, although they were the dregs of the air force, knew their equipment and were competent military fliers. What they lacked was a coherent air-ground tactical doctrine and proficiency in weapons and logistics delivery. They also had plenty of aircraft, particularly light transports, which was a refreshing change.

To create an air-strike capability, we rigged the T-6s with 30-caliber machine gun pods and racks for five-inch Zuni HVARs (high-velocity aerial rockets), as well as spotter rockets and even a few light bombs. The real value of these birds, though, was for FAC duty in placing artillery rounds and for the psychological boost their appearance gave Iranian soldiers. Having been on both ends of an aerial attack, I can affirm the extraordinary morale lift even a single, delapidated airplane gives to friendly forces and the feeling of dread it inspires when its weapons, however modest, are aimed at you.

I also learned a new respect for air-transport resources. The Iranian army was able to operate at considerable distances from their bases because of our ability to resupply them on demand from the air, a big factor in mountain warfare. We also rigged a loud-hailer on one C-47 Gooney Bird, and flew around enemy enclaves broadcasting propaganda and helpful hints on how to surrender. I tagged along on many of these missions, especially early on, just to get a firsthand, accurate feel for what was going on. The Iranian Goon-drivers were gutsy and competent, just what it takes to survive in mountain flying.

Both the ground and air campaigns were aimed at building the "sinews of war," which is a combat infrastructure of the type American servicemen take for granted: rapid, secure communication; wholesome field rations; plentiful ammunition; timely evacuation of wounded and adequate medical treatment; good real-time combat intelligence; and a sound doctrine for coordinated air-ground activity. With that infrastructure, the war becomes much easier. Without it, you're basically fighting like feuding bandits. You may not lose, but you probably won't win, at least in one lifetime. This lack of a button-down, systematic approach to war, I believe, is one reason multigenerational ethnic conflicts flourish around the world. The notions of individual glory, a warrior mystique, and fierce independence (as opposed to rational interdependence) make regional vendettas not only possible, but even profitable for their leaders. In my experience, when one side of such a dispute gets serious and adopts appropriate, systematic, war-winning methods, people suddenly find lots of new reasons to live peaceably together.

After six months or so, our reforms began to bear fruit. Although no big, decisive battles were fought, in the numerous firefights and ambushes the Iranians generally came out on top. By the fall of 1963, the threat to the Shah's government was gone. Barzani had lost a lot of men and knew he couldn't achieve his objective, which was to defeat the Shah's big divisions "in detail"—that is, break them up into smaller, more vulnerable units. Now, even those small units were more than a match for his irregulars, and he was forced to go on the defensive, always a losing proposition for a guerrilla army.

By spring 1964, the war was essentially over. More aggressive and effective Iranian patrolling had reestablished the Shah's sovereignty in contested areas, and the enemy no longer appeared in company- or even platoon-sized units. The hard-core Kurdish troops withdrew permanently to the Iraqi side. By the end of the first year, local police could once again enforce law and order without recourse to military firepower.

Eighteen months (and three TDYs) after we first arrived, we could declare total victory without fear of contradiction. The air advisors' job from that point on consisted primarily of documenting the institutions we'd created so that our 10-man replacement team could take over quickly and easily and keep the "railroad" we had built on track. General Azhari emerged a hero and went on to become the Shah's chief of staff. The rest of us were rotated back to the States, our wives, and other commands.

In retrospect, the 1963–64 Iranian war was the one and only clear-cut, unambiguous victory I would be associated with in my career. Perhaps it was the last such victory America would enjoy until the "great" Panama raid of 1990 or the rout of Iraq in Desert Storm—although even that one-sided victory left many regional problems unresolved. We achieved not only the military objectives we set for ourselves in Iran, but the political outcomes, too. Our philosophy was basically "keep it small and keep it manageable." To us secret warriors, escalation of such conflicts into big, conventional wars, as was happening in Vietnam under Lyndon Johnson, was just another sign of failure.

The taste of victory was sweet but, for me at least, it didn't last long.

# —5—

# CIA Station Laos

I returned to Hurlburt Field in mid-1964, confident I could help win a war but not so sure about my career.

Since that fateful interview with General Mundell several years earlier, I'd been too busy playing "Terry and the Pirates" to worry much about below-the-zone promotions—personnel maneuvers that can end with general's stars and offices on the E ring at the Pentagon. Although I'd seen action in a couple of secret wars, few people in authority knew much about it because "none of it ever happened."

I knew that unless I got back into a mainstream Air Force unit fast, I'd never rise to command the big conventional military units that I had been trained at the Point to do. Still, as John Lennon of the Beatles pointed out, real life has a way of happening while we're busy making plans.

While I was in Iran, Colonel Harry C. "Hienie" Aderholt had taken command of the Wing, and we finally had a CO who was not only a fine flier and officer but a superb combat leader as well. Hienie, who would become very important in my subsequent career and personal life, was a "mustang": a man with no college who rose through the ranks to become an officer-pilot and combat leader in World War II, Korea, and Vietnam. He was and is one of the most charismatic commanders I've ever known, and I've seen a lot of them. He had even been detailed for a number of years to the CIA; something I was soon to learn all about. He was eternally suspicious of the military bureaucracy, and although he disliked big staffs and the systems approach to defense problems, he always kept his own crew of highly educated officers (which he called his "back-room boys") informed, motivated, and on tap. His style was to tackle problems head-on; not in a bullheaded or foolish manner, but with intelligence backed by guts. He was a model for me and a lot of others who rose to positions of responsibility, and I think the Air Force and our country would've been a lot poorer without him.

52

Back at Hurlburt, I was assigned to train replacements for our ongoing operations in Vietnam, now going great guns after the Gulf of Tonkin Resolution gave Lyndon Johnson a virtual blank check to escalate the war. Our equipment included not only AT-28s and C-47s, but A-1 Skyraiders and a squadron of O-1 Bird Dogs (the Air Force version of the Army L-19), the preeminent FAC aircraft of the day. Before long I was assigned to collateral duties as a Wing staff officer and eventually became Hienie's director of tactical operations.

Before Colonel Aderholt was transferred to Southeast Asia to command the 56th Air Commandos at Nakorn Phanom in Thailand, he recommended me for the Air Command and Staff College at Maxwell AFB, Montgomery, Alabama. Command and Staff is the training college any officer hoping to lead bigger units must attend. I spent half of 1965 and the first half of 1966 at Maxwell, and graduated in June. While I was there, President Johnson began bombing North Vietnam and sent 3,500 U.S. Marines ashore at Danang, the first contingent openly labeled "combat troops" rather than advisors. War fever was in the air. Most of my classmates were angling for a tour, and career-enhancing combat experience, with our growing forces in Vietnam. That was when reality interrupted my plans.

Hienie had told me a little about his adventures as a CIA "detailee" in the late 1950s and early 1960s. In CIA jargon, a detailee is anyone from another government service assigned to fulfill a specific CIA need for which the Agency itself is not normally staffed, such as air combat. The CIA consists of "staff," or regular career officers; "contract" civilians with critical skills who free-lance for the Agency from time to time; and detailees. Detailees are viewed as "Christmas help," because that's just how they function, although some detailees wind up spending more time with the Agency than with their parent services. One detailee, in fact—Admiral Stansfield Turner—actually ran the store.

Hienie participated in this capacity in a number of CIA "black" programs, making clandestine drops into North Korea and, later, North Vietnam and elsewhere. The expanding war in Southeast Asia created more operational saddles than the Agency could fill. In the air war, many of the skills they needed were similar to things I'd been doing in Air Force special ops. There was a ring of glamour and intrigue to a CIA assignment (as well as a lot less bureaucratic claptrap), especially to an aging fighter pilot like me who was already finding peacetime assignments frustrating and confining while our country was at war.

When a request for a "detailee" volunteer came down from the CIA, I volunteered—and for no better reason than just to see what it was like.

Like the military, the CIA does its own psychological screening for covert operatives. It takes great stock in polygraph testing, and runs a baseline profile for every employee, even clerks. It's an exhaustive, exhausting process. They're concerned about screening out not only double agents and saboteurs, but anyone who might later be compromised through blackmail even if their heart remains true-blue. In those days, anyone who lived a secret life—homosexuals, heavy gamblers, alcoholics, chronic adulterers, you name it—were shown the door. Again, it seemed strange for an organization filled with spies to turn away people who were already good at keeping secrets, but experience was on their side.

After I passed the security scrubbing, I moved my wife and daughter back to Oklahoma and found myself once again boarding a transport for Vietnam. With the recent race riots in Los Angeles and violent antiwar protests beginning to erupt in almost every major U.S. city, it was not clear exactly *who* would be living in the war zone, them or me—but that was life in the sixties.

This time my destination was the CIA station at Saigon. I was told to report to J.R. Swasey, chief of what the spymasters creatively called the "air branch," which is just what it was.

J.R. was reputedly an "old China Hand," which meant that he had served covertly in Asia during World War II and was therefore entitled to a little extra swagger in his walk and a splash or two more gin with his quinine—as well as the unquestioned obeisance of new agents, and detailees like me. We were billeted in a small hotel, called the Duc, used exclusively by the CIA and guarded by Nung tribesmen, the agency's mercenaries of choice (a kind of American Gurkha). We went to work in short-sleeved shirts and slacks at the American Embassy, which was the headquarters for local CIA activities.

J.R. said most of my duties would involve helping to superintend the fleet of aircraft used by Air America, the CIA's proprietary airline, in their routine "trash hauling" (personnel and resupply) flights all over South Vietnam. We also had contracts with China Airlines and Continental Airlines, which operated smaller STOL (short takeoff and landing) aircraft like the Pilatus Porter to do the same thing in the same area. Any way you looked at it, though, the job was the same: running a third-rate Oriental airline. Where were the birds that went *bang*?

I also got the job of coordinating the visits of VIPs from Washington and virtually anywhere else in the States. In addition to ensuring hotel and transportation accommodations, I usually pulled "souvenir duty" as well, which meant buying what we euphemistically called BUFs, Big Ugly Fellows, the god-awful ceramic elephants that were Saigon's equivalent to New York's Statue of Liberty figurines. In fact, I bought so many BUFs that I finally went to the factory near Bien Hoa, my old base, and negotiated a volume discount. Was this what a West-Point trained, veteran combat pilot was supposed to be doing? Where the hell was the war?

Part of the answer lay in Saigon itself. By 1966, the South Vietnamese capital had gone from being the "Paris of the Orient" to the "Las Vegas of Indochina." Or, more accurately, it was a combination of Atlantic City, the Ringling Brothers Circus, and Detroit during the riots of the sixties. Saigon wasn't exactly a city under siege; it was a city choking on its own gluttony for power, luxury, high living, and vice. Over 10,000 uniformed Americans of the highest and lowest ranks occupied the place like an army of imperious tourists. We dodged VC terrorist bombs by day and dined at world-class restaurants at night. Even the most menial American official lived in a splendor undreamed of stateside, with housemaids, cooks, and drivers all paid for by a weekly paycheck that would last most Vietnamese families a year. I mean, some of us were really *having a good time* here, and almost all of that high living came at the expense of the local population. Prostitution, a genteel industry even under the French, now flourished openly on Tu Do street and in a dozen previously respectable neighborhoods. The sweet odor of decay was more pungent on the streets of Saigon than it was in the fetid jungles—and our dollars and our fantasies were the fertilizer.

After six weeks on this silly assignment, I went into J.R.'s office to calmly and rationally discuss my low morale.

"I quit, goddamn it!" and gave him a brief but colorful summary of my complaints.

"The hell you are."

"The hell I am. I'm a volunteer—I can quit whenever I want, and I quit. There's a war going on and I came to fight. I'm one of the most experienced combat pilots in the goddamn Air Force and if you don't let me fly an airplane or give me command of people who do, I'll find someone who will."

J.R.'s eyes got real big when I threatened to go over his head to Washington, since I was plugged into a network of high-powered Vietnamese officials and he knew it. On my first tour, I had gotten to know Colonel Vinh, our liaison officer at Bien Hoa, who was now VNAF chief of staff. I also knew Nguyen Cao Ky, a C-47 squadron commander from my first tour, who was now the South Vietnamese prime minister. I had also been friends with Captain Su, a good AT-28 pilot who had separated from the VNAF and was now running Air Vietnam. I had rekindled acquaintances with all these men since I returned. Even J.R. had been impressed. I could use these contacts as sources of intelligence that J.R. himself could only dream about. If I wanted to make a big stink, the stench, he knew, could envelop his whole station.

J.R. said, "I'll see what I can do," which meant he'd try to find some make-work that would help me feel useful. These fellows had a cushy little empire going, and I don't think they wanted anyone to wreck it with blood and bullets.

As it turned out, J.R. entertained some Agency bigwigs shortly thereafter in his grand French colonial home near the Independence Palace. I attended, along with a number of executives who worked directly for William Colby, then the CIA's chief of Far East. After some initial cocktail party chitchat, I mentioned that I was leaving and repeated my complaints. The visiting officials seemed surprised and sympathetic. The next day a cable came in from CIA headquarters ordering me to report to CIA Station Vientiane, Laos.

J.R.'s face clouded up when he saw the bad news. He fired back a request for clarification, stating that I already had a "sensitive and important" job with his station and couldn't be spared until a replacement had been received. Headquarters responded promptly and curtly: *Referenced cable was not a request but directive in nature.*

I went directly to the Duc Hotel, slapped on the only summer uniform I'd brought with me, and threw a toilet kit and underwear in an overnight bag. I didn't even wait to ship my footlocker, but went straight to Tan Son Nhut and grabbed the first "scatback" T-39 shuttle flight to Thailand.

The trim little twin jet landed at Udorn, Thailand, home to a big Air Force contingent, including a 1st Air Commando Wing detachment (code name WATERPUMP), with 70 or 80 AT-28s and the 432nd Tactical Recon Wing flying RF-4s, F-104s, and A-1s. My instructions had said to report to "AB-1," and if that meant little to me, it meant less to the local troops. How do you even go about asking for a secret installation? Welcome to the CIA.

I figured the place to start was the Air America compound on the southeast side of the field. After a couple of inquiries, somebody finally took pity on me and pointed out a low, unmarked building on the edge of the field. There were no guards, just a locked door and a buzzer, which I pressed several times. A voice finally answered and asked what I wanted. Good question— I didn't even know who I was supposed to report to!

"Captain Richard Secord reporting for duty."

After a puzzled silence, the voice said, "Okay, I guess you want Bob."

Inside I met a young CIA staff officer named Bob Blake, an ex-USAF pilot and Air Force Academy graduate who left the service for a career with the CIA—permanent party, not Christmas help like me. Like J.R. Swasey in Saigon, Bob ran the tactical air ops, such as it was, for Laos. His staff consisted of one man: himself.

Bob was a nice fellow but pretty inexperienced, which helped explain the haste with which my orders had been cut at the Agency's headquarters. He decided to introduce me to our mutual bosses—the chief and deputy chief of the CIA's paramilitary base—right away. While we walked, he explained the rather streamlined organization CIA field operations used, which appealed to me.

The CIA had a three-tiered hierarchy, beginning with the chief of station, or COS. At Vientiane, the COS was Theodore Shackley, a rising star in the Agency who had a classical military and CIA intelligence background. His credits included the famous Berlin Tunnel (that conduit for Iron Curtain intelligence in 1961), and he had been the Miami COS after the Bay of Pigs. His handpicked operatives had uncovered the Russian IRBMs that led to Cuba II and to Kennedy's finest hour. Shackley's stock had gone way up in Washington, and he was put in charge of the CIA's paramilitary operations in Laos. Ted was about six feet tall, and light complected with sandy hair, earning him the nickname "blond ghost." He was articulate in many languages, especially the Slavic dialects, and had a wry sense of humor, which he tried to keep secret. Needless to say, he knew his craft inside and out. He was an aggressive leader and a helluva taskmaster. Although we eventually butted heads a few times, I respected him a lot.

Next in the chain of command was the chief of base, or COB, and his deputy. COB in Thailand was Bill Lair and his deputy, Pat Landry, who worked as an inseparable team and never stepped on each other's toes. Bill usually ran the war in Northern Laos and Pat was responsible for the Panhandle. When Bob took me in to meet them, their two beat-up desks were pushed together like a couple of supply sergeants', head-to-head, so that they could trade hand signals and notes while they talked on the phone. Next to Hienie Aderholt, Bill and Pat were the two best combat leaders I ever worked for. That always struck me as peculiar. Here I was, a West Point officer, trained in the wake of "Black '50" and the Cribbing Scandal, and my best command role models were an Air Force mustang and two CIA civilians!

Bill and Pat explained the third and last rung in the CIA field hierarchy as it applied to my new assignment. Each of Laos' five up-country military regions had its own CIA unit, headed by a chief of unit, or COU. The CIA eventually had over 80,000 troops, mostly Meo tribesmen, on the ground in Laos, so it was by no means the "sideshow" some analysts and historians have made it out to be. It was a real war, played for the highest stakes.

Bob and I were ordered to expand the clandestine helicopter infiltration and exfiltration system used for placing "road watch" teams on the Ho Chi Minh Trail. As most people know, the Ho Chi Minh Trail was the jugular that kept both NVA and VC troops supplied in South Vietnam and Cambodia. America had tried cutting it for years, but air interdiction could only do so much. Everyone knew that ground troops—in force—would be needed to permanently squeeze off the continuous river of replacements and materiel Hanoi sent south, but neither our MACV in Saigon nor our Joint Chiefs of Staff in Washington ever bit that particular bullet, which I think is one reason North Vietnam wound up winning the war. Three good divisions could've driven west past Tchepone to Savannakhet in southern Laos and parked across the Trail. The NVA would've been forced to play by our rules instead of theirs; but that never happened.

In the absence of a sizable ground presence, we had to do the best we could with air interdiction. The CIA's job was to provide intelligence about when and where suitable targets were moving, so Ted Shackley ordered our road watch teams to "cover the Trail like dew."

I was billeted in a Thai-style house (raised up on stilts), equipped with mostly native furniture, which I never really got to use because I spent so little time there. The CIA role in Laos was rapidly expanding from a country-store operation to a full-service supermarket, and Bob and I were right in the thick of things. In addition to collecting the aircraft and crews we needed for clandestine missions, we also laid out plans for a first-class operations center for interpreting photo reconnaissance, originating strike-order requests, and coordinating missions—especially the "exfills," or team extractions, half of which were unscheduled emergencies while the teams were under fire.

After a few months, just as we started to get a handle on the infrastructure, Bob was reassigned out of the theater. As if to compensate me for having to perform twice the work with half the labor, the Air Force promoted me to major. I had been a captain for six years—about as long as you could remain in one rank without facing involuntary discharge—but I was too busy to lament my fate. As soon as I accumulated enough rotary-wing assets and qualified crews to expand our service on the Trail, I was called upon to increase air support for the rest of the country. The war was really heating up, from the bombing of Hanoi itself, which had commenced in June 1966, to support for a large U.S.-ARVN offensive in the Iron Triangle region of South Vietnam in January 1967. Six months after I arrived, I was running a pretty big air war from one tiny office and a telephone. If I'd had two phones, like Ho Chi Minh was rumored to have had in his "tree house" command post in Hanoi, who knows what we could have accomplished?

North Vietnam viewed Southeast Asia as one big battlefield, and deployed their forces accordingly. We, on the other hand, created rigid bureaucratic, political, and military boundaries, and constantly made our commanders fight our own system as well as the enemy. Seventh Air Force ran air-combat operations in Saigon in association with MACV. The Navy, of course, never subordinated its command to anyone, and operated its carrier war with, on occasion, only nominal coordination with the other services. The war in Cambodia was supervised by the local "U.S. Military Equipment Delivery" office and was funded under MAP (the Military Assistance Program). And Thailand, which had significant "CT," or Communist counter-terrorist problems, was viewed by many as yet another completely separate theater of operations. The CIA was put in charge of its own "nonwar" in Laos, the proverbial "hind tit" on the great boar hog the war had become. Add to this a State Department ambassador in each country who thought, because the conflicts were all undeclared, that *he* was running the war, and you have a command and control system that only a Detroit whiz kid could understand—one reason the theater quickly became known as McNamara's war. Even the famous (or infamous) SEACOR (Southeast Asia Coordination) meetings, which I attended as chart bearer for Ted Shackley, quickly deteriorated into battles over turf, not strategies on how to effectively confront and defeat the enemy.

At least at the CIA we had the power to clean up our portion of this mulligan stew, and I came up with a few ideas.

Experience had taught me to keep things simple. At the COB level, we established three operational divisions: air, ground, and logistics. As the only guy with wings on his chest and buckshot up his britches, I became chief of air. A fellow I would wind up working very closely with and who would become a lifelong friend, Tom Clines, was appointed chief of ground. The logistics chief ran not only the supply-support role, but communications and administration. A fourth division, foreign intelligence, or FI, was already established at the chief of station level in Vientiane, and since this was a very specialized, centralized function and needed a spymaster like Ted Shackley at the helm, we left well enough alone.

Apparently all this appealed to Shackley's passion for making order out of chaos, and my plan was adopted as soon as Bill and Pat took it forward. Headquarters had even approved our request for a new, more secure home: a million-dollar, walled two-story concrete headquarters with state-of-the-art communications and on-site quarters. I detailed some of the partitioning (so that the right people could talk easily while staying out of everyone else's hair), but I was mostly concerned with the telecommunications system, our lifeline to the world. With a little forethought and a lot of on-site follow-up, we internetted completely with the existing Air Force system already on the base. Because we were in regular contact with people (such as Laotian tribesmen, Thai mercenaries, and others) the uniformed services either didn't know or care about, our system was easily the most comprehensive on the block. Many times, it was all that stood between success and disaster.

From late 1966 on, my relationship with our new chief of ground, Tom Clines, had a big impact on my tour in Laos and the rest of my career. Tom was a "foxhole buddy"—someone with whom you establish a bond born out of shared adversity and danger, and even a few successes. It has no real analogue in peacetime. About six foot four and fair, with prematurely grey hair and boyish charm, he reminded me a lot of Jimmy Stewart. When I met him, Tom had five kids, which was a minor miracle given the small amount of time he spent at home.

Tom was a CIA staffer, a GS-14 who had joined the Agency after combat experience as an Army noncommissioned officer in Korea. As a spook, he helped train guerrillas for the Bay of Pigs, and their abandonment by the CIA soured him permanently on Agency headquarters. He was also case officer on several operations in Africa and in Latin America. Just before coming to Laos, he had been assigned to the Miami station with orders to harass Fidel Castro. Because my job was using air to support the war on the ground, Tom and I spent a lot of time together. I like to think that our collaboration was as good as the teamwork developed between Bill and Pat. The record for our three years together shows that we came close.

My first concern as chief of Laotian air operations was the high number of sorties I was called upon to provide and support. As our coverage of the Ho Chi Minh Trail increased, demands on air assets went up arithmetically, as illustrated by this snapshot of a typical infil/exfil mission.

First, a suitable landing site had to be chosen based on aerial and ground intelligence. You wanted to be far enough from the enemy to get in and out unseen, if possible, but you didn't want to be so far from your objective that the team wasted a lot of time or took too many risks getting there.

Next, six to a dozen men had to be assembled and led. Our road watch groups were passive observation teams charged with radioing information about target movement on the Ho Chi Minh Trail in anticipation of air strikes. We experimented from time to time with our own special guerrilla units, or SGUs, who would attack trail targets directly, but we could seldom mount these in sufficient numbers, and they were no match for the NVA units guarding or transiting the road. As a result, air strikes weren't so much our tool of choice as the recourse of necessity.

Even without combat, our Little Guys, as we called the tribesmen who served on most of our teams and as light infantry irregulars, gave us special problems. Most were illiterate in their native tongue and virtually none read English. How could we get them to accurately report the quantitative and qualitative information they observed on the Trail?

We solved this in large measure late in 1967 with a program called, symbolically, Hark 1. The "Hark box" was a VHF-FM transceiver about the size of a brick with the alphanumeric keys replaced by symbols for troops, tanks, trucks, artillery—items commonly sighted on the Trail, with additional keys for multiplying the selected item by tens. After the observer figured out what and how many of something he'd seen, he entered it in the box and pushed a "squirt" button, transmitting the data in one pass.

The downside was that it took two Volpar (twin-engine Beech) aircraft circling constantly to catch and relay the data burst to either Savannakhet (from "red" orbit in the north) or Pakse (from "blue" orbit in the south), where the intelligence interpretation was made and sent to our headquarters in Thailand via teletype. It was an improvised answer to the lowest common denominator in the system, but it worked.

Team leadership was always a problem. Because these were clandestine missions with a high potential for combat, but *not* planned combat assignments, we needed leaders with self-discipline and resourcefulness as well as tactical skill and aggressiveness: the good judgment to get the job done without either running from or looking for fights. Some of our best team leaders came from the Thais.

Once a team had been trained for operations at a specific site, it had to be inserted—always with appropriate combat air cover—and supported. The NVA was constantly combing the Trail for our guys, so each team knew their stay was provisional. We didn't tempt fate and scheduled team removals before their chances of discovery got too high. This doesn't mean there weren't firefights, but emergency exfills to me were a sign of failure, and we took every precaution to avoid them.

Once the system was up to speed in late 1967, we had over 80 passive observation teams in place. Statistically, we were running one infill, one exfill, and one emergency extraction operation each day, every day, seven days a week.

The war in Laos was the reverse image of the war in Vietnam. In Laos, *we* were the guerrillas. The Pathet Lao (PL) and NVA held some of the towns and most of the roads, which they needed to move their larger units. The U.S.-backed forces were irregulars (mostly Meo tribesmen in the north, but with significant numbers of Thai volunteers and mercenaries) moving at night to harass the enemy and tie down his forces. Led in the north by General Vang Pao, the Little Guys inflicted a lot of NVA casualties and were a bone in Hanoi's throat throughout the war.

We had air superiority, but because the United States did not officially acknowledge our presence in Laos, we kept it low-key, which is not how air campaigns work best. In fact, the true scope of our operations wasn't acknowledged until the Symington hearings in 1972, during which Senator Stuart Symington professed shock at the CIA's success in both prosecuting and concealing the war. Symington's stage acting impressed me, because I had personally accompanied him on his Laotian tour, which included Site 36, a place we called "the Alamo" because of its numerous big unit battles.

As far as I know, I was the first person to more-or-less run a large-scale tactical air campaign *covertly*. When our ragtag little air force, numbering about 20 choppers and whatever WATERPUMP AT-28s and USAF A-1s we could muster, couldn't do the job, we called in air strikes from "7/13," the consolidated command post for the 7th and 13th Air Forces located at Udorn. As I would eventually find out, though, the assets we asked for didn't always show up.

My way of "managing" this mixed bag of airmen was to work among them as much as I could in order to understand their problems and give them confidence in my operations. This was especially important because my helicopter, Porter, C-7 Caribou, and C-123 pilots were mostly Air America civilians, and civilians, even very professional and disciplined ones, are better at saying "Drop dead!" than "Yessir!" when you give them a dangerous order. They weren't cowards, by any means, but you had to explain things to them thoroughly before they would buy into your plan.

The WATERPUMP unit was straight military and a lot easier to deal with. I flew with them as often as I could, frequently as an IP for Laotian and U.S. pilots. My call sign, "Tiger 96" (all IPs were called "tiger"), may have been heard on aerial frequencies more often and for more years than any other, given the time I spent in Laos.

One of our first big struggles against the military hierarchy came over so-called Dr Pepper strikes waged by 7th Air Force in Saigon. This exceptionally poor "strategy" was a typical bureaucratic response to a high-command mandate to generate the largest number of aircraft possible for F-4 and F-105 strikes into North Vietnam. Unfortunately, this otherwise laudable goal was pursued in a way that violated one of modern war's basic principles: the element of surprise. Under the "Dr Pepper" strategy, our main force missions were sent out at ten in the morning and at two and four in the afternoon, every afternoon, like clockwork—allowing the NVA gunners to eat their lunches in peace because they knew they were safe from air attack until the next "scheduled" raid.

The reason for this absurd practice was that fighter maintenance could be scheduled more efficiently if strike times were standardized. We tried to convince the Air Force that the goal in war is defeating the enemy, not optimizing logistics or racking up some arbitrary score—like sorties flown or bomb tonnage dropped—on an administrative tote board. Like many other field commanders, we fought to get the policy changed, but never succeeded. In a war that was increasingly dominated by statisticians instead of combat leaders, it was another sign of the times.

Because CIA's communications plugged directly into Royal Laotian Air Force (RLAF) as well as 7/13th and MACV channels, I could usually obtain air support for our guys in the field faster than my counterparts in the other services. This gave General Vang Pao the notion that I had magical powers. I was the first airman to support him effectively from the air. He used to call me "Colonel Deeck" even though I constantly corrected him and told him I was just a lowly major.

"That's all right," he would say. "In the Lao Army, you are a colonel!"

Some of our ground actions were pretty harrowing, with or without air support. In the handful of times I was up-country during these battles, I gained enormous respect for the Meo.

One telling incident took place in 1967, on Phou Mok Lok, a mountain over 6,000 feet high in northern Laos overlooking the only road out of Sam Neua south to the Plain of Jarres, a route usually choked with nighttime NVA traffic. Because our aircraft had been unsuccessful in interdicting these convoys, General Vang Pao decided to seize the mountain, which was defended by a squad of NVA regulars with 82 mm mortars in reinforced bunkers, and let his 105 mm howitzer do the job of clobbering the convoys for us.

Over the next week, Vang Pao moved his forces, about 200 men, onto the adjacent peak only 2,000 meters from his objective. Once he was in place, we airlifted the 105 howitzers (disassembled and in slings), as well as two 75 mm howitzers and some recoilless rifles to his position—all with the single Bell 205 chopper that was the only air asset available for his operation. His attack was led by Lieutenant Bac Ri, a Meo we called "the Squid" because of his talent for slipping out of NVA ambushes unscathed. This time, the Squid had his work cut out for him.

Vang Pao and Bac Ri launched numerous frontal assaults on the position and were repelled with high losses. Contrary to his usual tactics, the Squid decided that by hugging the mountaintop in close proximity to the enemy, he could keep his men safe from their deadly 82s. This worked fine, except for a poncho-wearing North Vietnamese (and probably more who imitated his methods) we quickly dubbed "Bat Man." Bat Man's specialty was swooping out of his bunker, rolling grenades onto Meo positions, and slipping back into his bunker as if he had wings. Unfortunately, the close proximity of Bac Ri's troops to the crest prevented Vang Pao from supporting him with concentrated artillery fire, and the smoky air, caused by slash-and-burn agriculture after the summer monsoons, prevented USAF A-1s from acquiring the target. In desperation, General Pao appealed to me for assistance—a little of "Colonel Deeck's" aerial magic.

I flew by STOL fixed-wing aircraft to Site 36, 30 miles to the south, and then by Air America Huey to Vang Pao's command post on the peak opposite the enemy position on Phou Mok Lok. Bill Lair told me to stay in the area only a few hours—just long enough to assess the situation—but the general, a consummate politician, had other plans. He had invited various village elders to his camp for a show (another assault by the Squid on the crest, which was quickly repelled) and a feast of roast pig with all the trimmings: fresh bread, rice, fruit, and White Horse scotch (all brought in on the ammunition chopper). Apparently a CIA officer once ordered White Horse in the general's presence, and Vang Pao forever after assumed it was the official drink of American warriors. Despite my orders to get back as soon as possible, I could hardly refuse Vang Pao's invitation—especially in front of his constituents.

After the battlefield banquet, I studied the NVA position through binoculars and decided that the smoke had thinned enough to try a napalm strike. The long axis of the bunker was parallel to our position, and if the pilot was good, he could toss a canister right into its aperture.

After making the assessment, I asked for the chopper to pick me up, but the bird had broken down after its last shuttle (the roast pig flight), and I was stuck there for the night.

I asked Vang Pao how he had arrayed his forces to defend the position against an NVA night attack.

"No problem," the general said. "The enemy stays on the road."

All his troops were positioned between us and the NVA bunker on the adjoining hill. Our flanks seemed undefended, which didn't strike me as very smart. But I was the air advisor, and the big general had guests, so I kept my mouth shut. Nonetheless, I got on my little HF (high-frequency) radio and asked the office in Udorn to give Colonel Hienie Aderholt at 56th Air Commandos at Nakron Phanom the following message:

"An old buddy from Hurlburt is stuck up at Phou Mok Lok and is lonesome for some company."

A couple of hours later, an A-26 attack bomber began circling our position and stayed there throughout the night. It was a fortuitous precaution.

Around midnight, 82 mm mortar rounds began falling near our position. Soldiers familiar with the *pop* of the standard 81 mm American mortar would be astounded, as I was, by the additional punch of that extra silly millimeter. The ground trembled as if we'd been hit by howitzers, and there was nothing I could do but jump into a hole with a couple of other guys, equally terrified, and ride out the storm.

While we waited, I turned my flashlight on the wooden slats under my boots. The stenciled letters showed we were crouching on several crates of 105 mm shells and fragmentation grenades. Figuring this was not the safest foxhole in camp, I borrowed an AK-47 and as much ammo as I could carry and took my chances on the perimeter.

Below us on the hill, I could see the muzzle flashes of NVA troops advancing on our right. I radioed coordinates to the orbiting A-26, which broke out of its pattern and made a couple of bombing and strafing passes. The bomb concussion was fierce and the A-26's machine guns really ripped up the foliage. One of the tracers started a grass fire and visibility got even worse, but most of the smoke rolled back on the NVA and blocked their view of the summit. The mortar fire stopped and things got quiet—at least for a couple of hours. Vang Pao, belatedly perhaps, sent out his skirmishers on the flanks.

Just before dawn, some of our Meos encountered an NVA patrol at the 5,500-foot level and a brisk firefight broke out. We couldn't support them by shooting down from above for fear of hitting our own guys, but the battle was never a contest. I called the A-26s for flares, and as soon as those big arc lights started swinging over the area, the enemy ran for cover. The NVA kept probing us in other sectors until well after sunup, but they obviously had no desire to storm the position in daylight.

I had been in a couple of ground firefights before, but never at night. This one scared the bejesus out of me—mostly because of the lack of control. You just don't know who is where, and between the eerie light of the drifting flares and brilliant flashes of the mortar rounds and gunfire echoing from all directions, you just want to pull in your head and hide until it's over.

Vang Pao and his elders, though, thought the whole thing made quite a show. He sent them down the mountain in the morning with a pat on the back, full bellies, and big smiles. I just wanted to get the hell out of there and bugged out with the day's first supply chopper. Back at Udorn, I phoned Hienie Aderholt to thank him for the "angels" that helped us survive one of the longest nights of my life.

Four days later, the visibility cleared enough on Phou Mok Lok for the A-1s to return. As it turned out, the very first bomb scored a direct hit on the bunker and wiped it out. "Squid" Ri slipped away to fight another day, and General Vang Pao was able to claim a victory in front of his constituents. I sent him a congratulatory message:

"You killed the dreaded enemy and got Bat Man in the bargain. Well done. Colonel Dick."

I flew back to the mountain the next day to estimate for Bill how long Vang Pao could hold Phou Mok Lok now that the crest was ours. The NVA hadn't forgotten we were there and were no less determined now to protect their traffic than they had been before. I didn't think the Meo could hold out for long, and the NVA proved me right. When the pressure got too tight, Vang Pao withdrew and made trouble elsewhere. It seemed like a lot of guys got killed and a lot of ordnance got expended without having very much to show for it, but that was the nature of the war.

One of my most satisfying operations was, to my knowledge, the only successful POW rescue staged during the entire Southeast Asia war: the freeing of a large number of POWs held by the NVA in eastern Laos. For such a successful raid, however, it did not have an auspicious start.

During my stay in Laos, MACV's Studies and Observation Group (SOG) was led by Colonel (later General) John Singlaub. SOG was really a cover for special operations, which cut a lot of mischief in South and North Vietnam all during the war. Singlaub and his staff met with us periodically at Udorn (sometimes we went to Saigon, but Udorn was nicer and I think they liked taking a break from the local scene) to coordinate covert activities, usually clandestine helicopter infiltrations into Laos and North Vietnam.

Singlaub was responsible for several POW rescue attempts between 1966 and 1968, leading eventually to the much-publicized Son Tay attempt in 1969 in which Singlaub was not involved. Sadly, not a single prisoner was sprung by these efforts. The reason they all failed, I believe, was a lack of real-time intelligence, poor security, and too much outside "hep," as we called it: "help from heaven" or "help from higher up"—from bureaucrats and pencil pushers. In Laos, we had plenty of intelligence, but lacked the high-quality ground forces and tactical leadership necessary to bring off such raids. We also had our share of "hep," which is why we needed two swings at the plate to hit this particular home run.

In late 1966 Pathet Lao informers (the CIA had penetrated parts of the local cadres; their commanders couldn't go to the latrine without our knowing it) gave us hard intelligence that three American pilots were being held at a well-known NVA site in north-central Laos. By "hard intelligence" I mean actual names of fliers that tallied with our own MIA lists. We knew this bit of information was a real windfall—as did CIA headquarters at Langley. They proceeded to inundate us with advisory cables and, before long, "hep" in the form of on-site supervision.

Combat intelligence is very transitory. What's true at noon today may not be true at noon tomorrow, or even at four that afternoon. The various Laos chiefs, including me, wanted to organize a raid (using handpicked Meo guerrillas led by a U.S. case officer) and bust the pilots out immediately while the information was hot and the element of surprise was on our side.

Our "hep" from Langley, however, decided that our foreign intelligence, or field spies, should attempt to bribe a Pathet Lao guard and spring our guys surreptitiously. This plan struck us as the administrative analogue to a "Hail Mary" pass in football. Three things can happen and two of them are bad: The bribe and break can work as planned, the bribe can work but the break can fail, or the bribe can fail and the whole thing becomes academic. These are pretty lousy odds, compared to the advantages of a well-planned, well-executed surprise raid.

Predictably, the guards were spooked by our agent's overtures and the headquarters plan blew up. Not only did we lose the opportunity, but the NVA moved the prisoners.

A year later, in the fall of 1967, we picked up the trail again. We were especially anxious to do the job right this time, because U.S. officials, including Deputy Defense Secretary Paul Nitze, monitoring American POWs in the North, had accused Hanoi of violating various provisions of the Geneva Convention, including use of prisoners for propaganda and denying Red Cross inspectors access to POWs.

We had known for some time that the NVA was maintaining a sizable POW facility somewhere near the heart of the Ho Chi Minh Trail. Our information came from locals who had been forcibly ejected from the area by the North (for security reasons), radio intercepts, prisoner interrogations, and occasional scuttlebutt from our Pathet Lao informers. The only real questions were exactly where the camp was, how many prisoners it contained, whether Americans were among them, and how well it was guarded.

Finding even a large facility was harder than it seemed. The area was heavily jungled—a morass of densely foliaged limestone hills, ravines, and gorges—and the North Vietnamese were very skilled at minimizing the telltale signs of a military installation: converging trails, smoke from kitchens, large gardens needed to feed prisoners and guards, that sort of thing. Through our informers, we eventually established that the camp, wherever it was, contained a large number of friendlies, and possibly several Caucasians. But we could never quite get a fix on it.

Then one day, routine photo reconnaissance revealed cultivated areas about 30 kilometers north of Route 912, the main east-west artery between Laos and North Vietnam—signs of habitation we had previously overlooked or that had just been excavated. We increased our surveillance but were careful not to reveal our suspicions. We didn't want to spook the enemy again.

Then, a minor miracle happened. One of our tribal patrols accidentally encountered two Pathet Lao corpsmen—medics—who claimed to be deserters from a "big NVA camp" a dozen miles away. The miracle was not so much that the deserters eluded their own forces or that our CIA guerrillas happened onto them, which was remarkable enough, but that they weren't killed on the spot by mines, ambush, or just plain cussedness (the Laotians did *not* like the Vietnamese, and our guys hated the Pathet Lao even more). Every patrol had standing orders to interrogate prisoners, and usually they did— sometimes brutally. But getting them to capture rather than kill the enemy in the first place was always a problem.

The patrol leader who captured the two NVA radioed his case officer for instructions, and within a few hours we had them on the way to Savannakhet in a helicopter for complete interrogation, which included "map walking," or reconstructing their escape route on a detailed topographical map.

When the CIA regional chief was satisfied that these two NVA were genuine, he flew them back over the target area in a Porter (a fixed-wing utility plane) before nightfall. Sure enough, the camp was there. The reason we had missed it from the air (in addition to the heavy foliage and normal NVA precautions) was that the prisoners were being held in limestone caves— there were simply no huts to give them away. All supplies were brought in by foot or pack animal, so there were no roads. The defectors gave us a complete layout of the camp plus a rundown on the number of guards (fewer than 40) and prisoners, which we realistically expected to number about the same.

Tom Clines, the chief of ground, was on leave in Bangkok with his family, so Pat Landry and I had to carry the ball in Thailand. We didn't think our recent aerial missions had tipped our hand (aircraft were always overflying the area), but the two defectors were bound to be missed and searched for. When their absence had been reported up the NVA chain of command, the camp would either be moved again or, at the very least, reinforced. We had a little breathing space, but not much—maybe another day.

Our first decision was to keep the information to ourselves. The last thing we needed was more "hep" from on high before we could even evaluate the raw data ourselves.

Our second decision was to authorize our field chief to put together the best team they could find while I had our photo interpreters out scouring the area for landing and extraction zones. We had the usual concerns, plus a few new ones. The infill site had to be far enough from the enemy camp so that the sound of our aircraft wouldn't tip them off. The exfill site had to accommodate the additional birds needed to remove the passengers. Our plan was simple: Get as close as we could on the ground, assault the camp's two gates simultaneously, neutralize the guards and spring the prisoners, then get the hell out to a much closer extraction zone.

Because tactical leadership would be crucial, we toyed with the idea of breaking one of our major rules of engagement and putting a U.S. case officer on the ground in command, but eventually decided against it. Our regional chief felt he had some good local candidates, and we decided we would probably risk more than we would gain by putting an American in a situation that could become a major international incident.

So far, for a change, things were progressing well. We had excellent real-time intelligence and surprise on our side, plus an experienced team to do the heavy lifting. Our remaining concerns were (a) Murphy's law—how to avoid screwing up something that ought to go like clockwork—and (b) how to explain a surprise raid to the higher-ups and still keep our jobs.

Regarding possible foul-ups, we had most of the detailed raid planning from 1966 to fall back on. This included bona fides, for instance: indisputable proof to show the prisoners that our native soldiers were really there to rescue them—things like photos of a prisoner taken before he was captured. It also encompassed obvious things, like bolt-cutters, to cut prisoners free if nobody could find the keys. We also had the best photo interpreters and helicopter drivers in the business.

As far as headquarters went, I told Pat about a term I hadn't heard since West Point, one that had been used throughout military history to cover a multitude of sins: "reconnaissance in force."

"You know, Pat," I said, "we've been mousing around with a squad here and a squad there. What we need to do is probe the area with an aggressive team to confirm or reject our intelligence—an honest-to-God *reconnaissance in force*."

Pat agreed that the term sounded fine, and that's what the raid wound up being called, at least in the written reports.

We worked out the details with the regional chief and by dawn the next day we were ready to go. He had selected a young lieutenant who had a reputation as a hot rock with a cool head under fire to lead the team. His squad consisted of 12 men, mostly seasoned guerrillas, dressed like peasants. They were skinny as hell, and lacked a complete mouthful of teeth among them—but they were tough as old boots and knew their business. As added insurance, a CIA case officer would orbit in a plane a discreet distance away in order to stay in continuous radio contact with the team and our command post. They'd be on their own, but they wouldn't be completely alone.

The assault force choppered in just before sundown. The anticipated four-hour march stretched into six, but they were able to get right up to the gates. About 3:00 in the morning, they launched their attack, catching most of the enemy asleep. They cut down the handful of NVA sentries and quickly dispatched the rest of the guards—asleep in thatched-roof barracks—with a few grenades. In seconds, the squad completely wiped out a force several times its size.

Now came the first real surprise of the mission, and it was a doozy. Upon entering the caves, the lieutenant ran back out and excitedly radioed the plane.

"*Mach! Mach!*" he said after counting the prisoners, "Too many! Too many!"

It turned out that our rescue squad had taken on a major facility that contained 82 captives, made up of Thai mercenaries, Filipino "kickers" (aircrewmen who discharged cargo from our Air America resupply aircraft), and various political prisoners, including several females. It was roughly *double* the maximum we expected, with many sick and injured who were not ambulatory. Unfortunately, there were no Americans.

The lieutenant and the orbiting CIA officer realized immediately that they'd never make it to the primary HLZ (helicopter landing zone) in a reasonable amount of time, and certainly not before half the NVA troops in the area had been alerted. In addition, I simply didn't have enough helos on hand to chopper them all out.

I called in Air America's chief rotary wing pilot and told him we needed about a dozen H-34s to go to Savannakhet (about 90 minutes' flying time from Udorn) no later than right now. As I expected, he started moaning about where he'd find that many choppers and crews. Then I dropped the real bombshell.

"By the way, our primary and secondary HLZs are no good," I said. "The POWs can't make the march, so we're going to have to pick them up on the nearest patch of open ground."

"Yeah? And where the hell is that?"

I thumped the wall map with a finger. "Right here—in the middle of the Ho Chi Minh Trail."

This did not make his day, but there was no other alternative in that neck of the woods, and he saw it, too. I waived the "two-pilot rule" (which said all choppers had to go out with at least a pilot and copilot), and between the two of us, and a lot of phone calls, we managed to scrounge enough helos—many of them straight out of maintenance—to make the mission.

Landing on the Trail would be gutsy, but it wasn't as foolhardy as it sounds. Our group would be extracted in midmorning, and experience showed that the Trail could be pretty quiet during daylight. Traffic moved only at night, which was when most of our aerial attacks took place, so the gunners and most of the NVA patrols would probably be asleep. As an added precaution, though, I arranged through 7th Air Force to have a couple of fully armed Thuds (F-105 Thunderchief jet fighters) stage a diversionary attack just as our choppers arrived, backed up by a flight of A-1s in case an enemy ground force turned up and things got sticky.

By the grace of God, our luck held. The 105s screamed in and clobbered the road just north of our touchdown zone, diverting enemy attention. Moments later, nine Air America helicopters landed line-abreast on the Ho Chi Minh Trail. It would've made one hell of an historic photo if anyone had thought to bring a camera.

In the end, we got everyone out without firing a shot on departure and without losing a man. Pat and I sent out our "reconnaissance in force" report to headquarters, mentioning how our intrepid band "happened" onto the POW camp and bent the bars on 82 friendlies. Although they couldn't breathe a word of it to the press—and to my knowledge, details of the raid have never before been made public (although it is used as a case study in classified training for modern special ops officers)—the CIA executives were delighted. We papered the walls with congratulatory TWIXs and official commendations. Tom Clines congratulated us, too, despite his great disappointment at missing the show.

When Ted Shackley, who was out of the tactical loop, heard the real story from Pat and me, he nodded grimly, agreeing that we did the right thing—although, he said, the move was very bold and dangerous, and landing on the Ho Chi Minh Trail, "a real stunner."

It was then that the first cardinal rule of covert operations, the one I had learned from Hienie Aderholt, really sunk in: *You can get away with anything—once.* Yeah, we did a toe dance on the Trail, but I wouldn't want to go back and try it again.

In a war as screwy as the one in Southeast Asia, even these little successes didn't come without a price. As time went on, I was saddled with more and more extracurricular duties.

Because I knew about airplanes and radios, the Special Intelligence Branch, or SI, was assigned to my division. In fact, anything technical was sent my way, which is why I bore the brunt of several later, great experiments from DCPG, the Defense Communications Planning Group—the cover name for the development and deployment of McNamara's famous "electronic fence" intended to block the Ho Chi Minh Trail. DCPG was a multibillion-dollar mistake founded on the faulty premise that you can defeat the enemy without facing him. This uniquely American misconception goes back to World War II and seems rooted in a market-oriented civilian culture that has little to do with the realities of war. This doesn't mean that technology can't give you an edge, even a decisive edge, but it can't replace *people* as war's primary instrument. Schwarzkopf knew this in Desert Storm, despite the fact that he commanded the most sophisticated high-tech armed force in history and fought over terrain that was a theoretical tactician's dream. The Iraqis may have been defeated by air power and technology, but the Grand Coalition didn't *win* the war until troops arrived to claim the field. In the mid- to late 1960s, the Defense Department's infatuation with technology seemed to have more to do with a president's promise of going to the moon than a nation's commitment to winning a war.

"McNamara's line," or "Igloo White," or "Mud River," or a half-dozen other code names it assumed over time, was really a collection of high- and low-tech strategies developed in a summer study in 1966 for monitoring and interdicting traffic on the Ho Chi Minh Trail. These "hobby shop" projects, as we called them, arrived with distressing regularity, and as the SI and technology guru, as well as chief of air, I was the person who was supposed to make them work.

My introduction to this heroic DCPG farce began in 1967 when Lieutenant General Starbird and his assistant, Brigadier General Antonelli, arrived at Udorn with an armful of slides and graphs to give Bill, Pat, Ted, and me a top-secret briefing on DCPG's task: a set of remote listening devices and sensors that would be programmed to screen out extraneous noise and detect enemy vehicles and troops with high accuracy without risk to human life, and without the errors of human observers.

To do this, General Starbird told us in his deep, dignified voice, they would need baseline data on what the jungle actually sounded like *without* NVA troops on the road. This included the sound signatures of wind in the trees, monkey chatter, rain on leaves, jet overflights, and so on. In other words, in addition to their usual road-spotting work, our Little Guys would be assigned duties as Hollywood sound men.

I looked around at my bosses and waited for someone to ask, "Is this a joke?" Nobody said anything. So I raised my hand.

"Yes? You have a question?" General Starbird asked.

"Yes sir, I'm Richard Secord, the local airman. I'll be responsible for putting your prototype equipment in the field. If I understand you correctly, you're talking about developing a very extensive, high-tech, real-time automated intelligence system."

"That's right!" General Starbird said. "That's exactly it. That's a good way to describe it."

"General, we have a pretty good system of road-watch teams already in place. We even have Hark boxes that—"

"Yes, we know all about that. We've been briefed by your people in Washington. The problem is, even the Hark reports don't always reach the tactical air commanders in a timely fashion, and humans, let's face it, can make mistakes."

"Yes sir, that's true," I continued. "The only reason I brought it up was to make sure you knew that a pretty good, reliable, and very near real-time intelligence system exists. Our real problem is that air strikes alone will never interdict the Trail, no matter how good our intelligence gets. We know where the enemy is. We really don't need any more intelligence. What we need is a lot more striking power and warm bodies in the path of the enemy. Otherwise, they'll always find a way to get through. If you like, I'll be happy to take you out to the Trail tonight and show you what I mean."

Ted Shackley gave me one of his "core meltdown" looks—a piercing stare, that said "Don't get cute, buster," but I was deadly serious and he knew I was right.

Starbird replied stiffly, "*Mister* Secord, it is not our task to make judgments about the tactical employment of this system. It is, instead, my charge, as given to me by the Secretary himself, to develop and deploy the system."

"Then General, with all due respect, *please* tell them it ain't what we need."

"That's enough," Shackley said.

When the meeting broke up, Generals Starbird and Antonelli went back to the Pentagon and Bill and Pat spent the rest of the morning trying to calm me down.

"Do you realize what they're saying?" I sputtered, still incredulous. "They either really believe this crap will work, or they don't care if it doesn't. They don't intend to put troops on the Trail—ever! They don't even intend to put more striking power in the air. We're going to be in this fucking war forever!"

Ted told me that the Director of the CIA had personally cabled him to give Starbird's team every cooperation with their project. Basically, he said, if these guys don't want to be confused with the facts, that's their problem.

I saluted and did what I was told. I had learned a long time ago how to keep a secret and keep my mouth shut, but this time it was hard.

DCPG and other "hobby shops" produced ideas that ranged from merely interesting to preposterous. If putting their ideas in the field didn't involve risk to human lives, I would've laughed at them more often.

One of the silliest ideas passed down to us was the notion of dumping dishwasher detergent on the Trail. This approach had supposedly been tested in the lab at CIA headquarters, Langley, and was ready for large-scale experimentation. The strategy was to dump big parcels of Calgon dishwasher soap directly onto the Trail at choke points—hairpin turns, constricted passes, and extremely steep grades—just before it rained during the monsoon. When the weather entered its "wash cycle," the treated roads, in theory, would become extremely slippery and impassable.

We received about 150,000 pounds of Calgon in steel barrels. The plan called for us to repackage it into a few thousand brown paper shopping bags, tape them shut, load them onto three C-130 Hercules transports dragooned from Taiwan, and kick them out the door onto the Trail. My orders were to take no casualties, but choke points, by definition, are heavily defended. We picked three good ones and prayed to God we could get in and get out without having to pay the likely toll.

Flying in extended trail position, my crews delivered the bags from very low altitude so they'd be sure to hit the road. We didn't have enough planes to hit all three points simultaneously, so we did one point each day for three days. The first two days went fine—in and out with no problems. On the third day, though, word had passed through the NVA, and the crews encountered heavy ground fire. A couple of the planes were shot up, though luckily, no one was injured.

A CIA photo-reconnaissance plane followed the last C-130 on each of the three missions and took pictures of the shattered bags at all drop zones to confirm for the brass that we'd delivered their soap on target and that if the idea didn't work, it wasn't because of us.

Lo and behold, the rains came, and observations showed that the soap just bubbled up and washed away. Traffic counts were normal, and even a little higher. All the enemy got for our trouble was clean hubcaps, compliments of Uncle Sam.

Still, the projects kept coming. It was as if somebody had opened a physics textbook and wouldn't be satisfied until every phenomenon known to science had been exhausted. We had truck counters based on seismic, audio, and electromagnetic detection. We had low-light-level television and infrared spotters that made the Trail, in places, look like Thomas Edison's workshop. We had minimunitions—explosive mini-mines the size of popcorn—sprinkled like pebbles across the Trail that, if they didn't blow off your foot, would at least take the shine off your brogans. In short, we came up with dozens of ways to make life difficult for NVA corporals but gave their generals very little to worry about.

Paradoxically, we verified our robots' reports by checking them against the observations of our road-watch teams—the human beings who had shouldered the load for the entire war and would continue to shoulder it until the last shots were fired.

It was this cavalier, if not callous, attitude of the top brass toward our men in the field—the ones who put the guts behind the technology and did the job in spite of it—that angered me the most. Toward the end of my last year in Laos, it contributed directly to one of the worst debacles of the war.

# —6—

# Disaster at Site 85

In early 1967, Bill Lair and I took refuge from the stifling heat of the summer monsoon at the 7/13th Air Force headquarters at Udorn in a briefing led by four-star General Hunter Harris, commander in chief of the Pacific Air Forces. On the agenda was an important new ground-based radar bombing system called Commando Club that promised to revolutionize the air war over North Vietnam.

The heart of the system, called TSQ-81, was SAC's Skyspot radar bomb scoring system, used for years to predict bomb impact points from simulated drops in training. Now, the same system would be used to radically improve all-weather bombing accuracy in tactical fighter "route packages" in North Vietnam, especially from October through April, when the enemy normally received a respite from sustained aerial attacks due to monsoonal weather. Attacking planes would simply follow the ground system's voice commands to weapons release: "Ready, ready, *now!*" and all the pilots would drop their bombs together.

To help safeguard the installation, secure voice transmissions would be made from the TSQ to a command and control airplane (usually a C-135) that would relay the bombing commands to strike aircraft in either code or plain English, making it appear as if the radar instructions were coming from the plane instead of the ground.

The system's biggest drawback was its location. To get the best accuracy, the ground station had to be as close as possible to its targets. The development team had already picked out a candidate site on mount Phou Pha Thi, a steep 5,500-foot ridge located about 30 miles southwest of the town of Sam Neua and an equal distance from the North Vietnam border to the northeast. Most important, the site was less than 150 miles as the crow flies from Hanoi.

We already had a 600-foot STOL strip three-quarters of the way up the mountain for resupplying local Meo guerrillas and a TACAN station (tactical

74

air navigation system, which broadcasts azimuth and slant-range information to planes in flight) and a low-frequency radio beacon on the summit, which the CIA called "Site 85." Adding the new compact TSQ equipment by helicopter would present no special challenges, but it would sure increase the site's attractiveness to the enemy if they ever found out what we were up to.

That raised the practical problem of security.

Site 85 was pretty remote and surrounded by unbelievably wild terrain. That would insulate it a bit from surprise attack, and the C-135 decoy ship would probably fool the enemy for a while, but hostile action wasn't our only concern. Laos was officially neutral, and the TSQ-81 represented a major escalation in a war that technically didn't exist. It also had to be manned around the clock by about 15 technicians who were rotated weekly from a cadre of 40 workers based at Udorn—a major new complication. The U.S. ambassador, William Sullivan, warned everyone involved to be sure that no violations of the 1962 Geneva Agreements guaranteeing Laotian neutrality were even inadvertently made. This admonition would later come back to haunt us, but at the time, the political concerns were the least of our worries.

As usual with technical projects, implementation responsibility for Commando Club on Site 85 fell to me, with assistance from Tom Clines. Our main job, in addition to clearing additional space on the white karst limestone mountaintop and heavy-lifting in new equipment, vans, and prefab crew quarters, was to defend the site from ground attack, and therein lay the rub.

One company (about 100 men) of Thai infantry was all we could obtain for full-time perimeter defense, plus a contingent of several hundred Little Guys—Meo irregulars—which would be adequate to foil NVA patrols and provide a trip wire for a large-scale assault, but little else. Because Bill saw right away that ground forces would be marginal, he and Tom agreed to alternate CIA case officers on site as tactical commanders, a very rare thing to do. Given that air power would be the major component in a serious confrontation, and because the whole project was obviously an "Air Force baby," I was the staff officer assigned overall responsibility for Site 85's defense.

My first glimpse of Phou Pha Thi had been in 1966. The place was right out of a travel poster. The crest ran northwest to southeast straight out of a lush valley filled with opium poppies waving scarlet in the breeze. Our elevated landing zone gave us a good view of the surrounding terrain, including the mouth of the valley to the northeast, the direction from which a North Vietnamese attack would most likely come.

Just to be cautious, we assumed that even if the enemy didn't figure out the site's function, all our activity—helo flights and construction and the presence of significantly more personnel in the area—would tip the NVA off that something big was going on, and they might try to neutralize the site on that basis alone. Therefore, one of the first things I did was to formally request through channels a unit of U.S. Army Special Forces (even a squad would do) to guard the site. That meant going through the embassy in Vientiane, which meant a run-in with Ambassador William Sullivan.

Sullivan, in my opinion, was one of those State Department careerists who could be dangerous precisely because of their outward air of competence and authority. In Laos, we CIA guys called him "Field Marshal" Sullivan because he constantly micromanaged military ops. We (CIA and the Air Force) would dogfight with him often on the validation of air targets—what we selected for strikes and why. He and his staff frequently vetoed our plans out of what I thought was a needless fear for civilian casualties—a good instinct, but only when you can separate fact from fiction, which they never seemed able to do.

For example, any time our photo recce showed a target in the general vicinity of anything with a roof, the embassy vetoed the bombing because it was "too close to a village." This was usually a needless precaution. When the NVA parked their trucks or dumped their materiel near a populated area, hoping to preempt an attack, the civilians would evacuate, knowing that *we knew* they wouldn't hang around to get blown up. This is aversion/survival training of a very low order. But the embassy people just never got it through their heads that "the natives" were at least as corrigible as Pavlov's dogs. This useless and arbitrary ground rule on hitting only "embassy-approved" targets was to cost us dearly in the coming months, particularly during the monsoon when the ability to visually isolate targets is drastically reduced.

Sullivan rejected out of hand our request for even a tiny contingent of SF troops to reinforce Site 85. He believed that if Washington wanted Special Forces to get in the act, it would have said so in the directives, which it had not.

His concern, of course, was political. Nobody minded Thai soldiers roaming the woods, and the Meo, after all, lived there. But American combat troops on the ground were verboten. Even the American technicians manning the site had been sanitized. They were what the USAF called "sheep dipped"—U.S. servicemen with critical skills posing as civilian contractors on a volunteer basis. That, apparently, was as far as Mr. Sullivan was prepared to go.

With the U.S. ambassador intransigent about using American ground forces to defend Site 85, I could see no way to hold it in the face of even a moderately determined NVA assault. My reaction was to draft a straightforward plan to get our guys out of there and destroy the classified equipment if things turned sour. This evacuation plan was based, in part, on provisions made by the CIA's TSD, the Technical Services Division (the "burn, blast, and blow" guys) who seeded the entire site with claymore mines and other pyrotechnics to be activated around the perimeter when an attack began, and later at the summit if the place was declared indefensible and our people had been removed.

Unfortunately, TSD's provisions turned out to be mostly smoke and mirrors. Tom Clines inspected the portion of their work at the base of the mountain designed to act as an enemy "trip wire" and declared that, with a little artillery support, he could take the hill "with a troop of Boy Scouts." Again, we requested Special Forces through the ambassador. Again, we were denied.

My next step was to get several USAF A-1 Skyraider pilots into the area to familiarize themselves ahead of time with the terrain, likely target locations, and the disposition of friendly forces, such as they were. If history was any guide, the NVA would sneak up and attack the hill at night or in bad weather, hoping to neutralize our air advantage. I wanted our pilots to know that region like the back of their hands—not only to defend the Thai and Meo positions, but to make sure our extraction choppers got in and out and to punish the enemy as much as possible in the process.

That, basically, was my plan for the defense of Site 85. It was less a battle plan than a non-battle plan, because nobody I talked to, including the guys who wrote the book on jungle warfare up north, gave the troops a snowball's chance in hell of surviving a determined NVA offensive, let alone one that would be conducted virtually in the enemy's own backyard.

I added to my plan what I thought was an innocuous but important addendum: arming the civilians. But when I brought it up with the embassy, the reaction was predictable.

"What? You want to *arm* the civilian, contract employees? Forget it. Civilians don't carry guns. That's a violation of our policy."

This was too much. It was one thing to send sheep-dipped Air Force techs out into a storm; it was another to leave them there without raincoats.

"At least give them a fighting chance to get to the evacuation area," I pleaded to my superiors, but my protests were shrugged off. The ambassador had decided: better a clean corpse than one found clutching an M-16 with Army serial numbers.

There wasn't much I could do about the Special Forces, but there sure as hell was something I could do about small arms. On my own authority, I drew 40 M-16s from USAF stock at Udorn, plus a number of CIA-issue Browning autopistols and cases of hand grenades (and lots of ammo) and delivered it to the case officer on-site with instructions for him to give the "civilians" a little refresher training in small-arms handling and marksmanship. I told the commander of the 7/13th Air Force that, as senior military officer directly involved with site defense, I had determined that the men in or associated with my command were in jeopardy and I wasn't going to let them face the Pathet Lao or North Vietnamese regulars without some means of defense. He listened to my speech, put his hand on my shoulder, and said, "Dick, we're with you."

It was refreshing to find an ally; particularly since that commitment would soon be put to the test.

Late in 1967, two ominous events took place.

In the Panhandle, in a previously sacrosanct area, one of our TACAN sites was overrun by NVA and some real (not sheep-dipped) civilian contractors were killed. We didn't know it at the time, but the preparatory phases of the North's theaterwide and soon-to-be historic Tet offensive of 1968 were under way.

A second piece of bad news came to us in November in the form of throwaway data—something so minor that it is often overlooked even by diligent analysts. Aerial photos showed what looked like a "trace," or the beginning of a mechanically cleared path, no wider than a goat trail, in the jungle about 25 miles from Site 85 at a place where several skirmishes had already taken place between NVA and Meo patrols.

I immediately arranged for FAC and CIA photo reconnaissance aircraft to take a closer look. The resulting evidence plainly showed that North Vietnamese workers were clearing brush and leveling terrain in an attempt to build a motorable road in the direction of Phou Pha Thi—a dagger aimed at the heart of Site 85. If it was allowed to get within 15 kilometers of the installation by the time the dry season commenced next spring, artillery could be brought up to blast the facility off the map. If they wanted to absorb the losses necessary to occupy the mountain, the enemy could use the road to bring up the men, supplies, and munitions needed for a large-scale infantry assault. Either way, we believed, the key to preserving the site was to stop the road in its tracks.

This discovery began a chain of events, known collectively as the Battle for Site 85 or the Battle of Route 602, that was subsequently documented in a variety of top-secret reports, one of which was recently declassified by the Air Force and called *The Fall of Site 85*, prepared, unfortunately, without the benefit of interviews with the CIA personnel involved. I reviewed this report, and although it is generally correct as to substance, it is full of factual errors and several mistakes in interpretation. I will attempt to set the record straight here. The disaster at Phou Pha Thi is a shocking story, a bitter pill that was tough enough for me to swallow at the time. It gets no sweeter in the telling. Still, it's a story that must be told, if only to let those who paid the final price rest a little easier.

Once the construction of Route 602 was discovered, Ted Shackley directed me to "stop the road." And that's just what we tried to do.

The official, embassy-approved defense plan for Site 85 went like this. If an enemy attack looked imminent—that is, once troops and equipment had been assembled within a reasonable striking distance—we were to notify the local Meo commander and, at the same time, request permission from William Sullivan's office for air strikes. Sullivan would then notify 7th Air

Force in Saigon that the local commander had requested aerial support. However, at Sullivan's insistence, only after the enemy was actually moving would blanket strikes be authorized, and at that point, the TSQ-81 commander, acting as his own FAC, would open a voice channel and provide bombing coordinates to whoever showed up to help. Seventh Air Force was tasked to respond as circumstances and time allowed, even if it meant diverting aircraft from other missions.

The flaw in this plan, of course, was that the longer we waited, the more force would be needed and the greater the danger would be to our troops, let alone the top-secret equipment on the site, which included not only radar-bombing hardware, but encryption devices, codes, and software.

Naturally, I requested 7th Air Force support as soon as we spotted the road. Our goal was to whack 'em hard whenever they cranked up a tractor, to obliterate the construction in the early stages and make it crystal clear that we would simply not tolerate a road in the area. Since the NVA was basically a "road-bound" army with no aerial support, this would preclude any movement of heavy artillery to the site and basically end the battle before it could start.

However, the response from 7th Air Force was underwhelming.

"I'm sorry, Mr. Secord, we have higher-priority targets," the strike coordinator told me—not once, but several times.

I finally replied, "You *cannot* expect us to hold this site unless you give us sufficient tac air to prevent the completion of the road!"

"Well, Mr. Secord, what would you have us do—assign a whole wing to your operation?"

"If necessary, yes sir!"

"For the duration of the war?"

"If that's what it takes, you're right!"

"Well, I'm sorry, we just have higher-priority targets."

Long weeks passed; more calls. A few strikes were authorized, but the road crept further and further, like a cancer, toward Phou Pha Thi. We'd knock off a bulldozer or tractor and another would arrive the next day to take its place. Burned-out "Cats" littered its shoulder like locust skins, but the road kept coming.

The enemy also began to show a lot of interest in not only the disposition of our forces around the perimeter, but also what was going on at the crest. Agents with cameras, posing as Buddhist monks, were apprehended near the summit, and on January 10, 1968, a five-man enemy patrol was encountered at the base of the mountain and dispersed. The NVA failed to get any substantive information from these forays, but it sure reinforced our conviction that the countdown had started for an assault.

In the middle of January 1968, one of the strangest episodes of the battle, if not the entire war, took place.

Observers near the site spotted four dark green, propeller-driven aircraft, completely unidentified, flying northwest at about one o'clock in the afternoon. When the formation reached a point about 30 miles away, two ships broke off and made straight for Phou Pha Thi. The people on the summit identified them as old-fashioned Soviet-made An-2 Colts—single-engine biplanes right out of the 1930s.

The two aircraft maneuvered into attack positions and dove on the mountain. As it turned out, one of our jet-powered Air America Huey helicopters happened to be en route to the site with a load of building materials. The site commander gave it a frantic radio call.

"Jesus Christ—firewall it, you guys! We're being attacked by airplanes from World War One!"

The Colts made three passes at the summit, raking the TSQ station with rockets and machine-gun fire. As they flew over, they dumped several bombs, killing two women civilians and two guerrillas, and wounding two others.

Then the Huey showed up.

The jet-powered helicopter was a little faster and a lot more maneuverable than the obsolete Colts, and its Air America pilot a lot more experienced. While the lead Colt drew a bead on the station for his fourth pass, the Huey popped up alongside. The Air America crew chief leaned out the open door and sprayed the enemy cockpit with an M-16. The Colt pulled up abruptly, fell off on one wing, and dove into the trees, exploding on impact. Meos arrived almost instantly on the scene, but little of any consequence was saved from the wreck, least of all the crew, which burned with the airplane.

While this improbable dogfight was going on, the second Colt lined up for its next pass. By now, all the troops on the perimeter, as well as everyone at the summit, had their weapons in hand and were banging away at the intruder. The second Colt roared in, shuddered under withering small-arms fire, and pulled up. It turned to the northeast but was losing power and didn't get far. After limping about 25 kilometers, it smashed into the trees while trying to clear a ridge. Meo guerrillas arrived at the crash scene shortly thereafter and found three dead crewmen, all Vietnamese, and numerous bits and pieces of the aircraft.

Our later analysis of this astonishing air raid—to my knowledge the only air strike ever launched against U.S. ground forces by the North Vietnamese during the entire war—revealed even more bizarre information. Witnesses at the site said the concussion of the "bombs" felt like 250s, but subsequent investigation by 7th Air Force G2 showed them to have been 120 mm mortars "converted" for aerial delivery—an ad hoc device that did not suggest a significant new threat was arising from Hanoi's (principally interceptor) air fleet. The Rube Goldberg ordnance was dropped, in fact, by the third crewman through tubes in the fuselage and was armed by the force of air pressure in the windstream. The rockets had been conventional Soviet-issue 57 mm fired from pods, which could—and did—pack quite a punch.

If nothing else, this crude and costly "experiment" showed that Hanoi took the site seriously, was feeling our attempts to interdict the road, and was willing to try just about anything to knock us out. What worried me was what the enemy might try when such quick-and-dirty efforts failed.

After the air raid, Ted and Tom got the Thai government to contribute an additional company of volunteers to the ground defense, which was now augmented to about 400 men. The Thai commander was a former acquaintance of mine from West Point, and I'm afraid I embarrassed the hell out of him by greeting him by name on one of our frequent inspection tours of the site. He had adopted a *nom de guerre* for his covert work in Laos, and I sort of blew his cover—or would have, if anybody but 10-inch bugs, poisonous snakes, and his own guys had been around to hear it.

The addition of these Thai reinforcements made a big difference in our ability to hold the site long enough to evacuate the technicians and blow the equipment. It was like Davy Crockett and his Kentuckians arriving at the Alamo, and I can tell you, everybody from the site commander on down to the lowliest Meo private was glad to see them. The U.S.S. *Pueblo* spy ship had just been seized by North Koreans, compromising a lot of intelligence equipment, and nobody was eager to have Site 85 follow in its wake.

We had been watching the Song Mai military district in North Vietnam west of Hanoi for months, waiting for the slowly massing battalions to make their move. We even knew the numbers of the units and the names of their commanders: two regiments of NVA regulars, about 3,000 troops—one of infantry and one of artillery drawing 85 mm divisional field guns. When it decided to take the field, it would be the largest concentration of heavy artillery observed in Laos since the siege of Dien Bien Phu against the French in 1954.

Now they were on their way, part of the general Tet offensive launched on January 30th throughout the entire theater.

Shackley sent a bulletin to "those listed"—everybody who had any connection with the project—stating flatly that the CIA could not guarantee defense of the site after March 10, 1968. How he arrived at this date, I'll never know, but he proved to be eerily prophetic. Naturally, the dispatch fell into a bureaucratic void.

Although we continued to fail in our requests for additional ground and air support, we couldn't just sit there and wait passively for the ax to fall. We told the local Meo commander to begin aggressive patrols around the perimeter, hoping to keep the advanced elements of the enemy forces off balance.

On February 18th, one Meo patrol managed to ambush and destroy an NVA survey party near the head of the road. They quickly searched the bodies and found they had bagged a field-grade officer in possession of a map that showed the NVA's intended artillery emplacements for the upcoming battle.

Naturally, this very valuable set of charts was whisked back to Udorn on the wings of eagles. I remember staring in disbelief at it. In elegant French, as if it had been inscribed by some student officer at *L'école Polytechnique*, were detailed specifications for the placement of every regimental gun and heavy mortar. In the margin were hurried pencil jottings in Vietnamese; and on the crest of the hill, high atop Phou Pha Thi, was a notation in ink, written in English: "TACAN." It did not mention radar, so the enemy—or at least the poor guy who drew this map—missed the whole point of the party. Yet here we were, about to go against each other hammer and tongs: me with a catch-22 order to defend our "highest-priority" site without dedicated air power or sufficient ground troops; and the enemy with World War II–era equipment and a lot of guts grinding out yard after bloody yard through the jungle guided by a French colonial map! Crying or laughing, you couldn't look at the thing for long without tears coming to your eyes.

As soon as we got this rosetta stone, I had the gun positions converted to bombing coordinates and told the powers-that-be what a gold mine we'd stumbled onto. I repeated my umpteenth request for air support—this time asking for saturation bombings, including B-52s, if necessary, which up until now had never been used in northern Laos.

But the Tet offensive was nearing full intensity in South Vietnam. Once again my plea was rejected.

Meanwhile, Shackley's bulletin had drawn some attention, but not the kind we wanted. From over the heads of the Saigon commanders—the same guys who were denying us air cover—we received the following message straight from CIA headquarters in Washington:

"You will hold the TSQ Site at whatever cost. It is of vital importance."

The American Embassy, Vientiane, was so advised.

"If we can't have Special Forces, then at least give us a couple of experienced SF officers and NCOs," I asked—begged, practically. "Give us a few guys right out of combat in South Vietnam, current in tactics and equipment, and let us put them on the summit. With a couple of guys like that, I'm confident we can at least hold the site long enough for an orderly evacuation and demolition of the facility."

Again, my request was denied.

By this time, Tom Clines and I were sleeping at the CIA building, with Pat and Bill spelling each other so that we would have command coverage—somebody actually awake and at the helm 24 hours a day. It was just after sundown on March 10th—I was getting a haircut in one of the offices—when the voice of Evan Washburn, the CIA case officer in command of the TSQ site that evening, came over the radio.

"Jesus Christ! They're shooting artillery at us!" We could hear the incoming rounds explode behind his voice.

I ripped off the towel and ran back to our little command post. Weather reports showed that a pall of smoke from local slash-and-burn agriculture had drifted over the area, which, in addition to scud and low ceilings, made air strikes very dicey, especially close to our lines. If this was, in fact, the start of a full-scale enemy assault, the NVA couldn't have picked a better time.

Without delay, I called 7/13th Air Force on the secure phone and asked for TAC air support ASAP. Seventh diverted a flight of F-4s, and, as we had rehearsed weeks before, they made some Skyspot-directed passes and actually knocked out some guns, but the visibility was really bad and it turned out to be too little, too late. In the absence of continuous and aggressive pressure from the air, the enemy had been allowed to set up their artillery, and rounds were now landing all over Site 85, setting off the defensive land lines and damaging the generators, cutting power cables, and generally wreaking havoc. Skyspot went off-line, and some technicians had to run outside and make splices, which, as we could well imagine, was like going up on a roof to repair a television antenna during a shrapnel hurricane. To make things worse, we couldn't get firm mission commitments from 7th, so when Skyspot was up, our aircraft often weren't, and vice versa. It was frustrating as hell—and potentially fatal.

By now our only hope was that the weather would clear enough for us to sneak in the evacuation helicopters. General Vang Pao was airlifting some reinforcements up from the south, but there was no way they could arrive in time to help. I ordered the Air America guys to move the choppers we had earmarked for the mission northward to Site 36, which was several hours away. Of course, that damn cable from Washington kept staring us in the face—*hold the site at all costs*. But heroism isn't suicide. Pat, Tom, and I were perfectly willing to withdraw our men, blow the site, and declare victory. However, time was now our shortest commodity, and I racked my brain trying to think of something that might buy us enough of it until the weather broke or the sun came up.

I called 7th Air Force again. "How about an AC-130 gunship?"

"We might be able to get a bird up from Udorn," a staff officer volunteered. "Let me see what I can do."

These gunships had been in the theater only a few months and were rapidly becoming the terror of the skies: mounting four 20 mm Gatling guns and in later versions, 105s and 40s as well. They spotted targets with low-light-level television and infrared, among other sensors, and so had a fighting chance to at least detect cannon and mortar flashes through the soup at Phou Pha Thi. That would be enough to aim the 20 mms and, for the NVA artillery under the resulting fusillade, that would be all she wrote.

However, word quickly came back down the chain. "Negative on the Alpha Charlie One Three Zero. It's got a priority mission on the Trail—"

"Then *divert* the sonofabitch!" I yelled. "Lemme talk to your boss!"

The authoritative voice of a colonel came on the line, but it was more of the same: The aerial dreadnaught was on a "mission with higher priority—"

Suddenly, the secure voice channel crashed—went out of business—as it sometimes did, but never before in an emergency.

I ran out of the CIA building, got in a car, and drove like a fiend to the other end of the base, where the 7/13th kept its headquarters. Ten minutes after I'd been cut off I was on the duty officer's secure line to the 7th Air Force in Saigon talking to the *colonel's* boss.

"Are you the officer who decided against giving us a gunship?" I asked.

The supervising duty officer, a brigadier general, replied, "We're working high-priority targets on the Ho Chi Minh Trail."

"Are you aware of Site 85? Are you aware of what it is? What the hell is your name?"

"I'm *General* Arnold R. Craig. Who the hell are you?"

"My name is *Major* Richard V. Secord, USAF, and I'm trying to defend Site 85—tell that to General Momyer!" In addition to evoking the name of his boss, the 7th Air Force commander, I added that a sizable contingent of American and Allied troops, and a ton of classified gear, was about to go down at Phou Pha Thi. I repeated my request as emphatically and urgently as I could and hung up. As I left, a dozen blanched faces followed me to the door. I paused and looked back at them. I was so angry and frustrated and so absolutely terrified at the bloody handwriting on the wall, that all I could say—whisper to them, really—was, *"We're gonna lose the fucking site!"*

I went back to the CIA building completely out of airspeed, altitude, and ideas. As soon as I walked in, Tom told me the artillery barrage had stopped, which was not necessarily good news. More likely, it meant the enemy's big battalions were moving up. Sure enough, reports began streaming in of fighting well within the defense perimeter, with some engagements a kilometer or two from the hill itself.

Still, Tom, Pat, and I worked the problem as best we could trying to think of something—anything—to get some tactical air *in* and our guys *out*. If prayers, drums, and feathered rattles would've worked—cleared the skies over Phou Pha Thi or cleared the cobwebs out from between the ears of the commander of the 7th Air Force—we'd have tried them. The secure channel came back on-line, but we had nothing new to say into it.

At three in the morning, we lost voice and teletype communication with the radar site on the summit.

We just looked at each other and thought, *Oh shit.*

But all was not lost. A few days earlier we had positioned an Air Force staff sergeant—a Sergeant Gary—at the CIA STOL strip two-thirds of the way down the mountain. He had a portable HF and an air-ground radio set and had been assigned to act as FAC for any planes that managed to get through to defend the site. I also figured he could coordinate the evacuation, if it came to that. Now we had more urgent things to do with his radio, provided Evan Washburn remembered it was there.

Within the hour, Evan came back on the air, speaking from Sergeant Gary's battery-powered radio at the STOL strip.

"The artillery's stopped," Evan said, "but—I can't believe it! We're picking up small-arms fire at the summit!"

Again we looked at each other, wondering what the *hell* was going on. With several hundred Meo and Thai veterans deployed around the mountain and a sheer cliff of a thousand feet on one side—not to mention the trip-wire pyrotechnics—there was *no way* an enemy assault force could've broken through that line without our hearing about it, let alone climbed to the summit without being seen.

Pat took the microphone and said, "Evan, get on top of that goddamn hill—and I mean right now. Take some Little Guys with you and find out what's going on."

I'm sure as far as Evan was concerned, that was going the wrong way, but he was a good troop, gathered up a squad or so of Meos from the defensive perimeter, and did as he was told.

While Evan was out reconnoitering, we ordered Vang Pao's reserves north to Site 36 in anticipation of the general engagement that would probably follow the loss of the site. A large NVA force was now in the field and the weather was still dry; they would likely go looking for additional fish to fry. I sent our chief photo-interpreter, a great guy named Pete Saderholm who was popular with the aircrews, over to the A-1 squadron to brief the pilots for a maximum effort against the enemy as soon as the sun came up.

"Tell them we're trying to get our guys out," I told Pete as he left the command post, charts and photos bulging under his arms. "And Pete—preach a goddamn holy war to those guys!"

He nodded that he would.

About four in the morning, we started receiving calls telling us that the 7th Air Force was now throwing "everything it had" into the defense of Site 85, beginning at sunrise. If it was true, the biggest danger to pilots over Phou Pha Thi would be a midair collision, the sky would literally be black with planes. Word had obviously gotten back to General Momyer from both up and down the chain of command that somebody had fumbled the ball. Now we were going to be embarrassed with too much "hep." We only hoped there would be somebody alive up there to benefit from it all.

I looked out a window and watched the sun come up. The A-1 Spads had long since launched, and the dawn broke with an eerie silence belying the hell breaking loose—or soon to break loose—200 miles to the north.

Before the sun's disk had cleared the horizon, Sergeant Gary was on the radio. The weather was clearing, he said excitedly, and it seemed as if every airplane in the world was descending, like a nest of angry hornets, on Phou Pha Thi.

While we waited to hear from Evan, Sergeant Gary narrated the battle, strings of 500- and 750-pounders crackling like firecrackers as he spoke. The winding road, Route 602, which had taunted and threatened us for so long in the distance, was obliterated in the first minutes of the bombing. The sides of the hills facing the mountain, and most of the valley in between, were set ablaze or obscured by smoke from American bombs. Our A-1s arrived, dropped their ordnance, and loitered in the area, acting as FACs for the jet fighters—F-4s and F-105s—that streamed in from the south and east like an endless conveyer. One Skyraider was hit by NVA ground fire and pancaked on a hillside. The pilot didn't eject.

Where the hell was Evan?

After what seemed like an eternity, we found out. An hour after sunup, the evacuation helos landed and Evan came hobbling down with his Meos and five wounded technicians. They piled into the chopper, along with Sergeant Gary, and lifted off just as a burst of fire from NVA automatic weapons ripped open the helicopter's belly between the skids. The chopper shuddered but stayed in the air. One wounded and extraordinarily unlucky technician was killed—shot through the back as he lay on the aluminum floor.

As soon as they landed at Site 36, Evan checked in to tell us how many guys got off the hill—only the six of them, plus the poor guy KIA'd in the chopper. He then hopped a C-123 for an immediate flight to Udorn, which we met at the ramp. Evan limped off with a bandage around his leg. "A clean shot through the thigh," the medics told him. "No sweat."

He debriefed us right there on the amazing, chilling story of those last hours before dawn on the summit.

Shortly after three that morning, as Pat had ordered, Evan had taken 10 or so Meos and started up the hill toward the gunfire. Unfortunately, by the time he reached the summit, his skirmish line had dwindled to himself plus a couple of others; the rest hung back until they could see what they were getting into.

Immediately on entering the radar site, they surprised what appeared to be a squad of enemy sappers who had apparently infiltrated the summit under cover of darkness and their own artillery barrage—the classic "troop of Boy Scouts" raid Tom had prophesied months before. Evan and his Meos opened fire and dropped most of them, then rooted out and killed several more after a stiff firefight during which Evan took the wound in his leg. Among the bodies they found many, but not all, of the technicians, including five who were still alive. They had been surprised by the sappers but had fiercely defended themselves using the weapons we had provided.

Evan immediately dispersed the squad to search for more survivors or more enemy, telling them to be careful which was which. He himself went to the karst wall and was astonished to find two NVA setting up a sandbagged gun emplacement—the bastards had hoisted a hefty antiaircraft cannon up the wall on straps! He raised his weapon, an automatic shotgun he always bragged about, but the damned thing jammed. The NVA saw him and dived for their rifles, but Evan had already yanked the pin on a grenade and got them both.

By this time the shadows themselves seemed alive, and Evan had no way of knowing how many enemy were actually on the summit, where they were coming from, or where they'd pop up next. He regrouped his Meos and withdrew with the wounded to the STOL strip, where the first rescue chopper found them shortly after sunrise.

Six Americans survived. Sergeant Gary was the only man among them escaping without wounds. Of the 10 left on the hill, most were confirmed dead by Evan, but a number were inexplicably MIA, even after a quick but thorough search of the site.

Evan left for the USAF field hospital and we went back to the command post. The Air America fliers returned to recover the bodies of the KIA and continued to withdraw Meo tribesmen and Thai volunteers from the perimeter, eventually extracting several hundred. Most of the casualties had been taken by the Thais, who bore the brunt of the fighting. The Meos, as usual, managed to escape relatively unscathed—but then, nobody expected them to "stand fast" under the pressure of heavy infantry and artillery; that just isn't how guerrillas fight. Those Meos not withdrawn by helicopter broke up into squads and melted into the jungle, to reappear magically at Site 36 with the reinforcements under General Vang Pao himself.

Bill, Tom, and I now had two new and perplexing problems. With the demolition system damaged by the artillery barrage, Evan had been unable to blow the site as planned. Destroying it should have become our highest priority, but we still had to account for the missing technicians, who might be dug in or hiding somewhere on the summit.

Although the aerial bombardment was still in progess against NVA in the valley, I ordered a CIA Volpar (a twin-engined reconnaissance bird) to photograph every inch of the summit and surrounding area for clues to the possible location of the MIAs. If dead, their bodies may have been overlooked in the dark. If alive or wounded, there would likely be signs of their survival and we could pluck them out with a chopper—unless, of course, the NVA had already captured them and removed them from the hill. It was only a matter of time before we'd have to reduce the site from the air, but I wanted to give those guys every second I could.

The Volpar's photographs, sadly, answered our question, but revealed yet another weird twist to an already unbelievable episode.

Most of the remaining technicians were found, apparently dead, on a small ledge a short way down from the summit on the karst wall. They had appeared to have descended there on aircraft tie-down straps (the straps Evan saw by the antiaircraft gun emplacement) in order to hide from the NVA. From the look of things, it was not a spontaneous decision but a maneuver planned in advance—unfortunately, without consultation with the site commander. These technicians apparently (and understandably) had little faith in the upper echelon's ability or commitment to save them, so they decided, in extremis, to help themselves. Unfortunately, their escape route may have been the very avenue the NVA used to infiltrate the site, or they may have hidden successfully only to be discovered later by the NVA gun crew on top. However it turned out, all had been killed, and we could only assume that those still missing fell over the narrow ledge after being hit. Unfortunately, with two NVA regiments still roaming around the base of the mountain, it would be a long time before a team could go back to search for the bodies.

This discovery at least allowed us to press ahead with the destruction of the site from the air. The next day, a flight of F-4s from the famous "Triple Nickel" (555) squadron roared in to take out the radar equipment, vans, and other facilities. Believe it or not, every last bomb they dropped missed the mountain entirely. To make matters worse, aerial recon now showed NVA all over the site, where they would remain for the rest of the week.

Ambassador Sullivan met with Laotian Prime Minister Souvanna Phouma on March 15 to give him the bad news: The sensitive facilities on Site 85 had not been totally destroyed prior to evacuation, and some Americans had been left behind—presumably killed, but possibly captured, although this was unlikely.

Observers said Souvanna Phouma winced and replied that the enemy could make "some pretty damaging disclosures" if they wished.

By now the battle around Phou Pha Thi had become one of trying to demolish the site while punishing the enemy before they dispersed, and the latter was going much better than the first. For several days, radio intercepts showed some of the most gut-wrenching communications ever to come out of the enemy camp—no brevity codes, just guys terror-stricken, absolutely panicked, shell-shocked, and demoralized.

One of the most pathetic calls I read in translation came from what had apparently been an infantry battalion-level officer: "My men are gone. I'm the only one left. Can anybody hear me? Can I come home?"

You and me both, brother!

Finally, Bill and I gave up on the jets and asked for propeller-driven assets to liquidate the site. The job was finally accomplished by a pilot named Bill Plank, an old AT-28 buddy from my first Vietnam tour. Flying nothing more sophisticated than an A-1 Skyraider, Plank stuck his prop in the weeds, stared down the gunsight, and—literally—blew off the top of the mountain.

Two days later, an Air Force lieutenant general, at the direction of Secretary of Defense McNamara, arrived to take statements about the battle: what happened, what led up to it, why it turned out the way it did. The whole affair was classified top secret by both the CIA and Air Force and that wasn't likely to change, but at least the truth could be made available to those "with a need to know." Shackley met with the general, then the Udorn team, Pat, Tom, and me—and I unloaded on him.

I told him the loss of Site 85, which during its existence had directed over a quarter of all bombing missions in North Vietnam, had been a major disaster made worse by the loss of nearly the entire team and the compromise of our TSQ technology and a variety of top-secret encryption systems that we could only assume were now safely on the way to Moscow. Even more infuriating, the loss could have been prevented easily at any of a dozen decision points over the past few months, beginning with Ambassador William Sullivan's inability or disinclination to deal with the problem realistically. Numerous warnings had been sent from the Laos Station to 7th Air Force headquarters in Saigon, to CINCPAC, and to Washington—the CIA and the Pentagon—about the deteriorating status of site defense, and a deaf ear was turned to them all. Instead of allocating assets needed to defend the site properly, or even withdraw from it in an orderly fashion, Washington had ordered us to "hold the site at all costs." Even worse, once the enemy attack was under way, critical air assets were denied until the site had been rendered indefensible and timely extraction of the team and demolition of the sensitive gear was impossible.

"Surely you may have misunderstood some of the commands and instructions," Mr. McNamara's inspector general said, looking very much like the forlorn, lonely soul he would be when—and if—he turned in this report. "I mean, in the heat of battle, and all that. And you yourself admit you were exhausted in these final hours . . ."

"General," I said, "I've been in the field a long time. I've been in a lot of battles. And I'm telling you, this just doesn't happen. It never should happen. It can't happen. But it did. And it's up to you to do something about it." He and I both knew I was talking about gross dereliction of duty, or worse.

I'm sure neither he nor any other inspector general had ever heard a lowly major talk that way about senior officers, and he left the room a very concerned man—at least as shaken, I hoped, as I was. Shackley couldn't believe what he was hearing, but he hadn't faced what we had that night. I figured my career was finished anyway, so I had nothing to gain by mincing words.

Coming on the heels of Tet and the siege of Khe Sanh in Vietnam, this was something the high-ranking general didn't want to deal with. He took other comments, other interviews, then disappeared in a blast of jet wash back to Washington. I felt sure something productive would come from his investigation—too much was at stake; but Shackley, who had a bit more experience with the bureaucrats, wasn't as sanguine.

We didn't have the luxury of mourning our dead or crying in our beer for long. We still had a major enemy formation in our gut, and the regrouped and reinforced enemy regiments were bearing down on Site 36, the staging area for our rescue forces and our last significant site in northern Laos—a much-contested strategic outpost we had long ago dubbed "the Alamo." The air campaign continued, and General Vang Pao made and broke contact with the enemy several times, cat-and-mouse, exacting a toll in men and materiel at every encounter. But to Hanoi's big regiments, he was never more than a distraction.

Then, on April 1st (no less), we heard that Lyndon Johnson had gone on national television and announced he would not seek reelection. Instead, he said he would devote his remaining months in office to securing an honorable peace in Vietnam. Along with this, he announced a unilateral bombing halt on targets north of the 20th parallel—Hanoi, Haiphong, and environs. We couldn't imagine this applied to Site 36, which lies north of the 20th, but in Laos, not Vietnam. We had to assume this omission was intentional—that nobody at the Pentagon, after the debacle of Site 85, would leave one of our strategic outposts undefended.

The battle for Site 36 intensified, and we called in requests for massive air strikes, including Arc Light (B-52) strikes, in its defense. In return, we received confirmation, from the director of the CIA, that the bombing halt meant a halt to *all* bombing north of the 20th parallel.

Incredulous, Tom and I flew up to Vientiane to meet with Shackley. He showed us a reply he had drafted to Richard Helms, director of the CIA, protesting the decree but basically surrendering to the "inevitable." He asked me how I liked his cable.

"Frankly," I said, "I don't."

Tempers were a little short in those days, so Ted threw a yellow pad at me and said, "Okay, you write a better one."

I wrote a blistering message to Helms that Shackley actually sent over his signature. The gist of that message was this:

"We don't understand the referenced logic: How can we announce a halt to bombing north of the 20th parallel in Laos when officially we're not even fighting in Laos? Surely the President means to halt bombing north of the 20th in Vietnam, where the whole world knows we're engaged in a desperate war against Hanoi.

"Since neither we nor North Vietnam acknowledge that we are fighting in Laos, why should we tie our hands with a public announcement of this nature? Request confirmation regarding Arc Light strikes in support of Site 36, in your next communication."

We know this message was cycled by the White House, because a reply was quickly received from the Joint Chiefs of Staff (whom Shackley had never contacted with respect to B-52 strikes):

"Your request for B-52 strikes in Northern Laos is denied. However, 7th Air Force is herewith directed to furnish friendly forces in northern Laos with up to 300 tactical air strikes per day until further notice and as required by CAS [which meant us at the CIA]."

We felt like starving men suddenly shoved into a banquet—relieved but overwhelmed. The day before yesterday I couldn't get 30 air strikes approved from Momyer. Today, I got more than we could reasonably target, at least in the short term. Perhaps the investigation into the Site 85 debacle had gone forward and was bearing fruit; we couldn't know. We had heard nothing from Washington, and Ambassador Sullivan was strangely silent.

We moved fast before this sudden windfall could blow away. We redoubled our on-the-ground and aerial intelligence efforts and apprised our Little Guys in the field of the approaching fire storm around Site 36. For the first time, we were able to institute a truly "fused intel" program in which intelligence from all sources was combined in support of an integrated campaign plan. Our strategy was to hold Site 36 by air—the Meo just couldn't do it against Hanoi's regiments—and methodically reduce the enemy forces wherever they were found on the model of the massive counterattacks at Site 85.

After the attacks began, SI again submitted translated summaries of NVA horror on the ground: whole battalions eviscerated in an afternoon, companies in attack positions around the site simply disappearing from the map. For the first time in history, a position had been held and a large enemy main force destroyed utterly by tactical air alone—23 years before Desert Storm.

More than a victory over one disputed site, it ended for several years Hanoi's successful big-unit maneuvers in Laos. It allowed our Little Guys next year to recapture, under Tom's guidance, the entire Plain of Jarres, the strategic plateau in north central Laos that the NVA had held since the early sixties.

The rainy season finally began in June, ending Hanoi's ability to reinforce its units; and I have to admit, I had a feeling deep inside that the war had ended for me, too. At home, Martin Luther King and Robert Kennedy had been assassinated. Peace talks had started in Paris but they soon stalled out. It was hard to keep a grip on who or what we were fighting for—what the war was all about.

I was simply burnt out, like one of the earth movers by Route 602. From Tet on, I joined the legion of walking zombies who had held the American war effort together with baling wire and bile—and the blood of a lot of good men in the field.

We never received a copy of the inspector General's report. Perhaps there never was one. As far as the top brass knew—or even cared—the fall of Site

85 was just another combat loss. War is supposed to be hell, even when God is on your side.

Ted made me take some much-needed and much-deferred leave, and I didn't put up a fight. We left Tom Clines in charge of the store and all of us—Pat, Bill, a couple of other CIA officers, and me—went to Bangkok, got smashed, and tried to forget the last 12 months.

We were not entirely successful.

Shortly after our too-brief R&R, Shackley, Bill Lair, me, and Tony Poe, a well-known case officer, were invited back to Bangkok for a secret ceremony at Thai army headquarters. There, the Prime Minister and his deputy presented us with the Most Exalted Order of the White Elephant, Thailand's highest medal for *farangs*, as we foreigners were politely called in that country, in honor of our "heroic defense of Phou Pha Thi" and other miscellaneous services for which the Thai government was suitably grateful.

I looked down at the ornate, gaudy thing on the pocket of my civilian jacket and whispered to Shackley, "Sonofabitch, Ted—this is the first time I ever got a medal for failing."

I could only hope it would be the last.

# — II —

# Crusades in the Puzzle Palace

# — 7 —

# Merry Christmas, Uncle Ho

Agamemnon was right: 10 years of war is too much. After a decade of on-and-off combat, the Greeks threw up their hands and captured Troy with a wooden horse. After almost as long in one war zone after another—Vietnam, Iran, and Laos—I, too, had had enough.

The first sign that stress and the elements were getting to me showed up in the spring of 1967 during the so-called dry monsoon. Tom Clines and I were on an inspection trip to southern Laos when I suddenly became very thirsty. I got a can of Coke from a cooler, took one swallow, and began to see stars—light-headed, as you get when your oxygen hose comes loose at high altitude. Then the lights went out.

I woke up hours later in a field hospital with a couple of doctors standing over me. At first they thought I had cerebral malaria, then changed the diagnosis to dengue fever, the on-again, off-again infection that felled almost as many of our guys in Southeast Asia as that bigger, nastier disease. They pumped me full of drugs and I was back on the job within 10 days, but the episode got my attention. Other than for physicals, I hadn't been in a hospital since West Point. I'd spent a lot of time in some pretty rough places, but between GI vaccinations and a sturdy constitution, nothing much ever bothered me. Until now. Looking back, it was one of the first signs that the stress of almost constant action—and, worse, the responsibility for *others* in action—was starting to take its toll.

Another blow came later in that year when I learned that an old friend from Detachment Two Alpha, Gene Connally, had been killed flying Thuds (F-105s) over the North. Gene was a great guy and one of the best fliers I knew. Somehow deep inside I felt really angry, frustrated, even betrayed by his loss. For the first time, war felt both intensely personal and supremely impersonal, like a force of nature.

The CIA did its bit to keep up our morale. In late 1966, Jo Ann and Julie had moved to Bangkok, which was considered "safe haven" for CIA and military personnel, although my family's arrival had been anything but festive.

Jo Ann was anxious to join me and had gotten used to Air Force life. She was beginning to see that raising her daughter as a "military brat" had some advantages—like living in exotic places and experiencing things other families could only read about in books. She was looking forward to seeing what the Far East had to offer and reported for her "security briefing" at the U.S. Embassy in Bangkok full of enthusiasm. Unfortunately, I hadn't quite gotten around yet to telling her that the CIA, not the USAF, now issued my paychecks.

When she came out, she looked like she'd been run over by a truck.

"What's wrong, honey?" I asked. "Didn't they answer all your questions?"

"My God, Dick! What's all this about the CIA? I thought you worked for the Air Force! Why didn't you tell me what you were *really* doing up here?"

I gave her my most charming grin. "Then it wouldn't have been much of a secret."

"Well, I knew you'd been involved with Air Force special operations, but the CIA? I don't know. I don't think I like that. I don't even like the *idea* of that! Can't you just go back to the States and take a regular Air Force job?"

That was the 64-dollar question, of course; and it became the $64,000 question by the time Phou Pha Thi had fallen in the spring of 1968. I had already been on station twice as long as most of my peers, and, for one reason or another, I'd even extended my second Laos tour by several months. "The company" was pressuring me to come back for yet a third extension. But enough was enough.

Not only had I made up my mind against a third tour, but by July 1968, I was seriously thinking of resigning from the Air Force.

Compared to my earlier successes, the debacle of Site 85 was an aberration, but it seemed eerily symptomatic of the way the Vietnam war had gone since America took over. Worse, it revealed some very unflattering characteristics of the U.S. high command—the top military jobs that every academy graduate was supposed to covet. I wasn't sure I was ready, or ever would be ready, to make the kind of compromises necessary to pin on colonel's eagles or, if I made the cut, a general's star. We'd heard nothing from the Pentagon's investigation over the loss of Site 85, and I was beginning to suspect we never would. The Air Force seemed primarily interested in averting its eyes from what to me had been a textbook case of dereliction of duty. The services didn't want to string the war out, of course, just come away from it looking as good as possible. If a young officer didn't like the way things were going in Southeast Asia, where else would he find the opportunity to command in battle?

While I mulled this over, trying to figure out what kind of career was left for me, I got a call from Hienie Aderholt, now deputy for operations in the USAF Special Operations Force (AFSOF) in Florida.

"What do you mean you're thinking about leaving the service?" he growled. "You're gonna let those idiots have the last word? Not a chance. I want you to come to work for me. I want you to be my deputy director of operations here at Eglin."

"Hell, I'm just a major, Hienie. That's a colonel's job."

"So? You got something against making below-the-zone LC? All I'm saying, Dick, is don't throw it all away. If enough young guys like you bail out, who the hell's going to run the show ten years from now? And I'll tell you, Southeast Asia ain't the whole Air Force. You owe it to yourself to give it one more shot."

Well, I decided Hienie was right, as usual. In September 1968, after the riotous Democratic National Convention in Chicago symbolized the nation's schizophrenia about the war and itself, we went PCS—permanent change of station—to Eglin AFB, Florida. Soon after our arrival, Jo Ann gave birth to our twins, Laura and John, in an American hospital. I felt good about my decision but bad about leaving my friends—Tom, Bill, and Pat, and also Ted Shackley, who taught me a lot about people and getting things done despite a hellish bureaucracy. That's one reason (along with the renewed sense of optimism about ending the war that arrived with the new Nixon administration) I volunteered in 1969 to return for a couple of months to help put the Laos air war back on track when my replacement didn't work out.

Things in Southeast Asia went pretty well after that—Tom seemed to have the ground war in Laos well in hand (at least until the major Communist offensive following Tet in 1970)—and I felt things were still pretty shipshape from my watch. We built a two-bit little Air Force that took the war to Hanoi and helped an important "neutral" country stay neutral. The peak of American commitment passed as Nixon announced the beginning of a phased reduction of the 543,000 U.S. troops in Vietnam. America landed the first man on the moon in July, and we finally seemed to be finding our way out of the long, dark tunnel of the 1960s.

Back at Eglin, I reported to Hienie's boss, a great guy named Joe Wilson— a brigadier general in a major general's job—and went right to work training aircrews for the kind of operations I had just left behind in the field.

In the fall of 1969, General Joe Wilson gave me the news of my below-the-zone promotion to lieutenant colonel that Hienie had kidded me about;

and shortly after that, I was given command of the 603rd Special Operations Squadron (a brand-new TAC outfit being equipped with twin-engine jet A-37Bs) at Hurlburt Field.

I was finally headed back toward the mainstream Air Force. More important, I was back where I felt I really belonged: in a jet cockpit.

Unfortunately, the A-37B Dragonfly was fated to become one of those "footnote" airplanes, a project that filled a particular niche brilliantly, then got trampled by events. The B-model Dragonfly was a beefy first cousin to the famous T-37A used to train generations of Air Force pilots. Because of its unusual side-by-side seating, the big-canopied, tadpole-shaped trainer was nicknamed "Tweetie Bird" or "Tweet" after the big-headed cartoon character. (It was also called the "Hummer," or hummingbird, probably because its distinctive, high-pitched turbine seemed to have been designed primarily to convert jet fuel into noise.) As Cessna's only combat airplane, the attack "B" version was refitted with General Electric J-85 turbojets (the same engine that powered the advanced supersonic trainer, the T-38 Talon), which made the souped-up and beefed-up "Hummer" a real humdinger to fly. It also had in-flight refueling capability, which the trainer version lacked, and was the only jet fighter in the inventory capable of refueling behind KC-130 tankers, making it the ideal choice for helicopter escort duty. Its straight wing held lots of ordnance and preserved the trainer's honest flying characteristics. It offered twin-engine reliability; turbine speed to station; and, with the new J-85s, enough power to get its driver out of just about any problem. All in all, the Dragonfly was tailor-made for close air support in Southeast Asia. Yet it was never deployed in significant numbers, despite the intensification of fighting brought about by Nixon's incursion into Cambodia and growing public disenchantment with stalemated Paris peace talks, now entering their third year. The A-37's demise is a case study in the kind of shortsighted "systems analysis" thinking that characterized the era.

In the late 1960s, Air Force doctrine was going through a grand debate. One school of thought—from those concerned principally with limited wars and the requirements of our third-world allies—wanted to see more light-weight, easy-to-fly, easy-to-maintain, and easy-to-buy fighters (like the A-37 and F-5E) provided to MAP (Military Assistance Program) countries and even operated by our own services in those environments. Their opponents, who eventually carried the day, favored big, expensive, complex, multirole aircraft, which, at that time, were best exemplified by the F-4 Phantom. In combat, and particularly night attacks in close proximity to the enemy, the F-4 (and its kind) would roll in from altitude, scare the hell out of friendly and enemy troops alike, unload the wrath of God on everything more or less within gunsight, then skedaddle home to refuel those big, gas-guzzling J-79 engines. The A-37, on the other hand, performed more like a World War II prop-driven fighter; that is, more like the A-1 or AT-28. It could take the time necessary to pick its targets under the flares and actually work with the FACs over the course of an entire battle.

During my three years in command of the 603rd, we worked hard to perfect the night attack mission for the A-37, fully intending to go to Vietnam and show the old Spad and A-26 drivers how it was done. Part of my job was to get every element of my command combat-ready, which meant weeding out some of the deadwood and misfits that accumulate with any stateside unit.

One particular airman, a maintenance staff sergeant, had been reported by his supervisor several times for erratic behavior aggravated by heavy drinking. I asked the squadron flight surgeon to get on the case right away, to get the airman back on track or give me enough reasons to transfer him to a place that could. But events moved faster than our good intentions.

My home phone rang one midnight. The base duty officer said the local police had just reported that "one of our guys" had flipped out at a trailer park where he lived: grabbed a rifle, shot up the place, then holed up in his trailer with a roommate (also one of our airmen) at gunpoint. We now had a hostage situation.

"Tell them I'm on my way," I said, then dialed the flight surgeon. I picked up the doctor and sped directly to the trailer park. It was like a scene from a B movie: County sheriff and highway patrol cars were parked everywhere, lights flashing, with spotlights playing across the beat-up trailer. A patrolman directed me to the officer in charge—a state trooper standing behind his squad car's open door.

"What's the status, officer?" I said, identifying myself as the sergeant's commander.

"He's been quiet for the last few minutes. As far as we know, he hasn't harmed the roommate. Maybe you can talk to him." The trooper handed me a microphone attached to a loudspeaker under the grille.

"Sergeant, this is Major Secord," I said, "your commanding officer. Look, sergeant, I'm sure whatever's troubling you can be worked out. But the longer this goes on, the worse things are going to be. Now listen to me, this is a direct order: Put down your rifle and come out of there . . ."

The bullet whizzed past my ear even before I heard the crack of the rifle. The next thing I knew, I was flat on my stomach looking over at the patrolman next to me on the ground.

I got up, microphone still in hand, and crouched behind the door.

"Okay, sergeant, that's enough! Put that goddamn rifle down right now or I'm coming in there and taking it away from you myself!"

The rifle cracked again, and again we dropped. The patrolman fished his carbine out from the squad car.

"You got another one of those?" I asked.

While he drew a bead on the window, I looked back at the doctor, crouched by a nearby trailer.

"Come on, Doc!" I shouted, waving him forward. "It's your turn, goddamn it! Get up here and talk this guy out!"

Amazingly, that's just what he did—after about 10 minutes and in a decidedly more conciliatory tone. The airman threw out his rifle, and the police had him in custody almost before the barrel hit the ground. The roommate was shaken but okay, like the rest of us. I gave credit to his supervisor, who diagnosed his dangerous condition even if the medics didn't. If I learned nothing else from the incident, it was that hostage takers aren't rational people. You may have to play by their rules for a while, but eventually you'll get the drop on them.

In June 1971, the Air Force in its wisdom decided to disband the 603rd without a combat tour. The "aerial battleship" proponents had won the policy day, and the unit was broken up. That almost three-year stretch as squadron commander was among the happiest assignments of my career. We had an important mission and just the right blend of old hands and new faces to make the work challenging and rewarding. Because we were a self-contained airmobile unit, I commanded an exceptionally large squadron—600 to 700 people—and had all the combat disciplines under my control, from flight-line mechanics and POL technicians to armorers and the motor pool.

My experience in joint command had more than prepared me for the varied responsibilities, and as a below-the-zone "light" colonel, I could now realistically aspire to command of an operational wing, the capstone of a mainstream Air Force career. But first, I had to get a final ticket punched: a tour at one of the senior war colleges, something an Air Force colonel needs on his transcript and absolutely required for anyone aspiring to the stars of a general officer. As a result, from August 1971 to June 1972, I was assigned to the Naval War College at Newport, Rhode Island.

A lot of officers look back on War College as the intellectual high point of their careers, but, for a variety of reasons, I did not. Perhaps it suffered in comparison to the rigor of West Point and its superb faculty, but I quickly came to regard the Newport school as a rather stodgy old "gentleman's club." I wasn't particularly challenged academically and felt the school was organized more along the lines of a low-threat executive "retreat" than a finishing school for the nation's future top warriors.

Not that the curriculum wasn't interesting, and often fascinating. We studied the tendentious whys and wherefores of national security policy, force structure, case studies about famous successes and infamous screw-ups in geopolitics, and a little world history. We simulated some wars and learned more than most of us wanted to know about Pentagon funding and the annual budget rites. We even had a few VIP lectures from the Chief of Naval Operations, the Chairman of the Joint Chiefs (and other service chiefs); Al Haig (who had by now moderated his views on the Air Force); and even journalists like John Chancellor—since television and politics were inseparable, even then. We wrote a few papers and read many, many books, but frankly, if Tom Clines hadn't been there at the same time (the CIA had several slots in each class for their career officers), I would've found the year pretty tedious.

The problem wasn't so much what was covered, but what was left out: the *guts* of high-level command. Like a uniformed mannequin, War College displayed the "ropes and whistles and scrambled eggs" of policy-level decision makers, but not their heart and soul. Perhaps those were things that couldn't be taught. That last bit of education, like any art, apparently, would come only by apprenticeship to a master.

In any event, the 10-month program left me with a great deal of free time, so I signed up for the master's program in international affairs at George Washington University. The GW program complemented the War College curriculum, and, as with my earlier adventure into English literature, I felt that if it didn't make me a better officer, it certainly didn't make me any worse. In fact, in a year that recorded such pregnant events as Nixon's historic visit to China, the aftermath of Nasser's death and Anwar Sadat's rise in Egypt, the record-setting peace march in Washington, the mining of Haiphong, and the Watergate burglary, a politically oriented university was undoubtedly the right place to be.

In June 1972, I was assigned to the Pentagon.

Normally, a first-tour colonel goes to work somewhere in the general staff of the Air Force Department; you can't be very useful until you learn the rules of the game and the names of the players. The reality of Pentagon duty, I discovered, was about as different from what was taught at the War College as an actual Super Bowl is from the pregame warmup.

I quickly discovered that the "big four" at the Pentagon are the OSD (Office of the Secretary of Defense), with all the assistant secretaries of defense and their staffs; the civilian service secretaries departments; the uniformed service staffs (Army, Air Force, and Chief of Naval Operations), and the JCS—the Joint Chiefs of Staff. Because of my extensive background in Southeast Asia, I went directly into the OSD, assigned to International Security Affairs (ISA), East Asia and Pacific Region, Southeast Asia Branch, as chief of the Laos desk.

My main duty, like that of most newly assigned lieutenant colonels, was carrying books and briefing papers for my superiors, at least for the first few months while I learned the batting order of the bureaucracy. Our charter was simple: to justify our budget. This meant advocacy as well as analysis, and, at my level, "devil's advocacy" to make sure our bureaucratic flanks weren't exposed to unanticipated criticism. To be fair, the Pentagon wasn't alone in playing this game. In an intensely competitive federal budgeting environment, every department works hard to justify its slice of the pie. When sharp-pencil analysis reveals some program or function isn't doing the job, it's usually dropped so that money can be "better wasted" elsewhere. It's a grueling process with plenty of room for error, but somehow it works. The real miracle isn't how much money and effort gets wasted; it's how many systems, plans, and components wind up working the way they should. As a newcomer with a strong field orientation and deep suspicion of bureaucrats, I was surprised to discover this—but in my experience, it's true.

After a month or so of chart bearing, a list came through showing my name, along with many others, as having been selected for promotion to full colonel. Not only was I just getting used to my new silver leaves, but I didn't have the time in grade or sufficient "friends in court," not to mention the kind of service record, that cried out for a way, way, way below-the-zone promotion to bird colonel. (Officers who complain about their bosses to the IG, as I did in Laos, usually find themselves swamped, career-wise, by the waves they created.) I was so sure it was a mistake that I phoned Colonel Aderholt's office, where I knew they'd have a copy of the list, and asked his secretary to confirm the Social Security number.

"Dolores," I said to Hienie's secretary after explaining my quandary, "please check your copy of the list. There's a transport pilot named Mack Secord who's also a lieutenant colonel, but no relation to me. They must mean him."

"Now, Dick," she laughed, "the colonel's right; you just don't know how to accept good news, do you?"

So, with a new pair of eagles on my shoulders (actually, I didn't pin them on until April Fool's Day, 1973), I took over a new job that my bosses (short-timer Rear Admiral Harry Train and his boss, Deputy Assistant SecDef Dennis Doolin, a long-haired hell-raiser who looked and sounded, but didn't act, like a Berkeley professor) thought was more befitting my lofty station: head of the entire Southeast Asia branch. At this level, I now had some civilians among the blue-suiters on my staff, including John Kelly, a talented State Department exchange officer who would later become Assistant Secretary of State for the Middle East.

Our main function was to prepare policy papers for Defense Secretary Melvin Laird—usually option analyses, which ranged from budget justification to military strategy. In late 1972, as Nixon was reelected, the U.S. ended its ground combat role in Vietnam, and the Paris peace talks were nearing their climax, the SE Asia branch was the place to be. Soon after I took over, in fact, instructions came down through channels that would change an important slice of world history—and directly contribute to the end of America's longest war.

Like the battle for Site 85, the true story of Nixon's "Christmas bombings," the so-called "Twelve Days of Christmas," has to my knowledge never before been told.

To understand the significance and scope of the Christmas bombing campaign, you have to remember what the world was like for America in late 1972. The Vietnam war had dragged on for over a decade, by Washington calendars, and over seven according to the public, who figured the war really began when U.S. Marines waded ashore at Da Nang in the spring of 1965. Although in tactical terms the Allies (ARVN and U.S., but also Australian, Korean, and nominal forces from a half-dozen other countries) had pretty much destroyed the Southern Viet Cong as a cohesive fighting force by 1969 and driven back or dispersed bigger NVA units, the general perception of the war after the 1968 Tet offensive was one of hopeless stalemate, a quagmire that the Allies could never win and the North would never lose. The U.S. had failed to take decisive military action (such as permanently occupying the Ho Chi Minh Trail and conducting a sustained, no-sanctuary, no-pause bombing of the North) to knock Hanoi out of the war. This allowed North Vietnam to pursue a classic "negotiate and strike" strategy against the South—punctuating its occasional truces and peace overtures with violent, and increasingly big-unit, offensives aimed at wearing down the South's, and America's, will to resist.

Nixon's management of the war reflected a personality and leadership style quite different from Lyndon Johnson's. Immediately after taking office, Nixon implemented his preelection "secret plan," which was really nothing more than offering Hanoi a carrot and a stick for joining America in achieving their mutual objective: America's withdrawal from the war. The carrot was a series of unilateral withdrawals of American troops and high-level, publically visible (as well as covert) peace talks between National Security Advisor Henry Kissinger and Le Duc Tho accompanied by high-intensity, visible (as well as covert) military punishment: the "secret" bombing of Northern sanctuaries in Cambodia and Operation Lam Son 713, the belated (and woefully unsupported) ARVN ground incursion against the Ho Chi Minh Trail.

By early 1972, the United States was heavily committed to Defense Secretary Laird's "Vietnamization" scheme: a code word for the unilateral American withdrawal portion of the Nixon plan. Hanoi was also committed, but to its own game plan, and kept up the pressure on what they perceived as a precipitous American rout.

On March 30, the NVA crossed the demilitarized zone in force, and captured Quang Tri a month later. Nixon responded by bombing the North and mining Haiphong Harbor. (That fall the famous "Linebacker One" campaign took place, in which B-52s were used for the first time over the lower reaches of the North.) This sudden flurry of large-scale violence sobered negotiators on both sides, and a tentative cease-fire was drawn up in Paris. Wisely, in my view, South Vietnamese President Nguyen Van Thieu, who was really on the hot seat, utterly rejected it, along with most of us in the Pentagon. As leader of the DoD's working-level delegation, I pointed out to my superiors that the agreement had no penalties for North Vietnamese violations (although the U.S. was absolutely forbidden to intervene again under any conditions) and that no provisions for punitive consequences (or even sanctions) existed in case of a later NVA invasion of the South. Even worse, it mandated no provisions for third-party inspections. It was a Christmas gift for the North and a time bomb for the South, and we recommended strongly against it.

Unfortunately, State (led at the working level by none other than William Sullivan, who was now Deputy Assistant Secretary of State for Far East), despite the refusal of Thieu and our own generals to sign off on the treaty, felt confident enough to declare, in the words of Henry Kissinger, that "peace is at hand." Our only question was, in *whose* hands?

In October, my group was asked to prepare a "talking paper" that outlined plans for a drastically expanded air war, to be delivered to the President by Mel Laird at Camp David. We assumed it was just an extension of our previous efforts; my group had been cheerleaders for the expanded use of B-52s in Southeast Asia ever since I arrived, and I had championed the backbreaking power of the BUFs (the B-52 Stratofortresses now had the same nickname as the ceramic Saigon elephants) long before that, since my first tour in Laos. Although we didn't know it at the working level, the paper was intended to show the President his options in case negotiations broke down.

Unfortunately, the Joint Chiefs disliked our proposals for wider B-52 use almost as much as the North Vietnamese did. The case the JCS (mainly the Air Force itself) made against our plan was based on a real catch-22: If we don't use our B-52s' wartime electronic countermeasure (ECM) settings to defeat the Soviet-made surface-to-air missiles (SAMs), we'll lose too many of them; and if we *do* use the wartime settings, we'll tip the Soviet Union off to the fact that we can generally evade their air defense system and give away a big, secret advantage in case of a nuclear war.

Our response to this paradox was, and always had been, a strong dose of logic: "Hey, guys, we *are* at war!" We couldn't understand why the JCS didn't just go back to the ECM vendors and ask them to come up with new settings to protect our B-52s if and when they roared into Soviet airspace to sweep up after a general ICBM nuclear exchange. To lose a real, hot war because of some contingency plan in an imaginary cold one seemed to us to be the height of folly.

We also had another ace up our sleeves, namely a copious supply of TAC air flown by highly experienced combat pilots who (along with the B-52s) could knock out the SAMs (even the mobile units) in a new Linebacker-style air offensive. With the SAMs down or unable to fire accurately, our BUFs and other attack planes could roam the North Vietnamese skies virtually unchallenged.

Anyway, that was the basic tenor of our paper. We (myself, Major Don McDonald, and another officer, who helped write it) appended a somewhat lengthy list of targets that had, for various bureaucratic reasons, been previously deleted from strike or heavy bomber target lists. *This* plan, for once, allowed few sanctuaries and no time-outs. It was the kind of plan the U.S. had used against Germany and Japan in World War II. We believed it would probably have similar results in 1972.

We dotted the *i*'s and crossed the *t*'s and kicked the paper upstairs and, given all the objections we expected the JCS to raise, promptly forgot about it.

It was now early November, and despite a few rumblings about the botched burglary at the Watergate Hotel in June, the nightly network news—especially from the Paris peace talks—was good enough for Nixon to clobber McGovern in the presidential election. In the office, I was getting ready to receive a new boss. Harry Train had left and was replaced by another two-star admiral, Tom Bigley, an old-school submariner.

It was time now, too, for Hanoi to learn a slightly different lesson about American politics and its influence on our foreign policy. Freed from the reelection blues, Nixon and Kissinger suddenly realized that Thieu's (and the Pentagon's) objections to the proposed treaty had merit after all. On November 20th, Kissinger went back to Paris not to sign the treaty, as everyone expected, but to introduce 69 new conditions for peace, virtually all of them critical to South Vietnam's sovereignty after the American withdrawal. Hanoi interpreted this as bargaining in bad faith and stormed out of the talks. Nixon decided to activate the "stick"—the B-52 raids—Laird had told him about in October and prod the enemy back to the table.

In mid-December, Doolin called me into his office.

"Dick," he said, a bit grim-faced, "do you remember that paper you guys worked up for the Secretary a couple of months ago—the one about unleashing the B-52s?"

"Sure do."

"Good. Dust the fucker off. We're going to use it."

"Are you sure?" I couldn't believe it.

"I just got it from the horse's mouth." He had just returned from the Secretary's office. "Think about what you need; work on an update and get back to me as soon as possible. We've got to get a paper in the hands of the Secretary immediately, including an implementation order."

In the hall I bumped into my new boss, Rear Admiral Tom Bigley. It was his first week on the job, and now Armageddon was about to break loose. We ducked into his office.

"Sir," I said, "remember that paper on B-52s I told you about? I just got the word from Doolin—we're going to war!"

His eyes got as big as portholes. He fired a broadside of questions about the plan, including the all-important one: "What's the position of the JCS?"

"They'll be opposed, I'm sure." I couldn't camouflage the obvious. Then I added, "On the other hand, they haven't done any real war planning since the shooting started. We'll just have to let the Secretary deal with them."

The next few days must have been very tough ones for poor Tom Bigley, since he seemed greatly (and justifiably) concerned about the lack of JCS consensus. Still, we had our orders.

These conversations began what was, for me anyway, my first experience with an "accession list," and until I had to deal with one personally, I didn't even know they existed. This is not a classified document control list in the usual sense, but an administrative tool used internally to keep sensitive information away from prying eyes, even when those eyes would normally have access to it. In a way, it was kind of a "career proprietary" or "office politics" list, but it predated my tour in government (and probably even Thomas Jefferson's) and sure didn't end when I left the service.

The accession list for plans and orders related to the Christmas bombing campaign of 1972 had a handful of names on it, including Laird, Doolin, Bigley, me, several of our officers, and the stenographers who typed it. More significant were the names *not* shown, namely the Joint Chiefs, who usually originated such plans. I understood completely why the Secretary had not included them—they would've torpedoed the whole idea based on their concern about SAMs and the security of the B-52 electronic warfare codes. Those fears seemed groundless, but it still felt like I was heading down the Black Diamond slope with my ski boots unlatched; a pretty big link in the chain of command was being bypassed not just in the planning, but eventually in the *implementation* of what was to become one of the boldest strokes of the war.

I called my staff in and told them the balloon was going up. The plan was later called Linebacker II, for obvious reasons. We already knew generally how things ought to unfold—the fighter strikes and MiG CAPs (Combat Air Patrols) and B-52 raids—but our target data was a little old, and our main obstacles at this point wouldn't be the enemy, but the inertia in our own command and control system: the reluctance of field commanders who had learned (in over a decade of half-baked planning and lousy interbranch coordination) the fine art of partial commitment, of holding back a little, of anticipating next month's missions or politicking for next year's allocation instead of going balls-out for victory today. That was going to change. But to do it, we'd have to get their attention.

We drafted the initial order in totally unambiguous terms:

"By order of higher authority, commencing on 18 December and continuing until further directed, you will make maximum effort utilizing all assets currently assigned, including all B-52 and Naval aircraft, to attack the following targets, which are validated for strike within a 48-hour period herewith. Further orders to follow."

A list of numbers accompanied the order, drawn from the "bombing encyclopedia"—the target data book that had been in use for a considerable time, although many of those targets made their actual strike debut on this list. We purposely used the term "higher authority" because these orders were signed by the Secretary of Defense on behalf of the President—the commander in chief himself.

We also chose a term that hadn't been heard in those hallowed halls since World War II: "maximum effort," something we push-button warriors had apparently forgotten about.

"What the hell does *this* mean?" bellowed one JCS staff officer who, as we expected, had trouble accepting reality. "Maximum effort?"

"I believe the Secretary means we are supposed to fly everything, sir," I replied. The institutionalized paper shufflers just couldn't conceive of an order that meant, reduced to its essentials, *Engage the enemy with both hands, kick him in the ass, and get this goddamn war over with!*

Other staffers were sent to see me in order to "clarify" things.

"Come on, Dick—what does that mean, *maximum effort*?" Their cajoling voices were brittle.

"It means use every airplane you've got. Fly 'em all!" I explained. "And by the way, we know you've got a hundred and thirty-two B-52s, G and H models, deployed at two bases. We'd best see them up there!"

"Our losses will be terrible!"

"Any losses will be replaced," I answered.

"But it'll screw up SIOP!" one officer protested, referring to the Strategic Integrated Operations Plan, the plan that allocated nuclear resources to World War III.

"So be it!" I threw up my hands.

Our guys finally got the picture. The might and majesty of the USA was going to land squarely on Hanoi's neck—belatedly, and, with a little luck, for the last time.

That initial order was followed by about six others over the next 12 days (we stood down only for Christmas—not for a holiday, but to read the diplomatic tea leaves). North Vietnam, which had been planning its own maximum effort to force President Thieu to rescind his new demands, was caught completely by surprise, unprepared for either the volume or the violence of our attack. The bomb-damage assessments and scuttlebutt from the theater would never be as satisfying as those received on that first day.

Radio Hanoi's anti-American broadcast was cut off the air in midsentence by a string of bombs from high-flying B-52s. The Gia Lam North railroad marshaling yard, long a privileged sanctuary owing to its location next to Gia Lam International Airport used by Aeroflot, the Russian airline, was obliterated, along with parts of the airport. The dock facilities at Haiphong, avoided for fear of injuring Soviet or third-world seamen, were demolished.

Similar reports streamed in for the next week and a half, like stock prices on ticker tape—24 hours a day.

The two railroad lines in northern North Vietnam over which supplies were obtained from Red China—demolished. The North Vietnamese Air Defense Command headquarters, for years not targeted because of its proximity to a building believed to be a hospital—blown up, severely damaging its civilian shield.

Two terrible instances of civilian casualties outraged world media during the campaign. One was that hospital; the other was a direct hit on the French Embassy (caused by a hung-bomb—a bomb that failed to fall properly from a Navy A-4), killing the ambassador's longtime mistress and sending the ambassador himself to the hospital and then to Paris where he eventually died of his wounds. It is cold comfort to those civilians and their families that these deaths were inadvertent, but such suffering may be the best argument I know for prosecuting any combat that's thrust upon you with sufficient force to win it quickly. That, in fact, was what Linebacker II was all about.

As far as the SAMs that so worried the Joint Chiefs went, by December 25th, American bombers and tactical fighters had either destroyed all fixed and mobile launchers or deprived those remaining of replacement missiles by interdicting the sea, rail, and highway lines into the country. Our fighters literally roamed at will over North Vietnam looking for targets. Not a missile or aircraft—even a blip from a ground-based radar—rose to meet them. It was the third time in the war we had systematically reduced the air defenses in the North, but the first time we had done it in all areas simultaneously. For the first and last time in the war, we were total masters of the Vietnamese skies, north and south.

As December slipped away, the bombing continued around the clock, "Desert Storm" style—19 years before Iraq invaded Kuwait and the world learned about Patriots and Scuds. It was the kind of aerial campaign we in the combat units had always dreamed about, particularly when the Triple-A and SAMs were flying thick and fast in our direction: a never-ending air raid, the kind in which the enemy simply throws away the sirens because they never stop. The "all clear" never sounds.

On December 30th, the 13th day of the campaign, while some Congressmen were crying for Nixon's impeachment, the *Washington Post* was claiming that the President had "taken leave of his senses," and North Vietnam was accusing the U.S. of waging a "campaign of extermination" against its population, Hanoi let Washington know privately that it "was willing to return to Paris." Mr. Kissinger's and Mr. Thieu's 69 points no longer seemed so noxious. Hanoi's single condition: the bombing must be stopped.

On December 30th, it was.

A week later, Kissinger and Le Duc Tho met again, and on January 23rd, a final agreement, still mostly a paper tiger but one that South Vietnam felt it could live with, was initialed.

On January 27, 1973, a "permanent" cease-fire was signed in Paris, and Secretary Laird announced that the selective service lottery in the United States was ended.

On March 29th, the last American troops left Vietnam.

Using wartime settings on their ECM, only 16 B-52s were lost (and none after the first week) out of a total combat fleet of 148—a 12 percent loss rate far below the rate of similar "maximum effort" heavy bomber raids in World War II. Several bomber crews were killed in action, along with a small number of fliers in tactical aircraft. Most of the survivors were rescued as soon as their feet hit the ground (or water), and the handful that were captured were released along with the other American POWs approximately three months later.

It is too much to say that the "12 Days of Christmas" won America's peace in Vietnam, but it certainly hastened the inevitable and, I believe, saved vastly more Allied *and* enemy lives than it cost. What made the campaign's success so bittersweet was that such a victory was completely within our power just about any time during the war. We simply chose not to make the "maximum effort" it—and most wars—required to be won.

Patton complained in Germany, as MacArthur complained later in Korea, that their jobs had been left half done. Others would make the same complaint after Schwarzkopf's liberation of Kuwait in 1991. In 1973, some in the Pentagon pointed out that our victory in Linebacker II, as effective as it had been, bore the seeds of future frustration. That January, we had within our grasp the destruction of North Vietnam as a regional power—as an agent of armed influence in South Vietnam, in Cambodia, in Laos—for at least the next generation. Although our ally in the south would continue to struggle for another two years, I believe we could easily have purchased for them eight or 10 or however many more years it might have taken for the indigenous factions to come to grips with this unusual new condition called *peace*. At worst, it would've meant a return to the same kind of low-intensity war I found there in 1962.

Instead, we used our aerial victory over the north to feather a few nests in Washington and get out of Southeast Asia while the getting was good. Talk about impeaching Nixon for the Christmas bombings would eventually be drowned out by popular praise. The Air Force (SAC in particular) and the JCS immediately took credit for the "12 Days of Christmas" as soon as the dimensions of the victory were apparent. If the success of an endeavor can be measured by the number of people who claim "parentage," then the 12-Day campaign need never worry about dying a bastard of history. Still, careful researchers will discover Linebacker II was pretty much a runny-nosed or-phan until the end of December 1972, hated like bitter medicine until the effect of the cure became obvious at the conference table.

In my view, though, the significance of the campaign, particularly how it was conceived and implemented, has had repercussions far beyond the end of the Vietnam war.

It has become conventional wisdom, at least in the military, to blame the mass media or politicians for America's failure to defeat North Vietnam decisively and to save South Vietnam, particularly when the glow of Desert Storm has given us back our pride in the U.S. military. I believe this now-accepted and all-too-comfortable view is dangerous and misleading—and I'm no fan of either the media or most politicians.

When I finished my first tour as a combat pilot in Vietnam at the be-ginning of the American military buildup, I began to realize things were going wrong with the institution responsible for South Vietnam's defense. In early 1964, Jim Ahmann, another attack pilot who later rose to the rank of lieu-tenant general, and I authored a paper proposing some organizational and doctrinal changes we thought might help America win the war. We thought that the command and control of air power should be somewhat decentral-ized. We wrote that it would be a big mistake to introduce conventional U.S. ground forces into the war since this would just spur the enemy to escalate their own involvement in the south (which it did) and change the focus of victory from simply "not losing" (which is the usual guerrilla objective) to one of having to destroy an entire nation's ability to make war—the politically unpalatable ground interdiction of the Ho Chi Minh Trail and systematic reduction of North Vietnam's military, industrial, and transportation infra-structure. Instead, Jim and I proposed a low-intensity counterinsurgency cam-paign that would be neither politically nor economically costly. It could be run by a cadre of highly trained, motivated, and experienced American vol-unteers who would act as combat "stiffeners" for South Vietnamese troops and fliers using their own equipment. Under such circumstances, we could afford to beat the enemy at their own game—going 30 years, if necessary, which was about the time horizon Hanoi had in mind.

Our proposal received a lot of attention at TAC headquarters and at the Pentagon, but it was quashed after a few months on doctrinal grounds. The "big thinkers" had already decided to introduce conventional forces and were unwilling to entertain any unconventional ideas like ours, especially when our proposals were tactical heresies. When these conventional forces finally went into Vietnam, our military did not commit the error of "refighting the last war"; it found a new way to lose this one all by itself. It simply refused to acknowledge that we were really at war at all. Gradually, our own top generals lost touch with their troops and were either unable to reestablish it, or unconcerned about doing so. When I finally left Southeast Asia and ended up in Washington, what I found at the Pentagon (not only at OSD, but in later assignments within the Air Staff and JCS itself) only confirmed what I had suspected.

The Vietnam war was lost by our Joint Chiefs of Staff, ably assisted by the DoD's civilian "micromanagers" and the White House. Although we can't blame politicians for acting like politicians, we sure as hell *can* blame generals who don't act like generals. Not one member of the JCS resigned in over 10 years of increasingly desperate, ill-conceived, and compromised warfare in Southeast Asia.

By refusing to fight an unconventional guerrilla war, and instead committing America to an ever-escalating conventional conflict that depended on conventional criteria in order to succeed, the military helped turn a sustainable low-intensity and domestically apolitical conflict into a virtually unwinnable U.S. political hot potato that resisted consensus and allowed nonmilitary factors to cloud the military objectives. Said another way, it was not the politicians alone who screwed up the Vietnam war effort; it was the Joint Chiefs who went along to hold their coats.

And civilian control over the military is no excuse, as many military people have claimed in the post-1975 rush to save face. The Constitution mandates civilian control of the military, but it does *not* mandate, or even assume, that all civilians capable of election or confirmation to high office have military skills or insight—in fact, quite the opposite is true. By the time a soldier or airman or sailor reaches a rank exalted enough to be a member of the JCS, he is expected to be able to bridge that sometimes yawning gap between professional competence and constitutional duty. A politician is no more empowered to "act like a general" and pick bombing targets from the Oval Office, as Lyndon Johnson did, than a general is empowered to count delegates at a convention. A politician may say, "I don't want to suffer the international repercussions of putting ground troops on the Ho Chi Minh Trail or bombing the north back into the Stone Age," but the general—at member-of-the-JCS level—*is* empowered to respond, "I'm sorry, sir, I cannot prosecute the war according to my oath under those conditions, and must respectfully submit my resignation." If enough top generals had said "No, I won't go along with this," even a president like Lyndon Johnson would have eventually been obliged to listen.

This pattern of politicians interfering with military decisions and the Joint Chiefs letting them get away with it, even when every professional instinct in their bones militates against it, began in Vietnam on Maxwell Taylor's (JCS chairman during the Kennedy years) watch and didn't change throughout the war. It didn't take long for the JCS example to produce a theater commander like William Westmoreland and his largely incompetent staff. In an army that had been conditioned to maintain "radio silence" when things went wrong, it's no surprise that things so seldom went right.

# —8—

# Iran Before the Fall

For the South Vietnamese, the 1973 Paris Treaty marked the beginning of a two-year slide into hell. For America, it meant the end of the war. At the Pentagon, Watergate (the Senate hearings would not begin until May) was not yet an all-consuming topic, so the nervous energy we'd devoted to wartime operations now shifted to other priorities.

In the spring of 1973, the postwar Office of the Secretary of Defense was drastically downsized, and I began to look for new opportunities. I interviewed for the executive officer's slot in the Defense Security Assistance Agency (DSAA), a little-known but very productive organization that began life before World War II as the "lend-lease" program and matured into a modern agency responsible for implementing American arms transfers to over 70 countries worldwide. It seemed a logical place to apply my experience, and the director agreed. I ended up working there for the next two years.

DSAA's mostly civilian staff is headed by a three-star military man (the directorship alternates among the services as does the Chairmanship of the JCS) who reports directly to the Secretary of Defense. When I came on board, the director was Vice Admiral Ray Peet, another old-school admiral who was an Annapolis classmate of Chief of Naval Operations Elmo Zumwalt and former commander of a nuclear warship. A lot of talent was available for the position, and I think Peet picked me because, having previously served two admirals and having graduated from the Naval War College, I "spoke Navy" while still being able to offer the West Point and Air Force perspectives. Admiral Peet was a nice guy as well as a good administrator—and one of the best, most professional officers I've served with.

During the Yom Kippur War of October 1973, we received a briefing by one of Defense Secretary James Schlesinger's staffers on Israel's strategy for handling a potentially dangerous two-front war. DSAA was making a number of emergency arms transfers, and everyone was concerned with the Israelis'

112

ability to resist the Syrians in the north and Egyptians to the south—either one of which outnumbered the IDF, the Israeli Defense Force, several times over.

The man briefing us described the Israeli strategy as a classic campaign "along interior lines": that is, they planned to hold the Egyptians in the south with a minimum force while they concentrated their strength in the north to knock the Syrians out of the war. Once that was done, they'd swoop south and bring overwhelming force to bear on vulnerable parts of the Egyptian army, defeating them "in detail." Golda Meir's order of the day was: "Hold the [southern] Bar Lev line at all costs," and everyone understood why.

When the briefing was over and Peet and I were getting ready to leave, he asked me my opinion of the Israeli strategy. We both knew Secretary Schlesinger would be calling on him continually for advice, and big tank and infantry battles weren't exactly standard fare at Annapolis.

"Well, sir," I said, "it sounds to me like history repeating itself—it's the Battle of Tannenberg all over again."

The blue-water admiral gave me that *How many battleships did we have at Tannenberg?* look, so I cleared my throat and continued.

"Of course, sir, you'll recall that at Tannenberg in 1914, the Germans defeated Russia's two-headed invasion of East Prussia. First, German generals Hindenburg and Ludendorff marshaled their forces against Rennenkampf in the north, then secretly withdrew enough troops to defeat Samsonov in the south, after which they returned and finished off the Czar's northern army. By maneuvering skillfully along interior lines and taking advantage of the enemy's inability to support each front, they completely neutralized the Russians' two-to-one numerical advantage. I'm only pointing out that by all relevant measures, the Israeli plan seems to have taken its blueprint from Tannenberg."

"Oh yes—Tannenberg," Peet muttered. "Quite right!"

We both had a good chuckle, but that little bit of West Point erudition stuck to the Admiral's hull. Midway through a subsequent Schlesinger briefing, Admiral Peet deigned to point out that, as anyone could plainly see, the Israeli strategy was basically "another Tannenberg," and given the quality of Israeli Defense Force troops, Moshe Dayan's leadership, and the lack of cohesiveness among their Arab opponents, it would likely be just as successful—which, indeed, it was.

As the United States energy crisis deepened due to the Arab oil embargo, Admiral Peet rotated out and was replaced, in the summer of 1974, by Air Force Lieutenant General Howard Fish (or "Jaws" as we called him, though never to his face). Fish's B-17 had been shot down in World War II, and he had subsequently escaped from a German POW camp. He was a Phi Beta Kappa economist and the only navigator I know of to make three-star general. He spent several years as the Air Force's budget director, and was no babe in the woods when it came to hacking his way through the bureaucratic underbrush. He already knew, for example, that Admiral Peet had recently sent me on a brief trip to Iran (in the company of two other Air Force three-stars) to conduct a low-key investigation into Project Peace Crown, a multimegabuck, developmental air-defense system for the Shah that had run into unexpected trouble. In Tehran, we found contractors and Iranians chasing each other around the Air Force MAAG chief's desk with, figuratively speaking, scimitars drawn. DSAA's world was one tailor-made for Howie Fish.

"Jaws" got his nickname just as you'd imagine: by constantly biting huge chunks out of the posteriors of subordinates, peers, and opponents. He was a taskmaster—a real workaholic even in that pool of Pentagon movers and shakers who thought a 24-hour-clock meant just that: no time off for good behavior. Although his style was the 180-degree opposite of Peet's, he was just as effective, although he burned through staffers like tires at Indianapolis and my scant seven months with him seemed more like seven years. Even so, I grew to like Howie Fish. Like Bill Casey, who I would get to know later, his brain often worked faster than his mouth. When he was in high gear, his words piled out in a jumble. Everything was crystal clear to *him*, of course; it was *our* problem if we didn't understand. The extra bit of thought we had to put into his projects as a consequence usually paid off in better results. I learned from him the value of not overexplaining things to subordinates who had fine minds of their own.

Naturally, his style didn't quite gel with the tall, slim, professorial Schlesinger, who liked to tent his fingers, puff his pipe, and mull over ideas. An economist by training and a historian by inclination, Schlesinger was fond of philosophy and always probed for the logic and hidden agendas behind an issue. When he finally spoke, he cast his words with machinelike precision. Although he had no field experience that I knew of, he was thoroughly self-confident and self-assured when dealing with our top generals and, especially, with a crisis. Howie seemed to realize that his usual mumbly, frothy-mouthed blitzkrieg wouldn't captivate Schlesinger, so he asked me to coach him a little before his "confirmation interview" with the Secretary.

"Secord," he snapped, "do you know what a 'murder board' is?"

"Of course, sir. I used one to pass my master's orals at the University of Oklahoma."

"Good. I want you to put together a murder board to get me through this damned interview with the Secretary."

"Sir, I wouldn't presume—"

"Goddamn it, you've worked with the man and know a helluva lot more about him than I do. Put a murder board together!"

For years I had assembled "what if" books for my superiors to take to Congressional hearings: tabbed briefing books flagged at places where the representatives and senators were most likely to ask probing questions. But that was a lot different from trying to second-guess the individual quirks of one very penetrating and protean mind.

I came back with an extensive list of issues and answers I thought Fish should know about for his meeting. His face darkened as he scanned my notes.

"What the hell is all this stuff about foreign intelligence, strategic planning options, and the USSR?"

Howie had spent his recent career in the Air Force comptroller's office. He thought DSAA was about budgets and materials lists, financial analyses, and foreign military sales (FMS) credit and federal laws, which it was. But that's not what the Secretary's interview would be about.

"Sir," I responded, "the Secretary used to be director of the CIA. I've never attended a meeting where he didn't ask something about intelligence or foreign security policy issues—how we know what we think we know and why we're sure it's true. He already knows you're an expert on the budget. What he really wants to know is if you can communicate on his wavelength."

Fortunately, Howie was a pragmatic guy and a quick study. He devoured the information; debated the hell out of my analyses and conclusions, adopting some and rejecting others; and showed a real genius for isolating big themes, transcending issues, and coping with the *human* side of the numbers. He sped off to his confirmation interview like a great white shark after a surfboard. He came back a few hours later with his tailfins intact—and a big grin on his face. I was probably the only guy in the building who got a pat on the back for "murdering" his boss.

I put in seven of my hardest years in the service at Fort Fumble, as the Puzzle Palace was alternately called. I would be exaggerating to say I hated every minute of it, but not by much. Physically and organizationally, the place is a gulag.

To begin with, the facility itself is not only depressing, it's unhealthy. Aside from my one attack of dengue fever in Laos, I had never been seriously ill in my life. During my seven years at the Pentagon, however, I would be hit *four times* by pneumonia. As the flight surgeon treating me said after my third attack, "Dick, it looks like you're as allergic to this place as I am!" I'm sure the constant stress of intra- and intermural politics had a hand in this, but I know the long, grey corridors, grey-green offices, cement walls, conditioned air, lack of natural light, and general prisonlike, bunker-style environment also played a role. As one popular D.C. bumper sticker says: "Happiness is seeing the Pentagon in your rearview mirror."

My ticket back to the Air Force arrived in the form of a inquiry from USAF personnel (the "Colonel's group"), passed to me through General Fish, asking how I would respond to an appointment as vice commander of an FB-111 wing, a strategic bomber unit based at Plattsburg, New York. Now,

I had been around the Air Force long enough to know there is a certain courtly dance that must be performed around assignments at this level.

First, you never ever tell the high honchos that you would "decline" an assignment, and you certainly don't turn an important one down once it's been formally offered. Just like they do when the Queen of England wants to confer a knighthood, an intermediary acting on behalf of the chief of staff contacts the candidate and lets him know that the royal personage "has it in mind" to offer thus-and-such to him. If the person replies that the offer would not receive a ready welcome, the whole thing dies quietly. In the Air Force, though, you're also expected to come back with a pretty good reason why not.

"It sounds like a fine offer, Dick," General Fish said. He had introduced me to the Air Force chief of staff, David Jones, and allowed me to do a few minor projects for him, so the groundwork had been set for my next assignment out of DSAA. "Sounds like they're grooming you for a wing commander's slot. And the FB-111 is no B-52. I imagine it's almost like flying a real airplane."

"I know, General, I know," I tried, but really couldn't warm to the opportunity, as desperate as I was to leave the Pentagon. "I just don't think I'd do very well up there."

"What do you mean? You could command a wing standing on your head!"

"That's not what I'm worried about. My problem is that I'm just not part of their culture. I haven't spent a day in SAC and I'd be competing with guys who spent their whole careers in bombers. I've got no patrons—no godfathers to look after me. I just wouldn't do very well, no matter how good a commander I was."

Howie had been around long enough to see my point, and word went quietly back upstairs that Colonel Secord would really be happier commanding from a seat that was all by itself in a single-engine airplane. Almost overnight, in early 1975, another offer came down about taking over as deputy commander for operations (DO) for the pilot-training wing at Craig AFB, Alabama. The former DO, Tom Kirk (a repatriated Vietnam POW), was moving up into the wing commander's slot.

By this time I realized that I was rapidly burning through my chits and needed to make up my mind. I gave Howie a hearty thumbs-up and by March 1975 was on my way back to beautiful downtown Selma, Alabama. As always, I blazed the trail alone and left the packing as well as the homesteading to Jo Ann and the kids, who followed me in June.

If a good commander can handle a SAC wing standing on his head, as Howie suggested, he should probably be able to command an air training command (ATC) wing in his sleep—and that is no aspersion on ATC or its fine commanders. By the mid-seventies, ATC had developed military pilot training to a fine art as well as a science. Most of their bases ran themselves like Swiss watches. All a good commander (or his deputy) had to do was deal with occasional personnel problems and keep the machinery humming.

The 29th Flying Training Wing at Craig flew T-37s (Tweets) and the T-38 Talon, the supersonic advanced trainer that was so sleek and fun to fly that NASA's astronauts still use them as the pilot-proficiency plane of choice. I went through what the IPs called the "colonel's refresher course" and flew regularly with the students in both airplanes. Needless to say, I had an absolute ball—at least in the air.

On the ground, I felt more like the night-shift engineer at a power plant: eyeballing dials and thermometers from time to time but basically trying to stay out of the way. Every activity in the wing was based on thick procedure books, and student ground and flight curricula reflected a well-planned and time-honored syllabus. If it weren't for the occasional personnel action (promotion or student flight board) and IG inspections, I'd have spent most of my ground time drinking coffee and telling war stories—that is, when I wasn't staring wistfully at orders assigning our better graduates to tactical fighter schools like Luke and Nellis.

Still, I needed to "depressurize" from the Pentagon (and the tension, shared by everyone in government, over Nixon's Watergate woes and his eventual August 1974 resignation, as well as the depressing fall of Saigon in April 1975) and recover, through routine and diverting work, from the shell shock of bureaucratic battle. I thought I had the game pretty well figured out when ATC—and life—threw me another curve.

A few months into my assignment, the wing commander experienced some family problems and went on emergency leave. That left me to run the store. Everything percolated along normally until we received word that the IG had scheduled a "short-notice" ORI (an operational readiness inspection) and that the team would be headed by ATC's inspector general himself, a Brigadier General Fox.

Fortunately at Craig, our department heads and flying-squadron commanders had things pretty much under control, and close day-to-day supervision, including IP "stan-eval" (procedure standardization and performance evaluation), kept all the nuts and bolts torqued properly. Aside from cleaning up the officer's club and showing my nervous face to the troops for encouragement, there wasn't much for me to do.

Just before the evaluation team hit town, though, I got a call out of the blue from my old boss, General Howie Fish.

"Dick, I thought you'd like to know you are one of several promotable colonels being considered for a high-level assignment in Iran," he said.

"You gotta be kidding!" I knew the Air Force MAAG post was a brigadier general's slot; that was too much to ask.

"No joke. Remember that little trip you took to Iran for Peace Crown? Well, the chief—General Jones—has decided to replace the current Air Force MAAG commander, a one-star named Humphries. General Jones is pretty embarrassed about the way things have gone and wants to choose a replacement himself. He asked me for a recommendation and I put your name in the hopper. I hope that's consistent with your wishes. You'll be receiving a TWIX shortly calling you up for an interview with the chief."

"That's great, General," I answered. "The only thing is, I'm acting wing commander and we're about to start an ORI!"

That was when I learned—very quickly—the power of the right phone call. The TWIX arrived with a copy to ATC's four-star commander, General McBride, who phoned Craig almost as soon as the teletype stopped clicking.

"What's going on up there?" he asked, referring to the Pentagon's sudden interest in one of his commanders.

I told him the situation, at least what I knew of it, and he said to tell General Fox, who had now arrived on base, ASAP. He added that if his IG had any problems releasing me during the ORI, he should call McBride right away.

It was now early evening, and I tracked General Fox and his team down at the officers' club, where they were having dinner. I told him I'd received an order to report to the chief of staff and had a T-38 standing by for an early-morning flight to Andrews.

General Fox looked at me quizzically, blotting his mouth with a napkin, then said, "Chief of whose staff?"

"Ours," I grinned. "General Jones at the Pentagon."

Fox was silent a moment, then replied, "Do you really *know* General Jones?"

Actually, I had met with General Jones a few times while I was at DSAA and respected him greatly, but he wasn't my "patron" and we certainly weren't personal friends, nor did I consider myself a shoo-in for the job. However, General Fox had absolutely *no* problem releasing me for a meeting the next day.

My interview with the chief didn't last long, and he did most of the talking. He told me that, due to protocol and tradition, the Iran MAAG advisor had to be a general officer, and that I was one of only three "promotable colonels" with the TAC air experience needed for the job. Also in my corner, he said, was the fact that I had already served in Iran as a junior officer and used to drink beer with some Iranian pilots who were now among that country's top generals. I also had the endorsement of a well-respected man like General Fish, who didn't give such things lightly.

General Jones couldn't afford to leave such an important, high-visibility post unfilled for long, so he told me he'd make his decision shortly. I flew back to Craig in time for the ORI's wrap-up briefing. We had passed with only a few discrepancies, and I'm sure it would only have been worse if I had stayed around to "hep."

Over the next few days I waited like a teenager for the phone to ring, but it never did. After a week or so I figured some other lucky, and undoubtedly more deserving, guy had won the appointment and put my mind back on business. Ten days after the interview, Howie Fish called again.

"Congratulations, Dick. You're it!"

It took me a second to recalibrate my thinking, then what he said hit me like a ton of bricks: I was on my way to Iran.

By September, my family was settling into a beautiful home provided by the Iranian government on Agdashi Street, about a mile from the Shah's Niavaron Palace.

By October 1st, I was sitting at the MAAG chief's desk in Tehran with a brand-new star on each shoulder.

The next three years were among the best of my career. Twenty years out of West Point, at a time when many regular officers (having made major or LC) decide those colonel's eagles are just too far off and take early retirement, I was one of the youngest—if not *the* youngest—general officers in the Air Force. As much as I would like to have credited that to my good looks and talent, I really had to thank a succession of historical forces, good bosses, good training, and plain old-fashioned good luck.

I would spend my time from August 1975 until July 1978—only six months until the Shah fell from power—running a variety of challenging programs. The work was important and the flying was great; I checked out just about everything in the Shah's inventory, including helicopters, which was a first for me. Best of all, I was in charge of the whole shooting match. The buck for virtually everything that happened in the air over Iran stopped at my desk.

Our government-furnished house (grey marble with 82 rose bushes, a swimming pool, and a walled compound) was located in the northern part of Tehran. We had two drivers and never went anywhere, at least in the city, without bodyguards—a security officer and three enlisted men. Julia, Laura, and John would be exposed to many exotic sights, sounds, and experiences over the next few years, not all of them pleasant. One of my predecessors had been attacked by a bomb, and the kids would learn to deal not only with the possibility of my not coming home one night, but also with the possibility that they themselves might face danger. But kids are resilient and a lot tougher and more optimistic than most parents think. Jo Ann and I knew they would do just fine, and they did.

My office was co-located with the headquarters of the Imperial Iranian Air Force in the southeastern quadrant of the city, in the foothills of the Elburz mountains. In Iran, your social status was measured not just by your access to the royal family, but by how high you live in the hills. Eventually, I would meet privately with the Shah about once every six weeks. Near my home was the office of General Toufanian, the vice minister of war—the closest thing Iran had to a secretary of defense. The general saw the Shah more often than I did, but our houses were just as high.

When I arrived in Tehran, Richard Helms, the ex-CIA director, was the U.S. Ambassador. Unlike Bill Sullivan in Laos, Helms was a good listener, and his instincts were usually right on the mark. He was tall and fit and had the bearing of a statesman, which sat well with the Shah, who treated him deferentially. I found Helms to be a good leader for the American contingent—firm but tolerant, and accessible to everyone. Although he knew the Shah's military problems well and was a good friend to the MAAG, Helms was preoccupied at the time with Congressional hearings on his handling of affairs in Chile while director of the CIA.

The local CIA boss was a 20-year veteran with a lot of that experience in the Middle East. The CIA kept close ties with the Savak (the Iranian secret police) and was our main listening post in surrounding countries. Most of the Shah's foreign policy decisions usually started with the CIA. My CIA "detailee" days were ancient history, and Helms and his CIA chief thought of me primarily as a blue-suiter. Consequently, I was never privy to the full extent of their activities, although this would change later in my tour.

My immediate boss was Major General Sandy Vandenburg, USAF, who was the chief, Army Mission and U.S. Military Assistance Advisory Group— or ARMISH MAAG, as it was said in Pentagonese. But Sandy left a couple of months after I arrived and was replaced by Air Force Major General Ken Miles. Ken never warmed to the job, though, and retired after 18 months, replaced at the beginning of 1978 by another Air Force two-star general, Philip Gast. The Iranians didn't appreciate these musical chairs, and because of it, my two-year assignment was extended to three. In fact, I was acting or de facto ARMISH MAAG chief so often, the Shah and his generals began looking at me as the one fixed star in the American firmament. In a way, this supported American interests better than if I had inherited the somewhat lower status of my predecessor. In 1970, after a 30-year emphasis on ground forces, the Iranian defense sector had clearly shifted its focus to air power and high technology.

The Shah, or "Majesty," as he was referred to by everyone from butlers to brigadiers, and his senior officers were all cut from the same cloth: the ancient Persian nobility. To the last they were full of pride (sometimes past the point of arrogance), strong willed, and intensely jealous of Iran's sovereignty and independence. Their xenophobia was in inverse proportion to the distance and direct proportion to the antiquity of their enemies, real and imagined. Consequently, they hated and feared the Russians and Iraqis and thought America was wonderful, although the sudden ingestion of Western culture during the Shah's last decade, as well as the Shah's own broken promises about reform, played a large share in undermining his long rule.

This mix of old-world culture and new-world technology came to a bizarre climax when the commander of the Iranian air force, General Khatemi, was killed in (of all things) a hang-gliding accident just after I arrived. This was a real blow to the nation because, in addition to being the Shah's brother-in-law, Khatemi was a living legend in Air Force circles: a talented pilot who had led the Shah's air arm for 15 years. The Shah appointed General Tadayon, a trustworthy older officer but a nonpilot, in Khatemi's place, but only as an interim step. As it was in my first tour to Iran, leadership would become the vital issue, and in this, too, the Shah proved to be his own worst enemy.

As U.S. representatives, our main objective was preserving Iran as a bulwark against Soviet expansion into the Gulf oil fields and the "warm-water" ports of the Persian Gulf and Arabian Sea. The wealthy Shah and his high-living ruling families hated Communism, for obvious reasons, but their distrust and dislike of the Russians went back for centuries, reflecting both cultural and religious hostility. It may seem odd to Americans, but the Iranians, who were spiritual heirs of the great polyglot Persian empire, thought nothing of employing foreign generals and alien soldiers on their soil; the 30 years of (sometimes sizable) U.S. MAAG presence was to them just another episode in a very long tradition. Adding up all of our instructors, planners, analysts, logisticians, and administrators, over 2,500 Americans served in Iran under Air Force control, and the Navy (which had its own high-tech, blue-water Iranian fleet-building program) and the Army had similarly constituted, if smaller, contingents.

Although we sometimes quibbled about specifics, the foundation of U.S.-Iranian cooperation was as solid as any outside NATO. Because these ties were not just legal or for political convenience, but deep and personal, the MAAG was often used to transmit information to, solve problems with, and coach the Shah on matters that were considered too delicate for "normal" (State Department) channels. But this communication was never a one-way street, nor did it devolve, as the Shah's critics claim, into a South Vietnam-like dependence on the U.S. In the Shah's mind, America and her military representatives were kindred spirits sharing a warrior's code of honor and independence that was completely compatible with Iranian society. Even more important, he saw us as agents for beneficial change in his country, and because of our influence he brought about the so-called White Revolution in 1962 that introduced women's suffrage, universal education, and government-sponsored college for any Iranian who could gain admittance to the best universities in the West. Our very presence was a kind of laboratory for the twentieth-century values he espoused for his people. We socialized regularly with Iranian officers of all ranks—played tennis with them and went skiing at Dezin in the mountains north of Tehran. We hosted them at formal and informal dinner parties, and they invited MAAG people to all their important ceremonies and holiday events—except, of course, those confined to the Muslim faith. Jo Ann and I weren't alone in making many lifelong friends among the Iranians, although too many of those friendships were cut short by firing squads during the revolution. Iran's air force officers were particularly hated and feared by the Ayatollah's ministers. They represented not only the most significant military threat to the revolution, but they were cultural leaders in the effort to break away from the country's stifling traditionalism. I think it is significant that the Iranian air force officer corps, which was relatively free of corruption while I was there, was the one segment of the Shah's leadership most closely associated with the Great Satan—America.

And corruption was always part of the equation, especially in the mammoth procurement programs that characterized those years. No cocktail party or luncheon began without a flurry of gossip about who was "fiddling" which project—skimming money from government programs from radars to runways to roads. As I would find out, the Shah's immediate family led this unsavory parade, especially his twin sister Ashraf and the high officials in the various ministries charged with bringing their nation into the twentieth century.

In the civil sector, huge housing projects were completed with substandard materials and shoddy workmanship after substantial delays, all to increase the contractor's profit and potential rake-off for the decision-making elites. Nuclear power stations and highways and experimental agriculture, from irrigation projects to herds of imported dairy cows, bloomed, but only when they put money into the right pockets.

In the military sector, where I had responsibility, our quick access to the Shah allowed us to abort these instances as soon as they were discovered—but uncovering them through the layers and layers of bureaucratic red tape on *both* sides of the table was time-consuming and often more costly than the crime itself. Through our vigilance at MAAG, though, we were able to rebate to the Iranian people close to $50 million from Grumman International Corporation for improper "agents' fees" attached to the already lucrative F-14 program. This success was mirrored in many smaller programs, and its example was not lost on stateside corporate executives.

Still, companies of every foreign nation, the U.S. included, persisted in hiring "fixers"—agents of influence—to push their pet and most profitable programs with the Iranian hierarchy. For too many people in too many high places, corruption, inefficiency, and mismanagement were just too profitable to clean up, at least right away. The Shah continually made speeches about corruption, undertaking one drive after another to rid business and the bureaucracy of such practices, but they were deeply ingrained in the culture. After a while, it became evident to me that the Shah had no *real* intention of challenging such a fundamental trait of Iranian society.

Most of the complaints about corruption came from the new Iranian middle class—nonexistent before the 1960s, and now fairly numerous due to skyrocketing oil prices and the benefits of the Shah's early education initiatives. By the late 1970s, the Shah's dictatorial rule ran counter to everything these enterprising people had learned in their Western universities. "Majesty" never understood this, and seemed to believe that if he could deliver an ever-increasing standard of living and a few cosmetic reforms, like confirmation of the prime minister through popular elections and women's suffrage, his people would accept his rule indefinitely. It was a significant miscalculation on the Shah's part and, in the end, one that contributed greatly to his demise.

I first spoke to the Shah in October 1975 at an Iranian air force ceremony, although he shook my hand (as he did with the other American military advisors) after our victory over the Kurds in 1964. A lot had happened in the region since then, not all of it good. After the Baghdad Pact fell apart in 1959, Iran's old enemy, Iraq, drifted further and further under Soviet influence. Another U.S. clandestine operation began shortly after our 1964 war ended, this time managed by the CIA *in support* of the Kurds. The case officers in this instance were Israelis (perhaps with a handful of American advisors, but I have no documentation for this, just scuttlebutt), with U.S. dollars financing the whole thing—although disbursements were made and supplies provided by the Iranians. Thus by 1972 the Kurds had been "turned" once again and were in action against Iraq.

By the time I arrived in Tehran in 1975, this "low-boil" strategy was working quite well and Baghdad (the Ba'athists and Saddam Hussein were now in power) was forced to contemplate a treaty establishing certain rights and prerogatives for ethnic Kurds—all at Iraqi expense. Unfortunately, the U.S. (with the Shah's concurrence, although it was clearly a U.S. initiative) decided to capitalize on the Kurds' military success and cut its own deal with Baghdad, promising to withdraw Iranian support from the Kurds in exchange for border adjustments favorable to the Iranians and other concessions. Iraq's embarrassment at having to swallow these humbling conditions was felt throughout the Arab world and helps explain (although it can never justify) Saddam's subsequent brutal actions against both of his old enemies, the Kurds and Iran, in the 1980s.

Now, as Air Force MAAG chief, my first private meeting with the Shah was scheduled for just after New Year's in 1976 at the Niavaron Palace.

A majordomo escorted me to where His Imperial Majesty (we referred to the Shah in writing simply as HIM) was relaxing in an ornate, French-style sitting room filled with Louis XIV furniture, richly embroidered silk drapes on the high windows, and, of course, priceless Persian rugs. He was about 60, short, and very spare—a foretaste of his almost cadaverous appearance in the last year of his life. He was a man literally born to be king, with a hawklike visage, long Persian nose, and regal bearing.

The Shah rose, smiling, straightened the silk tie under his smart, London-cut, double-breasted suit, and gave my hand a solid, practiced shake.

"*Teemsar* [General] Secord," he said in nearly perfect English, "I'm so pleased to be able to talk with you. Won't you have a seat?" He gestured to a gilded chair opposite his own. A liveried waiter in white gloves poured tea for us both.

Ever since the appointment had been scheduled, I'd worried about in-advertently committing some faux pas, but Majesty made me feel as though he wanted nothing more than to spend the afternoon with his "new friend from America." *Royalty* to the Shah meant obligation as much as privilege. He had spent a lifetime mastering social protocol, and, although he was used to dealing with high-ranking officials and royalty from many countries, he was also used to putting "commoners" at ease. Also, the Shah was a pilot himself and had great respect, if not preference, for military fliers.

After initial small talk about my family's arrival and the wonders of Iran, he got right down to business.

"We have two things to discuss today," he said, finishing his tea. "The morale and leadership of my air force, and the strategic situation our two countries face in the Persian Gulf."

By the word *morale* I knew Majesty was referring to his generals, not the rank and file.

"As you know," he continued "my air force is expanding very quickly. I have many young generals, some of whom you already know, but no one seasoned enough yet to replace the great General Khatemi."

"I understand General Tadayon is an extremely loyal officer with a long record of exemplary service," I replied, referring to his interim commander in chief.

"Yes, and he is a good administrator as well. That's why I appointed him. Soldiers like to see a few grey hairs on their commanders, isn't that so? But I am more concerned with the younger officers. A long-term commander will come from their ranks, and I want them to get as much experience as possible over the next few years. Does this seem to you like a reasonable objective?"

"Indeed, Your Majesty. It has worked well for other air forces in the region."

The Shah smiled lavishly. "Ah, yes. You refer to the Israeli air force; I quite agree. I view our air arm as Iran's first line of defense. If we are attacked, our aircraft must buy time for our ground forces to mobilize. They must bleed the enemy and slow his advance—ruin his lines of communication. After that, we must be able to finish him with combined air and ground attacks, or at least resist long enough for our allies, like the United States, to come to our assistance."

Now it was my turn to smile. "Such wisdom is not shared by your opponents, Majesty. Moscow, for one, believes in jamming the front with big divisions at the first sign of a crisis."

The Shah laughed and shook his head. "In my opinion, you Americans have never fully understood the objectives of the Soviet empire." This was not the last time I would hear the Shah refer to the USSR (and Marxists in general, with whom he had had many tussles) in imperial, colonial terms. "Iran sits at the crossroads of the Middle East. The great Russian bear—now the Soviet Union—has always understood this and coveted us because of it. They have always been ready to employ force against us, and our neighbors in Afghanistan. My will to resist them is well known. Your presence here is proof of that. I'm not so confident, though, about the *old man* [Afghanistan President Mohammed Daoud] in Kabul. And the Soviets are too friendly, I think, with our counterparts in India; and their strong position in Iraq is well known. Brezhnev is well on his way to grasping two of our region's three pillars. President Nixon knew this, but I'm not sure it is appreciated by his successor. Like most American presidents, Mr. Ford sees little beyond Europe. A clever enemy never attacks the best-watched gate, isn't that so?"

It was true that while the Nixon doctrine saw Iran as central to Eurasian stability, conventional wisdom was preoccupied with NATO and the Warsaw Pact. Although I didn't say so during the meeting, because my own superiors had a solidly Eurocentric outlook, I tended to agree with the Shah.

My audience lasted about half an hour. We touched on many subjects, such as Iranian ground and air support for the Sultan of Oman in a border dispute with North Yemen, and I went away with the feeling that the Shah was a studied strategic thinker who valued his American "window on the West" highly and was prepared to show me, personally, as much confidence as I could earn through effective leadership and discretion with his generals.

I reported the details of our discussion to Ambassador Helms and expressed mild surprise that the Shah hadn't broached these issues of high policy before a bigger American audience.

"Don't worry," Helms said. "That's just how Majesty does things. The air force is his baby and he wants to have complete confidence in its American advisor."

From this and many subsequent one-on-one meetings, I would become even more privy to the Shah's ideas and more impressed with his grasp of relevant details and commitment to building Iranian air power. Before, I had always viewed the Shah as a remote and forbidding character, embodying more of Iran's "ancient soul" than its contemporary human spirit. He and his beautiful wife, Farah (considerably his junior), and three children appeared before my arrival to be a figurehead royal family, like the British Windsors. In person, though, I found him to be a very intelligent (though not intellectual) person who thought ruling, even in a hereditary monarchy, was an active verb. He valued education, training, and pragmatic experience and used his own to full advantage. His character and his system had its weaknesses, to be sure, and these would eventually undo him—with some inadvertent help from us. He was not especially religious, for example, which did not sit well with some factions, and he avoided meetings, preferring to deal with all his high-ranking ministers, generals, and advisors one on one. This kept him at the hub of the authority wheel, but it also bred suspicion among his underlings.

I had a full plate that first year in Tehran, and my ration of responsibility seemed to get even bigger as time went by. The Shah did not doubt General Tadayon's loyalty, but he couldn't trust (and rightly so, I thought) a nonpilot's opinions on air force matters. Tadayon was very sensitive to this, but the more he tried to involve his subordinates in his decisions (which was infrequent at best, owing to the Iranians' stiff martial pride), the more he felt these young pilots were sniggering at the "old man's" deskbound limitations. Things never got as bad as Tadayon thought, but given the size of his command and the kinds of upgrades we were trying to make, even a little static was too much.

When I arrived, the Shah had almost 200 Northrop F-5E fighter bombers and a like number of F-4 Phantoms, both fighter and reconnaissance versions. He had the best aerial tanker fleet outside the United States, mostly new, re-engined Boeing 707s, and also the only three KC-747s ever built. In tactical transport, the old Gooney Birds of my first tour had been replaced with 60 C-130s and a large fleet of helicopters, giving the Imperial Iranian Army a forward deployment capability that was the envy of the region.

A big part of my job would be to integrate all 80 state-of-the-art F-14 Tomcats the Shah had ordered into this inventory. The F-14 sale had been highly controversial, and its implementation would be scrutinized closely, since Iran was the only foreign country to be trusted with the Phoenix missile, the F-14's ultrasmart air-to-air system that was, and still is, the most sophisticated weapon of its type in the American arsenal. But this was only the beginning.

Spurred by Israel's impressive example, the Shah wasn't out simply to revamp his air force; he wanted an entirely new and leakproof air defense system. This meant a state-of-the-art SAM network and the combat doctrine, command and control, and unit- and depot-level maintenance capability needed to give it teeth.

This lucrative, developmental, fully automated, 360-degree air defense system, called Seek Sentry, was what we in MAAG referred to as a "contractor's delight." Like many third-world nations (as well as Israel), Iran was enamored with high technology and viewed state-of-the-art weaponry less as a true contribution to national defense (which was often questionable) than as an ornament designed to overawe their populations and enemies and make their generals, presidents, or potentates feel, as much as possible, like full-fledged members of the global power club. In such circumstances, their decision makers were ripe for the slick presentations and sophisticated chartsmanship of Western contractors. All the usual suspects—Westinghouse, GE, Litton, Northrop, General Dynamics, Lockheed, Boeing, etc.—had gathered like sharks around my predecessor's, General Humphries's, raft.

A civilian consultant (actually, a professional "systems critic" who, as a retired Army colonel, first came to my notice when I worked for Admiral Peet) named Richard Halleck was collaborating with Iranian General Toufanin to throw out the current cast of vendors and replace them with Halleck's own team. From where I sat, it looked like a clear conflict of interest since Halleck was supposed to be advising Secretary Schlesinger. The program was well enough along to reveal significant "absorptive" problems with the system—Iranian airmen, technicians, and commanders just hadn't received adequate training with the complex equipment—so many of Halleck's criticisms were justified, although his solutions weren't. Uncle Sam (meaning *me*) was caught in the middle.

My solution was to rework what was clearly a too elaborate, too expensive system with one that would be both effective and manageable from the Iranian perspective. Halleck wanted to do the same, but his plan was for a complete "dumbing down" of the system, sacrificing certain modern features I knew the Iranians would not only want, but need if a shooting war started. For our solution, the MAAG dipped into America's own air defense history and came up with a system called RAMIT (Rate-Aided Manually Initiated Tracking) that was built on the same tried-and-true principles as the old SAGE (Semi-Automated Ground Environment) system used by our Air Defense Command for 20 years. With human decision makers retained in the loop, we not only accommodated the top-down Iranian leadership style, but drastically reduced both deployment time and operational expense. This initial success instantly endeared me and my philosophy to the Shah and his top generals.

The major ground-based weapon of this system was the so-called Improved HAWK, or I-HAWK, surface-to-air missile—an advanced version of the venerable American SAM, first sold to Iran in 1974, that was a real terror to high-speed planes coming in below 300 feet but could also snag aircraft up to 35,000 feet, although less reliably. In all, the Shah ordered 16 batteries of I-HAWK missiles, more than the U.S. Army itself had deployed. These were to be integrated with 22 long-range ground-radar sites and a far-reaching "C cubed" (command, control, and communications) system.

Still, advocacy was high among the old Seek Sentry supporters, and the new system found detractors at all levels. To make the bugs in the system abundantly clear, despite the contractors' brochuremanship, I authorized a "red-team" exercise after the first few HAWK sites had been selected. The red-team approach is used widely by the Pentagon (and by aerospace contractors, too). It's simply a group of independent experts assembled to assess and critique a plan, program, or system whose corporate parents believe has been perfected.

In this case, my red team was a half-dozen EWOs (electronic warfare officers) and F-5 pilots who had F-4 and F-105 combat experience penetrating air defenses over North Vietnam. I told them to study the Iranian deployment scheme and set up an attack plan to counter it—pretty much standard fare in red-team analysis. Where I differed was in ordering my guys to actually get in their planes and fly it.

In a blitz the Iranian crews and their contractor mentors are probably still talking about, these hunter-killers swept in from "below the boulder tops" and inside the creek beds and absolutely overwhelmed the system in a simulated attack—with no computed air losses. As a result, the whole Seek Sentry team went back to school on tactical doctrine and came up with a system that was, from a war-fighting and war-winning standpoint, vastly superior to the original.

Majesty was pleased.

In my second year, though, some of the Shah's personal shortcomings became more evident—and burdensome.

Despite his Western orientation, high-tech ambitions, and flexible strategic thinking, the Shah embodied many of the traits of a stereotypical "Oriental despot." He had trouble delegating real authority and collected a menagerie of sycophants and toadies on his staff. He was paranoid about coups (he had been wounded in one attempt) and consciously pitted one general against another lest they combine against him. More than anything, this disunion among his leaders prevented the kind of bold, concerted effort needed to foil the 1979 revolution. It made my job more difficult and, as my tour wore on, those troubles only increased.

We had just brought the technical problems in the air defense system to heel when its organizational side began to unravel. It started at the top, with General Tadayon. Although his actual age was guarded like a state secret, we all figured the Shah's chief nonflying flier to be at least 70 years old. This was no barrier, apparently, to his sudden decision to become a pilot.

"What do you think, *Teemsar*?" Tadayon asked me with his heavy accent, eyes glowing like a little kid. "What is the best way for me to proceed?"

"General," I said, trying to be as patient and diplomatic as I could, "you know, this really isn't necessary. Majesty knew you were not a pilot when he appointed you. Like the rest of us, he respects your long career as an officer and administrator. You really don't need to compete with these younger specialists."

But he was persistent; so to keep him from trying something too dangerous, I suggested he begin with one of the light, single-engine airplanes used for primary training. The old general found this not only distasteful, but insulting. After all, didn't civilian beginners fly these little "puddle jumpers?" No, he wanted to start in a real soldier's airplane. He chose the twin-turboprop "Hawk" Commander—a particularly bad choice, although it was still better than a Phantom or Hercules, which is what the old fellow really wanted to fly.

Predictably, Tadayon's slow progress only engendered new jokes and derision, so he switched to helicopters, which most of the top-ranking officers piloted like taxicabs. Tadayon figured that rotary-wing aircraft must be easier to operate, since the U.S. Army allowed noncommissioned personnel like warrant officers to fly them. Unfortunately, his instructor, a young first lieutenant, was totally awed by the task of teaching the commanding general himself how to fly. Worse, Tadayon vocally blamed most of his problems in the Hawk Commander on his old instructor, so the young IP was quickly bullied into submission.

Every day after work, Tadayon left his office, climbed into the Bell 206 with his young protégé, and terrorized the local neighborhood with careening low-level passes, death-defying autorotations, and nail-biting hovers. This was especially dangerous because in the winter months night fell quickly, and it was only a matter of time until "General McGoo" tangled his rotors in tree branches, power lines, or something worse. Things finally got so bad that several Tadayon staffers asked me to intervene.

"You know, General," I said, "helicopters are damned tricky machines. They're much more sensitive than fixed-wing aircraft, and most of us need a lot of formal training to fly them safely, especially at night. I'd be much more comfortable if you would slow down the pace of your lessons and pick a more experienced instructor to fly with."

The old general just grinned. Undoubtedly, all the complaints and jokes he'd heard just reinforced his opinion that we "regular" pilots were worried about having to admit him to the club. He went right ahead with his hell-for-leather program.

On a frosty morning in late January 1977, a short time after the new U.S. President, Jimmy Carter, had been sworn in, General Tadayon took his helicopter on a crosstown flight to meet with the Shah. That afternoon, a snow flurry developed over northern Tehran, and Tadayon and his young instructor crashed on his return flight to the base. Both occupants were killed.

Tadayon's executive officer notified me by radio of the general's death, and I immediately informed General Rabbii, commander of the Shah's tactical fighters. The accident was bound to throw the Iranian air force's high command into turmoil, and Rabbii was understandably upset. At his request, I joined him immediately at the Iranian tactical air command headquarters in Shiraz.

We were sitting in his office when the call came through from Majesty: Lieutenant General Rabbii was to be the Iranian air force's new commander in chief.

This decision, made by the Shah without any American input, placed a superior pilot-leader in what had previously been an administrator's slot. Rabbii was a young (in his mid-40s), charismatic fighter pilot—a kind of Iranian Moshe Dayan. We worked well together, and he was one of two candidates I would've recommended had I been asked. Because of our friendship, Rabbii thought I was somehow behind his promotion. That simply wasn't the case. You don't go around giving Majesty that kind of unsolicited advice.

However, it wasn't long before even this talented new commander's inexperience began to show. Despite (and partially because of) his aggressive new policies, 1977 was marred by a long string of aircraft accidents, most of them easily avoidable. Once again, Majesty called me in for another audience.

"General Rabbii is destroying my air force!" he wailed. "How are we going to stop this?"

I had at least one answer, an obvious one, but I was afraid it would bring me into direct conflict with an age-old Iranian tradition. That tradition was the single biggest impediment to lasting technological change in most monarchical, oligarchic nations I was familiar with; namely, that noble birth is some kind of guarantor of competence. One of the privileges rank doth *not* have is an exemption from the laws of gravity.

"I think what you need, Your Majesty, is what we in the U.S. Air Force call a standardization and evaluation program. It involves giving all pilots both scheduled and no-notice written and flight examinations, including checks on tactical proficiency, regardless of rank. Any pilot who scores below a certain percentage is automatically grounded until he accomplishes remedial training."

After a long silence, the Shah said, "And this program will stop all these accidents?"

"It's the only way I know, Your Majesty."

After another long pause, the Shah replied, "I will give the order."

Of course, this was pure heresy in a culture that equated good birth and high rank with ability. Not only was it impolite in traditional Middle East society to challenge an aristocrat or high official on his competence, it was seditious. Iran was no different, and it meant creating new values based on merit. No Iranian stan-eval major was about to ground his wing commander colonel for "busting minimums" (descending below safe altitude) on a missed approach. I knew, therefore, that for the first year, the evaluators would have to be all-American.

We wrote up some pilot-evaluation procedures and criteria and made sure it was published up and down the flying hierarchy. My director of operations, Colonel Rod Beckman, was made chief of our "hit" team, and they literally dropped in unannounced at air bases all over Iran with our own version of an ORI. We would have the wing stand down from normal operations and assemble all its rated personnel, from the wing commander to the lowest second lieutenant, in the base auditorium and administer a written exam on tactics, normal and emergency procedures for the specific aircraft, and air traffic rules. After that, we'd randomly select a half-dozen or so pilots for check rides, always making sure at least one was a squadron commander or higher. Most of the pilots were competent, but we discovered some that were disasters waiting to happen—General Tadayon's heirs.

After a few months, we had grounded dozens of pilots and became known as the "black hats," more hated and feared than any enemy air force. But the program worked. By the end of the year, the accident rate was down to three or four per 100,000 flying hours, competitive with major Western air forces.

Later that year, the Shah and his slowly "professionalizing" air force faced a different sort of emergency.

In late 1977, the Soviets intervened in Afghanistan and deposed Daoud, the "old man" Majesty had been watching cautiously since I arrived. The Shah asked me and one of his high-ranking generals to go deep into the desert in eastern Iran, near the Afghan/Pakistani border, and survey locations for a new fighter base. This was an adjunct to another high-tech program, Project IBEX, an electronic intelligence-gathering system being installed under the tutelage of the CIA.

IBEX was a good program, not as complicated or goofy as some of the Igloo White projects we had to fret over during the Southeast Asian war. In essence, IBEX collected data from a network of automated sites and fed it, along with information about enemy radio communication and radar signals, to the CIA, who provided the Iranians with real-time analysis and interpretation. I had only two complaints about this otherwise fine system.

First, I didn't think it was appropriate for the CIA to shepherd the program, since its use was intimately tied up with the forward deployment bases, and I had discovered through sad experience that extra organizational boundaries in a war situation just didn't make sense—as we Americans had proved often enough in Southeast Asia.

Second, key Iranian leaders still tended to view these advanced systems as just another sort of Porsche or Mercedes; and IBEX, despite its pluses, was no different. I advised the Shah to slow his deployment of I-HAWKs from three years to six, mostly because he and his generals never really took into consideration the astounding effort needed to recruit, train, equip, deploy, and sustain the technicians required to operate, repair, and overhaul the system and its components. This effort was further complicated by the fact that the system had to be manned by indigenous, working-class Iranians, most of whom had only a rudimentary education and poor to nonexistent skills in reading and speaking English. Even in Western countries with an adequate educational infrastructure, qualifying and fielding such technicians requires three to four years of intensive electronic and mechanical training. This was doubly true for the F-14s, AWACS (Airborn Warning and Control System) aircraft, and, later, the F-16s Iran would buy (although these would never be delivered because of the revolution). All the Shah's planners saw was a country of 40 million people—more than comparable to the populations of the "sophisticated" European nations that Majesty wanted to emulate. They just didn't understand that a population used to weaving rugs and hand-irrigating crops might have trouble repairing jet engines and fine-tuning radars without remedial as well as advanced training.

Such "bureaucratic detail" never interested the Shah. Perhaps this was the time when the Shah and his top leaders turned that irreversible corner into fantasyland that eventually destroyed his regime. Majesty's excuse, of course, was that with the deteriorating situation in Afghanistan, he didn't have time to delay deployment of these sophisticated systems until his people were adequately trained. Although he took my advice and changed his mind about *doubling* his F-14 fleet to 150 planes, he stuffed his understrength support units with half-trained youths and contract labor and hoped shepherd boys and civilians would be able to hold the line against Russian tanks should they ever rumble south of the Elburz mountains. Every dime of his oil money went for newer and shinier military toys, and it was all we could do at MAAG to convince him to slow down the flow of gadgets until his people could absorb the ones that were already in the pipeline.

However, what was only good military common sense seemed anathema to the marketplace. The big aerospace and electronics contractors constantly criticized us to Congress for impeding sales to a "willing and waiting" Iranian customer, and many of these complaints were forwarded to us under the official U.S. wrapper. Ironically, Congressional staffers from both parties *also* criticized us for building up Iran's military too rapidly. Although these latter critics usually had their facts mixed up, their complaints were right in substance: Uncle Sam was trying to force-feed 10 pounds of high-tech equipment into a 5-pound Iranian bag, and it just wasn't working. Any one of these glossy, big-ticket programs from Seek Sentry to I-HAWK to AWACS to IBEX to the F-14—and these are only a few—would've taxed even the mainstream American military to implement safely, efficiently, and effectively in the time allowed, let alone a third-world nation with too few qualified personnel.

Under such circumstances, the State Department, and especially the ambassador in Tehran, should've been our best ally and clearest voice for rationality, but such was not the case.

About 18 months into my tour, Dick Helms was replaced by a new ambassador. This new representative, theoretically the top-ranking American in Iran, was fresh from an unbroken string of disasters. Most recently, as ambassador to the Philippines, he had allowed Ferdinand Marcos's war on Communist insurgents to languish and exerted no leverage on that worthy to help U.S. negotiators hammer out leases for our extensive military bases in those islands. Before that, as one of Kissinger's chief negotiators, he helped forge the 1973 Paris Treaty, the terms of which contributed directly and inexorably to the fall of South Vietnam in 1975. Prior to that, he virtually personified every flaw in the Southeast Asian theater, from civilian micro-management of military operations to a preoccupation with interagency turf wars rather than the enemy. At the dawn of his career in 1954, he helped Averell Harriman establish the treaty that got the French out of—and us into—the Indochina quagmire.

I refer, of course, to William Sullivan, a man who seemed to plague my career around the world. I stood with his welcoming committee on the ramp at Mehrabad Airport as the air-stairs rolled up to his plane, cast my eyes heavenward and wondered, like Job, "Lord, why me?"

For the first few months of Sullivan's stay, we had no problems. To be fair, Sullivan was the consummate bureaucrat and a terrific communicator—urbane, charming, distinguished looking, well-liked and respected by many. Unfortunately, jealousy often raged behind the scenes at the American Embassy, since in Iran, the MAAG was by far the biggest show in town, in terms of both dollars spent and strategic importance to the United States. Even worse from Sullivan's perspective, the various MAAG chiefs' personal rapport with Majesty preempted that one-on-one intimacy with the head of state that most ambassadors strive to achieve. Sullivan's response to this dilemma was to increase the embassy's political/military (pol/mil) officers' oversight of the MAAG. The atmosphere from late 1977 on became more tense and contentious.

Our first real confrontation came when it was time to "do something" with the Afghan border/forward deployment plan the Shah's generals and I had been working on. The Shah told me he wanted to give the Soviets in Afghanistan a "show of force," which in Iranian terms meant a show of aerial force—a display of raw air power in which he had made such a tremendous investment. It was determined that a sizable detachment of F-4s (the equivalent of a full squadron) would be deployed for several weeks of "exercises" (practice bombing and strafing) in the area north of Zahedan where the borders of Iran, Pakistan, and Afghanistan come together. Not only would this make a suitably impressive show for the Soviets and their Afghan quislings, but it would also give us the first practical opportunity to test Iran's ability to field its now significant aerial assets. The Iranians requested extensive on-site MAAG support and I was happy to oblige—and reported same, as was required, to the U.S. Embassy.

Unfortunately, Ambassador Sullivan didn't like this plan at all.

First, Sullivan feared the maneuvers were too bellicose, too threatening at a time when the Carter administration was preaching a peaceful settlement in Kabul. (As it turned out, the Soviets were no more willing to cede Afghanistan from their sphere of influence in the late 1970s than the U.S. was Vietnam in the early 1960s.) Second, he hated the idea of uniformed U.S. advisors accompanying "locals" on the ground, just as he did in Laos. He feared an American serviceman might be drawn into some as yet unspecified incident and complicate U.S.-Soviet relations. On the strength of his authority as the President's personal representative, Sullivan *ordered* the MAAG to withdraw from the exercise.

Almost as soon as I heard his decision, I appeared in Sullivan's office. The more we argued the merits of the decision, the more I became convinced that Sullivan was less concerned about the geopolitical implications of the exercise than the necessity for the embassy to make all decisions, particularly if the Shah was involved. He really didn't have a strategic or military leg to stand on, so (as I'm sure he expected) I bucked the dispute upstairs to my boss, four-star General Dutch Huyser at headquarters, U.S. European Command in Stuttgart, Germany. This started a brouhaha in Washington, but ultimately the MAAG advisors were deployed on schedule.

About this same time, the Tudeh, the outlawed Communist party (which had been active in Tehran for years, although less so in the countryside) staged a bold attack right outside my office. Three U.S. contract intelligence technicians with the IBEX program were being driven to work when their car was blocked in the crowded street by an old Volkswagen. Two gunmen dashed out and told the Iranian driver to run, which he did. They opened fire on the occupants in the backseat, severely wounding them. One American managed to get out but was gunned down in the street. The attackers then approached the wounded men and administered the coup de grace: one shot in the head. They took the technicians' briefcases which, contrary to regulations, contained some classified documents.

These assassinations, the first to succeed against Americans in over two years, were like a splash of ice water in our faces. The Savak was chagrined and went right to work to repair what they perceived to have been a breakdown in their system. Within a week they surrounded what they purported to be the terrorists' hideout (just a block from the MAAG compound!) and, after a raging gun battle, killed a number of Tudeh operatives.

The OSI chief, who reported to me, was a bit suspicious that this quick and conspicuous "victory" might've been staged for our benefit, but the Savak recovered both the briefcases and all our classified papers at the site, so, given our own security lapses, we were hardly in a position to criticize anyone. As acting ARMISH MAAG chief, I convened all American military personnel and their families in several separate sessions in a Tehran auditorium and briefed them on the incident, reviewed security procedures, and tried to quash the usual rumors that crop up after such events.

"The main thing to remember," I said at the conclusion of each speech, "is that we're not the Department of Agriculture. We're the Department of War—the American defense establishment. That's why the Communists want us out of here so badly, and that's why we're going to stay."

I announced mandatory refresher training for everyone in antiterrorist tactics, and said I intended to arm all American military personnel under MAAG command in Tehran. This was not an offer, not a suggestion, but an *order* from the highest-ranking military officer on the scene.

I was barely back in my office after the first speech when the phone rang. It was the embassy's pol/mil officer.

"Dick, the ambassador says you've *got* to rescind that order. It's blatantly provocative and will just incite more violence. Besides, you're going to kill or injure more people through accidents and panic than the opposition ever could."

I responded, resisting that sense of déjà vu, "I'm the senior military man in Tehran. I've been given command—not management, not trusteeship, but *command*—of this group. The first duty of any commander is to see to the welfare of his troops. This is not a rash act, but a well-considered military decision."

The pol/mil guy promised my decision "would never stand" and hung up.

Sullivan's knives were obviously sharpened for another bureaucratic tussle. Fortunately, I had already informed my superiors in Europe and the Pentagon.

While the cables began flying between the Tehran embassy, Washington, and all our ships at sea, the arming and refresher training went ahead. Like most self-defense programs, the real value came less from the distribution of hardware and target practice than the alert, self-confident mind-set it engendered. Morale went up and the rumormongering ceased. Productivity in work-related areas, far from slipping because of a preoccupation with terrorists, actually increased.

I didn't see the cable traffic or other correspondence, but I was informed by General Huyser in Europe (with copies to the Pentagon) that the higher-ups supported my plan and that my orders would not be countermanded. Sullivan was so informed through State Department channels.

This episode had a chilling postscript.

The Tudeh struck again, shortly after I returned to Washington in July 1978. This time, their target was a pair of American F-4 pilots about to drive to an Iranian air base. As soon as the terrorists showed their weapons, though, the first F-4 jock dove from behind the wheel and started blazing with his sidearm. The startled terrorists returned the unexpected fire wildly and beat a hasty retreat. One round notched the pilot's ear, but both Americans escaped with their lives and a colorful war story to tell their grandchildren—a big improvement over the last such encounter.

As the Shah himself had said, "The enemy seldom attacks the best-guarded gate."

Although my tour was supposed to finish in the summer of 1977, General Huyser persuaded me to stay an additional 12 months. He didn't have to twist my arm. He was concerned about repairing the revolving-door image America's top military posts had earned in the region, and I was interested in completing the work I had begun: perfecting an operational readiness and war-fighting structure for MAAG and our Iranian ally.

Unfortunately, for the Shah, time was already running out. Although the storm clouds that ultimately washed away his regime were still only distant rumblings on the horizon, they precipitated a tempest in a teapot that came to dominate much of my remaining time.

A few months before the end of my extended tour, right after the U.S. signed a contract to deliver 160 F-16s to Iran, Majesty let it be known that his oldest son, Reza—a bright, proud, and good-hearted young man of 17—required "regular" training as an officer and pilot in the United States. Like General Tadayon, Reza had undergone a very nontraditional initial pilot instruction program supervised by no less than General Rabbii himself. The boy had started in light, single-engine aircraft but quickly (too quickly, we all knew) progressed to bigger airplanes. Too proud to show his natural apprehension and aware that nothing was supposed to be beyond the reach of the Shah's son, Reza asked to solo in a jet fighter. This caused Rabbii one beat short of a heart attack, but valor once again triumphed over good sense.

On the big day, the commander in chief of the Iranian air force called me out to the runway supervisory unit at Mehrabad Airport while the prince made a quick circuit of the flagpole in an F-5E. I couldn't do a damn thing except hold Rabbii's hand. Perhaps he just wanted me there for insurance in case the worst happened and he needed somebody to plead for mercy on his behalf. Although the short flight had a happy ending, it was the final catalyst for a long-overdue, candid discussion between the general and the Shah. Shortly thereafter, I received a message from Majesty through Rabbii saying he "had it in mind" to send his son to the U.S. for pilot-officer training. Did I think my superiors would object?

I went up to the Niavaron Palace with Rabbii to see Majesty. I told the Shah, "The U.S. Air Force would be proud to train your son, Your Majesty—just as it has trained hundreds of sons of our allies over the last thirty years." The Shah knew, too, that over 150 Iranian student pilots were currently undergoing flight training in the U.S. However, I informed him that aside from security precautions, special dispensations—a customized training program, a "royal road" to Reza's silver wings—would be impossible.

"You and Prince Reza must realize," I continued, "that he will have to go through the same standardized undergraduate pilot training program (UPT) as everyone else. I know my government and the Air Force will insist on this. Of course, special security arrangements can be made, but he cannot live luxuriously and must participate in all academic and physical as well as flight-training activities without exception."

The Shah didn't expect his boy to be "pencil-whipped" through UPT the way many privileged young men are passed through name-brand civilian colleges with a "gentleman's C," but it was clear that he, and especially the Shah's wife, had not given adequate consideration to Reza's English, which was poor and vastly inferior to the French he had learned from a tutor imported from the continent when Reza was a child.

To his credit, the Shah entered his son in an intensive technical and colloquial English course, and the boy did quite well, applying himself as diligently to his studies as he did to the stick and rudder. I expedited his paperwork through the Pentagon and onto the desk of ATC's new commander, General John Roberts, who decided that Reese AFB in Lubbock, Texas, met the stringent security needs that, almost daily, seemed to become more urgent. Many Iranian dissidents found asylum in the U.S., and Reza would make a tempting target for demonstrations, or worse. In fact, a few Iranians *did* organize some protests in late 1978, but they were met well outside the base perimeter by the local sheriff and carted off to the hoosegow.

"Project Reza" succeeded, but not without its own peculiar problems and loose ends. Some of the bean counters at Reese had trouble justifying Reza's girlfriend (a Swedish knockout named Ann Marie) as part of the official party, but the Iranians solved that by identifying her as "governess" to the children of the Prince's aides. And even before he went to the States, Reza himself took exception to some of the UPT requirements, figuring that if he had already soloed in an F-5 (an airplane very similar to the supersonic T-38 advanced trainer), he should be spared the indignity of primary training in slower airplanes, namely the subsonic T-37.

This potential impasse raised a very real problem that threatened to torpedo the whole project. The Shah and General Rabbii trusted me *personally* to look after the boy. In their eyes, it was not a responsibility I could delegate to another officer. Unfortunately, the rules and regulations Reza would have to live with were made and enforced by ATC. I found myself wasting *hours* every workday placating the royal feelings and cajoling the guys in the States who ultimately would have to shepherd him through the program. It was time stolen from what I perceived to be my real task in those last months: preparing a strong legacy for my replacement.

The only solution was to create an opportunity for the trust the Shah and Rabbii felt in me to be transferred to others through personal contact. Since the Shah and the Iranian air force general staff couldn't very well travel to Lubbock, the mountain, so to speak, would have to come to Mohammed.

Through General Rabbii, I arranged for the Iranian government to invite the ATC wing commander, Charlie Bishop (an old friend who drove Thuds in Vietnam), Reza's IP—and anyone else ATC thought might be needed—for a short "orientation visit" to Iran. While they were here, they'd be introduced to Rabbii (who was still caught between the hound and the hydrant with respect to the Shah) and the royal family. If the chemistry was right, they would establish the rapport needed to resolve Reza's issues and handle any future problems in the Prince's American flying career without my hand on the stick.

The plan worked wonderfully. Bishop tactfully explained the facts of life and leadership, American Air Force–style, to young Reza, the Shah, and the Queen, and by the time the team left, Reza had bought into the program. Better still, nobody gave Dick Secord a second thought.

Eventually, Reza went to Reese and did well, winning his USAF wings in less than the prescribed time of 53 weeks. Ironically, in 1979, by the time the royal pilot was qualified to receive further training in his father's aerial fleet, that air force—even the Shah's Iran—would no longer exist. Later that year, Reza's father himself would be gone.

I knew a little about such family losses myself. In May 1978, one month before the end of my extended tour, my own father passed away in America.

I left Iran at the end of June 1978 after a cumulative total of four and one-half years (including the Kurdish war tours) in that country. I went back to Washington, D.C., to assume a new post: director of international programs for the U.S. Air Force, administering the grant and sale of defense materials and services to U.S. allies. My replacement, Brigadier General George Kertez, was a seasoned fighter pilot and a perfect candidate to lead the MAAG. During my tour, I had administered over $17 billion in FMS programs, about 35 percent of which had been delivered and paid for, with substantial down payments having been made against the others. Jo Ann and I also made a number of close personal friends among Iranians in and out of government and the military; some, like General Rabbii, would come back into our lives sooner than we expected and in a very tragic way. The Imperial Iranian Air Force was well on its way to becoming the best in the region, although I was still convinced that they were trying to do too much too quickly. I felt my one significant failure had been my inability to convince Majesty that even the biggest and most modern fleet of aircraft and missiles in the world would be useless if spare parts and trained technicians were unavailable to service them. Those views proved to be prophetic—for the Ayatollah, if not for the Shah.

By the time Jo Ann, the kids, and I left, a few antigovernment demonstrations had broken out in the smaller cities of Iran. Muslim religious leaders were now vocally opposing the Shah's modernization plans and demanded the return of mosque lands confiscated under his land-reform program. In Abadan, a theater had burned down under suspicious circumstances with heavy loss of life. It was a bad omen for the Shah, although nobody in Tehran—the Savak, CIA, and OSI included—foresaw a revolution.

Six months later, the government would be toppled, revolutionary mullahs (a radical, Bolshevik-like minority in what was generally one of the *least* devout of the Muslim countries) would be in power, and Majesty would be wandering among his former so-called allies, deathly ill and broken.

How did it happen? Why did it happen? What could we have done differently to preserve a key ally and prevent the debacle from degenerating into what became known as the Iranian hostage crisis?

First, the "outsider" Carter administration, in its populist zeal, seemed to have forgotten that Iran had been solidly within the American sphere of influence for almost 40 years. As a strategic crossroads and source of some of the largest proven petroleum reserves in the world, its significance as a buffer to the Soviets and bastion of American national interests was vastly greater than our interests in Vietnam—yet we sacrificed 58,000 American lives defending Vietnam and gave up Iran without firing a shot.

Instead, we should have annunciated a policy of direct intervention clearly and forthrightly, just as the Shah made his important "show of force" when the red balloon went up in Afghanistan. Rather than sending Europe-based General Dutch Huyser to Iran in late 1978 and early 1979 (Huyser was not known by the Iranian generals and did not have their personal or professional confidence), a special envoy from the President himself, such as the National Security advisor or the Chairman of the Joint Chiefs of Staff, should have gone to Tehran to explain the facts of life to the Shah and his key generals and ministers.

He should have told the Shah that continued American support for his regime would be contingent on reforms to the current system that was causing grass-roots discontent. The Shah had a Majlis—a rotating legislature—but that Parliament needed to be based on a true democratic constituency. And the Shah had to clean up the corruption. We'd made a start with the huge DoD contracts; these could've been used as models for managing projects in the civilian sector as well.

This envoy should have told the Shah, also, and in no uncertain terms, that civil disorder must not be tolerated. Even valid grievances can't be redressed after law and order breaks down. We should have insisted that the

Shah take control of his army, police, and gendarme units and exert his considerable personal authority.

The U.S. should then have assisted the Iranian government with advice and information related to martial law and security. The Shah would have had to stop playing one general or police agency against another and build a cohesive team that could properly defend the government and execute its laws. Also, with the Carter administration's big push for human rights, the reforms of the 1960s curbing the Savak's brutal tendencies should have been furthered and made more visible to the international community.

The special presidential envoy—*not* of ambassadorial status—should have stayed in Tehran to represent U.S. interests until the crisis was over.

In private, this special presidential envoy should have added:

"Look, Your Majesty, the disorder in your country has got to stop and permanent reforms must be put into place. We believe you have been acting uncharacteristically these last few months—indecisive and weak—and we know this is not your nature. We believe you need help. If necessary, we are prepared to evacuate you to Geneva for medical treatment."

This last comment would have been enough to put the fear of Allah into Majesty, no matter what his health. He heard it before in the 1950s and again in the 1960s when disorder threatened Iran and jeopardized U.S. interests. If the Shah still didn't get the message, we shouldn't have hesitated one day in brokering a military junta to take his place. All the key generals were congenial with the U.S. and worked well together. They were Iranian patriots and could, in extreme necessity, separate their loyalty to one man from their loyalty to the state. A core of tough, reform-minded, honest leaders *was* available in Iran in late 1978. Instead of seeking these people out and supporting them in a firm coalition, Ambassador Sullivan spent his time writing "dispatches from the front," like a war correspondent or play-by-play announcer, and never got into the game. This attitude, coupled with the use of envoys who were several steps removed from the U.S. President, seemed to the Iranian generals like a solid vote of no confidence in the Shah's regime or even in the future of the Iranian people. The Iranian generals needed and wanted American leadership; and before that time, they always had it.

We had no excuse save our own incapacity and muddled thinking for losing Iran to Khomeini. I believe history will excoriate the Carter administration and, to a lesser extent, Sullivan for their failure to act decisively in Iran—for losing irreversibly a strategically vital area with barely a word of protest. Worse, I fear the United States has not yet paid the final price for its folly.

In my opinion, the Carter Administration helped lose our embassy—our sovereign, national soil under international law—to the Iranian radicals not once, but twice. Before the second incident, the JCS dispatched a company of Marines to be airlifted into the compound from a base in southern Turkey to collect our people, demolish sensitive material, and get the Americans out. But the troops were stopped in Lajes, the Azores, after the State Department received Sullivan's plea that such an act would result "in a bloodbath."

A bloodbath might have happened, but it would have happened to the Iranian "students," radicals, and flag-wavers who at that time posed no threat to any organized military unit, let alone to U.S. Marines. But the Marines never landed. The U.S. "cavalry" never arrived.

Once again, Sullivan played and won the bureaucrat's game. Once again, other people paid the price. Not even President Carter's admirable moral sensibilities could save the country from what was bound to happen next. The capture of our embassy personnel began an era of hostage taking and American insecurity that never should have occurred.

In early 1979, Reza came back to the Iranian Embassy in Washington, D.C. His two sisters soon joined him and were taken under the wing of Ardeshir Zahedi, the Iranian ambassador. I visited them there several times and saw them off at Andrews AFB when they left on an Iranian air force 707 to join the Shah and the Queen in Morocco at the beginning of their politically awkward, and ultimately tragic, exile. The long line of Persian kings reaching back 2,500 years to the time of Cyrus the Great would end with both the bang of revolution *and* a whimper of a tired, dying old man.

One of the last times I saw General Rabbii was in October 1978 at the Iranian terminal at McGuire AFB, New Jersey. He was on his way to Europe amid televised reports that the Ayatollah Khomeini was going to leave Paris for Tehran to vie, in his own way, for Shah-like powers over his people. While the reporters talked and the images of the shrewd, sullen Ayatollah flashed on the screen, I could see the warrior's fire kindling in Rabbii's eyes.

"I wish I was in Europe right now," the commander of the Shah's aerial host growled, almost under his breath.

"Why?" I asked, feeling depressed myself at the prospect of seeing all our work—and the work of a generation of Americans—going down the drain in Iran. "What could you do?"

"I could shoot down that son of a bitch!"

Rabbii went on his way. A few months later, my good friend would be dangling, dead, from a firing squad's post in Tehran.

Although I had spent the last three years in Iran, working at the highest levels and in close cooperation with the Near East intelligence community, that fall was the first time most of us had heard the name Ayatollah Khomeini.

Sadly, it would not be the last.

# —9—

# The Raid That
# Never Happened

Unlike some Pentagon programs at the time, my crew at Air Force International Programs was pretty lean considering the herculean tasks we faced, with only 130 people to manage several hundred billion dollars worth of defense programs in over 60 countries. All together, USAF international programs in those years were comparable to the sales volume of General Motors and Ford combined—the largest in the U.S. Security Assistance Program. The funds we administered exceeded the GNP of many countries, Thailand and the Philippines included. As the Air Force focal point for this great transfer of technology and wealth, I was either courted or vilified by everyone who had a stake in it, from the CEOs of vast aerospace conglomerates to one-man entrepreneur-consultants such as Iran expatriate Albert Hakim, one of a legion of "knew-you-whens" who stopped by to congratulate me on my new job. I don't want to sound too cynical, but it's hard to imagine all these people taking the same personal interest in me and my career had I been made a commander of some air division in Timbuktu. It's often difficult to separate the person from the position, particularly when you're the guy on the "throne," or hot seat, depending on the situation. Whenever I began feeling too high and mighty, I reminded myself how quickly a well-placed burst of flak had brought down better men than me.

One of the reasons I received so much attention from the outside world was that our charter required us to screen bids on foreign military sales (FMS) contracts, which we administered. Aircraft manufacturers base the price of their product (including spare parts and support services) on the grand total of their direct and indirect costs, factory overhead, contingency reserves, and profit. Because every contractor puts his thumb on the scale (a little bit or a lot) as a hedge against the unexpected, estimates for these already expensive

142

and exotic products can quickly become exorbitant. One of our most important jobs was to "disassemble" these data into their constituent parts so that we could test them for reasonableness, to determine how much aircraft, spare parts, or support services really "should cost."

A couple of these pricing brushfires were already smoldering in my in-basket when I arrived.

Near the end of my tour in Iran, ISA had shepherded through Congress the so-called Peace Sun program: the sale of F-15s to Saudi Arabia. Buying jet airplanes isn't like buying a car, or even a new fleet of vehicles for a corporation or municipal bus line. Modern aircraft require specialized care and feeding, and the logistics—spare parts, documentation, unit- and depot-level maintenance, airworthiness, and technical upgrades, to name only a few factors—run into many, many times the aircraft's purchase price over the fleet's life cycle. This after-sales support is a very lucrative part of any FMS deal, and a big flap had been raised over whether McDonnell Douglas (the F-15's manufacturer) should be awarded a sole-source contract for these services or whether they should be put out for competitive bid.

Now, it may seem strange that another organization could support a competitor's product more cost-effectively than its maker, but it happens all the time. (Just think about the cost of 10 years' worth of maintenance at a new-car dealership versus obtaining those same services from a neighborhood garage.) We analyzed some of McDonnell Douglas's (or "Mac Dac" as they've been nicknamed) cost elements and decided that a few were as inflated as the Goodyear blimp. For example, they had estimated the cost to supply maintenance technicians to the Saudis at over $300,000 per technician per year, *plus* all sorts of infrastructure "taxes" the Saudis would have to pay to support the workers, such as modern, air-conditioned housing in special "Americanized" compounds with swimming pools and recreation facilities and so on. If Uncle Sam could position GI technicians for the same aircraft all over the world for a fraction of that cost, what were the Saudis really paying for? We sent the results of our analysis to the manufacturer and informed the Air Force chief of staff that the validity of the McDonnell Douglas price would have to be verified by competitive bidding; it was just too far off the mark to be acceptable to us.

The industry didn't like this, of course, and neither did we. Earlier sole-source procurements for the Saudis had a bad history of cost overruns, and this looked to be no exception. Our relationship with Saudi Arabia was fragile enough in those days, and even the appearance of collusion between the U.S. government and its major industries to rip off our FMS partners would be enough to send them elsewhere in the arms bazaar, with the attendant loss of national influence that would involve. If it was simply a matter of Saudi Arabia versus McDonnell Douglas in a commercial contract (such as a deal for typewriters or computers), we would've bowed out. But in arrangements like this, the U.S. government was a contracting party, and we at international programs were charged with protecting the public interest. With a sole-source contract, the incentive to be both good *and* cheap was close to zero, regardless of the manufacturer's brochure. My point—which I made clear to both company reps and the air staff—was that if the Mac Dac cost estimates were truly competitive, they'd have no problem prevailing in a head-to-head competition.

They did not see it that way.

Our first obstruction was within the Air Force itself. By getting the USAF logistics command to oppose my office on the matter, sole-source proponents were able to pit a four-star general against a one-star general. Their argument rested on the logical premise that the people who make a product should be best at supporting it in the field. I thought they were unnecessarily padding their price; and in absence of a detailed "should-cost" audit, which they *really* didn't want, competitive bidding was the only alternative.

After months of wrangling, the Air Force general counsel finally ruled that I was right: Competition was in the best interests of the U.S. government and Saudi Arabia.

The sole-source advocates immediately appealed the decision to the Air Force vice chief of staff, another four-star general, General James Hill. Air Force logistics command (AFLC) gave a colorful and complex slide show that purported to prove that the F-15 was so complicated and sensitive a creation that only its "mother," McDonnell Douglas, could care for it properly. I responded with a few plain-vanilla vu-graphs that told the story the way I saw it: Airplanes are airplanes and the U.S. Air Force had plenty of experience supporting them—at a fraction of Mac Dac's price. Besides, nobody was suggesting that the winning contractor would not use the manufacturer's spares, technical manuals, parts catalogs, and factory experts (as required), just as the Air Force had used them in the past. I rhetorically asked that if contractor-supplied product support was really essential, why hadn't AFLC written up a proposal for the Air Force to fire its enlisted maintenance troops and farm out the labor to the manufacturer, which it had *not* done, even for the F-15? "Given the great comparative advantage in favor of McDonnell Douglas as described here today, and a reasonable profit margin," I said in my conclusion, "I would expect them to win hands down in a fair competition."

The vice chief of staff retired to consider his verdict. I thought we had won until he came back and ruled in favor of the AFLC. No rationale for the decision was offered.

Orders were orders, and I'd just gotten mine. It was a frustrating experience, particularly since my desire had not been to *exclude* the manufacturer, but simply to test its questionable bid against free-market forces. That's when I learned that big business wasn't about competition; it's about *evading* competition, and anybody who thinks otherwise, and tries to enforce that view, is just a voice crying in the wilderness.

The battle didn't enhance my image among contractors. After Iran, they respected my technical and combat experience but believed I was a "bleeding-heart" missionary more concerned about third-world dictators than American profits. In truth, I never saw FMS in adversarial terms—it was just a question of duty and fairness.

In 1979, after the Carter-Begin-Sadat accords, I was assigned to lead the first military delegation to Cairo to help the Egyptian high command allocate its first U.S. FMS credits, one of Sadat's tangible rewards for doing the right thing at Camp David. It was a daunting task, given Sadat's huge shopping list—M113 armored personnel carriers, M60 tanks, and top-of-the-line F-4E Phantom fighters—and previous (almost exclusive) reliance on Soviet-bloc equipment going back to the days of Nasser.

Most of our work was accomplished at Egyptian Forces headquarters in Cairo. It was one of those few times and places where the idealism at the top gets converted to practical results at the working level. When we were finished, my host (a counterpart Egyptian general) politely asked if there was anything he could do for me before we returned to Washington.

The customary response to such ceremonial questions is "No, thank you; your hospitality has been most generous" because you're usually anxious to get home; or, if the situation seems to call for additional rapport building, "Yes, I've always admired the so-and-so palace" or "Your outstanding national ballet is very famous in America" and so invite yourself on a VIP tour of some famous building or to the theater and thus get to know your hosts better in an informal environment.

This time, I surprised us both by saying, "Yes, General, there are two things I've always wanted to do: see the headwaters of the Nile and fly a MiG-21."

The sleek, delta-winged Russian fighter had been for years the standard by which Western warplanes were judged. In Vietnam, the MiG-21s (at least those flown by Russian pilots) had given American fighters a run for their money. And I don't know of any U.S. fighter pilot who had ever gone "up North" who didn't harbor a secret wish to climb into a MiG-21's cockpit and see what that baby could do.

Understandably, my host looked a little stunned. More than a few eyebrows would be raised in Moscow should the remains of an American Air Force general be found in the smoking wreckage of one of the Soviet Union's most famous fighters. However, saddling up a couple of MiGs for a hop around the Beneseuf Air Base flagpole was a lot easier to arrange than an expedition to Victoria Falls. After a couple of phone calls, a takeoff time was set, and the Egyptian general shook my hand with a big, nervous grin.

A nation's personality—its assumptions about people and life and death—is mirrored in its weapons of war. Most modern American warplanes come in dual cockpit versions for easier, safer pilot transition training. They also have reliable safety and escape mechanisms, few of which were reflected in the single-seat Soviet plane I soon found myself strapping into.

My preflight orientation was nothing more than a quick tour around the cockpit by an English-speaking crew chief. Since most Russian aircraft designs are based on Western models, nothing was too alien to comprehend, except the ejection-seat system, which had more lockouts and safety pins and guarded switches than I could count. The whole thing seemed a lot safer if I just left it alone, which is what I did, and took off with the seat disarmed. It was a reasonable compromise. I still had a parachute, and the MiG was notoriously short-ranged. Neither plane in our two-ship formation had drop tanks, so I knew our flight would be short. My host had seen to it that I wouldn't have too many opportunities to get into trouble.

From the moment we lifted off to the time I reluctantly parked the aircraft, I saw why the MiG-21 (and probably most Mikoyan-designed fighters) were so popular with third-world air forces. Light on the controls and extremely honest (meaning it had no hidden, nasty surprises when it approached a stall, pulled Gs, or flew at high speed), the sleek little bird showed itself to be a true pilot's airplane and was unlike any other aircraft I'd flown—something of a cross between an American F-102 and a French Mirage fighter. It was very maneuverable (which our pilots in Vietnam discovered whenever they closed in to use their guns on one), and if you like to turn, this plane was your baby. Unfortunately for Mr. Mikoyan and his customers, modern fighter tactics no longer reward agility alone, but rather acceleration, speed, and avionics—the sophisticated fire control and electronic countermeasures that employ or evade the deadly new species of air-to-air missiles that dominate jet engagements from increasingly longer distances.

Still, the export version of this legendary airplane was fun to fly, and I gained a new understanding of what must go through the enemy's mind when he squares off against our pilots. My biggest challenge, in fact, wasn't Russian aerodynamics but the MiG's metric flight instruments. The "kilometers per hour" on the airspeed indicator weren't so bad, but the "meters of height" on the altimeter got my attention *real* fast, particularly as the featureless Egyptian desert raced up at me at the bottom of my first loop!

I would've been happy to fly that beauty all day, but dry tanks and business called me back to earth.

Our highest priority was getting the first F-4 squadron in place and ready to fly, with at least minimally qualified crews, in time for Egypt's annual October parade. It was a task worthy of the pharaohs, and we barely made our deadline. The sight of first-rank U.S. equipment in Egyptian markings roaring over the reconstituted Egyptian forces proved conclusively to the world, I think, that a new age in Middle East history truly had begun.

Unfortunately, it was the same celebratory parade that would, on October 6, 1981, see the assassination of Anwar Sadat, whom, when we met on my previous mission, I found to be intelligent and friendly—an engaging leader with an acute sense of his place in history. I also became acquainted with his successor, Hosni Mubarak, whose less gregarious, more formal and aloof (and thus more Near Eastern) style is often mistaken by Westerners for arrogance, which is not the case. But Sadat was not Nasser and Mubarak was not Sadat, although each man has played a unique and crucial role in shaping the destiny of his country.

After a few more bruising battles with a variety of U.S. defense contractors (such as one with Sikorsky in Venezuela, where we again had to put national interest and regional stability ahead of contractor dollars), I received, in early 1980, a promotion to major general. As that second star joined the first in a brief Pentagon ceremony, I couldn't help but think about my interview with another two-star general in Oklahoma before my assignment to Jungle Jim. Neither General Mundell nor I could've foreseen the path—half a career in special ops—that had brought me to this moment, but for such a notoriously bumpy road, it turned out, for me at least, to be a surprisingly high-speed turnpike.

My biggest disappointment in an otherwise absorbing and challenging job was having to watch Iran go down the tubes during the 12 months bracketing the Shah's January 1979 departure from his country.

I was in fairly regular contact with General Rabbii and others until the end, and it was hell to watch the growing confusion and despair overtake what had once been a thriving, vital U.S. ally. Demonstrations against Prime Minister Shahpur Bakhtiar's government intensified until the Ayatollah Khomeini was allowed to return two weeks after the Shah's departure. Bakhtiar himself resigned shortly thereafter, and Khomeini's government began imposing the first of a series of draconian Islamic laws regulating everything from banks to broadcasts. The ailing Shah, in a losing struggle with cancer, stopped for treatment in a New York hospital, enraging 500 Iranian extremists who stormed the American Embassy in Tehran twice, the second time seizing 52 hostages, two-thirds of them American. Not long thereafter, President Carter evacuated all nonessential personnel from our embassies in 10 Islamic countries and, later, froze Iranian assets in the U.S. until such time as the Tehran hostages were released. Months went by and nothing happened. Carter stuck close to his phone in the White House, quickly becoming a prisoner of events precipitated by his own inaction.

On April 24, 1980, the nation was shocked to learn that a rescue raid had failed even before it started in a desert staging area deep inside Iran. The details were sketchy at first, but then got worse as more facts became known. The mission, dubbed Desert One, had been aborted because of unspecified "equipment failure," and during the withdrawal, two aircraft—a C-130 transport and a Marine helicopter—had collided on the ground, killing eight GIs and seriously injuring five others. Secretary of State Cyrus Vance resigned in protest over the botched mission a few days later. U.S. voters were disconsolate and enraged. As would be ratified in November, the presidency of Jimmy Carter was all but over.

Despite my familiarity with Iran and years in special ops, the Pentagon top brass did not include me in their plans to rescue our embassy hostages. Consequently, the only thing I knew about our tragic reaction to that crisis was what I read in the newspapers or heard through intelligence channels, and that was frustratingly little.

When news of the failed Desert One attempt broke, I was as heartsick as everyone else. It was inconceivable to me that eight men could die without seeing one hostage or confronting one hostile Iranian. It was even worse for me, in some ways, than the battle for Site 85, since in Laos I at least had a chance to influence the outcome. The Desert One fiasco was more like the fall of Saigon in 1975. As detail after detail slowly emerged, it was like watching a terrible automobile crash in slow motion.

The media, of course, had a field day. America's military establishment, a fumbling giant that couldn't even bring off the kind of raid Israeli commandos performed in their sleep, was going from bad to worse. A great sense of impotence and frustration descended on everyone at the Pentagon: a communal, institutional depression so thick you could slice it with a bayonet.

A couple of days after the tragedy, Chairman Jones called me into his office. Given the things I knew he had on his mind, I steeled myself for the worst. I half expected to be drafted onto some red team or audit squad to analyze the failure and present a mea culpa to Congress. Those particular wheels *had* been set in motion, although I—thankfully—would not be one of its cogs. I couldn't think of a worse assignment.

Until General Jones told me why I was there.

"This comes right from [Secretary of Defense] Harold Brown," he said stolidly, "who got it straight from the President. We're rebuilding a new task force to go back to Iran and do the job right. Lew Allen [the four-star USAF chief of staff] and I think you'd be a key man for that task."

Two thoughts immediately popped into my head, both of them disturbing.

First was the old saw every schoolkid learns from his teacher: "Nobody's got time to do things right the first time, but everybody's got time to do it twice." Why hadn't I been included in the first attempt?

The second was Hienie Aderholt's old dictum about special ops: "You can get away with anything—*once*." As far as an Iranian hostage rescue was concerned, that card had already been played; our hand had been tipped and the enemy alerted. To go back now with anything less than the 82nd Airborne and a couple of very large, rabid dogs seemed to me inordinately risky.

I hope General Jones took my stunned silence as a flood of patriotic zeal, because all I could ask, with a very dry throat, was, "What job do you have in mind for me?"

The JCS chairman paused, apparently thinking over his reply very carefully. We had built a pretty good rapport over the last few years. He went to bat for me more than once and expected me to do the same for him when I was asked. I knew he felt terrible that things had come down to this.

"I can't offer you command of the operation, Dick. The Secretary's already decided to keep Jim Vaught [the Army major general who led the first attempt] in charge, and I agree. But we all want to beef up the organization, so we want you to be Vaught's deputy commander."

He might as well have said, *Hey, it's 21 to 0, fourth down, 80 yards to go, with 10 seconds on the clock—let's send in Dick Secord! And by the way, Dick, the old quarterback will continue to call the plays from the sidelines.*

I winced like I'd been shot and managed some sort of reply appropriate to the situation and required by military etiquette, but my feelings, I'm sure, showed plainly on my face.

General Jones continued in an upbeat tone, "One of the changes we've already made is to create the new post of air component commander. That'll be your job, too: If it flies, you'll be in charge of it. But it's a joint task force— we call it the JTF. That's why I want you to wear the deputy JTF commander's hat. I've got every confidence in General Vaught, but we need somebody like you to get the mission off the ground, to get to the target and back with all our people."

I knew I couldn't say *no thanks*, so I promised to give it my best shot. Jones set up the first planning session for later that same day in Secretary Brown's office. He told me to come with a wish list, and a few good ideas.

"And by the way," General Jones said as I got up to leave, "this is all top secret. You'll be detailed to the new JTF, but you've got to keep your current shop running as if you were there. I hope you've got a good deputy."

I did, but that wasn't what worried me. The more I thought about it, the more problematic the whole deal looked. I didn't know General Vaught except by reputation. Before Desert One I thought of him as just another crusty old Army guy. Now he seemed to be another crusty old Army guy who had been given his big chance and blew it. Politics seemed to be raising its ugly head again. Carter, I thought, didn't want to admit his mistake and fire the man in charge, so he'd keep the coach and change all the players—a bass-ackwards way of doing things. I felt like Abraham's son being led to the altar with a knife at my neck, and there wasn't a damn thing I could do about it.

The kickoff meeting with Secretary Harold Brown, though brief, was a real eye-opener.

Brown's long, rectangular office was serious, like its occupant (a former nuclear physicist), despite the obligatory sofa and coffee table. The slightly built, bespectacled Secretary sat behind an enormous desk (reputed to have belonged to General "Blackjack" Pershing), looking like a hanging judge at a tribunal; or worse, like a bereaved father at a child's funeral. Chairman Jones, General Vaught, and I sat on chairs before the desk, balancing note pads on our laps like nervous schoolboys called into the principal's office.

"The President will give you his full support," Brown said, never one to mince words even when things were going right. "You'll get all the resources you need to effect the rescue. Everything we have is at your disposal."

This was a surprise, given the fact that half the generals at the Pentagon expected to be fired in the aftermath of Desert One, whether or not they were blameless. In Pentagonese, "resources" meant money, and the President himself had just given us a blank check. I hoped my new CO realized that blank checks had to be cashed in a hurry; they had a way of being filled in or canceled by other people. I needn't have worried.

Brown spoke solemnly for 15 minutes, giving us our orders. He invited no discussion, so mostly we just listened; then we were dismissed. After the meeting, General Vaught asked me into his office. He eased into the chair behind his desk looking older than his 55 years.

"Look, Dick," he said, "we can probably agree on one thing. This building is filled with conventionalists, and the only two unconventionalist generals in the Pentagon may be sitting in this office. How do you want to proceed?"

I could only smile. "Well, sir, I'll admit, after two hours on the project, I haven't quite finalized my plan."

We laughed together. I'd half expected General Vaught to be contrite—feel and act defeated or ashamed, perhaps even ask me openly to shoulder his load—but I was mistaken. Instead, he impressed me as the tough old pro he was, before and after Desert One. He was more frustrated than anyone about how things had turned out and just seemed grateful that the gods of war had given him another chance. I think he saw me in the same light, as a no-bullshit guy whose addition to the team may have just improved the odds.

We agreed that the first order of business was to decide between us what had *really* gone wrong with Desert One. Our agenda was not the same as that of the Holloway board of inquiry. We weren't interested in finding scapegoats or writing apologies to Congress or redeeming the Carter administration with the American people. All we cared about was discovering any flaws inherent in the system. We wanted to be dead certain that, in restaging the mission "the right way," we wouldn't somehow perpetuate the seeds of the earlier disaster.

So, while General Vaught peeled off to battle the official blame seekers (where, unfortunately, he would spend much of his time over the next three months), I met privately with each of the surviving principals to hear *their* side of the story: What, in the opinion of those who were there, really sabotaged the mission?

The answers were illuminating, and in many ways contrary to the "official findings" of the Holloway board, which would be published several months later.

The three main reasons the board came up with for the failure of Desert One were as follows:

1. *Overemphasis on OpSec.* The board found that a preoccupation with operational security resulted in poor command, control, and coordination among the services and participating units. Joint exercises were cursory, and key commanders felt they were being "left out of the loop."
2. *Inadequate Navy maintenance.* The care and feeding of the big H-53 heavy-lift helicopters was found wanting during transportation and staging from U.S. Navy carriers. This resulted in an excessively high mechanical breakdown rate, endangering the mission.
3. *A BIM warning light caused the abort of the critical fifth helicopter needed to launch the mission from the Iranian desert staging area.* To increase structural integrity, the H-53's rotor blades are filled with high-pressure nitrogen. If this nitrogen leaks out, a light comes on in the cockpit warning the pilot to land at the nearest suitable airfield for repairs. This malfunction occurred in one of the helicopters (five was the minimum number of helos called for in the plan), leaving only four operational, which caused the on-site commander to scrub the mission.

My own investigation came up with entirely different reasons for the failure, representing the consensus of the people whose tails were on the line at the time. Its results have never before been published:

1. *The infiltration failed because not enough backup helicopters were available.* The eight specially configured H-53s used in the raid constituted "all there were" of this particular kind of helicopter. Everyone agreed that eight helicopters simply weren't enough. Either additional types of rotary-wing assets should have been employed or the mission should've been replanned.
2. *The Marine helicopter pilots were insufficiently trained for formation flight under instrument meteorological conditions.* Hard as it is to believe, the Marine Corps pilots had had only rudimentary formation-flying training (even under daylight, contact conditions), and *none* were competent to fly formation at night, in the clouds. You can't blame troops for failing to do what they haven't been trained for, and I didn't. As a matter of fact, I rehired the Marine pilot (a major) who

was at the controls of the helicopter that hit the C-130 and caused the big fire. Refueling two big pieces of whirling machinery next to each other with an 80-foot piece of hose was, in my opinion, an idea just this side of lunacy. That was a planning mistake, not a pilot error, and I could see no reason for holding the Marine driver responsible for it.

3. *The field commanders (particularly the Delta Force commander) showed a lack of aggressiveness that ultimately cost them the mission.* This was another tough one to accept, but I could come to no other conclusion. Under the Desert One mission ground rules, surprise was the first objective: Get into the embassy compound with an adequate force to take control of the hostages. My analysis showed this was possible even if only *four* of the original eight helicopters actually reached the target. Extraction was no problem, since the plan called for a battalion of Rangers—the finest light infantry in the world—to be inserted into an auxiliary field only 40 miles southwest of the embassy. Thus, four choppers could have done the job, although more would've been desirable. Additionally, the bird with the BIM light should have continued—or been ordered to continue—the mission.

This third point puts the BIM-light abort in its proper perspective. The nitrogen-leak warning is fairly common among H-53s. Even in peacetime, the helicopter is capable of flying many dozens of hours with such leaks before any problems are encountered, and its pilots know this. Further, this was a combat mission, not a routine training exercise. Many lives hung in the balance. It was apparent from the top (a commander who did not improvise to accomplish his mission) to the bottom (a line pilot who aborted the critical ship because of a minor problem) that the whole mission was abort-oriented, more interested in avoiding problems than accomplishing its objective. Unbelievably, another helicopter pilot had aborted because his TACAN receiver malfunctioned, and there was *no* essential need for TACAN where he was going!

After completing my analysis (and while the Holloway board was still arranging its chairs), Jim Vaught and I decided that, since equipment and leadership were so important, the next thing we should do was prepare an "order of battle": define the rotary and fixed-wing assets required to do the job and sign up the personnel we'd need to make them fly and fight.

I reminded General Vaught about Harold Brown's "blank check." I also remembered the lessons I'd learned in Vietnam and Laos, that "dotted-line" organizational relationships just don't work in combat. Any aircraft we drafted had to be permanently assigned to us, the JTF. Any pilots, gunners, electronics technicians, crew chiefs, and so forth that we'd need to go with them had to be transferred to us, too. We knew that would irritate more than a few generals in most of the major commands, but our guys *had* to know they belonged to us, body and soul, because that's what combat leadership—and followership—is all about.

I began with the H-53 heavy-lift helos, which the Air Force used mostly for air rescue. We contacted my old boss, General Dutch Huyser, now commander of MAC (the Military Airlift Command), and said, in essence, "Gimme all the heavy-lift choppers you've got," along with their crews. Before this, Dutch had been one of my boosters; he backed me up any number of times in Iran and did what he could to prevent the Shah's fall, although the deck was stacked against him in that job. Now I must've seemed like a real Judas, robbing his command of a major asset without explanation. He bucked the order all the way to the JCS and—knowing General Jones was behind us—to the SecDef himself. I got a call from Harold Brown's office asking me to draft a reply to General Huyser's "request for clarification" of my requisition. I could only fall back on the one example I had seen for such a reply—the answer made by the CIA Far East division to my old pal J.R. Swasey, who tried to foil my transfer from Vietnam to Laos:

"Referenced message was not a request, but directive in nature."

Initial inspection of the H-53s showed we had a lot of work to do, in terms of both field modifications and crew training. I had been away from special ops for about 10 years, and although I was a little rusty on all the new gadgets and gizmos, the basic laws of physics and human nature were still in effect. In Laos, I ran (or tried to run) a good part of the air war, much of that with helicopters, for over two years without a fatality. Of course, we lost birds and took casualties, but none that were fatal. I chalked that up to a big dose of good luck fortified by a little forethought and common sense. The main principle I came away with was that all helicopters—even the little ones—are temperamental, unstable, unreasonable beasts. You can turn your back on some fixed-wing aircraft and they'll forgive just about anything: rough handling, severe weather, hard landings. You choose the wrong time to glance away in a "fling-wing" aircraft and it'll bite your head off. Unfortunately, helicopters do things other aircraft can't; so, as a commander, you're stuck with them if you want the biggest toolbox possible. The key to success is staying on your toes—and making sure everyone else does, too.

The jewels in the crown of our helo fleet were the six (*all* six) PAVE LOW H-53s, just delivered to the Air Force, which I intended to use as pathfinders—to get in first and mark the way. These birds were specially configured for sensor operations and had a ton of state-of-the-art equipment, from forward-looking infrared (FLIR) and low-light-level television (LLTV) to Doppler/inertial navigation systems and terrain following/avoidance radar. The long pole in this tent, unfortunately, were the crews, who thought they were pretty hot stuff when in reality they were far from combat-ready. That would change.

I next hopped a T-39 to Hurlburt—a sentimental journey to the field where it all started, at least for me—to take a look at the special ops wing I had just commandeered, lock, stock, and barrel, from TAC. The wing commander, whom I didn't know, was understandably shaken by this sudden and disruptive reassignment of his wing, but managed to give me a decent briefing on the status of his unit, at least as he saw it.

They say you can't go home again, and I'm afraid this visit proved it: My memories had definitely aged better than the wing. They flew AC-130 gunships (the only ones in the Air Force) and special MC-130 "Blackbirds" configured for covert operations. But the AT-28s, A-26s, and A-37s were long gone, and so was the spirit of the crews who once animated them. The ground crews were sluggish and the pilots indifferent—rather like high-tech postal workers. Worse yet, the helicopter squadron was having growing pains from a recent expansion and had leadership problems of its own.

That, too, would change.

I gave the key officers a little lecture on what was coming up for them: some hard training and a few modifications to their aircraft, particularly the C-130s, many of which had no aerial refueling capability. I also told the wing commander I wanted a secure communications transceiver (SAT comm) and radar warning receiver system mounted on each ship, including all our helicopters, which drew nothing but wails and head shaking.

"Can't get there from here, General," one engineering officer said. "We'll have to do a radiation pattern study to find out where to place the antennas, and God knows what EMI [electromagnetic interference] problems we'll run into with the black boxes."

I sat there grinding my teeth in silence, mastering the moment, and then said, "You all know where the Desert One force got its enemy radar detectors?" Blank stares. "From Radio Shack. They used goddamn retail fuzz-busters! Right now, I'm pulling our best EW [electronic warfare] systems off the F-16 production line so that you guys can have them. Rivet the son-of-a-bitch to the fuselage and if it doesn't work, find another place to put it until you get it right. Any other questions?"

I later found out that, since the end of the Vietnam war, the conventionalists in the Air Force had held funding for Hurlburt to a minimum. What they got for their lack of investment was a unit that was being allowed to gather rust on its equipment and moss around its feet. Instead of being number one in the Pentagon arsenal—a valuable asset that could be taken off the shelf, combat-ready, when it was needed—it had become obsolete, like a gun everyone was afraid to touch and so ignored until nobody remembered how to use it. This was a tangible symptom of the post-Vietnam syndrome.

While lamenting the depths to which my old unit had sunk, I went on to inspect the Army's first operational company of Blackhawks (the only 20 the Army had), which we promptly transferred, along with some supporting

CH-47C Chinooks, from the 101st Airmobile to the JTF. What I found, fortunately, was enough to make an old West Pointer's heart leap for joy.

The Blackhawk was a superb helicopter, built for battle and with plenty of power. The birds were clean and well maintained, and their crews were proud and on their toes. Unlike his Air Force counterpart, the Army commander (a Colonel Allen, now a general) was ready to try anything and seemed happy to be getting a shot at combat. I wanted to clone him and send a copy to all my other units.

All in all, we assembled almost 4,000 troops and more than a hundred aircraft of all types. The Desert One force went to war with eight helicopters; we had 95. We used everything from the H-53s (PAVE LOW and "slicks," or "vanilla" birds, which had no special equipment) to the tiny Hughes 500, which we discovered could carry several fully armed Delta Force troopers (although some guys had to cling to a special outside platform: no great shakes in summer, but I wouldn't want to try it in winter).

The basic plan that evolved was to seize Mehrabad Airport in Tehran using Airborne Rangers and, once the runways were secured, land jet transports—C-141s, C-130s, and C-5s—carrying the assault helicopters. The attack helos would then be run out (already fueled and fully armed), and readied for flight while the pilots strapped in and prepared to crank up. Our goal was to have them on their way to the various hostage holding areas within two minutes of the time the transport's loading ramp hit the tarmac.

Overhead (and at two other major airfields where Iranian fighters were based), AC-130 gunships would orbit, ready to blast any Iranian warplanes (their F-4s were our biggest worry) that tried to taxi or take off. Assuming Murphy's law would be operative, as always, I had a "Phantom CAP" of four F-14s flying overhead with two long-range Phoenix air-to-air missiles each—a match for any squadron of less sophisticated fighters that might be dispatched into the area. This precaution forced us to refit our KC-135 aerial tankers for probe-and-drogue refueling, since the Navy doesn't use the Air Force's rigid boom method. Little details with big operational ramifications like these can drive you crazy in a closely timed, covert operation. You hope like hell that you've at least thought of the ones that can hurt you most and pray that the rest show up during training and dress rehearsals.

The actual grunt work would be done by two Ranger battalions (the 1st and 2nd of the 75th) with well over 700 trigger pullers each, plus Delta Force, as well as several other special ops units whose identities remain secret to this day. It was a convention of the elite's elite, and woe betide any Iranian who got in their way.

Besides assembling the hardware and personnel, Vaught and I went to work on our operations and planning staff.

For director of operations, I recruited Colonel Bob Dutton, a fine officer and A-26 pilot with whom I had served in Vietnam and Iran. Our staff would comprise senior officers from the Army Rangers, Delta Force, Special Forces, and one chief each for logistics, intelligence, and communications.

We also added a function called "cover and deception" (C&D), which Desert One lacked. C&D is widely used in the CIA but little known in the Pentagon. Just as the name implies, C&D's prime function is to keep an operation under wraps during the assembly and training stages and to ensure that the enemy gets no inkling of the developing plan's timing or intentions. Given the size of our force, the scope of our mission, and the fact that the enemy had already been spooked by one failed attempt, I gave C&D as high a priority as any other staff function. No order went out of our shop to the operational units without being cleared by these guys: two majors who were absolutely fabulous at their jobs, diligent and creative. Their task was to come up with a plausible cover story for any contingency and, when necessary, manufacture evidence to support it. We even set up our own communication system independent of the Pentagon's DCS (defense communication system), which controls the flow of secure military information worldwide.

Without going further, you can see that we already violated the first finding of the Holloway board, which targeted a preoccupation with security as the cause of Desert One's poor coordination and planning. I agree that the previous attempt's planning may have been poor and training inadequate, but that had nothing to do with security. In that raid, surprise was everything; in our raid, it would be even more important. Besides, security is like pregnancy. There's no such thing as keeping a secret "just a little bit"; your operation either is secure or it isn't.

We held our first get-acquainted session with this staff, and things went well—with one exception. Vague (and in some cases, very specific) criticism of Delta Force had already surfaced from my personal investigation of Desert One, although little was forthcoming in that regard from the Holloway board. The SecDef's approach was to try it again with many of the same cast of characters. This idea had never struck me as wise, and after this first meeting, I believed it was absolutely the wrong thing to do.

After introducing me as his right-hand man and the guy everyone would have to deal with in matters related to air, General Vaught handed the meeting over to me. I explained that, because I hadn't had time to study every officer's 201 file the way I'd like, I wanted to go around the table and have each man give me a brief summary of his service record. This proceeded apace until I came to Colonel Charlie Beckwith, Delta Force commander. His expression made it plain he thought the whole procedure a waste of time, especially for him.

After giving me a cursory review of his training and experience, Beckwith said, "I spent two years in Vietnam, all in Special Forces, then went to school with the SAS in England. I spent a lot of time with special ops in Vietnam,

General Secord, but I don't remember running into you. Would you mind telling me what you did out there?"

Even asked in a conversational tone, the question would've been impertinent. The way he asked it, though, was positively insubordinate.

"Well, Colonel," I said, feeling the heat rise in my cheeks, "I started in combat operations there in 1962 and was involved directly or indirectly with Laos and Vietnam until the very end—but I never once ran across *you* over there. Where were you all that time?"

Beckwith shifted uneasily and I marked him right then as a guy to keep my eye on.

After the meeting, Jim Vaught tried to smooth things over.

"Don't let old Charlie get to you, Dick. He just likes to get a rise out of the senior officers—you know, a kind of rite of initiation. The Army chief of staff thinks he walks on water, so do me a favor and cut him a little slack, won't you?"

I replied that sure, I'd give him as much slack as I'd give anyone who already had two strikes against him. I said I'd wait and see how things went during the Delta Force inspection I would be making in a couple of days.

When I arrived at Fort Bragg, Beckwith gave me the usual VIP briefing and then walked me through the grounds, visiting a small-arms firing table and his "shooting house"—the live-fire mockup of a terrorist hideout. On an individual basis, at least, the Delta Force soldier was probably the best I'd ever seen.

Toward the end of my tour I said, "I notice a lot of your men—the junior officers and sergeants—call you Charlie."

"Yeah," he said, "we're pretty informal around here—lots of camaraderie. Good for morale."

"I see." After thinking about his response a moment, I probed deeper into the leadership question. "You know, a lot of guys were surprised that, on the Desert One raid, you didn't press on with four choppers."

Beckwith shrugged. "The op plan showed we needed five."

The more I asked, the more this seemed to be the party line: "It wasn't in the plan." As a guy who had seen my share of combat—the vicissitudes of battle and the fog of war, as well as plain bad luck—I knew that the plan was everything and it was nothing. Often, success comes down to the judgment of the commander in the field; and in the Desert One force, that all-important piece of equipment just wasn't in the kit. Beckwith may have been a fine training officer (his crackerjack individual troops were a testament to that), but he ran his show more like a sergeant major than a commanding colonel. Camaraderie is no substitute for discipline once the lead starts flying. Without it, even a well-tuned, high-horsepower machine like Delta Force would only spin its wheels in combat. In my opinion, Charlie Beckwith's time to go had come, and that's what I told General Vaught.

Within a month, he had been reassigned.

The raw materials of the raid—the men, materiel, and leaders—were things I could handle. What worried me more were the yawning gaps in our knowledge about the Iranians and the location of our hostages.

We had four basic sources of information in this regard: the CIA (which was terrible); the field operations group, or FOG, which was our pathfinder team headed by an Army colonel (they had good language and intelligence skills, but not much to do until they got in country); G2 military intelligence headed by Lieutenant Colonel Rod Lenahan, a very smart operator who turned out to be a jewel and a still-classified, highly reliable team which was excellent. In this group I also included General Vaught's aide, Tom Seaman, a jack-of-all-trades whose expediting and scrounging skills really accelerated our combat-readiness. I hated to go anywhere without him because he kept people honest and got things done. Our JTF-NSC liaison man was William Odom.

In May, I got word from our intelligence staff that the CIA had lost track of the hostages. Since Desert One, the kidnappers had been playing a shell game with the hostages, breaking them up and moving them from site to site, but this had not been a particularly big problem. Now, suddenly, it was.

I made an appointment in Washington with Stansfield Turner's deputy director of operations, John McMahon (later, deputy director of the CIA under Casey) and took Tom Seaman along as my witness. McMahon had his own deputy with him, and I could tell immediately from their rather tense demeanor that something terrible had happened.

McMahon told us in terse, ascerbic terms that the CIA had simply lost much of its ground intelligence capability in Tehran. No further information was available about the hostages' latest moves.

"This is appalling," I said; I found no way to sugarcoat my reaction. "It's unsatisfactory."

"Well, General," McMahon asked, "what would you have us do?"

I took a long breath. "Well, first of all, I'm not here to lay blame. I spent several years detailed to this agency and I'm one of its biggest boosters. But the fact is, we're not exactly dealing with the Kremlin. Tehran's still a fairly open place, even after the revolution. What I want is for you to review every NOC [nonofficial cover] operative in the world and insert a few of the better ones to find out what the hell's going on over there. I want to know who's sleeping with who and who's got the Swiss bank accounts. I want pathfinders put on the ground *now*, and I want a supergrade CIA officer with combat experience assigned as our personal liaison with the Agency until this thing is over."

McMahon smiled. "Sounds like you have somebody in mind."

"No, I don't. That's up to you."

It was not a cordial meeting, and McMahon knew full well I was prepared to buck this thing past Turner to Brown and the President.

The next day, May 1, Rudy Enders, a 50-ish marathoner and CIA GS-16 with plenty of ground-ops experience, reported for duty. McMahon was moving. The CIA was back in the game.

The task I gave our intelligence crew was simple. The Carter administration had eviscerated our on-the-ground human intelligence network just about everywhere in the world. Our satellite coverage of Iran was spotty. This was our chance to begin reconstructing what we should never have torn down in the first place. I told Enders his top priority was getting his wall-to-wall intelligence operatives, and then our pathfinders, inside Iran. When the hostages were located and those locations verified, I wanted on-scene beacons, IR (infrared) panels, reception committees, eyes-on coverage of the landing zones—the works—set up to greet us. I knew some of this was wishful thinking, but if we got only half of what we asked for, our chance of success would easily double. To my great satisfaction (and mild surprise), this table thumping launched six months of what was probably the most intensive and focused U.S. intelligence-collection effort in modern history.

Although the basic plan (airport seizure, multiple helicopter sorties and rescues, return and extraction) was set, we had of necessity *twelve* operational scenarios for the rescue and at least *five* possible locations where the hostages might be kept. This was to be the Carnegie Hall of raids, and getting there meant practice, practice, practice. Vaught and I decided right away that the Mehrabad assault would require a full dress rehearsal, no matter what combinations and permutations might arise after that, so the search was on for a suitable location—a more difficult task than it might appear. We required a site with not only a similar density altitude and physical appearance to Mehrabad, but one that could be screened from outside eyes.

The best candidate was Reese AFB in Lubbock, the same base where the Shah's son had trained, although he (and my old friend Charlie Bishop) were long gone by this time. The runway and taxiway configurations were almost identical to those at Mehrabad, and as an ATC base in the middle of nowhere, it would be free of civilians (at least on weekends) and had a base perimeter that was easily sealed.

Raid rehearsals can't be halfway. You do as much as you have time and resources for because experience shows that little, unexpected things can really cause you trouble. Consequently, our "raid" on Reese was conducted under full wartime conditions: blacked-out runway, no lights on the aircraft or on the ground, soldiers firing blank ammunition with staged resistance—"war games" with as high an adrenaline factor as we could create.

The first rehearsal was not a success. Not only did we run into a lot of unanticipated mechanical problems, but, in the middle of the night with motorcycles racing, trucks roaring, helicopters screaming in and out, and gunfire rattling every which way, we were noisier than hell. This would be a problem in the actual raid, but in Lubbock, Texas, it was a disaster. We hadn't been on the ground 10 minutes when the Reese switchboard lit up with phone calls from local citizens, police, and media. Here's where our C&D team really earned their pay.

"Not only do we have to explain this," I told them, "but we've got to do it in a way that kills their curiosity. In other words, what's the most obvious, least intriguing, and most believable story they could hear?"

My majors thought for a moment, and then one of them joked, "Why don't we tell them it's the Texas National Guard on maneuvers? Everybody knows how screwed up *they* are!"

We had a good laugh in the spirit of interbranch rivalry, but the more we thought about it, the better the idea sounded. The team got on the horn to the Guard Bureau in Washington. Asking one of your own units to take the rap as a bunch of yahoos couldn't have been easy, but the Minutemen understood our emergency, bless 'em, and got right with the program.

"Don't say any more," the local Guard commander replied after receiving our cryptic request through channels. "Whatever you want, you got it!"

And so the "Battle of Reese AFB" became a minor footnote in Guard history (as well as a monumental PR headache), but the story did the job. Security held, and a lot of important training got accomplished.


After a couple of weeks of additional rehearsals at this and other locations, I tagged along on a practice mission being staged from an old World War II–era facility high in the Rockies. I hitchhiked in on one of the Army Blackhawks that, much to the pilot's consternation, aborted because of a bad APU (auxiliary power unit). It was an inauspicious beginning to a day that would only get worse.

After the exercise, I called all the helicopter pilots together into a hangar and gave them a little speech. It was the first time they'd all been together, and I felt I owed them at least a cursory explanation about what was going on and what would be expected of them. Since they had by now been reassigned PCS the new joint task force, I also wanted to give them a look at the sorry SOB who had made their lives miserable and answer any of their questions that I could.

The session started well enough. I talked to them about the importance of long-duration, all-weather night flying to the mission and the necessity of keeping formation integrity, no matter what. Although they knew our task force had something to do with a hostage rescue in Iran, I told them that our main concern was injecting a large force on top of the enemy with total surprise. That's why security was tight and Air Force OSI and Army counterintelligence was watching them like hawks, monitoring phone calls and even too much loud talk in local bars. With a little luck, though, it wouldn't last much longer.

The pilots seemed well motivated, but outside, after the session, the colonel who was Hurlburt's assistant director of operations approached me with a number of his compatriots. With a long face he said, "General, I know what you're saying, but you don't understand. You just can't fly these helicopters in tight formation like jet fighters, especially in large numbers. It's just not safe. Now, if you ask me—"

I glanced at his buddies—all pilots or staff officers. Some looked sympathetic, others disgruntled. All looked unhappy.

"Colonel," I interrupted him, "will you come on over to my office?" I motioned toward an old shack.

When the others were out of earshot, I said, "Colonel, you are relieved. Report back to your wing commander for reassignment out of this operation."

I walked away with the poor guy blinking in disbelief. I went straight to the makeshift command post and sent a direct order for the special ops wing commander to fly up to the site immediately. Early the next morning he reported in a military manner. I gave his salute a perfunctory return.

"As an old Hurlburt alumnus," I said, "I've been watching your unit closely, Colonel. Frankly, I'm not impressed. You've got no mobility, your kits aren't ready, and your GIs look like shit. The Blackhawks fly rings around your people—the goddamn *Army* puts you to shame! When will you people understand that this is serious business? You guys couldn't fight your way into Cincinnati Municipal, let alone a heavily defended airport halfway around the world! I'm ashamed I used to be in this unit. Dismissed."

After he left, I phoned General Vaught.

"I just reviewed the Hurlburt wing CO's record, General. Did you know the wing commander is a *maintenance* officer? He's never seen a day of combat in his life. I can't use him."

Two weeks later, the special ops wing had a new commander, and a new staff. The C-130 assault landing training—in the dark, in close formation, on parallel runways—went ahead as scheduled. To everyone's surprise and considerable pride, they *were* able to land in close trail under those conditions. And the helicopters could indeed fly in tight formation. Not like the Thunderbirds, perhaps, but close enough to do the job.

In July, world events again overtook us, and I thought, with some hope, that the exercise might become academic. After being turned out of six countries, including the United States, the last Shah of Iran finally joined his fabled ancestors, and died in Egypt. Since the Shah's New York visit triggered the embassy storming in the first place, everyone thought that the remaining 52 hostages might be released; but our hopes were short-lived. A spokesman for the Ayatollah said the demise of his arch rival would have no effect on hostage "policy." Even in Tehran, the captives were becoming an institution.

Near the middle of August, after 10 major exercises, the consensus of our staff was that the JTF was combat-ready. We passed the word upstairs to Secretary Brown and Chairman Jones. All we needed now was a fix on the hostages and we would be on our way. The mullahs would never know what hit them.

In early October, the CIA Near East division chief called Rudy Enders on our secure phone. "We found them!" he said.

We immediately scheduled a briefing between the CIA man (and his assistant) and myself, General Vaught, Bob Dutton, and Colonel Lenahan, our chief of intelligence.

"We've found them," the CIA man repeated triumphantly for all our benefits. "Except for the three individuals still kept in Khomeini's Foreign Ministry, who were never moved, the hostages have been relocated at the embassy compound and at a villa in northern Tehran."

He showed us hand-held snapshots of the villa and added that those returned to the embassy were being kept not in an old embassy building, as before, but in the chancellery and ambassador's residence.

I looked at the wary faces on the JTF side of the table and saw we were all thinking the same thing. It was a pretty story, but it lacked even *one shred* of corroborating evidence from any other source.

We asked where the CIA had obtained this information, particularly since it didn't match anything we had learned through other channels.

"We can't reveal our sources; you gentlemen know that," the CIA's Near East Chief replied.

"Well, *you* know we can't afford to launch and come up with a dry hole," I said.

"Dry hole?" he shook his head. "I doubt it."

"Let me put it this way," I continued. "Suppose we blast our way into Tehran and inflict a lot of casualties—and I assure you, there *will* be heavy enemy casualties—and come back with only the three guys from the Foreign Ministry? Aside from the two generals you see here twisting in the wind on flagpoles outside the Pentagon, what else do you think would happen? What would happen to the hostages we *didn't* get?"

He didn't answer.

After a brief caucus, General Vaught agreed that without a sources-and-methods analysis of the CIA report, he had no choice but to take the information to General Jones and, through him, to the White House. Although we'd recommend waiting for confirmation, if the commander in chief said *go* based on the CIA report alone, of course, we'd go.

The CIA guys put their photos away, and the briefing was over.

After they left, I said to our group, "Remember Mr. Archimedes? These guys must've been soaking their heads in the same bathwater: 'Eureka—we've found them!' "

Nervous laughter went around the table, and from that moment on, the episode was referred to as the "Eureka briefing," although the situation was far from funny. The JTF was on a razor's edge: Morale was high, the equipment was ready, and we were raring to go. All we needed was for somebody in authority to push the alarm bell and show us the fire that went with the smoke, and we'd be on our way.

Chairman Jones referred our report on the Eureka briefing to the White House, where Zbigniew Brzezinski, President Carter's National Security Advisor, undoubtedly gave it serious attention. The next day, word came back down the chain of command:

"The CIA can't provide their bona fides. The JTF will continue to stand by."

The Eureka briefing and its aftermath effectively killed any chance of rescuing the hostages before the Iranians achieved their personal and political revenge against Jimmy Carter. We stayed on alert for another month, hoping new information would break (or the old information would be confirmed), but it never happened. To make matters worse, the Iran-Iraq war broke out after 10 months of skirmishing over the Shatt Al-Arab waterway, further complicating our calculations for any raid.

Fortunately, or unfortunately, it never came to that. After Carter's defeat in the November election, everyone expected a softening of the Iranian position, and Chairman Jones ordered us to stand down from alert.

On January 20, 1981, minutes after Ronald Reagan was sworn in as President of the United States, and after 444 days of captivity, the 52 hostages were released. A few days after that, the JCS ordered the major units of the JTF disbanded and returned to their parent organizations. The residual part, and a good deal of its doctrinal and tactical legacy, would be retained as a permanent antiterrorist outfit.

I expected to feel the usual mixed emotions of an aborted mission—a combination of relief and frustration—but I didn't. I knew we could do the job. No force like this had ever been assembled or was so well trained and equipped for its mission. Mostly, I felt just relieved. No more people on either side were going to be killed or endangered over this one, and I was glad about that. My only disappointment came from missing our chance to correct the public's view of the military, which was at its lowest ebb since the Vietnam war. But that was the luck of the draw. Architects seldom live in the buildings they create. As quick as I could, I hung up my deputy CO's hat and went back to my Everest-sized in-basket at International Programs.

As it turned out, the returned hostages confirmed that the information in the CIA's Eureka briefing was false, and probably planted by the Iranians. Had we followed it, our troops would not only have come up empty-handed, but might have flown into a trap.

The basic JTF infrastructure—namely the staff organization we had built—became the core counterterrorist capability now attached to the U.S. Special Operations Command in Tampa, Florida. Most of the personnel changes we made and tactical innovations we developed became permanent. The specially equipped MC-130s, AC-130s, and long-range helicopters we dragooned from various units would provide a superior surgical attack capability for any future task force. The technology, techniques, and tactics we developed during that long summer in 1980—and many of the same crew members—were employed in the clockwork airfield seizures in Grenada in late 1983, and in Panama in 1989. In addition, special operations units and some of the gear we mandated for use, such as night-vision goggles, were widely employed throughout operations Desert Shield and Desert Storm in Kuwait and Iraq. Other hands may have been at the throttle, but our invention finally got off the ground.

Gary Sich, a Carter NSC staffer, and others have speculated widely about an "October Surprise"—whether or not Reagan campaign representatives such as Bill Casey, Reagan's campaign manager, and vice presidential candidate George Bush cut a deal with Iranian officials to hold the hostages until after the 1980 presidential election. Some of these investigators point to the mysterious "disappearance" of the hostages during the fall (and thus our inability to get a green light for the JTF raid) as one more bit of evidence supporting this conclusion. Given my experience as Deputy Commander of the Joint Task Force, however, that conclusion just doesn't wash.

First, from the time Chairman Jones tasked General Vaught and me to build the JTF in April—and certainly after my first meeting with McMahon and the CIA in May—every operative in the Western intelligence community was focused on Europe and Iran. If anything so complex and difficult to arrange as a high-level meeting of politicians on both sides had been attempted, let alone carried off, we would've known about it. The fact is, we received no inkling, even the indirect sort that must be pieced together retroactively, that any such meetings were ever discussed, or arranged.

Second, few people keep secrets more poorly than Iranian officials. They'll talk to anybody about anything—and go on for hours. Even under the mullahs, what and who you know is a badge of status, and among officials in that part of the world, personal status is everything. The biggest problem we had in monitoring unsecured Iranian telephone communication was not finding enough secrets, but sifting through all the "secrets" we had. If any Iranian officials of requisite stature had been in contact with the movers and shakers of the "Great Satan," especially that soon after the revolution, we would've known about it. As subsequent history in Lebanon as well as President Reagan's Iran Initiative shows, it is far simpler for a tightly knit band of low-level radicals to keep hostage whereabouts secret than it is for their "supervising officials" to keep the supporting political machinery under wraps.

Third, as anyone familiar with the Iran Initiative knows, we had enormous trouble finding proper opposite numbers to deal with inside the Iranian government even six years later. Had there been any preelection contact between Bill Casey or George Bush and a responsible mullah, the two or three years the Israelis, Ollie North, Bud McFarlane—and later, me—painfully spent probing for a reliable channel in the Iranian government would have been unnecessary. As appealing as the October Surprise sounds to conspiracy buffs, it just doesn't fit the facts.

The painful truth is that a massive failure of on-site, ground-level human intelligence tuned to the physical movements of the hostages prevented the second rescue attempt, not Republican skulduggery or cleverness by Iran's ruling elite. This is the gist of the message I wrote in a memorandum to Secretary of Defense Caspar Weinberger in 1982 in order to try to increase pressure on the CIA to improve our HUMINT (human intelligence gathering) in Iran.

My suggestion—my plea, in fact—was that the U.S. launch a two-pronged intelligence and bridge-building "offensive" into Iran after the hostages were returned. One initiative would have been the restoration of classic HUMINT resources in that country. The other was a government-backed program of commercial contacts such as we used during my years with the MAAG in Tehran, an approach whose value has been proven time and again in many nations.

Our first objective should have been to collect sufficient information about the new, postrevolutionary players and their organizations and leadership styles to rebuild solid relationships based on meaningful quid pro quos within the Iranian hierarchy. The Israelis worked hard during and after the revolution to keep their contacts open. We supported them in this and should've done some of the same ourselves.

If we had, a lot of painful history that was about to unfold might very well have been avoided.

# – 10 –

# Where No GI Has Gone Before

After President Reagan's inauguration, it was as if Iran had fallen off the edge of the world—my 1963–64 and 1965 Iranian combat tours, assignment as Air Force MAAG chief in Tehran, and stint as deputy commander of the JTF all nothing more than vivid dreams. I went back almost immediately to the bureaucratic trenches at the Pentagon. It was as if I had never left.

My deputy director, Colonel Ed O'Donnell, did a great job keeping our key projects afloat during my absence. However, my tour at Air Force International Programs was rapidly running out. I began to fantasize about that most magical moment in any brass hat's career: when I'd see the Pentagon in my rearview mirror for the last time. If I'd been smart, I'd have started trolling then for a good operational command in Europe or the Far East. I had almost forgotten what military commanders did for a living, and the JTF reminded me of all those things I had joined the service to accomplish. Battling the parochial interests of congressmen and contractors and arguing with bean counters about the price of rivets hadn't been among them.

But that idyllic capstone to my career was not to be. In retrospect, what happened next was as big a turning point in my life as my first unconventional assignment, Jungle Jim.

Early in 1980, Secretary of Defense Harold Brown met with the Prince Sultan of Saudi Arabia and agreed in principle for the U.S. to sell airborne warning and control system (AWACS) airplanes to the Saudis. To understand the significance of this decision and the absolute hurricane of protest it would create in Washington and Tel Aviv, one must appreciate the significance of AWACS in modern war, as well as the pivotal changes going on in the Middle East at the time.

166

In the opinion of many experts, AWACS has changed the nature of aerial warfare as much as the forward-firing machine gun or jet engine. It's one of those nonglamorous, behind-the-scenes syntheses of technologies that, like the telephone, we now take for granted and can't imagine ever having to do without.

Since the dawn of organized warfare, commanders have always striven to "take the high ground." From the top of a hill, you can see the enemy's evolutions while concealing your own. A millenium later, this tactical "high ground" has become the airspace above the theater. A suitably equipped AWACS aircraft can orchestrate a massive air or combined air-ground operation with an efficiency and effectiveness undreamed of in prior wars.

Naturally, the Israelis feared the effect AWACS could have in the hands of potential Arab enemies. Word that the U.S. was even considering such a sale to Saudi Arabia would hit Tel Aviv like a miniature Pearl Harbor. Why, the Israelis would wonder, would Uncle Sam do such a thing to its "oldest and best" ally in the region?

There were several good reasons for the sale—even from the Israeli perspective.

In the early 1980s, the Middle East was undergoing two fundamental changes. First, the Camp David accords between President Carter, Anwar Sadat, and Menachem Begin (wherein Egypt and Israel basically ended their generation-long war) showed that perpetual conflict was not inevitable in the region.

The second fundamental change was the loss of Iran as a U.S. ally and its corollary event, the Iran-Iraq war. Before the revolution, Israel and Iran sat like two great pro-America bookends at either end of a contained "Arab nation." Without Iran, the U.S. position in the Near East had become dangerously lopsided. Israel had survived (and could survive) as an island in a hostile Arab sea only so long as those Arab states did not act effectively in concert against her. America's goal, one that several administrations felt was in Israel's best interest, too, was to build a "surrogate Iran" by improving relations with select Arab states. Since the idea of a united "Arab nation" is more myth than reality, this strategy would actually *stabilize* the region and create a counterbalance to Arab radicalism.

The AWACS sale was the first and most highly visible symbol of a new era in America's Near East policy. Some Israelis, however, saw it as a treacherous betrayal of the special relationship their country had cultivated with America since the foundation of the Jewish state. Both sides decided early that the AWACS issue was one "we just can't lose."

I got involved with AWACS early on under the Carter administration, which initiated the sale. Carter wanted to make progress in the $7 billion sale while keeping it from the public, at least until after the 1980 election. Carter's concern (and it was a valid one, in my view) was not so much

American grass-roots opposition to the sale, which never materialized, but the wrath of AIPAC—the American-Israel Public Affairs Committee, the umbrella group for a variety of pro-Israeli lobbies that could exert enormous pressure on the executive and legislative branches whenever the U.S. seemed likely to adopt policies perceived as being contrary to Israel's self-interest.

My assignment was to meet with Prince Bandar (then Saudi air attaché, later ambassador to the U.S.) to work out some language for Secretary of Defense Harold Brown to use in a formal statement intended to (a) reassure the Saudis that the deal was under way, while (b) keeping Congress and the Israeli lobby off Carter's back. General Jones chose me not only because I was in charge of Air Force international programs, but also because I had a good reputation in the Middle East, knew Prince Bandar fairly well already, and had a good sense of the courtly toe-dancing that goes into "pre-wiring" such agreements with Arab countries.

To the Saudis (and most Arab nations), indirect communication is a fine art, and mastering it is half the battle. If a typical blunt, impatient American can track along with them through all the posturing that goes into even the smallest decision, that person will likely be accepted into the club. The purpose of such gavotting is to sort out personality differences and character flaws early in the game rather than trying to resolve conflicts after the fact, and often in court. If you've got the patience, it isn't such a bad system.

Bandar was recuperating from back surgery at his Western-style, elegantly furnished villa on Lake Leman, Geneva, Switzerland. I took Major General James Ahmann with me to meet Bandar for exactly the same reasons General Dave Jones picked me: He was personally known and respected by the Saudis and for a much longer time than I had been. Our task, which Bandar fully appreciated, was to find a way to tell the Saudis of our intention to sell the AWACS to them without publicly announcing that intention. It was a Byzantine court puzzle tailor-made for a Saudi prince, and I think he enjoyed the two days of intense discussion. A typical session would go like this:

Jim and I would propose some language for a statement from Harold Brown, we'd all discuss its ramifications, and Bandar would relay it by phone to his father, Prince Sultan, in Saudi Arabia. After discussing it up one side and down the other, they would come back to us with all kinds of problems and concerns, nuances and complications. We would listen intently and nod knowingly. Jim and I would then come up with another approach, run it by General Jones on a secure telephone, and then start the minuet all over again.

The discussions with Bandar were held in very plain, colloquial English, not the stilted, formalistic language of the State Department (although that is the dialect in which our final statement would have to appear). Bandar is a jet pilot and, I think, what most Americans would call "a regular guy." He has a great sense of humor and, while recognizing the foibles of both cultures, remains true to his own traditions and stays respectful of ours. For example, one of us would suggest a phrase, another would say, "Hell, no—we can't say that!" and the third would ask, "Why not? Old so-and-so said it just before they fired him!" We'd all laugh like hell, and then go around again.

After two days, we finally came up something pretty close to this:

"The President has this under active consideration and is favorably inclined, but no final decision can be made at this time."

The agreed-upon meaning, however, was this:

"America will sell you the AWACS immediately after the election. If the Carter administration loses the election, it will do its absolute best to persuade the new administration to honor our agreement."

Naturally, this injected a large dose of personal trust into the proceedings, which put Ahmann, Jones, and myself on the spot. If Carter lost and the Reagan administration decided it didn't want to dodge the kind of mud Congress was bound to throw at it over the issue, the deal would've died in the cradle, along with our personal credibility with our Arab counterparts. In such circumstances, it's doubtful that U.S. overtures to the key Arab states in the area would've borne much fruit over the next few years.

Reagan, of course, won the election; and to the new administration's credit, it honored Harold Brown's commitment. I don't know how much effort Carter, Brown, and Brzezinski put into selling the AWACS deal to the incoming Reagan crew, including Al Haig, his new Secretary of State, but it may have been considerable.

Haig was sensitive to Israeli reaction, and I dealt with him several times in July 1981 while I negotiated the "rules of engagement" with the Saudis for their use of the AWACS. Haig was at the peak of his political career now, but the wear and tear was showing. We were on opposing sides of many issues regarding AWACS, which didn't bother me, but he was often truculent—needlessly agitated—a characteristic that was only aggravated by the yes-men on his staff. He chain-smoked cigarettes and frankly, having known him since the early 1950s, I was worried about his health and wondered whether he was still the same self-assured, confident leader we thought Reagan had selected. Just over a year later, on June 25, 1982, Haig would resign on "policy differences" with the President, his remarkable career at an end.

When you reflect on all the legislative battles that awaited the ambitious Reagan agenda (massive cuts to well-entrenched social programs; the biggest military buildup since the 1950s; deregulation of dozens of American industries), the fact that they would risk yet another bruising fight on an issue of strategic, but less visible, concern, is a credit, I believe, to the institution of the Presidency—Democratic and Republican alike. The continuity of American leadership and the integrity of its commitments abroad took precedence over what must've been an almost overpowering political urge to simply look the other way.

Now, however, it was time to pay the price for that noble commitment.

About the time of Reagan's inauguration in 1981, General Lew Allen, Air Force chief of staff, told me that because of my familiarity with AWACS, I was being transferred to the Office of the Secretary of Defense, now led by Caspar Weinberger. We had already begun building the briefing books and sorting out the technical arguments needed to reassure the willing and persuade the doubtful, so my deeper association with AWACS, even on a temporary basis, was not totally unexpected. What did surprise me, though, was the post itself; I was to be acting deputy assistant secretary of defense for Near East, Africa, and South Asia—some of the most incandescent hot spots in the world. More significant from a career perspective, it was a political appointment that had never before been held by an active-duty military officer. (America is one of the only nations on earth that penalizes its generals by prohibiting them from holding certain political offices. While we don't want an active-duty general as Secretary of Defense, military officers should be considered for appointments as defense assistants and deputies because they're often the most qualified and experienced people for the job.) Oddly enough, this singular show of confidence in my abilities put me in something of a career quandary.

According to the "rules," I was due (if not overdue) for an operational assignment. The JTF assignment didn't really count since it was still top secret and was never launched. If I didn't get back into the field quickly, I'd be tagged (if not tarred) as a "Pentagon general." I got things done in my bureaucratic jobs because I had a solid sense of what was needed in the field, but I never liked politicking for its own sake, although a lot of senior officers did. Part of me wanted to leave the AWACS political battle to those horses who liked to draw that wagon, while the other part worried that if I didn't accept the yoke, who would? The other candidate for the job, a civilian named Noel Koch, was strongly backed by the pro-Israeli lobby—a group that had sworn to oppose the Arab AWACS concept. Frankly, I couldn't imagine an important program like this ever hatching if the foxes guarded the henhouse.

On the positive side, I had the opportunity now to blaze a new trail—to do what no military man had done before—and work directly and on a daily basis with some of the top policymakers of a new administration. My immediate boss would be Bing West, assistant secretary of defense for international security affairs. But on Arab-Israeli issues, I would report directly to Weinberger and his deputy, Frank Carlucci. It would be a job with enough new challenges to keep life interesting, even in the Pentagon, and carry enough horsepower to actually get things done. In the end, it was an opportunity that was just too big and too challenging to pass up.

In April 1981, the temporary assignment was made permanent, and I officially held two U.S. government commissions: one as a regular Air Force officer, the other as a political appointee.

Normally, a resolution like the AWACS sale to Saudi Arabia is shepherded through both houses of Congress in a series of time-honored steps. The first is a 20-day period of "informal notification" of intention to sell the major system. It consists mostly of schmoozing, wheedling, and cajoling politicians in order to find allies and isolate opponents; this is followed by 30 days of formal notification, required by the Arms Export Control Act, during which the all but scripted drama of "advice and consent" is played out in committee (in both the Senate and the House) for the benefit of constituents, lobbyists, and special interests. A lot of schmoozing goes on during hearings as well, and it includes the vote-counting process. If everything goes wrong despite your best efforts, and Congress disapproves the sale, the President can now veto the resolution, forcing Congressional opponents to muster the two-thirds vote needed to override the veto—a much more difficult task than obtaining a bare majority. In 1981, however, before the 1983 Supreme Court decision outlawing the so-called Congressional veto, this was not an option.

One of Reagan's amazing qualities as the "Great Communicator" was his ability to sway key votes in the House and Senate even when the committees and media coverage were stacked against him. This is even more astonishing when you consider that, except for a few years following the off-year election of 1982 when the Republicans gained a majority in the Senate, both houses were controlled by Democrats and the administration was regularly harassed by a media that was generally hostile to the Reagan ideology.

At the time of AWACS, however, Reagan's track record had yet to be established. The "Teflon President" still had plenty of cracks in his armor from the presidential campaign, and as one of the early legislative hot potatoes, AWACS would get very hot indeed.

The first (and possibly biggest) blunder the Reaganites (and especially Richard Allen, his articulate, telegenic national security advisor) made in those early months was to pick former Senator Jim Buckley, then undersecratary of state for security assistance, science, and technology, to lead the attack on the Hill. Buckley's heart was in the right place, but he didn't seem to pack the firepower for the mission.

After assembling the interagency team, Buckley announced his revolutionary approach to legislative liaison.

"The problem before has been a lack of consultation between the executive and legislative branches," he said, as if we were kids in a high school civics class. "That's why we get involved in these big Congressional floor fights. The solution is to approach Congress in a more collegial way."

We glanced at each other in astonishment. *Whose Congress is this guy talking about?*

"We're going to consult with *all* 100 Senators, plus their staffs, during the informal notification period," Buckley continued. "We're going to give them the whole story—all the background, all our data, all our reasons. They really want that. After the Senate, we'll consult with as many people in the House as we can before the vote."

In other words, our strategy was to tip our hand, lower our guard, and then give away our secrets—to pretend there was only minor opposition to the sale, which was obviously not the case. We accepted our marching orders, but most of us felt like lemmings headed over the cliff. We filed our notice and began to make the rounds of our "colleagues" in the Senate, as well as their staffers, and anybody else who Buckley thought might listen to us. After telling them everything we knew about the project (very little of which had to do with what they *really* wanted to know, namely, how they could vote for us and keep the Israeli lobby off their backs), we began to feel our wheels spinning in the slippery Potomac mud.

One factor Mr. Buckley had not foreseen was that as AWACS' opponents found more reasons to put us off and delay our progress, practical logistics problems began to surface. One was that many of the players changed after the elections, and we had whole new sets of officials and staffs to deal with—and with the massive Reagan agenda, AWACS was not their highest priority.

With insufficient progress (that is, lack of assured backers), Buckley wisely decided we couldn't afford to go to hearings. As a result, the 20-day "informal notification" period stretched from one month into two, and then three. Suddenly it was spring.

After wasting about four months on Buckley's ill-conceived "collegial approach," the President finally withdrew the notification (the only time I can recall such a thing happening) and declared a "cooling-off period"—a chance for both sides to collect their wits, votes, and energy for another try after Congress's August 1981 recess.

The main problem during this cooling-off period was that the longer we went without a vote, the more time the Israeli lobby had to spread its disinformation and distortions, and even to intimidate a few of those who balked at the party line. Just before we suspended our effort in the Senate, I was visited in my office by Thomas A. Dine, AIPAC's executive director.

He arrived for his appointment punctually and greeted me pleasantly. He began by explaining how technology like AWACS in Arab hands posed a major security threat to Israel, America's staunchest ally in the region, the Middle East's "only democracy." As he spoke, his tone got progessively darker. Finally, he said that when the American Jewry was informed of this breach of trust, a decisive rebuke would be dealt to the people involved. It would be a real political bloodbath, he promised. This was one contest Israel was just not prepared to lose.

He then offered me some personal advice. Given that he had heard good things about me and given that I was new at this game, he would give me a break. He explained how I would be crazy to get involved in such a bitter fight, how I should step off the playing field and leave the contest to the big boys. If I didn't, I'd wind up getting whipped and whipped bad.

From the way he said it, I realized he meant *me* personally. It was, in other words, a career decision.

I listened to Dine with my fingers tented patiently, doing my James Schlesinger impression, concealing my slow boil. When he finished, I leaned forward and said, "Mr. Dine, apparently you've been misinformed about me. I don't mind you making your case; in fact, I expect it; that's your job. But I don't like intimidation. I don't like to lose and I don't intend to lose this one. We don't have much more to talk about, do we?"

My relationship with AIPAC went downhill from there. I was prepared for a hard fight, but was I prepared for what might come after?

When Reagan's "cooling-off" period expired, the gloves came off on both sides. Dick Allen had resigned to avoid negative publicity over a flap about Japanese gratuities, and Buckley's role became less prominent and my responsibilities as Defense Department's team leader increased in anticipation of an October vote. I had by this time completed negotiations of a memorandum of understanding—still secret—with the Saudis that detailed the "rules of engagement" for using the Saudi AWACS: the sine qua non of the whole deal. Because of that, and because of the good personal rapport I was building with Secretary Weinberger, I was better able than most to coordinate Defense Department AWACS efforts with Congress.

I found Caspar Weinberger an easy man to work for, one of the best bosses I'd ever had. My early respect for him quickly expanded to admiration, owing mainly to his strong principles and willingness to stand behind them. This occasionally came out in public as the kind of lantern-jawed combativeness that eventually became his media trademark, but behind the scenes he was always kind and considerate, at least in his dealings with me.

Weinberger's personal commitment was important because our fight for Congressional support would be uphill all the way. Each and every vote was crucial, and we took none of them for granted. For example, all summer, the Congressional liaison groups in both the NSC (which included a Marine Corps major named Ollie North) and OSD held one key state's two senators in the "no" column. Nothing we said to either them or their staffs could shake them. One Friday night as the vote neared and we were all working our short lists, I called an old friend of mine from Command and Staff College who was now the commander of his state's Air National Guard.

"Dick, how the hell are you?" he answered my greeting.

"Not so good, I'm afraid. We've got word up here that your senators are going to let us down on the AWACS vote."

"*What?!*" I thought the poor guy had fallen through the floor. "You've got to be mistaken, General Secord. I'll guarantee you our senators would *never* vote against *our* President on such a high-priority matter!"

He then launched into one of the best pro-AWACS speeches I'd ever heard and I thought, *Dick—you've found your man*. I finally interrupted him and said, "Hey, I hope you're right. I can only go by what our people tell me."

After a short pause, he said, "Okay, Dick. I'll talk to you tomorrow."

The next morning, two Air Guard fighters landed at Andrews. A staff car bearing general's stars soon departed the base for my surburban home. After several hours' consultation with me and another day spent reflecting on the issues, my old friend visited the Senate office building early Monday morning. Around noon, I got a telephone call from Andrews' base operations.

"Dick—don't worry. You *were* misinformed about our senators' votes."

I didn't hear from the general again, but the NSC/OSD polltakers continued to carry at least one of his state's senators in the "no" column until the actual vote was cast. As with several other senators, we believed they were fully capable of changing their minds even as they stood up to vote. Vice President George Bush, the Senate's presiding officer, promised to be present in case he had to break a tie.

On October 28, 1981, the motion was presented and the vote was called. Both of my old friend's senators voted to support the President. AWACS passed, 52 to 48.

The downside of our AWACS victory, apart from bruised knuckles and a lot of used-up chits, was the unbelievable amount of time it took away from other necessary projects. For months, under almost the same conditions as the JTF sideshow the previous year, the central focus of my professional life had been on something other than what I was supposed to be doing. Talented deputies and resourceful staffers are a godsend under such conditions, but in my area of OSD responsibility—the Middle East, South Asia, and Africa—too much was at stake for me to really afford the time and energy AWACS demanded. In this region alone, for example, there were *nine wars* going on, many of which were heavily backed by Cuba or the Soviet Union. I also led numerous U.S. delegations to the Middle East to negotiate various bilateral military agreements, such as the U.S./Oman Access Accords, which turned out to be so useful in Desert Shield and Desert Storm.

Amid all this travail, one completely preventable war broke out despite our best efforts to stop it.

In May 1982, Israeli Defense Minister Ariel Sharon came to Washington to explain the "dire threats" to Israel that had suddenly materialized. Although it was never stated explicitly in his briefing, he was there to lay the groundwork for the Israeli Defense Force invasion of Lebanon less than one month later.

Sharon was a talented combat leader, a colorful character, and, I felt, an absolute demogogue. He was a divisional commander in the 1973 Arab-Israeli war and point man for the campaign against Egypt. His tanks actually threatened Cairo before hostilities ceased, making him a hero in Tel Aviv and self-professed scourge of the Arab world. He's a big-boned, bluff man with a commanding presence and booming voice, which he uses like artillery to shatter those who disagree with him—one of which happened to be me.

The "prelude to war" briefing was held in Weinberger's conference room, a long hall on the third floor of the Pentagon's E ring, sometimes used as a dining room. In attendance, besides Secretary Weinberger and his deputy, Frank Carlucci, were his deputy assistant secretary for the region (me), JCS Chairman General Jones, Bing West, the U.S. ambassador to Israel (Sam Lewis), and an assortment of note takers from within the Department. Sharon entered with his chart bearers and stood commandingly behind the small podium near the conference table. An aide put the first briefing board on the easel, and the show got started.

Sharon first reviewed recent terrorist threats to Israel, as well as threats perceived from nearby Arab states supporting those terrorists: so many "attacks by fire" against northern Israel; so many weapons of this or that type tracked from nation to nation, signaling a buildup; and so on. After only a few minutes it dawned on me that 90 percent of what Mr. Sharon was telling us was total bullshit, a figment of his imagination. I raised my hand.

"Excuse me, Mr. Sharon," I said, wondering why none of my bosses, who read the same intelligence reports I did, hadn't stopped the show before now. "I have a question. Your data ascribes to the Jordanians a number of modern tanks that, according to our intelligence, is approximately *five times* the total number of tanks of any sort they actually have. You state that the Saudis have cooperated with unnamed parties in reinforcing Iraq with 155 mm artillery, but Iraq doesn't operate 155s. You also say that you have traced a batch of captured M16 rifles to Saudi Arabia, but we traced those identical serial numbers and found them to originate with the Lebanese army. Besides, the Saudis don't even use M16s—they use G3s made in their own factories. Could you explain how Israeli intelligence came up with these estimates, particularly since Ambassador Lewis has already presented you with these other facts—"

"We don't need anyone to tell us how to deal with our ambassador!" Sharon blustered, red-faced. I glanced around the room. Every face was pale and slack-jawed, except for Weinberger's and Carlucci's, both of which looked ready to break into a smile. "And we don't need anyone to tell us how to conduct our diplomatic relations!"

Sharon drifted into a minor tirade on Israel's rights and prerogatives, ignoring the real issue, which was his specious evidence. When he figured his audience had forgotten the original question, he went back to his script. The episode seemed to me a microcosm of the relationship between our two governments during Sharon's administration: the fabrication and distortion of facts by Sharon that usually went uncontested by our highest officials.

Some of that reticence might be explained by diplomacy, but when war and peace are at stake, that rationale wears a little thin. I respected Weinberger, Carlucci, and General Jones a great deal, and felt it was my duty, as their regional expert, to put the facts on the table.

Accompanied by poor Sam Lewis—a great guy and Israeli cheerleader, but a man hard pressed to represent American interests in Tel Aviv in this environment—Sharon repeated his performance for Al Haig at the State Department. I'd like to think that Sharon amended or abbreviated some of his hyperbole, but I doubt it. The focus of the Haig session seemed to have been Israel's perceived need to create a "sterilized zone of security" along the northern frontier. I later investigated, formally and indepth, Sharon's claims about "attacks by fire" on the northern Galillee area. We discovered that these were utter and complete falsehoods. However, the U.S. never formally said "no" to Sharon's plan, so the Israelis took it to mean "yes."

On June 6, while world attention was otherwise focused on the British-Argentine war in the Falklands, now entering its third month, numerous Israeli divisions and brigades, arrayed in columns and preceded by armor, blitzed into Lebanon and drove all the way to East Beirut. On the way, they encountered, dispersed, and defeated in detail the Lebanese Armed Forces (LAF) and Syrian troops hastily assembled to meet them and scored some hundred-odd aerial victories without the loss of a single plane—although the cluster bombing of civilian "terrorists" in southern Lebanon was a clear violation of the U.S. Export Control Act governing the use of those weapons. We at the OSD strongly recommended sanctions against Israel because of this, but the request was quietly tabled and was mostly ignored by the media.

Sharon got his "zone of security" that conveniently took American eyes off the Gaza Strip, the Golan Heights, and other issues coming up for final resolution under the soon-to-expire deadlines of the 1979 Camp David agreement. Frankly, I believe Sharon's motive for invading Lebanon was to allow Israel to evade its commitments from the Camp David accords.

During the invasion, Israel captured a large cache of Soviet-bloc weapons (over 100 tons of arms and ammunition) that the IDF couldn't use. Following proper channels, the CIA asked whether I would approach Israel and see if at least some of the weapons could be obtained by the CIA for use in its various covert operations. The U.S. Army also expressed interest in the windfall, since their "OP For" (Opposition Forces) program pitted regular ground forces against special aggressor training units armed with realistic Soviet weapons, of which there was never an adequate supply.

These both seemed like reasonable requests, so I assigned a young civil servant on my staff, Richard Dudley, who had come over from the Defense Intelligence Agency, to contact Israeli Major General Mendy Meron, who was stationed in Washington, and inquire about transferring the weapons. Meron replied that Israel could not donate the weapons, but would sell them at a substantial price—several million dollars. This irritated me and other top U.S. officials greatly, and I told Meron personally that not only was his price too high, it showed a real lack of gratitude to the U.S. for its past aid and forbearance in the Lebanese invasion.

"Besides," I said, "as one military man to another, our need for them is much greater than yours."

To his credit, Meron seemed chagrined at his government's action, but there was nothing he could do about it at his level. The opportunity passed— at least for the moment.

As we learned in Vietnam and the Soviets learned in Afghanistan, nasty, undeclared wars tend to breed nasty, indefensible atrocities that eventually alienate even the most ardent patriots. After the massacres at the Lebanese towns of Sabra and Shatilla in 1982 in which over 100 Palestinians, including women and children, were killed by Lebanese militia that were supposed to have been restrained by Israeli troops, the world (and a substantial part of the Israeli population) said enough is enough. Sharon, halo tarnished, was forced to resign, and the U.S. stepped in to do what we could to clean up the mess left by our "best ally" in the Middle East.

As part of the Israeli shakeup, General Mendy Meron was promoted to Director General of the Ministry of Defense and transferred to Israel. One of his first official acts was to reverse the IDF's position on the captured Soviet weapons; he had them transferred, without cost or fanfare, into Richard Dudley's hands, where they were then distributed to the CIA and U.S. Army. This "back-door" arms conduit was so useful to both sides that Dudley was eventually assigned to run it full-time under the code name of Project Tipped Kettle.

Meanwhile, the Israeli shakeups did little to improve the situation in what had now become a three-way war zone in Lebanon: Christian against Muslim militias; Israelis against Palestinians; and extremists on both sides (Palestinian terrorists and Israeli hard-liners) against the rest of the world. Their wrath was felt not just by the multinational peacekeeping force that had been sent in by the United Nations, but by diplomats and civilians in many home countries. The age of the terrorist was about to begin.

At the end of June, the Israeli government had offered to withdraw from Lebanon if the Palestinians left, too, but the plan had been rejected by the Palestinian Liberation Organization (the PLO) in July. Later that month, the PLO won official UN recognition, pouring salt in Israeli wounds. The IDF had intensified its shelling of West Beirut in August and the Israeli cabinet agreed to an evacuation by sea of Palestinians from the Lebanese capital, thereby facilitating its own extrication from a more and more intractable problem. That month, too, a task force of U.S. Marines had been sent into Beirut (over and beyond the UN's multinational force in South Lebanon) to serve as a "force of interposition" to keep the warring factions apart.

On September 1, 1982, Cap Weinberger and I went to Beirut, and then Israel, to confer with Ambassador Lewis and President Reagan's special envoy, Philip Habib. Habib was a knowledgeable, professional diplomat who came out of retirement in his middle 60s specifically to help sort out the Lebanese mess—a situation that was gradually being called "Israel's Vietnam." Out of the spotlight, Habib could be pretty gruff, but I liked him. The Israelis never did because Habib thought for himself and wasn't afraid to challenge their facts.

As part of our official visit, Weinberger announced that all U.S. forces would be removed after 30 days. I strongly disagreed and argued forcefully against it up until the moment Weinberger made his speech. It was the first and only time the Secretary and I disagreed on any major issue. Along with others in our party, I had at least 15 practical reasons to keep the Marines there, beginning with the cold reality that if the U.S. left, so would the other MNF peacekeepers. But fear of the "Vietnam syndrome" was just too strong, even in the Reagan administration.

One symptom of this malady was Weinberger's famous "nine tests" for deploying or committing U.S. troops in a crisis abroad. Many people applauded this policy, but most of us in uniform couldn't believe a good man like Weinberger actually believed such a theory. We nicknamed the nine tests the "82nd Airborne Threshold" since it allowed an aggressor a pretty clear assessment of just how much he could get away with before Uncle Sam did anything about it. If nothing else, the Iraqi invasion of Kuwait in 1990 shows that if a country feels it can anticipate the U.S. response, they're more likely to act than if our national wrath hovers silently in the wings, incalculable to adventurers like Saddam Hussein—or Sharon.

The big failure of that policy in Beirut, of course, was that shortly after the Marines withdrew, they had to return because of the infamous Sabra and Shatilla massacres that cost Sharon his job. Out of a dire fear of another disaster like Desert One, or perhaps a deep concern that Lebanon should not become another Vietnamese swamp for the U.S. (as well as Israel), the JCS overrode the best judgment of their on-scene commander and decided that the Marine detachment should principally guard the airport rather than the port facility further north, even though the Palestinians were departing by ship, not plane. The buzz phrase on the Hill at the time was that we needed an "air head" for covering our ingress and egress. I thought it more appropriately described the policymaker who dreamed it up. It seemed to me another case of the planners worrying more about avoiding criticism than accomplishing their mission. It was bad enough that our pullout contributed to the loss of so many civilian lives. It was even more tragic that our return to the Beirut airport area (as opposed to downtown Beirut) would end a year later in the violent and needless deaths of 265 Marines in a suicidal terrorist attack on their barracks.

It was a terrible price to pay for keeping politely quiet while the red flags of an unjust war were being waved before our eyes.

# – III –

# High Noon in the Cold War

# – 11 –

# CBS Strikes Back

The Reagan administration's 1981 AWACS victory angered and offended two powerful groups in the U.S.: the pro-Israeli lobby and America's major broadcast networks, who at the time tended to support the Israeli view.

The Israeli boosters, led by AIPAC, the American-Israeli Public Affairs Committee, felt betrayed because, for the first time on any significant issue, a group of policymakers in the White House and defense bureaucracy had persuaded Congress that the dynamics of a changing world (and, in particular, a changing Middle East) made the old calculus for regional stability obsolete.

The major broadcast media, on the other hand, had a slightly different reason for criticizing the AWACS sale to the Saudis. To assess it properly, you must understand the political climate of the times.

Nixon's resignation was seven years old. The Watergate crew had been in and out of court, jail, and the news throughout the late 1970s. Ford had pardoned Nixon, and Carter had pardoned the Vietnam-era draft dodgers, so people at both ends of the political spectrum still fumed with a sense of injustice. The U.S. had vetoed a UN Security Council resolution condemning Israeli policies in the occupied territories (captured during the 1967 Six Day War) and vetoed another resolution calling for the establishment of a Palestinian state. The U.S.-Israel "special relationship" was especially close; the inconveniences and economic pain (a price-shock recession, for one) caused by OPEC's oil embargo was fresh in everyone's mind; and Arab states were depicted more than ever (that is, when they were depicted at all) as wild-eyed holdovers from the Middle Ages.

The major media were basking in their perceived twin victories over Vietnam hawks and their old nemesis, Richard Nixon, after Watergate. Popular wisdom attributed both events to the vigilance and perseverance of the U.S. media, especially television. It was a glorious time to be a journalist and a lousy time to wear a uniform, as American politicians and broadcasters

183

knew well. Anything connected with the executive branch or military was automatically suspect. Our network television producers, editors, and anchormen were no longer a "fourth estate" monitoring the game of nations from arm's length; they were major players with a big stake in both the process and the outcome.

This was the world of power politics into which I was unceremoniously dumped after the AWACS battle. If nothing else, I learned from these pros that the surest way to knock out an opponent was to leak some wild charge against him, claim to have substantiating evidence until the crisis (or vote) was over, and then let the whole thing drop. The victim may take you to court, but vindication comes years later, and if it's publicized at all, it's on the back page after the hog prices.

Shakespeare's Marc Antony summed it up correctly: "The evil men do lives after them, the good is oft interred with their bones." He should've added that if evil survives, innuendo *thrives*—in fact, it's damn near immortal, as evidenced by the now-legendary Edwin Wilson affair.

The AWACS vote was on October 28, 1981. On November 9, a scant 12 days later, "The CBS Evening News" with Dan Rather (a network that had been critical of the new Reagan administration in general and of the AWACS sale in particular) ran a report by correspondent Alan Pizzy concerning the then-evolving story of Edwin Wilson, an ex-CIA agent who was on the lam for smuggling arms to Muammar Qaddafi. (Wilson would later be convicted of selling C-4 explosives to the Libyan dictator and threatening his Justice Department prosecutors with death.)

As a mediagenic event, the Wilson case had all the ingredients: a villain from a shadowy government agency—one that had been "officially" discredited recently by the Carter administration; dealings with an unsavory foreign power; and the potential for a wider "conspiracy."

I had been following the Wilson story with interest, as had many other government officials who had met him during his rather meteoric passage through the Washington scene. I knew Wilson casually and recalled he was an impressive guy: outgoing, friendly, tall and athletic, handsome. Although he was no longer with the CIA, his record there, according to those who knew him, was exemplary.

For the first few minutes, the CBS report was unremarkable. It concentrated on excerpts from Pizzy's interview with Douglas Schlachter, a man who once worked for Wilson the civilian and claimed to be intimately familiar with his nefarious schemes. Halfway through the broadcast, though, I was astounded to see my own name and picture flashed on the screen.

Naturally, my ears were riveted to the voiceover: ". . . Secord's participation, according to Schlachter, in a plan to buy Russian equipment from the Libyans and help Wilson sell equipment in Iran."

CBS then switched to a conspiratorially tight close-up of a chain-smoking, shifty-eyed Schlachter answering Pizzy's questions. Schlachter accurately identified me as having been a key official in the Iran military assistance advisory group. Then, as Pizzy prompted him with suggestions that I may have been connected to Wilson, Schlachter said:

"Secord was definitely helping Wilson. Wilson sold intelligence ships to Iran," and that "he told me he made a lot of money on that. And it was done through Naval Intelligence."

The impression was clearly that I had somehow made a lot of money with Wilson selling intelligence ships to Iran. I was flabbergasted!

As soon as the piece was over, my phone rang and would keep ringing for the rest of the night: calls from reporters and supporters—the empathetic, the mildly curious, the suspicious. Somewhere, behind my back and out of sight, accusations had been concocted to pull me down into the political muck.

But by whom? And why?

I first met Wilson in the late 1960s or early 1970s through Tom Clines when both men were still with the CIA. They went back a long way together in the Agency (Ted Shackley knew Wilson, as well—and would be tarred himself because of it), and since I liked Tom and respected Ted a lot, I had no reason to be wary of Wilson. All together, I must've visited Wilson's Virginia farm just outside the Beltway three or four times during my first Washington tour. In doing so, I wasn't alone, or even in very select company. Wilson was still with the Agency and was considered one of its stars—an impression his polished, politician's style did nothing to contradict. He also seemed very ambitious and struck me as a bit of a climber. Still, there's nothing special about that, particularly in Washington. Half of D.C. must have shuffled through his suburban door in those years. The fact is, I never visited his home again after 1974.

Although my acquaintanceship with Wilson was purely social, Tom's was not. Three years after retiring from the CIA, Tom borrowed several hundred thousand dollars from Wilson to start a trading company. A year or two later, Tom became a coventurer with a shipping company called EATSCO (the Egyptian American Transport and Services Corporation). Tom's idea was to run a freight-forwarding business specializing in transporting FMS equipment. The "Egypt" in EATSCO stemmed from the fact that Tom's associate was an established Egyptian shipping executive. Together, they hoped to be among the first private companies to benefit from the new FMS credits allotted to Cairo after the Camp David accords.

I thought it was a good line of work for Tom's "second career." He knew a lot about doing business in other countries and had contacts worldwide. He was also a pretty tough cookie—a prerequisite for doing business in an industry known as one of the roughest there is. Activities that aren't kosher in more polite businesses are perfectly legal in ocean shipping, particularly kickbacks. I figured that if anybody could paddle through that particular scum-covered pond and keep his oars clean, it would be Tom.

In late 1978 or very early in 1979, after I had left my assignment as Air Force MAAG chief in Iran, Tom called and told me he had heard a shipping contract was going to be let soon for Iranian air force purchases. I was happy to give him what information I could about it, which wasn't much. Later, as an outgrowth of the Wilson allegations, I'd be accused of giving Tom a "sweetheart deal" on the freight-forwarding job. But even if I wanted to help a pal, my hands would've been tied. Ever since Lend Lease, the U.S. government has required the *recipient* nation to subsidize its own transportation for FMS goods. The best I could do was tell Tom what I knew about the structure of the Iranian air force—how they went about procurements, and so on—as I would for any other American bidder. I recommended he see Dick Helms, another CIA alumnus and former U.S. ambassador to Iran, who was now a private consultant. Helms was well known and widely respected by high-level Iranian decision makers. I knew that if anybody could help Tom prepare an effective proposal and get it into the right hands, it would be Helms. I also recommended that Tom make an appointment with General Rabbii, the Iranian air force commander in chief.

Because Tom was a good friend, I gave him permission to use my name as a reference while he meandered through the labyrinth of Iranian officialdom trying to make connections. However, I specifically told him *not* to imply that we were in business together, because (a) it wasn't true, and (b) that relationship carries special weight with businessmen in the Middle East. Tom said he would comply.

I gave Tom this caveat not because I thought he'd abuse our friendship, but because half the aerospace contractors in that part of the world dropped my name when it suited them in those days. Fortunately, most of our Iranian counterparts were pretty savvy, knew my reputation, and recognized a vendor con job when they heard it.

Nothing ever came of Tom's initiative. He traveled around Iran with his German-American venture partner, but the Shah's regime was crumbling and, to my knowledge, the particular contract Tom wanted was never awarded.

A couple of years later, in 1981 or 1982, the Justice Department began investigating a claim that EATSCO had overcharged the Egyptian government some $8 million. These allegations were never substantiated and were resolved by way of a corporate plea bargain. However, the investigation included interviews with people who had known both Tom and me, and my name was again bandied about by a few disgruntled contractors whose empires and egos I had upset.

I told the investigators I had no business interest in EATSCO, had made sure Tom would not suggest that I did, and received no kickbacks or other payments from him of any kind. Eventually, somebody at Justice read the procurement regulations about freight forwarding and realized I was right. The most I could have done to help Tom would have been to endorse him to the Iranians or Egyptians (which I did only indirectly, by giving him permission to use my name as a reference). But I couldn't give EATSCO or any other shipper a dime's worth of business. Normally, that would've been more than enough to close the case.

That was when the infamous Edwin Wilson resurfaced. By now Wilson had left the Agency and, unlike Tom, who merely transported equipment already purchased by foreign countries, was actively involved in putting deals together himself. Unfortunately, Wilson was using my name in Iran and elsewhere *without* my permission and freely suggesting (and sometimes stating outright) that I was a silent or limited partner in his business, which was patently untrue. Thus, the Justice Department found no shortage of people who recalled, with complete candor, Wilson's self-proclaimed and fraudulent connection to me.

The circumstantial evidence was impressive:

1. Clines had already been tainted with charges in Egypt, so the Justice Department considered him fair game.
2. Wilson, a world-class crook, was one of Clines's investors—more guilt by association.
3. I admitted freely to knowing both Clines and Wilson, so I must be involved in something, too.
4. Numerous Iranians and American contractors were willing to state for the record that, in one form or another, both Clines and Wilson had mentioned some connection to me.

The details were a little fuzzy, of course, but that's how "conspiracies" go.

To this day, I believe Wilson claimed he had a special relationship with me only to further his own business interests in the Middle East and elsewhere—the same motivation that caused lots of other vendors to mention or imply that they were "good friends" or "had an understanding" with the Iran MAAG and later Air Force international programs chief. I don't think Wilson was out to "get" me or to intentionally cause me grief. In fact, as the media has steadfastly refused to report, when Wilson was finally brought to trial, he never once named me as a business partner, co-conspirator, or anything else—even when it might've bought him some concessions from the prosecutors.

The only explanation I can think of for the longevity of the so-called Wilson-Secord connection was that somebody, in the media or elsewhere, remembered it and dusted it off after AWACS. By that time, of course, the story had matured and mutated into a much darker and wider-ranging "conspiracy."

The post-AWACS version held that I and a very senior OSD comptroller (a very capable guy named Eric Von Marbod, with whom I had worked closely on several occasions before and during AWACS) had put together a sweetheart deal for Clines and EATSCO and were lining our pockets with kickbacks from the shipping contracts we authorized. As I said, this was an idle fantasy beyond the capability, let alone intent, of everyone accused, but that "little detail" wasn't made known by the media.

The days after the CBS–Alan Pizzy story aired were some of the worst I ever spent, in the Pentagon or anywhere else, including a war zone. When I wasn't trying to "prove a negative," as they say—that I had no business or political or under-the-table connection to Wilson whatsoever—I was trying to do the job for which I was being paid by the taxpayers, but with less and less effectiveness.

People I used to deal with expeditiously now said, "I'll have to get back to you" or were continually "on the other line." People I used to see casually after hours or on weekends, the times when things really get done at the Pentagon, now required appointments, made sure witnesses were present at our meetings, or, worst of all, claimed to be too busy to give me the time my projects needed. Even my own staffers, who tried to be cheerful, began to keep their distance.

After a week or so of this, I began to realize it was only a matter of time until people who were simply late returning phone calls wouldn't return them at all; and coworkers who were now just worried and supportive would become worried and suspicious. Sympathetic comments would give way to gossip, and those innuendos would eventually turn into "facts"—in Washington, a faster way to die than by assassins' bullets.

I had seen it happen to other people, but, as with a terminal illness, I couldn't believe it was happening to me. By the end of the "CBS Evening News" November 9 broadcast, I was already dead politically. Like a dinosaur stabbed in the tail, it was just a matter of time until my brain got the message.

I finally realized I had only two choices left: give in, or try to do something about it. And if I wanted to keep working in government, there was really no choice at all.

To launch an effective counterattack, you have to assess the enemy's position—his order of battle and strengths and weaknesses. The assistant U.S. attorney running the Wilson/Clines investigation was a guy named Ted Greenberg. Like many in that department, his legal tenacity seemed matched only by his political ambition. Cap Weinberger's Defense Department general counsel, Will Taft IV, looked after the department's institutional interests, which I quickly learned didn't extend to specific employees. Taft was the great-grandson of President William Howard Taft, although I found the noble blood to be running a bit thin after three generations. From our first meeting, Taft proved to be a minor-league political animal who seemed more concerned about keeping the oil spill off his boss's shoes than saving the critters it imperiled.

Part of the problem, oddly enough, was the fact that I hadn't been charged with anything—and never would be. That kept the ball out of the courts and in the playground of the rumormongers. My opponents' strategy wasn't to resolve things, but to draw them out. Consciously or not, Taft's bungling and procrastination played right into their hands. As long as he could confine the damage to one or a few fall guys, he felt he was protecting the department. If this sounds familiar, it should. After Watergate (and certainly after Iran-Contra) it has become standard operating procedure in the government. Political animals don't just eat their young anymore—they sell them to the butcher.

Taft recommended to Weinberger and Carlucci that I should be placed on administrative leave—effectively suspended—until things were sorted out. As far as I could see, that only isolated me even more from the institution that was supposed to defend me. Of course, the real goal was to insulate the rest of the department—understandable, perhaps, unless you're the person being asked to take a phony rap. I walked out of the meeting where this plan was presented to me with a suspended job and a paycheck, but not much else. I realized that if I was ever going to get out of this mess, I would have to do it myself—and fast.

First, I asked Weinberger's deputy, Frank Carlucci, for a U.S. attorney who would defend *me* and not just the department. I explained that, as I saw it, some pro-Israeli supporters (whom I couldn't name for lack of proof) had concocted the Wilson connection and leaked it to an all-too-receptive CBS in retribution for my spearheading the administration's AWACS victory. I was confident the investigators had no legal leg to stand on, so Taft's Fabian tactics made no sense and would only feed the rumor mill, playing into the character assassin's hands.

My bosses' response, although personally supportive, turned out to be a tactical disaster. Taft argued that since I hadn't been charged with anything, I really didn't need (and he couldn't justify) a government attorney—although I could retain any lawyer I liked if it made me feel better. I was assured that Taft would work with whomever I selected, a promise that went unfulfilled.

This decision was a real setback for me, since it now pitted my pocketbook against the resources of CBS, the Justice Department, and who knew how many other people behind the scenes. After a few inquiries, I hired Tom Green, a Washington attorney who would later restore at least part of my faith in the legal profession.

After reviewing the case, Tom's advice was simple, if a bit taxing on my patience.

"Sit back and relax," he said. "Actively cooperate with the investigators, and let the whole thing die of its own weight."

He wasn't quite as sanguine as Carlucci, but he shared my conviction that, as far as the law was concerned, the case against me had nowhere to go.

Weeks, then months, dragged by without resolution. The networks continued their spotty coverage of the pursuit of Edwin Wilson and his eventual arrest. My polite correspondence with the Justice Department explaining the facts—including a primer on the relevant procurement regulations that showed the impossibility of the allegations—was politely filed and disregarded. The storm clouds continued to hover but the lightning never struck.

Finally, Tom began applying pressure on the attorney general's office for the prosecutor to either file charges or drop the investigation. Greenberg eventually offered to give me a polygraph test—hoping, we assumed, that I would refuse and add fuel to the innuendo fire. We surprised Mr. Greenberg and took his bait—on one condition.

"General Secord agrees to take the polygraph test," Tom said on the phone to Greenberg, "provided that if he passes, your office lifts any objection to his immediate reinstatement at the OSD."

Greenberg replied, in essence, not only no, but *hell no*—he wouldn't even *think* about doing that.

Tom's cheeks turned purple. He swore into the phone and slammed it down.

Until that moment, I don't think Tom had realized—I mean *really* realized—how pointless and vindictive the whole investigation and its attendant publicity had been. At least that was now finally out in the open.

Tom relayed the result of the conversation, in a more genteel way, to Taft; and Taft relayed it to Frank Carlucci, who took Greenberg's reneging on the deal implicit with the polygraph offer even harder than us. Carlucci, by virtue of his CIA experience, thought highly of polygraph testing and believed it was particularly reliable for people like me who had been given extensive baseline tests. Without waiting to hear from Justice, Carlucci reinstated me himself on his own authority, which was later endorsed by Weinberger.

Two and a half months after my suspension, I was back on the job.

As far as my superiors were concerned, that was the end of the Wilson affair. Carlucci's action carried some weight with the Justice Department as well, because many months after I went back to work, I received a form letter stating in terse, businesslike terms that no basis was found for any of the allegations and that no charges would be filed. The investigation was closed. What had swung in, arm over arm like King Kong months before through the media jungle—the CBS airwaves and headlines of the *Washington Post*—now crept out quietly like a spanked puppy, in the semisecrecy of a personal letter.

By the spring of 1982, my phone calls gradually got returned and people again asked me out to lunch. On the surface things seemed to return to normal.

In July 1982, George Schultz replaced Al Haig, and in September, I was sent to a secret meeting with delegates from other Middle East states to confer on Reagan's little-reported "President's Peace Initiative." The plan, backed strongly by Schultz, was based on UN resolutions 242 and 238, which the administration saw as a possible foundation for Arab-Israeli peace. Unfortunately, the initiative was rejected by Israel within 24 hours of its receipt, and that rejection, I believe, affected the new Secretary of State's relationship with Israel profoundly.

Schultz was very different from Haig. Despite his strong reputation from previous Cabinet service and the private sector, I was not particularly impressed with his political acumen or personal leadership style. My impression was mainly that he came to his office very ambitious and anxious to win laurels right away. He was terrified of interdepartmental leaks, which to me was the telltale sign of an administrative turf-builder.

When Israeli Foreign Minister Yitzhak Shamir came to see Schultz after Begin's rejection of the President's Peace Initiative, I was asked to sit in for Secretary Weinberger and was astonished at how easily Shamir dominated the meeting. When Weinberger asked me how things went, I replied, "In my opinion, it appears Mr. Schultz has never had to swim with the sharks."

That first bad experience with Israeli rejection, I believe, forever colored Schultz's view of that government, which he came to regard as an obstacle to achieving his personal goals.

Also on behalf of Weinberger, I attended a number of meetings with CIA representatives, including Robert Gates, and then Vice President George Bush, who sometimes chaired the President's crisis response group. On later occasions, I would attend meetings where Bill Casey, Reagan's CIA Chief, was present. Casey was undoubtedly a brilliant man, but enigmatic—not only because of his famous mumbling, but because of his Byzantine thought processes and preference for ambiguous statements. Bush was a strong performer in every meeting I attended: a quick study and very familiar with most issues. I never once had the feeling that he was, or desired to be, left out of the loop on any substantive question. His actions also made it clear that he viewed his role as one of gathering and sorting information for the President. He was, in short, a strong team player—no ornamental chair-warmer or usurper of his boss's power or prerogatives.

I was around the top man, President Reagan, only a few times, and those were mostly ceremonial occasions. I found him well informed but personally aloof. He seemed to concentrate on key issues and was content to let others—principally Jim Baker, Mike Deaver, and Ed Meese—manage things on a day-to-day basis. While I served in his administration, I thought he was a good president whose instincts on domestic and defense issues were generally on target.

In any event, after the summer of 1982, everyone at OSD was busy with the crisis in the Middle East—General Sharon's invasion of Lebanon and the aftermath. Nonetheless, the Wilson affair weighed heavily on me.

It didn't take a genius to see that my career, post-Wilson, was sputtering along on only a few cylinders. I hadn't been "defeated," but I had incurred a lot of battle damage. It seemed to me that those who wanted to punish me and the department for AWACS had gotten in their licks and danced away unscathed. I felt worn out by the whole process and embittered by its injustice.

As usual at a time of doubt or indecision in my life, I held a full-fledged "program review" to diagnose the situation with my wife Jo Ann (my indispensable chief advisor) and a few friends who understood my situation. We spent a few quiet evenings in the living room, around the kitchen table, or lingering over coffee at our favorite Washington restaurants sorting everything out. Here's what I came up with:

I was 50 years old and counting. I was having more and more trouble finding reasons to tumble out of bed and into the bureaucratic trenches each morning. While I had broken new ground by becoming the first military man appointed Deputy Assistant Secretary of Defense for Near East, South Asia, and Africa, my job there was a political appointment, and going further in that direction necessarily meant the end of my military career. I thought I had a better-than-average shot at achieving a higher rank in the Air Force, although that would've meant an indefinite stay in the Pentagon—another poor choice, considering that I had just suffered my third case of pneumonia in as many years.

Except for many of my fellow West Pointers, some of my Pentagon colleagues had severely disappointed me by their lack of support during the Wilson crisis. This was especially true in the case of Will Taft. I can understand career officers wanting to keep their records clean, but loyalty is a two-way street. Frankly, I just couldn't find it on any of the official Pentagon road maps.

The Middle East situation was grinding on me, too. Since my first tour in Iran, I'd felt a special affinity for that region. I could see it was entering into a new and lethal phase involving the Iran-Iraq war; the rise of Sharon and the Ayatollah Khomeini (similar, destabilizing forces on opposite ends of the Arab world); the invasion of Lebanon; and the beginning of organized hostage taking. Given how vulnerable I was to further attacks in the media, I could see only frustration and heartache in place of future accomplishments. Anyone who wanted to knock me out of a Congressional hearing would only have to dredge up the CBS "news clips" and any of a dozen defaming newspaper articles. Surrounded by innuendo and false allegations, I had become, in political lingo, *a liability* to the administration.

I also had over $22,000 in legal bills to pay off, and three kids who hoped to go to college. Although my salary was good by military standards, even major generals have trouble making ends meet in the D.C. economy.

In short, all the auspices seemed to point in one direction: Enough is enough.

I had 28 years of military service (plus four years as a West Point cadet) and could retire at any time. I was reluctant to drop the ball I had been given at OSD and I sure as hell didn't want my opponents to be able to say later that I had been "forced out of office." I made an appointment with Secretary Weinberger and told him I would give the job one more year. After that, I would try my luck in the private sector.

The Secretary did not like my plan.

"I think you're overreacting," Weinberger said. "I think you should stay on for the duration," meaning the rest of the Reagan administration. At least five times after that, he asked me to tough it out.

It's hard to say no to someone you respect and admire—and truly like—as much as I liked Weinberger. Our only real personal clash came over Will Taft, whom I admitted to Weinberger I could no longer work with. In essence, I told the Secretary his arguments against my retirement would carry more weight if Taft "went away," got another job or was simply kept away from me. It was a favor Weinberger couldn't or wasn't prepared to grant. I suppose, in retrospect, I was secretly glad he didn't.

My last hurrah in uniform came in April 1983.

By now Israeli Defense Minister Ariel Sharon had been dismissed, and the dimensions of his folly (and its cost to the world) were well known. Israel was gradually being called to account by the same criteria used to measure the behavior of other nations. I thought it would have a healthy long-term effect on the region, for Israel internally, and for the world. F-15s were now in place in Saudi Arabia and that, combined with their AWACS, seemed to be restoring the regional balance of power that was skewed so abruptly by the fall of Iran. Pakistan, for the moment, had moved even closer to the Western camp, another part of our strategy that was beginning to bear fruit.

One of my last projects involved shepherding through Congress the sale of F-16 fighters to Pakistan—a kind of "mini-AWACS fight" that tested my post-Wilson credibility in the face of pro-Israeli opposition.

AIPAC's big issue now was the so-called "Islamic bomb"—not only the possibility of a nuclear weapon in the hands of the Islamic world, but the rumblings of an enormous jihad that would wipe Israel off the map. It was extremist talk that did nothing but whip up irrational feelings on both sides.

In the case of the F-16 sale to Pakistan, our opponents claimed that both U.S. and Israeli security would be harmed if the F-16's ALR-69 radar warning system were made available to the Red Chinese, Pakistan's benefactor of long standing. This case was made during hearings of the Senate's Foreign Relations Subcommittee, chaired by John Glenn, in the special, secure "classified information" rooms built under the Capitol dome.

My approach, as always, was to let the facts speak for themselves. I brought along experts to defuse the Islamic bomb issue and debunk the disinformation that had been circulated about the F-16's black box. Our three principal witnesses were a deputy assistant secretary of state; Chuck Cogan, the CIA officer who had worked with us in the JTF days and who was still the CIA's chief of Near East; and myself.

When it came time for the technical discussion, I explained that we had carefully considered the national security implication of every system on the F-16, as we always did, and had determined no substantive risks were involved. I added that an earlier ground-based radar-intercept system, previously approved by this same committee and sold to the Pakistani army, contained *exactly* the same microprocessor as the ALR-69—the component that our opponents now tried to tell us would create a grave new risk to Western security.

The hearing room went silent. After a startled pause, Senator Glenn asked, "Then why weren't we informed of that?"

I replied, "Frankly, Senator, I myself wasn't informed until yesterday. The point is, a parallel analysis came up with the same conclusion." I closed by saying that we simply had nothing to fear and much to gain by proceeding with the transaction.

The Senate's subcommittee recommended passage, and the hearings went on to the House. By now the date set for my retirement (actually, the *second* date; it had already been extended a month to accommodate the hearings and a meeting in Jordan) was looming, and I was anxious to finish the hearings and get on with the rest of my life. I met early with Representatives Charlie Wilson and Baltimore Democrat Theodore "Doc" Price (chairman of the House Subcommittee on Appropriations) and their staffers to work out the agenda, sequence of witnesses, and so on just to be sure the hearings would stay on track and terminate as quickly as possible. Unfortunately, Doc Price had other ideas.

His closed-session hearings convened amid a circus atmosphere. Our first witness from the State Department was summarily dismissed. Instead, Doc Price said he wanted to hear about "our covert aid to Afghanistan" that had recently hit the news, and called our CIA witness instead.

The poor CIA guy could only say, "We've briefed the House Select Committee on Intelligence previously on this matter," but old Doc wouldn't be put off.

"Don't tell me how to run this committee!" he sputtered, banging his gavel. "I'm telling you, we'll hold up FMS credits until we get this information!"

"Can I at least have a recess to call the director?"

Price said okay, but it just resulted in another acrimonious exchange.

For two hours we tried to get Price back on the subject, but nothing was going to deter him—not even (and especially) the facts. When I finally realized our "mini-AWACS" would turn into another months-long, bruising battle over surrogate issues, I leaned into my microphone and said:

"Mr. Chairman, this hearing was called to examine the Defense Department's review of technical aspects of the F-16 sale to Pakistan—"

"We'll get to that," Doc Price said. "We'll get to it!" He banged the gavel again.

"Mr. Chairman," I continued, "I'd like to be heard. Apparently there's been some misunderstanding on our part as to the content of these hearings—"

"Now, Mr. Secord, I'll make those determinations—"

"Mr. Chairman," I said with as much finality as I could muster, "these hearings are at an end!"

I slammed my briefing book loudly—you'd have thought a cannon went off in the place!—and stood up. Price sat back in his chair, too stunned even to rule me out of order. The committee laughed; Charlie Wilson and the others just grinned and quietly applauded.

I packed my briefcase—one last time—and walked out. The whole room was buzzing, but I never looked back.

The Pakistanis got their F-16s, and the Defense Department muddled through without me. My retirement ceremony was convened in Caspar Weinberger's conference room, officiated by the Secretary himself. He made a great speech—a real tearjerker—and presented me with my second Defense Department Distinguished Service Medal, the highest peacetime award the department can offer a military man. (The first DSM had been authorized by the President for service above and beyond the strict call of duty in the AWACS battle. The second was initiated personally by Secretary Weinberger.)

Naturally, there were no cameras—nothing on "The CBS Evening News" or in the next day's *Washington Post*—about old Secord retiring: bloodied but unbowed; honored, yet in a quiet way, betrayed. Even by ignoring me, I learned, my opponents could deliver heavy blows.

But Weinberger made a good speech—the kind that gets interred with your bones.

Edwin Wilson was brought to justice in late 1982, before I retired. I was subpoenaed to testify by both the prosecution and the defense, and did so—ironically, as a *government* witness. The only substantive question I was asked related to a proposition Wilson had once made to my office. He proposed to steal a MiG-25 fighter from the Libyan air force and turn it over to the U.S.

for flight testing and engineering analysis. I told him at the time it was an "interesting idea" but that we would need a lot more information on his plan if we were to give it any serious consideration. That was the last I heard of him until his name and mug shot appeared in the media.

So the question remained, at least in my mind: Who created the fictional Wilson-Secord connection in November 1981? And why?

With Tom Green's assistance, I set out in late 1982, before I retired, to find an answer.

Tom, rightfully concluding that I was too indigent to tackle CBS head-on, recommended we bring suit against the guy who defamed me in public, Wilson's ex-employee, Douglas Schlachter.

One expensive lawsuit later, in April 1983, the Federal District Court in the District of Columbia awarded me $2 million in a default judgment against Mr. Schlachter, who at the time was in the Justice Department's witness protection program. We had asked for $1 million in damages, but the judge thought the lies were so egregious and the damage to my career so severe that she doubled the amount. Of course, I never collected a penny. Mr. Schlachter was indigent himself and you can't get blood from a turnip—but I was interested in neither Mr. Schlachter's blood nor his money, but the truth.

Four years later, in 1987, I obtained the videotape of the entire two-and-one-half hour interview between Schlachter and CBS correspondent Alan Pizzy. Comparing that to the segments broadcast by "The CBS Evening News" on November 9, 1981, some astonishing discrepancies appeared.

First, what appeared to be a contiguous sequence of questions and answers turned out to be a splice of information taken out of context from several points in the tape. As Schlachter himself later affirmed, the interview that was broadcast—the statement CBS put into his mouth through video editing—was "a lie, not correct" that resulted in great damage to him as well as to me.

The tape suggested that I helped Wilson by "burying" a file prepared for the CIA by another of Wilson's employees, a guy called I. W. Harper, when he was transferred to Iran. In fact, I never heard of such a file, assuming it even existed. The whole story was the product of Schlachter's admitted misunderstanding and misreading of some of Wilson's esoteric and bizarre activities. The managing editor of "The CBS Evening News", Dan Rather, wouldn't go on the air with such a mangled story, but that didn't stop it from making the rounds of the Pentagon rumor mill.

Regarding the "ton of money" Wilson and I supposedly made on the sale of an intelligence ship to Iran, that portion of the broadcast came from a later segment where Schlachter described (then U.S. Ambassador) Dick Helms's role in helping Naval Intelligence sell not two ships but one to Iran. In effect, CBS had taken Schlachter's comments about Helms, edited it to delete Helms and implicate me, and then spliced it into Schlachter's earlier comments about "Secord helping Wilson." The tape should have won an Emmy for creative news editing.

(Expert video editors who have examined both the original interview tape and the one subsequently broadcast state unequivocally that the resulting "message" connecting me to Wilson could not have been the product of accidental or careless editing—or even a misunderstanding. Their conclusion was that a deliberate attempt was made to reshape a primary record to support a predetermined editorial slant.)

I can only guess why the tape was edited the way it was. All I know for certain are the facts:

Wilson and I had no business connection. Wilson, after his arrest and during his trial, did not implicate me in his activities. Schlachter himself— the guy whose "interview" started the "Wilson affair"—says all such allegations about me are untrue. The Justice Department, after a prolonged and biased investigation, gave me a clean bill of health.

To these facts, I might add another: You probably won't see a retraction, an apology, or even an explanation of any of this on "The CBS Evening News."

# — 12 —

# "Hello, Dick, This Is Ollie . . ."

At the end of May 1983, I took that not-so-wistful last glance at the Pentagon in my rearview mirror. For the first time since I was 18, I was a civilian.

For my first six months of retirement, I was too numb to make much headway into the "rest of my life." Like most military retirees, I was way too young for a rocker and knew a lot more about what I didn't want to do than what I did.

The most obvious choice was the first one I forswore. Federal law prohibits high-ranking officers working in or around procurement from accepting private-sector jobs related to those projects for anywhere from one to many years, depending on their rank and the nature of their last assignment. This is supposed to prevent government decision makers from feathering their own postretirement nests: making sweetheart deals with contractors who employ them later or buy their insider's knowledge. In my case, I had been in too many battles with contractors and had seen too much of life in the big aerospace and electronics companies to want any part of it.

My reputation as a hard-nosed bureaucrat who refused to play contractors' games also preceded me. Although retiring Pentagon generals usually get numerous job offers from industry, I received not a single one—which I would've appreciated, just for the satisfaction of turning it down.

I was also used to working with top-level government decision makers on a daily basis—the people who got things done, including Cap Weinberger, Frank Carlucci, and JCS chiefs—as well as regular interaction outside the Defense Department with men like Bill Casey, George Schultz, and numerous Congressional leaders. Although each of these men had their own strengths and weaknesses, all had risen to their current positions of power through strength of will and political savvy; they were all professors emeriti of human

The dashing young plebe cadet, West Point, 1951.

As a newly commisioned second lieutenant, I "defected" to the Air Force in 1955.

My first covert assignment, as one of the fighter pilots stationed in Vietnam in the early 1960s executing the Air Force's Project Jungle Jim.

As Deputy Commander for
Operations, Craig Air Force
Base, Selma, Alabama, 1975.

Ambassador to Iran Richard Helms congratulates me upon my promotion to
brigadier general while my wife, Jo Ann, pins on my first star.

Here an Iranian Air Force base commander greets me during a stan-eval (standard evaluation) visit. Our "black hat" inspections were more hated and feared than any enemy air force.

Iran, 1977.

Lieutenant General Kelly presents me with my first Distinguished Service Award at the Pentagon in 1978.

In Egypt in 1979 inspecting a Soviet-made MiG 23. Wringing out its predecessor, an Egyptian Air Force MiG-21, was a high-point of my flying career.

President Reagan congratulating me for successfully spearheading Congressional approval of the sale of controversial AWACS aircraft to Saudi Arabia, 1981.

At my retirement ceremony at the Pentagon in 1983: bloodied, perhaps, but un-bowed.

I found Secretary of Defense Caspar Weinberger an easy man to work for—one of the best bosses I ever had. (UPI/BETTMANN Newsphotos)

CIA Director Bill Casey raised ambiguity to an art form. (UPI/BETTMANN Newsphotos)

George Bush has claimed to be ignorant of the Iran Initiative as a whole. That simply is not true. (UPI/BETTMANN Newsphotos)

Bud McFarlane announces his resignation as National Security Advisor while President Reagan and Vice Admiral John Poindexter, who will succeed him, look on. (UPI/BETTMANN Newsphotos)

Ollie's five days of testimony before the Iran-Contra hearings galvanized the nation. It began a tidal wave of anti-incumbant feelings that continues to re-shape the American Congress. (UPI/BETTMANN Newsphotos)

As the lead witness at the Congressional hearings into Iran-Contra, I went in to explain what our mission was, and how we carried it out. Instead, I received a crash course in bare-knuckles politics, Congressional-style. (UPI/BETTMANN Newsphotos)

nature. I had been privileged to participate with them in events that not only shaped our times, but might, I hoped, influence future history. It was a difficult way of life to leave behind, and one I never shook entirely.

Nonetheless, I tried to make a clean break with government service, at least in those early months. I quickly noticed, though, that without the daily infusion of intelligence reports and briefings, I experienced the opposite of "information shock," a kind of sensory deprivation when I discovered that all I was going to learn about the world or national policy would have to come from the media, personal contacts, or friends on the periphery of those events. This was especially frustrating when big stories broke, such as the car bombing of the U.S. Marines barracks in Beirut, or the October 25, 1983, coup de main in Grenada to rescue 600 Americans and stop Soviet-Cuban encroachment in that part of the Caribbean.

My family probably sensed my restlessness more than I did. Jo Ann, previously the consummate Air Force wife, seemed happy enough to lose a general and gain a full-time husband. She was never particularly fond of the cloak-and-dagger stuff—those special operations that lionized my time and sent me off to god-knew-where for days or months at a time. She turned out to be a very skilled "crisis manager" in her own right, however, and gave me all the space I needed to maneuver in these uncharted waters, offering empathy, advice, and the occasional kick in the pants when I needed it.

Our twins, Laura and John, were starting high school and, like most kids that age, were absorbed—thankfully—with their own lives, as was Julia, our first daughter, now married and out of the nest. The hoopla, such as it was, about their dad and this guy Wilson seemed to have slid off their backs. If they were concerned about this "stranger" who was now hanging around the house, bugging Mom, making phone calls, and growling at the newspaper, they never let on. Rediscovering my family after a decade of exhausting work and exotic distractions went a long way toward reassuring me that my decision had been the right one.

Despite my background with weapons and procurement, I shared most Americans' distaste for the commercial arms business and its "merchants of death" image. What fascinated me were the *strategic* aspects of that industry: ferreting out balance-of-power and trade issues; crafting the complex deals; and diagnosing and overcoming technical, cultural, and administrative obstacles to achieving political objectives, particularly in the Middle East. It occurred to me that, given my extensive knowledge of the technology, players, and issues in that area (particularly what it took to meet U.S. government political and procurement requirements), I could—with the right business partner—establish a viable trading company. In time, it might even rival the big houses in Europe and Hong Kong; the trade potential was that great.

Fortunately, in the winter of 1983, new Congressional legislation removed some of the self-imposed, nonmarket constraints encumbering American firms trying to operate internationally—particularly old rules preventing financial institutions from participating as venture partners. If I could find an experienced money man who understood the culture and customs of the Middle East, I could probably put my trading company plan into effect.

The "right partner" turned out to be Albert Hakim, a U.S. citizen of Iranian birth.

At this time, Albert was in his late 40s, of medium height, a bit stocky, with thinning hair and a clear, penetrating gaze. He had a friendly and articulate manner without a lot of glad-handing, an excellent salesman in a field dominated by boors and con men. He was raised in Tehran, where his Jewish father ran a small store; and later lived in Tabriz, near the border with Turkey, his mother's native country. The Iranian Jews were persecuted from time to time, so Albert's father encouraged him to seek his education (if not his fortune) elsewhere. He went to college in the United States, and finally emigrated permanently to California in the late 1970s, becoming a U.S. citizen in 1984.

In the 1960s and 1970s, Albert represented a number of American companies in Iran, mostly communications and defense electronics firms, but also a major ammunition manufacturer. He helped form Motorola of Israel, a communications company that grew rapidly and now sells equipment throughout the Middle East. His first U.S. entrepreneurial effort came with the formation of Stanford Technology Corporation (STC), a Swiss company that he later dissolved and resurrected (under the same name but with different officers) in California in 1974. He also set up Expandtrade in Switzerland with the help of a fiduciary company, *Compagne des Services Fiduciare*, or CSF, led by an American lawyer, Willard (Bill) Zucker.

With this network of firms and financial backers, Albert started doing business on his own in Iran. Aside from a possible introduction while I was MAAG chief in Iran (which Albert remembered but I did not), I had no direct business contact with him or his companies until he called on me a few months after I retired.

At our first meeting, Albert confessed he was undergoing a bit of a career change himself. He had recently sold a high-tech company specializing in nonmilitary computer-enhanced sensor imaging and had grown weary of running companies himself. His flagship firm, Stanford Technology, dealt in security systems such as electronic fences and anti-intrusion devices (like LLTV, IR sensors, and similar equipment), which it integrated into comprehensive systems for government and commercial users.

"Right now," Albert said like a proud entrepreneurial papa, "we're working with Westinghouse to install a security system for Korea's *first* nuclear power plant."

"That's quite an accomplishment," I smiled, getting a kick out of his enthusiasm.

"It's only a start," Albert said modestly. "My real goal is to create an American trading company that rivals the Japanese."

My ears perked up.

Albert continued, "I want a central company that contracts with other firms—manufacturers, shippers, banks—to import and export security systems on a large scale to other parts of the world, principally Asia and the Middle East, taking payment in oil or minerals or foodstuffs and disposing of them in other markets. In many ways, you would make an ideal partner for this venture."

He was right. I had a lot of experience with "offset deals," FMS contracts that were paid for by the exchange of raw or finished products. Countertrade (as such arrangements were also known) was a sophisticated form of barter and was, perhaps, the only way many third-world countries could afford the defense systems the U.S. wanted them to have. If a trading company could master the regulatory and commercial intricacies involved, countertrade projects such as Albert envisioned could be a very lucrative business.

Albert then presented me with an offer. He would give me a 50 percent share of a new company called Stanford Technology Trading Group International (STTGI) and finance it himself for the first three years if I would run the operation. I was prohibited by law from ever working on projects I had been connected with in the service, which eliminated most significant Pentagon programs. For me, in fact, this was tantamount to a lifetime ban, given the long lead times and high degree of technical integration of modern defense systems. The fact that Albert's business specialized in something other than arms, yet would benefit from a military man's perspective, made it unique; and to me, very appealing.

I told Albert I would consider his offer carefully. As someone who had been privy to a lot of classified information, I had to be cautious. But a routine check of his bona fides showed STC and Hakim to be just what he represented. I could find nothing in my research to spoil my growing enthusiasm for the venture.

A few weeks after that first meeting, we shook hands, drew up a contract, and went shopping for office space.

We settled in Vienna, Virginia, in October 1983. As he promised, Albert provided the venture capital: a loan of several hundred thousand dollars (from his own pocket and his fiduciary company, CSF), paid out over the course of the next several years. I hired a secretary and authorized myself a salary of $60,000 (raised to $72,000 the next year)—about what I had been making as an active-duty major general at the time I retired. The move was a real tonic for my spirits. I may not have been back in the cockpit of a jet fighter, but I was definitely going places. Best of all, *my* hand was on the throttle.

Albert was the archetypal capitalist. He had no hobbies that I could see; cultivating deals was avocation enough for him, and he honed his skills constantly. Within a few months, I discovered that Albert's interest in company operations was just about zero; what he liked was putting together "the package" on a particular venture, project, or contract. Although he proved himself to be a thoroughly honest guy and had great visions for his business, he was not particularly idealistic. I learned he still owned a company in Iran, despite the revolution, and ran it in absentia "just to keep a foot in the door" with a small staff—it was too dangerous for anyone connected with the U.S., especially expatriate Iranians, to even consider going back.

He also admitted he had been contacted by U.S. government intelligence during the hostage crisis and had offered them the flat roof of his Tehran building, only a few blocks from the U.S. Embassy, as a staging area for the rescue. Although the rescue never came off, I was pleased to hear Albert had made the offer, a sign of the patriotic instincts that belied his businessman's self-interest.

In due course, he completed the Korean nuclear power plant project and marketed ourselves to a dozen other companies. Our first significant client was the Marwais Corporation, an American steel company specializing in overseas turnkey defense construction projects, principally hardened shelters for aircraft and other military support facilities. Marwais retained us to market their products in the Middle East, most in Abu Dhabi and Saudi Arabia. After a bitter competition, we lost the Abu Dhabi project to a West German company; and the Saudi project (like so many programs in that area) would languish because of a leisurely government procurement schedule well into 1985. By that time, we would both be distracted by other, weightier affairs.

In late June or early July of 1984, I received a phone call out of the blue from Oliver North.

North identified himself in a friendly, casual way—a sort of "Hello, Dick, this is Ollie" kind of greeting, as if we knew each other well, though it took me a second to place him. As I would later learn, this was merely Ollie's style. He was an engaging fellow who had learned early as a junior NSC staffer how to get people on his side.

North had worked briefly as one of the NSC liaison guys on the AWACS interagency team in 1981. I remembered him mainly as a pleasant young major (he was now a lieutenant colonel) who was a dependable scheduler and coordinator, but a man without significant responsibilities in the organizational sense. He had accompanied some of our AWACS briefing teams (our "flying squads") as they collared congressmen and senators before the AWACS vote, and I don't recall anyone ever complaining about his work. Bob Lilac, an Air Force colonel I recruited to the Pentagon and who later went to work on the NSC staff, reintroduced me to Ollie at a social function at the White House just after I retired, but we didn't talk about anything consequential. North was an engaging young officer, very fit, with good military bearing and a lot of what seemed to be nervous energy. He walked with a slight limp, which I later found out came from a serious automobile accident about the time he graduated from Annapolis, although he had also been wounded in Vietnam.

Now, apparently, Colonel North had something important on his mind.

Obviously, my desk phone was unsecure, so North asked if I could come by and see him in his office in the old executive office building, known affectionately as the EOB. He said it involved a national security matter, so how could I refuse? In retrospect, I probably should have said, "Sorry, I'm in the private sector now. Do you want to buy an airplane hangar?" but I didn't.

Ollie greeted me warmly in his cozy, shopworn little office. He respected my time and got right to the point, explaining what I had been following casually in the newspapers: the saga of the Contras and Sandinistas.

Before I left the Pentagon, I had sat in on many of the classified briefings related to Central America. I was no expert on the region, but I had a pretty good feel for the military situation, which was poor from the American perspective. The Sandinistas (named after Augusto Sandino, a legendary hero to Nicaraguan nationalists) had expelled the Somoza regime in the summer of 1979. The new government promised democracy, which the Carter administration supported with aid, but the Sandinistas quickly turned to their Soviet mentors and, in cooperation with Cuba, began exporting their revolution to neighboring countries like El Salvador while stifling individual freedoms at home.

After a few years of Marxist rule, a coalition of Nicaraguans, from exiled Somozans to disenchanted Sandinistas, formed, with CIA help and leadership, a counterrevolutionary force nicknamed the Contras, which began a low-intensity guerrilla war against the Sandinistas. Despite the threat of Nicaragua becoming a mainland Cuba—a staging area for Soviet troops and weapons—I thought the CIA had no business trying to run an overt war covertly, and said so several times, but that was a bureaucratic turf battle and at the time I had my hands full with the Middle East.

The disclosure in April 1984 that the CIA had supported mining of Nicaraguan harbors woke up the media (evoking memories of Haiphong), and Congress, always tuned to that channel, started backpedaling from the Contras.

On October 12, 1984, what became known as the second Boland Amendment was passed after continuous debate since May. It was, pure and simple, an anti-appropriations measure aimed at U.S. government intelligence agencies. It clearly affected neither the activities of private citizens nor the NSC, the President's personal "lobby" to Congress and the bureaucracy. The amendment represented a complex compromise between those who wanted to abandon the Contras and accept the Marxist Sandinista government in Nicaragua, and those who believed in the Contra cause. It contained no penalties for its violation, nor did it abridge the ability of the U.S. intelligence community to collect and share information with the anti-Sandinista fighters.

The quid pro quo that allowed the continuing resolution (of which Boland II was an appendix) to escape a Reagan veto, in fact, were the very provisions that left the door open to private contributions; and wording that excluded the NSC and other agencies from its injunction just as had been done in other statuatory enactments. The idea that Contra support was intended to be an illegal "end run" around the Boland Amendments, and not something painstakingly conducted in compliance with them, was a myth created later by the media and repeated so often that it eventually took on the color of truth. In fact, the legislative history shows quite the opposite.

Even before Boland II formally passed, money to keep the Contras going had become tight. North had been on the private fund-raising circuit a while, offering big donors a photo opportunity with the President in exchange for a check. But a shooting war is even more expensive to produce than television campaign ads. It was clear the Contra leadership, in absence of the CIA aid that had previously sustained them, was going to need a lot of financial help.

I listened to Ollie's review of the situation with interest, but wondered openly what it all had to do with me. I was no expert on Central America, as I pointed out to him.

"That doesn't matter," North said. "You're an expert in special ops. You've been all over the world, know how to size people up. And—according to Bill Casey—you know how to keep your mouth shut. As a matter of fact, you're one of several special ops people I've been consulting."

Another such person, I would discover, was General John Singlaub, a man known to the public for his florid 1977 showdown with Jimmy Carter over the President's order to reduce U.S. forces in South Korea. I had dealt with Singlaub when he was a Special Forces colonel in Vietnam and, although he seemed competent, I wasn't overly impressed with him. I was even more leery of him after the Carter brouhaha since I'd never known a special ops guy (or even a ranking field commander) who was worth much after developing a taste for the spotlight.

What North wanted most was somebody who could meet with the Contra leader, Adolfo Calero, the head of the Nicaraguan Democratic Force (or FDN), on an upcoming Washington visit and give North a quick reading: Was there anything I could do to help?

It didn't seem like an outrageous request, and might even be kind of interesting. I answered, "Sure, what the hell?"

We shook hands and the meeting was over.

After an initial introduction to Calero in North's office in July 1984, I picked Calero up at the D.C. Sheraton Park hotel and drove around while we talked. Calero is a big man, the kind of "Spanish grandee" you'd imagine running a small Latin American country—or at least sipping tequila on a veranda while the *peones* did the work. His English was perfect, as you might expect from a Notre Dame grad, and he spoke with a certain eloquence. After a while, he asked me to drop him off at the Key Bridge Marriott, where he said he had another "very important meeting." I laughed when he told me. I knew instantly he must be meeting with the CIA, which he was. The Agency frequently met out-of-towners at the Key Bridge Marriott, which undoubtedly simplified things for anyone who wanted to keep track of the CIA's comings and goings. Maybe that was part of their system—so they could surveil the surveillance.

After a 45-minute wait, I picked Calero up again and bought him a glass of white wine at the Crystal City Marriott, where we got better acquainted. He mentioned a number of problems his soldiers were having, chief among them being a pressing need for ammunition and reliable firearms at "relatively cheap" prices.

"What do you mean by cheap?" I asked him. I hadn't even thought about commercially available small arms and ammunition since my days at the MAAG in Iran, but I knew several people in that business—not back-alley smugglers, but reputable dealers who handled volume purchases for governments and other security organizations around the world. I thought I might be able to steer him onto a better supplier.

He mentioned some prices the Contras had paid the CIA for firearms, and they sounded pretty high. We agreed it was a pity that the CIA was pulling out without developing the Contras' own resupply ability. According to North, and now Calero, the CIA had provided everything for the Contras, from weapons and price lists to airline tickets. Logistics may not seem glamorous, but they are the true sinews of war. Unfortunately, the CIA always paid two or three times what an item was worth, just to ensure security. Even their own purchasing agents and case officers knew they were overspending, but that was how they operated.

I asked Calero for some examples of the quality problems he had experienced.

The big man rolled his eyes and said, "You wouldn't believe it! We bought some Brazilian hand grenades for eight or nine dollars apiece, but they were very touchy. Your advisor, General Singlaub, told us to tape the handles down, since some of the first few guys who tried to use these grenades blew their hands off and were killed."

I almost choked on my wine. I couldn't imagine an experienced infantry officer telling his soldiers to go into battle with grenades that had to be un-wrapped, like Christmas presents, before you threw them at the enemy! Besides, I'd heard about that grenade problem before and it had nothing to do with the handles. It reflected a quality-control problem with the fusing, something a guy like Singlaub should've known all about. That was when the little voice inside of me started carping: *Are you going to leave these guys to twist in the wind like we did to the Laotians?*

When I dropped Calero off to catch his plane at Washington National, I told him I would check the CIA prices for reasonableness and see if I couldn't locate some sources for reliable weapons. Afterward, I stopped by North's office to give him my impression of Calero, which was, essentially, that he seemed to be a well-meaning plutocrat who was out of his depth trying to run an army.

I told Ollie, "You know, it's a crying shame we've left those guys the way we did. It just isn't right."

I suspect that was exactly what Ollie wanted to hear.

So that's how I backed myself into the Contra support effort. I would like to say Ollie talked me into it, but that's only partially true. My main motivation, in retrospect, was the nagging sense that things were getting screwed up again in our covert operations, and there weren't a lot of guys around who could fix them. Congress was vacillating once again between doing what was right and doing what was expedient and had predictably made the wrong choice, at least for the moment. I didn't feel I had to save the world, but I realized I'd have to live in it with my conscience. And what Ollie was really asking—helping the Contras with their supply problem— wasn't so much in the larger scheme of things.

North and I devised a brevity code (simple words or letters that meant previously determined things) for sending secure messages over commercial telephone lines or radio, and I took a code name, "Copp," to keep eavesdroppers—mostly Soviet and Cuban intelligence that was shared with the Sandinistas—from guessing our team's lineup.

We also used fake identities to prevent these same people from detecting us on travel records. Ollie's name was "Goode," for which he had a complete set of CIA-furnished dummy documentation: U.S. passport, driver's license, and other pocket ID aimed at satisfying a casual inspection.

When we had to talk about something for which a code word didn't exist, we used a simple alphanumeric key (letter or number substitution) for our messages. This is the type of "spy code" the public is most familiar with. It works fine as long as the message is short. If it goes on too long, however, or if there is some misunderstanding or discussion, somebody will eventually say too much; so the idea is to keep it simple.

Because Albert and our company, STTGI, handled fairly big-ticket, sophisticated noncombat systems, we hadn't considered relatively poor Central America as a viable market. Now, I was out pricing hand grenades and

7.62 mm ammunition for jungle guerrillas. Obviously, this was a sideshow as far as we were concerned—a favor for North and the administration to help the Contras bridge the gap until Congress's on-again, off-again funding could fall in sync with the President's policy. I told Albert I'd promised North to do what I could, which wasn't much, and then get back to business as soon as possible.

One of the first things I did was to get a hold of somebody who knew the region; and for ground combat in Central America, there was nobody better than Tom Clines. Despite his problems with Edwin Wilson and his unhappy experience with EATSCO, I still considered Tom a close friend and valued his infantry combat and CIA experience, much of it in the Caribbean as well as Laos. Tom was also an expert in the foreign arms market, which, because of the endless period that would be required for us to obtain a license under the U.S. Arms Export Control Act (especially given the negative climate toward Nicaragua in the regulatory agencies), was the place I determined Calero's munitions would have to be purchased.

Tom and I agreed that standardization and field delivery were the Contras' most pressing logistical problems. In terms of weapons, the Contras used a bit of everything: G3 rifles from Belgium, Spain, and Portugal; Soviet AK-47s; a smattering of U.S. M16s; and a real grab bag of machine guns—always a logistical nightmare. They also had LAW antitank rockets, a variety of hand grenades, and some American-made mortars, all 60 and 81 mm.

Ideally, we'd have used one model in each combat category, preferably equipment made in the Soviet bloc since that's what the Sandinistas used, and guerrillas always do best when they can use captured enemy arms and ammo. Besides, Tom said, the bloc countries (particularly dealers in Poland, Czechoslovakia, and Romania) were always eager to do business. They needed the foreign exchange, and weapons were one of the few commodities produced in Communist countries that the outside world demanded. Portugal was an ideal country through which to broker arms. They understood the facts of life and were dealing with both sides in the Iran and Iraq war, although they never trumpeted it openly.

I set Tom up in business with Rafael Quintero, a Cuban exile in his early 40s. "Ralph," as we called him (his close friends called him "Chi-Chi"), was a guerrilla war expert who had known Tom since the Bay of Pigs. Quintero, a pathfinder for that abortive invasion, escaped a month later in a CIA boat and was Tom's operative during his long campaign of covert harassment against Fidel Castro. After Ralph's CIA tour, he worked with various intelligence agencies in the U.S. and was highly regarded by them as well as by the Miami Cuban community and many Central American leaders.

Ralph was, in essence, our "customer rep": the guy who would stay with Calero and the Contras and get to know the Contra organization, including its armory and needs. We would then compare his information with the information we'd get from Calero. One of the ways we knew Calero was getting questionable advice from others was the fact that he never requisitioned certain spare parts or cleaning materials—things we knew would eventually prove essential. Quintero was what we call a "high-fidelity" reporter—a meticulous observer whose value is enhanced by the pains he takes to stay out of the limelight and pass unnoticed in almost any company. He spent a lot of 1985 and 1986 traveling through El Salvador, Honduras, Costa Rica, and Guatemala laying the groundwork for our operations (such as arranging landing permission for our ships and aircraft coming in from overseas) with government authorities and intelligence agencies.

I paid Quintero a salary of $4,000 a month, plus expenses, as well as an occasional bonus when cash was available. Tom didn't want a salary and instead made a commission on our arms sales. Over the two years we ran the operation, he made about $600,000, from which he had to pay most of his own expenses. His principal role was to arrange for Contra arms procurements in Europe, including Eastern Europe, and make sure they got to the Contras. He also made a number of invaluable suggestions regarding Contra combat operations; I would be hard pressed to put a price tag on his services in that regard, but the number of dollars and lives he saved with his ideas were considerable.

As far as Hakim and I were concerned, Albert was paid a commission on earnings that went straight into his Geneva accounts—a total of about $1.5 million during the whole Iran and Contra support period. I originally discussed with Albert a formula for splitting the profit we'd earn, but that never came to fruition. After I worked with Ollie and Calero a while and saw the dire straits the Contras were in, I realized a lot of effort and a lot of money would be involved. Anyone in my position who got rich would be crucified as a profiteer when information about the program was made public, which we all assumed would be after the resumption of Congressional funding. I was doubly concerned about this, since the more I worked with Ollie, the clearer I could see the day when I might be offered another high-level government position, perhaps as deputy director of operations for the CIA—the place where I felt my wealth of experience could make a significant and beneficial difference to that then-troubled agency. I had even gone as far as to discuss this prospect with Ollie, and rumors circulated not long after that I was, in fact, being considered for that position.

Albert used to tease me about this ambition. "Okay," he joked, "you take the medals and I'll take the money!" To him, arms trading (as opposed to the nonlethal security systems we began with) was simply another form of business—and nothing to be ashamed of.

"We are doing a valuable service for our country," Albert said. "We're helping the people down there, and we're doing it at a price cheaper than they've been able to get in the past."

Be that as it may, I learned enough from the Edwin Wilson affair to know the media and one's political opponents weren't always so scrupulous about the facts. Like Caesar's wife, I would have to avoid even the *appearance* of profiteering for my chance of returning to government service to be realized.

With each successive arms deal, we tried to work Calero closer to standardizing his weapons, a goal we knew would be crucial to keeping the Contras in the field—although Calero never seemed to appreciate this. I often told him, "Look, Adolfo, you've got all this crap—why not stick with one weapon, say, the Russian AK-47?" and then point out the virtues of this approach.

He'd only reply, "No, no, we like the G3 because of this and the M16 because of that," as if he were on safari and wanted one gun for elephants and another for gazelle. The whole principle of standardization for purposes of training, combat effectiveness, and logistics efficiency just seemed to escape the Contras.

Our first shipments went to Calero in December 1984 and January 1985 from the People's Republic of China, which had just entered the international arms market and offered terrific prices on high-quality goods—even ammunition for Western weapons manufactured to NATO specs. (They had set up two quasi-government agencies and got into the arms business with both hands, which really drove down world prices.) We later got arms from Poland using the same end-use certificate (EUC) system every other arms dealer in the world uses and every government winks at, including the United States and the then Soviet Union. In this case, the Poles wrote up false EUCs for South Yemen, Guatemala, Honduras, Nigeria, or, their favorite place for some reason, Somalia. The Polish government even provided "the paper," telling us, "We'll take care of everything." It was big business for them, and they didn't want little squirts like us to screw it up.

Our markup ran about 20 to 30 percent; and after our costs for shipping and middlemen, we never made more than about 20 percent on each order. That may sound like a lot until you consider that department stores and other retailers routinely mark up items 100 percent or more. Albert thought we were nuts charging as little as we did, but if he ever had second thoughts about leaving such operating decisions up to me, he never mentioned them. I've included an appendix at the end of this book detailing all of these financial dealings, including one made by Singlaub for comparison.

All told, we shipped about $9 million worth of M26 grenades (at $7.50 per) and AK-47 and G3 ammunition (starting at $130 a thousand, then dropping to $100 per thousand rounds)—a minuscule amount on the arms market but dear enough for Calero. He paid from his Ollie-augmented donations via wire transfer to the Swiss account of Energy Resources, Inc., a Panamanian company created for the purpose by Hakim and Zucker but controlled by me.

Most important, the Contras were happy with our weapons; although Calero, after coaching from Singlaub, thought they had to wait too long for delivery. His complaint arose from a meeting in North's office attended by me, Singlaub, and Calero, during which Singlaub said (to Calero, in front of Ollie and me):

"Secord's system is taking too long to deliver the arms. The ship has been delayed many times." He was referring to the shipment of Chinese arms due to arrive that week in Guatemala.

I mildly disagreed but did not engage in a lengthy rebuttal because I didn't want to give away our sources. Singlaub then expressed a desire to get directly involved in the weapons supply and delivery scene in Honduras (a Contra safe haven), which, given his penchant for publicity, I thought was a terrible idea and said so.

Later, Ollie told me this incident earned me Singlaub's animosity and I never met with Singlaub again, which was fine by me. For my money, he was a walking security violation, and his value to Contra operations increased in direct proportion to his distance from it.

Despite later assertions, Calero never complained about our markup. He and other Contra officials had no reason to squawk, especially when some of their leaders, including Calero's brother Mario (the Contras' New Orleans purchasing agent), lived better than they probably should have, and at their soldiers' expense. This was exemplified by the well-known case of substandard goods (rotten rain ponchos and unusable combat boots) Mario procured and sent to the guerrillas.

Ron Martin, a kingpin in the Central American arms trade, was furious with us because he thought we were intentionally undercutting him—"dumping" material at sale prices just to corner the local market. Martin had something of a monopoly on arms channeled through Honduras, where the Contra shipments terminated. He tried to give the CIA an ultimatum: Buy from me or find another country as safe haven for your freedom fighters. He apparently didn't know that, because of the Boland Amendment, the CIA was currently out of the loop. His threat resulted only in a renewed legal investigation of his activities, although, as far as I know, he has not been formally charged with anything.

Of bigger concern to Calero at this time was the source of funds to pay for the arms, ammunition, and supplies. North had been working hard since Boland II to raise cash from private sources and third-party countries, and to overcome the narrow margin of opposition at the State Department and in Congress to restoring Contra aid.

I discovered through our frequent contacts that Ollie was personally stretched very thin by these and other duties. He began to rely on me for information about the Contras, obtained during the normal course of business from Quintero and Clines, which I provided—including reports of financial corruption and military ineptness among the Contra leadership. He also asked me for help, from time to time, with his fund-raising efforts among the various officials and heads of state I knew in the Middle East, and I was happy to oblige.

Given my popularity among the Saudis, for example, I lobbied with them for support of the Contras in 1985. They eventually did make a sizable contribution after the king's U.S. visit. (The report on the Iran-Contra hearings puts this amount at $30 million, but I think $15 to $20 million is more like it, knowing the Saudis, although I can't be certain.) Jeff Garth, a reporter at the *New York Times*, later speculated on the newspaper's February 4, 1987 front page that "King Fahd and other top Saudi Arabian officials agreed in 1981 to aid anti-Communist resistance groups around the world as part of the arrangement allowing them to buy sophisticated American AWACS radar planes..." but such an arrangement was never made, and I'm the man who would know. This report is a good example of the media's propensity to reconstruct history to fit conspiracy theories. Such a condition on the AWACS sale to the Saudis would've made no sense in 1981, since the U.S. government wasn't prohibited from funding the Contras at that time.

Ollie and Calero always complained that funding was close to the margin, and I saw no reason to doubt them. From the Boland II cutoff in 1984 to the time the CIA got back in the game in late 1986, the Contra force had grown from about seven or eight thousand men to well over twenty thousand.

The growth of the Contra force exacerbated their second-biggest problem: resupplying themselves in the field. It also underscored the biggest, most absurd paradox of the whole affair—the need for the nation with the greatest air power in the world to provide such support *covertly*. I don't think it was a factor in his decision to first call me, but Ollie would wind up having in his network of helpers one of the few people around who had ever organized and run such an operation before. Me.

My involvement with the Contra air-supply operation began in July 1985 at an all-night meeting in Miami between Calero and his field commander, Enrique Bermudez, and Ollie, myself, Tom Clines, and Quintero. Ollie (who arrived at about 10 P.M. and looked like he hadn't slept in a week) was all worked up over his somewhat latent realization that the Contras were squandering their donated money and, worse, using part of it to line the pockets of some of their leaders.

He opened the meeting, which was intended as a comprehensive "program review," by laying into Calero about his leadership failings and these suspected improprieties. North pointed out such strategic failures as the Contras' inability to support a southern front, poor security (the Contras were riddled with Sandinista agents), and lack of any sort of special ops capability (a must in that environment), as well as gross inefficiencies—including a $5.6 million order for 10,000 AK-47 rifles, made by Calero to placate Singlaub, when the Contras already had thousands of rifles in storage and needed food and clothing (and just about everything else) a lot more. Ollie even brought up the old story about Calero's brother Mario and the rotten ponchos.

The rest of us just sat there, thunderstruck. It may have been the right thing to do, but it sure was the wrong way to do it.

The problem was Ollie's complete misreading, perhaps owing to his inexperience, of Calero's—and, indeed, the entire *latino*—mentality. Calero and Bermudez may not have been swaggering strong-men, but they had plenty of Hispanic *machismo*. You just don't disassemble someone like that in public, let alone in front of the gringos, and expect him to keep working for you.

Naturally, Calero was deeply offended and embarrassed and denied everything Ollie said; how could he not, even if he knew it was true? North's solution (a good one before the meeting and absolutely imperative afterward) was to have Energy Resources receive *all* future third-party donations and simply remove temptation from any sticky-fingered Contras. Ollie didn't mention this plan specifically to Calero in the meeting, but after a few months of receiving boots and bullets instead of greenbacks, the commandante got the message. Had this discipline been imposed a year earlier, I think an additional $8 to $10 million would've been available to the field soldiers in tangible aid, including food and clothing. The real downside was that Ollie's semipublic tongue-lashing only drove Calero closer to Ron Martin, who wasn't about to criticize him, and created a general atmosphere among the Contra leaders that what they really needed was not to be better stewards of their resources, but to be more careful about getting caught.

Eventually our discussion got around to the problems the field commanders were having because of a lack of airdrop capability. Some of the Contra units were a month or more by foot from their Honduran or Costa Rican bases and had no way to sustain themselves (particularly with consumables—food, medicine, and ammunition) in the field. The Contras had some light aircraft and seven or eight pilots, but they could operate only in daylight and couldn't penetrate to forward drop zones inside Nicaragua, where both Sandinista antiaircaft batteries and missiles were becoming increasingly effective. Back when the CIA was on board, they tried remote drops staged from Miami with predictably bad results.

We recognized that if the air resupply capability didn't improve—and rather quickly—the Contras would soon have to quit the field. Unfortunately, by this time it was dawn, and Ollie had to jet back to Washington for a staff meeting. We adjourned with a general understanding that I, somehow, would make everything better.

This meeting was another turning point for me personally. Up to then, I had been strictly a commercial supplier—someone who offered friendly advice when asked, but was there mainly to keep the shelves stocked to the extent that I was able. Now, I was sitting around the table with Tom and Ralph trying to sketch in plans for a complete air force on a blank sheet of paper. I was shifting, subtly, from supplier and advisor to player. I probably wouldn't have noticed the transformation had Tom Clines not injected a sage word of advice:

"Don't get involved, Dick," he said. "It will be nothing but misery."

"I know," I answered, "but that's not the point. The whole thing is going down the tubes!"

Spoken like a true Contra.

Because I was still "air chief" and "the general" to Tom and Ralph, they indulged my little fantasy. We pored over military maps of the region, much of which Tom and Ralph knew firsthand. The U.S. had training sites on the Atlantic Coast in Guatemala and Nicaragua, and Quintero had actually walked over much of the ground we were concerned with in Costa Rica and Nicaragua. He also knew some of the Indian leaders in the eastern part of Nicaragua. Together we designed at least the skeleton of a system: a forward air base (preferably three—one each in Honduras, Costa Rica, and El Salvador—but at least one emergency strip below the border to support the southern front); a secure main operating base and staging area (Ilopango in El Salvador was the natural choice); some warehouses; a few new airplanes; and the air/ground crews to man them.

After our bare-bones plan was complete, I rolled up the papers and stuck them in my hip pocket. Without more money, it was all academic, and cash like that wasn't gushing in from North's donation machinery. On the flight home, I agreed more and more with Tom: It just wouldn't be worth the headaches to get involved.

A short time later, while Ollie and I were talking on the phone, he again brought up the matter of Contra air support.

"Well, Dick," he asked, "do you think you can put something together?"

I replied with a quick review of our needs and concerns and told him the whole thing just didn't seem practical. Nonetheless, he was persistent.

"Now Dick, don't tell me a couple of old Laos hands like you and Tom can't scratch together something that'll keep a ragtag band like that in the field for at least a few more months!"

"Okay," I said in frustration. "If you can find the money, I'll do it." I figured that would end the conversation.

"How much money would you need?" North asked.

"A lot!" Next topic.

"How much is a lot?"

"I don't know," I sighed. "We'll have to study the matter."

That was the wrong thing to say. Having failed to say no, I sort of said yes—which to Ollie was like an oath in blood. He promised to find the funds for the operation somehow and asked me to begin getting my act together. Grudgingly, I agreed to be the "founding father" of Air Contra but made it clear that I didn't want to be saddled with its actual operation.

Famous last words.

To make a system like this work, we needed someone who knew how to manage night operations—someone on the scene to launch and debrief the crews and handle the dozens of screwups and emergencies that constitute even *normal* operations. I told Ollie that I would not go down to Central America and personally run his airline, and I stuck by that decision. I added (now that we were close to actually having an airline) that I also refused to try and run it from Virginia or Miami, which was a recipe for disaster. I would be willing to hire the on-site director, though, and had a colleague in mind, Richard Gadd, who was an excellent choice. Ollie agreed, and Gadd was hired in August 1985.

The first element in our "temporary" air campaign was the completion of an emergency airstrip at Santa Elena in the extreme northwest of Costa Rica near the Nicaraguan border. We set up a dummy company, the Udall Corporation (named, appropriately, after Morris Udall, the noted conservationist), which purchased the 15,000 acres for a paper value of about $3 million, financed by the sellers, under the cover of building a game preserve and tourist attraction.

In reality, of course, we built a dirt-surfaced emergency airfield with private funds deposited in Energy Resources. This was done with complete knowledge and cooperation of the Costa Rican government (Security Minister Ben Piza approved the construction) since we, in essence, ceded the field to them for use both with their main civil guard training camp, which was about 15 or 20 kilometers away, and as a base for drug-enforcement missions.

A more important asset was our main facility at Ilopango, on the eastern edge of El Salvador's capital of San Salvador. Ralph Quintero skillfully convinced the commanding general of the Salvadorian Air Force that it was in El Salvador's best interest to go along with the plan, and he agreed to provide security and basic facilities for a small logistical air operation. In practical terms, this meant the Salvadorians sold us avgas and provided parking space for our aircraft on the ramp. They also provided space (plus expansion area) for our warehouse and helped locate and rent three houses to be shared by our ground and air crews.

Most important, they fulfilled their agreement without the assistance of any U.S. agencies—although the U.S. Ambassador, U.S. Military Group Chief, and the local CIA chief knew about our operation. The CIA had a presence at Ilopango and occasionally spoke with our people. Still, we never established any formal reporting system with them. The reason for this was the CIA's bureaucratic fear of the Boland Amendments, although we assured them these amendments specifically *permitted* the gathering and exchange of intelligence with the Contras and their operatives. Despite this latitude (and despite my frequent requests for such cooperation through Ollie's and Bill

Casey's offices), neither the CIA nor any other U.S. government agency provided the necessary air intelligence (threat analysis, enemy order of battle, weather information) for our operation.

While the Costa Rican field was being completed, we assembled a small fleet of surplus transport planes: two C-123K Providers (a jet-assisted, twin-prop military cargo plane used widely in Vietnam); two C-7 Caribous (a slightly smaller twin-engine transport with good STOL—short takeoff and landing—capability); and a new Maule "Rocket," an extremely STOL light plane, a kind of souped-up Cessna. The Caribous we obtained from a dealer in Canada, where the planes were made, for $700,000—the first in December 1985, and the second in February 1986. The C-123s (purchased in March and June 1986) and the Maule we bought from a U.S. dealer for a package price, including spares, of about $85,000 each.

Like the money for the emergency air base, the cash for these outlays came entirely from private and third-country contributions deposited to the account of Energy Resources. It was a bedraggled little air force, but with the right crews, we hoped it would keep the Contras going until the CIA's Air Branch or U.S. Air Force reentered the picture.

Supporting FDN forces in the north was relatively straightforward. Aircraft from Ilopango would be staged for several days at a time at Aguacate, the Contras' Honduran air base on the north-central section of the Nicaraguan border.

Supporting the 2,000 or so troops under Eden Pastora, and later other commandantes, in the south would be another matter. As we later learned from the CIA's Costa Rica chief of station, Joe Fernandez, alias Thomas Castillo (a U.S. citizen of Hispanic background with 20 years of CIA experience; a man well thought of by Casey and his colleagues), the south had been given short shrift by the FDN owing to factionalism and poor CIA planning. Now specially trained Sandinista counterinsurgency forces had concentrated in the north, where they perceived a greater threat. We believed that a revitalized threat in the south would force the Sandinistas to disperse these elite battalions and make them more vulnerable to guerrilla attacks.

These more remote southern Contra forces would be supported via the Atlantic or Pacific coasts, by nonstop flights which would punch inland over the northern border of Costa Rica, service the drop zone, and then return to Ilopango. Our plan required a seven- to eight-hour flight by the C-123s—a demanding maximum-range mission even without the added burden of covert operations—but the potential rewards would be well worth it.

The problem was that the Contra high command still viewed the southern elements as a splinter group (which was pretty much how they viewed themselves). Getting Calero and Bermudez to share resources with the South and getting the southern force to coordinate its actions with the FDN was like

mixing water and oil. This is an all-too-typical problem in insurgency movements; we ran into it in Laos, and history shows North Vietnam had similar
troubles with its "uppity" Viet Cong allies in the South. As the Vietnamese
proved, though, such problems are not insurmountable because, when resources are scarce, even a little cooperation can make the difference between
survival and defeat.

I also invested in a little legal work. I was now getting out of the product
and into the service business. This gave me real concern that we could, as
American citizens participating indirectly in the combat operations of foreign
nationals, violate the U.S. Neutrality Act when we started operations. I hired
a well-known Washington law firm, Patton, Boggs & Blow, to prepare a legal
opinion on the matter and made sure that our system was set up and run
within the parameters of that opinion. It was a sensible precaution and one
I was thankful for a thousand times over. Although the media still refuses
to acknowledge the legality of our operation, including our compliance with
the Arms Export Control Act, the U.S. legal system has done so, much to
the consternation of the special prosecutor.

I then took the additional precaution of meeting with each of Ollie
North's solid-line and dotted-line bosses at the White House to make sure
the Contra support operation was on the level. While I admired Ollie and
found him to be the hardest-working public servant I'd ever met, I wasn't
about to commit other people to tasks and risks like this on the assurances
of one recently promoted lieutenant colonel, as earnest and persuasive as he
might be.

In December 1985, I met with Bud McFarlane, President Reagan's National Security Advisor, and Bill Casey, Director of the CIA.

Bud and I never saw each other socially, but we knew each other well
professionally, beginning in 1972 when he was a lieutenant colonel on Kissinger's NSC staff and I was a colonel in the Pentagon. A decade later during
the AWACS battle, he was counselor to Secretary of State Al Haig and was
a member of the interagency team led by then National Security Advisor
Richard Allen. As the man in charge of the Pentagon's team, I met with Bud
often. McFarlane went on to serve as deputy NSC advisor under William
Clark, and we worked together in the interagency group on Lebanon.

I had found Bud to be a straight shooter who, despite his lack of extensive
field experience, was a master of the Washington bureaucracy—somebody
you could count on in a pinch. Strangely, his organizational savvy didn't
seem to extend very far into the political world, despite the fact that his father
had been a congressman. Bud's notion seemed to be that politics meant
compromise, which it often does, but he reached for that tool too often, even
when he held all the cards. He was always a better analyst than decision
maker, which probably explained his longevity in Washington and his rapid
rise to the top.

My agenda for the meeting with Bud, as well as the meeting I intended to have with Casey, was more or less the same. I wanted to cover the scope of our intended operations, how they were funded, and the risks as I saw them. In each case I intended to emphasize the short-term, "bridging" nature of the operations; I didn't want to be in the clandestine airline business longer than six or eight months, the time Ollie thought it would take to restore Congressional funding. I also wanted it to be crystal clear that all the assets we had accumulated (from aircraft, spare parts, and crew contracts to airfields and warehouses) would be turned over to the U.S. government once the CIA got back in the game.

As it turned out, in late November 1985, the content of these discussions would be expanded dramatically. Before I could meet with his bosses, I received another call from Ollie.

"Dick, can you come down here? We have to talk."

The subject would be Iran.

# — 13 —

# Iran Redux

Ollie sounded worried, and even though I was up to my neck in alligators (trying to keep STTGI's marketing going while starting up Calero's Contra airline), I got down to his office as fast as I could. He looked as perplexed as he sounded, like a guy locked out of his car in a bad neighborhood wondering what the hell he was going to do next.

"We've run into a big problem on an Iranian project we've been working," he said, smiling bravely, as if the *project* were nothing more than a mixed-up airline reservation and Iran wasn't number one on the President's chart of terrorist nations—a dubious distinction it had held since January 1984. Ollie was being cryptic, very un-Northlike, and wouldn't say much about the project other than that it was some kind of "ongoing joint venture with the Israelis that had been approved by the President" for the transfer of I-HAWK missiles from Israel to Iran, possibly via Portugal.

The "big problem" was the fact that the Israelis seemed unable, for some reason, to arrange for the required air shipment of these missiles.

Ollie said that Bud McFarlane, who was with the President in Geneva for an economic summit, had passed along Israeli Defense Minister Yitzhak Rabin's plea for help on the matter. Gradually I was able to piece together the essence of the project—and the problem.

The Israelis had pursued their own policy with Iran for years, which was no secret to anyone familiar with the region. Even the 1979 U.S. arms embargo against Iran was no barrier—another example of the many ways American de facto foreign policy was shaped to accommodate its ally. That the U.S. should now attach itself to Israel's ongoing relationship in an attempt to restore old ties with Iran didn't surprise me; in fact, it was long overdue. It didn't surprise me, either, that North would call me about a problem like this. Both he and McFarlane knew I had been instrumental in establishing Project Tipped Kettle (some of those weapons had gone to the Contras, too, prior to the Boland cutoff). They also knew of my extensive experience in Iran.

I told Ollie that Portugal might make a good transshipment point, the only problem being that the new Silva Cavaco government was in the midst of taking over in Lisbon. Most of the Portuguese officials Clines and I had dealt with were either gone or on their way out. Because of that, we would have our hands full just keeping material in the current Contra pipeline, let alone patching Iran into the system, and that's what I told Ollie.

He could only repeat that I was the agent of choice, named by McFarlane as the only guy with the knowledge and contacts to pull this thing off in a timely way. He gave me one of those patented *Sorry, pal, it's your problem now* kind of smiles. I sighed and said I'd do what I could. Later the next day (November 19, 1985), "Copp" (as I was now known on such missions) and Clines, who happened to be in Washington, were on a plane to Lisbon.

Our first task on arrival was to determine the true scope of the problem. The CIA's senior local official and the U.S. Ambassador's deputy had been given a very limited, top-secret briefing on the situation—just enough for them to know they should do all they could without asking too many questions. North had also given me the name of his Israeli contact: a man named Al Schwimmer, whom I knew by reputation as one of the founders of Israel Aircraft Industries.

From Schwimmer (on an unsecure trunk phone line) I learned that we weren't talking about jury-rigging a false manifest for crated equipment or anything simple like that. Their plan was to off-load 80 very large surface-to-air missiles from an El Al 747, store them at the Lisbon airport to "wash," or launder, their paper, and then ferry them to Iran via a series of chartered flights on smaller 707s.

The status of the mission was this: The original plans to fly to Iran from Israel had been scrapped because no contractor would undertake the mission. The missiles were all sitting on the ramp in Tel Aviv while the flight was replanned to go through Portugal. Now, the new Portuguese government was showing reluctance about getting involved in a hastily contrived and, in my opinion, harebrained scheme. McFarlane had spoken directly to the new Portuguese foreign minister, but to no avail. Also, Schwimmer was running into trouble lining up narrow-bodied cargo planes for the final leg to Iran. None of the charter carriers could obtain insurance for such a flight, another niggling detail that should have been foreseen.

My first communication back to Ollie was, "This looks like a busted flush. Why don't you send the merchandise by boat?" That would solve both the manifest and security problems. But Tehran wanted the missiles immediately.

North asked, "How much would it cost if you chartered the necessary aircraft and took the missiles to Tehran yourself?"

Schwimmer had planned on taking about 25 missiles on each 707 or DC-8, so I figured four airplanes (or four trips by one airplane) would do the job at about a quarter of a million dollars per sortie—provided I could find a carrier that would self-insure. Call it a round million.

Amazingly, when Schwimmer was informed, he had the money instantly deposited to Lake Resources' (which had, by late 1985, replaced the now too-visible Energy Resources) account via Yakov Nimrodi, another private citizen acting as an Israeli intermediary.

The only airplanes I could get on such short notice were two 707s from a CIA proprietary, which explained why they didn't need insurance. The first plane landed at Tel Aviv but could hold only 18 HAWKs. That plane went on to Tehran, via Cyprus. After the Iranians examined the missiles, however, they rejected them the same day because they were "the wrong kind." This was not because they weren't compatible with the Iranian air-defense system. Rather, the Iranians wanted high-altitude SAMs, not low-altitude I-HAWKs, which they already had coming out their ears. They accused the Iranian acting as their conduit to the West, Manucher Ghorbanifar (whom we called "Gorba," although his Mossad [Israeli intelligence], NSC, and CIA code name was "the Merchant"), of pulling a fast one and complained that some components still bore Israeli Air Force markings—bad PR in revolutionary Iran, to say the least.

After learning of the I-HAWK debacle, North asked whether I would go to Tel Aviv ASAP to get the full story from David Kimche, then director general of Israel's Ministry of Foreign Affairs and a former high official with the Mossad. North wanted to know what went wrong, why, who screwed up, and what Israel planned to do about it. I had previous dealings with Kimche when I worked for Weinberger and believed him to be a reliable man.

Part of the problem seemed to revolve around Ghorbanifar. Ghorbanifar had been used by the Israelis as part of their ongoing attempts to open a dialogue with the Iranians on matters of strategic interest to the West, and Israel in particular. Ted Shackley had met Gorba in Hamburg, Germany, in 1984 in connection with another matter, and Shackley's impression was that Gorba was a can-do sort of man—the first to raise the possibility of using Iran's influence with the militants in Lebanon to release the American hostages. It was an intriguing but self-serving suggestion, since Ghorbanifar also indicated that he was the only person who knew the right Iranian buttons to push to get the hostages released. He certainly knew which of Shackley's buttons to push: Ted suggested that William Buckley, the CIA's Beirut chief of station, should be the first hostage freed through this channel. (Buckley was later tortured and died in late 1985.)

Since time was of the essence, I flew to Israel via chartered Lear jet to meet with Kimche. During our 45-minute debriefing, I reassured him that I was not in town on a fault-finding mission, but to prevent any problems from recurring. He was genuinely puzzled about why the Iranians turned down the I-HAWKs, which the Israeli team supporting Ghorbanifar assured him were what the Iranians wanted. After we finished, I took a cab to Schwimmer's residence near Ben Gurion Airport and interviewed him, hoping to get some answers. His reaction was a lot different from Kimche's.

"Look," he said, "I'm an old friend of Prime Minister Shimon Peres— I'll tell you and I'll tell him the same thing: You can fire me now if that's what you want. I'm not in it for the money and did the best I could. I was told you'd be able to get us political clearance through Portugal—so what happened?"

He went on like that in a very defensive vein, glossing over the fact that when Iran received the missiles, they rejected them out of hand. It turned out that the Israeli team had just assumed the "I" in I-HAWK mean that the "improved" HAWK missile had high-altitude capability, which it most certainly does not. If any of them had consulted their own ministry of defense, they'd have learned that it simply means the I-HAWK is better than the basic model at sniffing out low-flying, high-speed aircraft from the surrounding ground clutter. Schwimmer admitted that Gorba's contact, Mosen Kangarlu (code named, imaginatively enough, "Kangaroo"), an official in the Iranian Prime Minister's office, had gone crazy when he heard the shipment was the same I-HAWKs that Iran already had in copious quantities, and not high-altitude SAMs. He accused everyone, from Ghorbanifar to Schwimmer and the horses they rode in on, of being crooks, cheats, and liars. Kangarlu wanted the missiles removed immediately and all his money refunded.

Schwimmer was supposedly an aviation expert, and Kimche and Nimrodi weren't; so maybe he felt they were trying to lay the blame for the screwup at his feet. It wouldn't be the first time Israeli "overconfidence" got in the way of their good judgment. Schwimmer was understandably embarrassed.

Later, Kimche and I met with Major General Mendy Meron, now director general of Israel's Ministry of Defense, and Amos Lapidot, commander of the Israeli air force—both officers I knew well. After we talked a while, it became clear that what the Iranians really wanted was a SAM that could hit MiG-25 reconnaissance aircraft and Soviet-made Blinder bombers above 40,000 feet. Somehow this gap in information occurred between the technical advisors in the defense ministry and the nontechnical intermediaries in the field. I didn't blame Kangarlu one bit for losing his head. In revolutionary Iran, people had lost them—literally—for a lot less.

The second chartered 707 arrived in Tel Aviv, but, because we now knew the basic cargo was no good, we never used it. The tab came to $160,000, plus $40,000 for a chartered Lear jet used to shuffle people between Tel Aviv,

Lisbon, and Paris. This left a balance of $800,000 in the Schwimmer account, which I expected to refund. Schwimmer said to hang onto it because he believed the operation would continue.

I learned that the 80 I-HAWK missiles had been drawn from Israeli stock and made available to Iran through the private sector (the Schwimmer-Nimrodi-Ghorbanifar connection), each stage being further removed from the visible seats of power in Israel. I didn't know at the time what they were charging Iran for the missiles, but I saw intelligence reports later that put the price at between $500,000 and $1 million each. Based on Schwimmer's original estimate of 25 missiles per plane, Iran had already ponied up $40 million (the amount agreed upon for 80 missiles plus transportation), for which they had received only 18 units—and those weren't what they wanted. Now, Iran was demanding *all* its money back, which put the Israeli team in an awkward position. Aside from the million they paid me for the planes, they had blown another couple of million on the original 747 they had chartered from El Al. Now, Ghorbanifar, Nimrodi, and the Iranian oil minister were holed up in a Geneva hotel arguing over the finances. Although Ghorbanifar later claimed he never received his commission, a lot of the Iranians' money was disbursed. Nobody knew how the Israelis were going to refund it.

The Israelis picked a bad time for a financial dispute with the Iranians. Throughout 1985 and well into 1986, every con artist on the planet seemed out to make a buck at Iranian expense. The mullahs had been burned early and often but kept coming back for more; their lack of sophistication in these matters was matched only by their dire need for the equipment and munitions after five years of war with Iraq. The FBI and U.S. Customs Department actively tracked these cases and actually busted a few. Ollie passed whatever scuttlebutt we picked up from the Iranians about prospective black-market deals to his counterparts in the law-enforcement agencies.

Based on information we provided, U.S. agents shut down a TOW (optically sighted, wire-guided antitank) missile scam in Madrid and foiled an attempt in Texas to steal TOWs from the Army and ship them to Iran. Most of these (and other) crooks had already extracted some cash up front (the worst thing you can say to an arms dealer is "C.O.D."), so the Iranians were more and more wary about checking credentials and postponing payments.

I learned that in August and September of 1985, before Ollie brought me on board, Schwimmer and Ghorbanifar had sold 508 TOW missiles to Iran. They had flown 100 Israeli TOWs through Turkish airspace to Tabriz, Iran, and moved another 400 the same way to Tehran. These shipments were apparently clumsily handled because the Turkish authorities raised objections after the fact—one reason Schwimmer decided to launder the missiles in Portugal. Our 707 was able to overfly Turkey because of its CIA connections, but I doubted that would work on a regular basis.

This still left open the question about how the Israelis would be compensated for the 500 or so TOWs they shipped from their own stock. Based on assurances by Bud McFarlane, they clearly expected the U.S. to replenish them. As I told General Meron in our earlier discussion, the U.S. couldn't "just ship weapons" without Congressional approval. Although it was really none of my business, I was more than a little curious about where the money the Iranians paid had gone. If the deal had been handled in the same manner as the I-HAWKs, the Iranians must have paid somebody in advance for the missiles. I later learned that somewhere between $6 and $10 million had, in fact, been paid for the weapons and had just evaporated into "the system" established by Schwimmer, Nimrodi, and Ghorbanifar. To my knowledge, the question was never resolved.

I gave Ollie an update on all this by brevity code over commercial phone and he, Kimche, and Schwimmer decided to set up a meeting in London to sort through the issues. As the guy who was now nominally in charge of the air operation, I was asked by Ollie to attend.

On the way to London, at North's request, Kimche and I stopped in Paris, and I met Ghorbanifar and Nimrodi for the first time. As a new player on the American team, I merited a lot of "attention" from Ghorbanifar, who would, over the next four months, do everything he could to ingratiate himself to me—all of it unsuccessful.

Although I did not know him from my MAAG assignment, Ghorbanifar's history as a private intelligence operative went back to prerevolutionary Iran. In the early 1970s he was a contract agent for the Savak, in which role he operated a freight-forwarding business, Starline International—a kind of oceangoing Iranian "Air America." Sometime in the 1970s he had become close to Yakov Nimrodi, who was then military attaché and Mossad station chief in Tehran (the Israelis did not have an embassy per se). That was when Ghorbanifar was recruited, formally or informally, to serve as an Israeli operative.

Ghorbanifar fled Iran to Europe after the revolution but stayed in contact with both his Iranian and Israeli friends, particularly his old boss, General Hashemi, a high-ranking Savak department head who was also exiled in London. By 1985, the Israelis decided to expand their ongoing arms business to Iran with diplomatic initiatives and chose Ghorbanifar as their agent. Iran's war with Iraq was going badly, and since Israel, too, opposed Iraq, it seemed like the old Arab proverb that "the enemy of my enemy is my friend" would overcome the Ayatollah's well-known antipathy toward Israel. Kimche, Schwimmer, Nimrodi, and an American NSC consultant named Michael Ledeen met several times that year to formulate an approach that could then be coordinated with Ghorbanifar. This, apparently, was the genesis of the original 508 TOW missile deal.

A key element in this plan included assurances that the TOWs would go to Ghorbanifar's contacts in the Revolutionary Guards rather than the regular Iranian army, since this was where political power was concentrated in Iran and the conduit for influencing Islamic revolutionaries in other quarters, including Lebanon. Ghorbanifar claimed he was dealing with a "project officer" named Kangarlu in the office of Iranian Prime Minister Mushavi, which was one of the few Ghorbanifar stories that turned out to be true. The connection between his Iranian contacts and the Lebanese hostage takers was confirmed with the release of Reverend Benjamin Weir on September 15, 1985, after the delivery of the first batch of 508 TOWs.

This initial success sparked a lot of enthusiasm in the White House. At this point Ollie North became involved—inherited and extended, as it were, Ledeen's efforts on behalf of the NSC. Everyone felt America's entrance into the previously Israeli-Iranian project should start off with a bang. The I-HAWKs were picked by Schwimmer and Ledeen as the subject of the next batch, since the air war at the time was going badly against the Iranians. Obviously, this had been a mistake.

Ghorbanifar was staying at the opulent George V Hotel on the Rue George V off the Champs Elysées in Paris—another tip-off as to the kind of guy we were dealing with. I suppose old money and the unspeakably nouveau riche like places like this, but, despite my past working relationships with shahs and sheiks, I never had the wherewithal to cultivate a taste for them, so I checked into the Hotel Warwick next to the Chicago Pizzeria down the street. I met Kimche, Nimrodi, and Ghorbanifar late that afternoon for lunch—the George *Cinque's* dining room had about cleared out and we virtually had the place to ourselves. I must've looked pretty out of place, a corn-fed Ohio boy squinting at the elegant French menu, so Ghorbanifar ordered for me—a delicious fish dish that took two-and-a-half hours and two different kinds of wine to consume.

Ghorbanifar was a very, very slick operator. He was fluent in English, but he turned that fluency on and off as it suited him. When he was challenged on a point, for example, or was caught double-dealing, he suddenly had language problems, which bought him time to dissemble. We would soon learn he also had a tendency to "drop off the scope" when problems occurred and we needed him most—to go underground and disappear for weeks only to resurface when the problem (usually one he'd created) had been solved. Fortunately, we had a collection of telephone numbers Gorba habitually used, and intelligence usually apprised us of his activities, if not his whereabouts, during these periods. This information was a mixed blessing, for half the time he was promising people—particularly the Iranians—the moon when he could deliver only moonbeams. The key to understanding Gorba, I discovered, was that he was motivated almost exclusively by money. The one thing he was eternally afraid of was being cut out of the deal, and he went to extraordinary lengths to keep the game alive—to give people the impression of movement even if the new plan was dead on arrival.

At the time I met him, Ghorbanifar was in his mid-40s but looked older: the stereotypical Middle-East sophisticate, with a well-trimmed Vandyke, graying temples, five-hundred-dollar shoes and thousand-dollar suits, and a little of Albert Hakim's elegant, old-world manner. He liked the high life, including casino games like blackjack and roulette, and was a member of several private, world-class gambling clubs. He would later be described by the Senate's Intelligence Committee report as a "talented fabricator" (and they should know), but to me he was the grossest, most bald-faced liar I've ever run across. Many Middle East businessmen and officials like to quibble and prevaricate at least a little, but for Gorba it was an art form.

Nimrodi, who struck me at first as something of a clown—50-ish, with a big round face, round eyeglasses, and unruly fringe of hair—quickly took on the role of Ghorbanifar's "handler." He would preempt Gorba's comments and answer my questions on Ghorbanifar's behalf, and try to keep the conversation light by injecting humor and irrelevant stories about this and that. Had I gone by first impressions, I would've dismissed him as a lightweight, which would have been a mistake.

In fact, Nimrodi had been a Mossad field agent operating against Arab targets in the early years of Israeli statehood, when Israel clung with bleeding fingernails to a tiny chunk of the Holy Land. He had been born in Palestine and spoke Arabic like a native. In the early 1970s he was sent to Tehran as a military attaché for the Israeli mission, where he learned to speak Farsi as well. During his six years in Iran, he did business with virtually all Iranian leaders of consequence, especially in the defense establishment—including Albert Hakim and Ghorbanifar. When he retired, Nimrodi became an arms broker for Israel and other countries and quickly made his fortune.

All they really knew about me, other than my name, was that I was a general who knew his way around clandestine operations and had spent some time in Iran.

When the discussions got serious, they got *very* serious and went into all sorts of detail about future Iranian arms transfers—more TOWs (called "trucks"), HAWKs (which Ghorbanifar pronounced "Haaags"), and even super-sophisticated Phoenix missiles (which Ghorbanifar referred to in brevity code as "Volkswagens"). When I brought up the I-HAWK debacle, they just shrugged and began talking terms for another deal. From the naive way they talked about the Phoenix, a complicated air-to-air missile for the F-14 that the Iranians couldn't employ anyway because of lack of technical expertise, it was easy to see where the technical misinformation had begun.

I did pick up some lore about the project to date. Ghorbanifar habitually referred to "Line One" or "Line Three," and so on, when he talked about key players in the new Iranian regime. Line One contained the radicals, murderers, and thieves—the tough customers who put the muscle behind the revolution. Line Twos were the more pragmatic people who, although strongly nationalistic, worried about Iran's future in a hostile world and were willing to make compromises. Line Three people were the clerics—leaders motivated solely by religious principles. Obviously, the whole Iranian Initiative was aimed at Line Two. Ghorbanifar claimed, though, that he had to make payoffs to people in each line, including Ayatollah Karubi (a Majlis and War Council leader who oversaw Iran's nationalized companies) and Hashemi Rafsanjani himself, speaker of the Iranian Parliament. I discounted these claims as a cover for additional profiteering by Ghorbanifar himself, but who knows. Kickbacks are common throughout the Middle East, and, let's face it, virtue needs a bankroll as much as vice.

I could accept Ghorbanifar's political shorthand—but with a couple of modifications. First, there were more than three political factions in post-revolutionary Iran, and *all* the groups clung to the same religious hierarchy and rationales, although none of the leaders were purely religious in the sense of a Catholic Pope or Tibetan Dalai Lama. They all had their own temporal axes to grind, social and political programs, and some of the mullahs were known to be so venal as to make our own mafiosos look like Boy Scouts. In essence, the potpourri of reformers, nationalists, fundamentalists, zealots, and terrorists that formed the revolutionary core were much like the Bolsheviks in 1917.

Throughout the long lunch, Kimche didn't say much and I knew why. Nimrodi was sitting in for Schwimmer, but Kimche had none of the confidence in Nimrodi that he felt for the Israeli industrialist. Ghorbanifar and Nimrodi kept referring to "Mikey" this and "Mikey" that, assuming I was Mike Ledeen's replacement, which, in a sense, was true, although I hadn't discussed the project with Ledeen. In a way, Ledeen had become Ghorbanifar's sponsor with the U.S., and I think Gorba was afraid he'd be cut out unless he cultivated a similar friendly relationship with me. Mike Ledeen wasn't a stupid guy, and I think he clung to Ghorbanifar, as the Israelis did, because he thought Gorba could deliver.

I gave Ollie a brief, coded telephone summary of the luncheon and went on to meet him in London at the Intercontinental Hotel near Hyde Park on December 5. We discussed the Paris meeting at length, and I confessed that I found Ghorbanifar and Nimrodi the original "odd couple." They seemed pathologically averse to discussing the I-HAWK fiasco (water over the dam, they said) and cared only about future deals—and they were not thinking small. I told Ollie my concerns were twofold.

First, despite all the lip service, the bigger strategic issue of reestablishing high-level, government-to-government contact between the U.S. and Iran, which I had been told was the whole purpose of the initiative, often got sidetracked by their tendency to equate batches of arms with specific hostage releases. This tended to make the hostages bargaining chips for Iran rather than a quid pro quo or sign of renewed institutional trust—a significant difference in negotiating strategy. Ghorbanifar liked to cast these bigger issues as a kind of boilerplate, assuming that the U.S. and Iran were both "hostages of the hostage situation" and that the only thing we really needed to discuss was how many and what type of snazzy weapons would be equated with each hostage—a ransom deal if I ever heard one. I told Ollie that my gut-level instinct, drawn from a fairly extensive background with Iran's culture, material, and military needs, told me that Iran's higher leadership was probably a lot more interested in strategic rapprochement and bread-and-butter defense issues, like protection from the Soviets, than were these particular intermediaries. Almost all revolutionary regimes go through early radicalization followed by a period of reaction when more temperate heads take over. The current group of intermediaries seemed completely insensitive to this fact and the opportunity it presented.

Second, I felt their focus on high-tech arms (we eventually called this the "Star Wars" approach) would eventually backfire on everyone involved. Not only was obtaining that equipment a bigger hassle for us, but it really wasn't what the Iranians needed, thus indirectly hampering the Iranian war effort. Someday, some Iranian general or colonel would point this out, and Ghorbanifar's "Line Two" contacts would find themselves wearing blindfolds and tied to a post.

As far as the problem with high-altitude SAMs went, I had told Gorba and the others that the U.S. relied on manned interceptor aircraft and didn't really have any high-altitude SAMs, although the Soviets did—the famous SAM-2 that brought down Francis Gary Powers's U-2 or the newer SAM-8s. These could be procured at great price through the Eastern bloc countries if Iran thought it just had to have them, but I had a better suggestion.

I knew the Iranians had large numbers of Swiss-made Oerlikon 90 mm antiaircraft guns in their existing inventory. This triple-A was slaved to their gun-laying radars and, under favorable conditions, could give a helluva surprise to Soviet and Iraqi aircraft as high as 40,000 feet. Aside from these, the F-4s Iran operated could try pop-up maneuvers from around 40,000 feet and bag some of the high-flying bad guys with their AIM-7 Sparrows—as American pilots had been trained to do. Although I had never flown with an Iranian pilot who had mastered this technique, I knew it could be taught.

Ollie listened intently and nodded his agreement. He looked a little sobered by this—I think he had bought into the Ledeen/Ghorbanifar version of Iran's need—and agreed it was time to put the railroad back on track.

On December 8, 1985, the whole cast of characters was assembled in London at Nimrodi's row-house duplex on Exhibition Street near Hyde Park to discuss the status of the Iran Initiative.

Ollie and Schwimmer arrived late, so the meeting began with me, Nimrodi, Kimche, and Ghorbanifar. Ollie had asked me to begin by discrediting
the Star Wars approach Gorba had been pushing, which I did, suggesting that
the Iranians might find basic infantry, armor, and artillery support a lot more
useful—things like spare parts for wheeled and tracked vehicles, artillery munitions, tactical radios, and so forth. Recalling the problems the Shah had
right up to the end with qualified maintenance technicians, I also suggested
that some form of advisory or training aid might be helpful, too—a good way,
from America's viewpoint, to begin reestablishing our grass-roots intelligence,
although I didn't say this.

Ghorbanifar dismissed this out of hand. He said the Iranians already
had suppliers for this kind of stuff, largely through the Soviet bloc countries
and China, which really meant through suppliers other than himself. As a
result he didn't want to talk about it. At this point I demurred and said I
was too new to the project to render an opinion on what could be dismissed,
but it seemed that confining ourselves to high-tech equipment was just one
more way of limiting our flexibility.

As it turned out, after that December, the Soviet Union would concentrate almost all of its aid on Iraq, leaving Iran to turn more and more to
Spain, Portugal, Israel, France, West Germany, and South Korea for its war-
fighting materiel. Oddly enough, it seemed like the U.S. was the only major
nation *not* supplying substantial war materiel to Iran on a regular basis, giving
even greater irony to Iran-Contra critics who accused us of somehow "be-
traying our allies' trust" and violating our own arms injunction, which was
already a laughingstock around the globe. With the single exception of Jordan,
which was deeply committed to Iraq in the Iran-Iraq war, the Arab countries
would understand the Iran Initiative and support it. Beneath the public statements of concern would ring private applause, led by Egypt and the Gulf
Cooperative Council States—the same support for U.S. leadership that later
materialized as the Grand Coalition against Saddam Hussein.

North and Schwimmer finally arrived, and we turned to the I-HAWK fiasco.
They reviewed the record to date, attributed the release of Reverend Weir to
Ghorbanifar's efforts on the TOW sale, and concluded that the success more
than compensated for the "minor slip-up" of the I-HAWKs. The self-congrat-
ulation, which seemed premature to me, quickly gave way to a discussion of
how the team was going to refund the Iranian money paid to the Israelis for
the I-HAWKs and to replenish the Israeli TOWs. Everyone in the room looked
at Ollie and me, as representatives of Uncle Sugar, to bail them out.

That was Ollie's cue to take charge of the proceedings and read them the
gospel according to Uncle Sam—mostly a summation of the points Ollie and
I had talked about earlier. He also added a new carrot for the Iranians.

"It's possible," he said, "that we [the U.S.] might make some of our
regional intelligence available to Iran if sufficient progress is made."

By "regional intelligence" Ollie meant information about Iraq and the Soviets. Intelligence professionals and diplomats familiar with the region knew that Iraqi use of tactical intelligence was gradually giving them a leg up in the five-year-old war. Iran seldom achieved a surprise, whereas the Iraqis regularly mauled Iranian units on the southern front. This struck me as a powerful wartime inducement, but it was received noncommittally by Ghorbanifar and Nimrodi—another sign, perhaps, of their military inexperience.

After this offer fell flat, Kimche and North met privately to discuss ways to proceed, but nothing substantive came of it. At this point, the meeting was adjourned, to reconvene when McFarlane arrived.

An incident now took place that would have a profound effect not just on the course of our covert operations but on the future lives of everyone involved. It was the single event that, as Ollie would later say, "put the hyphen in Iran-Contra."

While we were waiting in London for Bud to show up from Washington, I pointed out to Ollie that we had approximately $750,000 in the bank from the HAWK deal, and it looked as if there would be no future transactions.

"What do you recommend doing with the balance?" I asked him.

"Use it to support the Contras," Ollie said. "You're starting an airline and you're going to need it."

This idea was far less exciting at the time than it appears retrospectively. At the time, although I knew the Israelis had contributed large quantities of arms and ammunition to democratic rebels in both Afghanistan and Central America, I still considered the residual funds to be Israeli. Even if Ollie felt the same, he obviously concluded that they had already been administratively committed—morally commingled, so to speak—in these joint U.S.-Israeli covert operations. To him it didn't really matter if this or that bit went to one program or another, provided all parties agreed to and were committed to supporting them.

I let the comment slide, at least for the moment. The Iran operation thus far had been so screwed up that I was in no mood to bend over backward to please the Israelis, who in my opinion created most of the mess.

McFarlane, now the lame-duck NSC advisor, arrived on the morning of December 8, and he, Ollie, and I had breakfast together at the Intercon. Bud seemed pretty relaxed considering he had just wrapped up Reagan's first summit in Geneva, had jetted down to visit the Pope, and then made a quick trip back to Washington to check his messages before flying on to London.

Ollie gave him a good, concise briefing on what had transpired, and I followed that with my own impression of events, stressing the problem I saw about replenishing the 508 TOWs and Ghorbanifar's obsession with high-tech weapons.

"It seems to me," I concluded, "that Mike Ledeen has just brought more technical ignorance to the party, and Kimche is more worried about keeping his skirts clean with Shimon Peres than getting personally involved. I've also got some problems with Ghorbanifar, Nimrodi, and Schwimmer. It seems to me we're dealing with some very slippery characters."

Bud just listened and seemed disinclined to discuss any of the specific problems, although that was no particular indication of his thoughts. He isn't much for small talk and tends to play his cards—and share his ideas—only at the last minute. Fortunately, at my request, Bud had spoken briefly with Israeli Prime Minister Peres and Foreign Minister Shamir and, now that our briefing was over, probably had a fair picture of how things stood. His main purpose for coming to London was to get a firsthand impression of Ghorbanifar and to see how strongly the Israelis were committed to using him.

But Bud was also taking heat from another quarter.

"I've been under great pressure from the President to get the hostages out," he said grimly. "There are a lot of reasons for this, not the least of which is the fact that he criticized Carter on that very point."

That explained to me why our counterparts emphasized this aspect of the initiative at the expense of the broader issues. Like all good horse traders, they were quick to spot an opponent's weakness and exploit it.

Under a weathering sky, we took a cab to Nimrodi's white-columned house and resumed the meeting about 1 P.M. I hoped the overcast wasn't a bad omen.

Bud and Kimche chatted briefly, one on one, before joining the rest of us in Nimrodi's office. While they were caucusing, a short, spirited argument broke out between Schwimmer and an Israeli general sitting in for Defense Minister Rabin over who should have the final word for Israel in the session with McFarlane. Schwimmer, speaking English, not Hebrew, angrily shouted at the general:

"I have been placed in charge of this project by the Prime Minister, and if you do not accept this, then I will pick up the phone right now and call Shimon Peres!"

The general, obviously embarrassed, demurred, saying they would thrash it out later in private. I'd heard others describe Schwimmer as something of a bully, although in our brief meetings to date, he had seemed quite reasonable, if defensive. This argument was a real breach of protocol, particularly in the presence of foreigners like myself and Ghorbanifar. It was also confusing, since Kimche was undoubtedly the senior Israeli official present. I could only conclude the dispute had something to do with Defense Ministry issues rather than state policy, which was more or less confirmed by what followed.

When McFarlane and Kimche came back, Nimrodi arranged everyone's chairs like a hostess at a tea party: Bud in the place of honor, behind Nimrodi's desk; Kimche beside the desk like a witness in a courtroom; while Ghorbanifar sat directly in front of them like a prosecutor—a great study in proxemics. Ollie stood by a radiator behind Bud (it was getting pretty cold outside) while I sat in the gallery comprised of Schwimmer, the new Israeli general, and Nimrodi, who finally sat down after pouring everyone coffee.

The meeting began with Ghorbanifar's inflicting his Paris lecture on Bud, joined by Schwimmer and Kimche as a kind of Greek chorus punctuating his story with mea culpas about the I-HAWK debacle. Nobody wanted to raise the issue about paying for or replenishing the 508 TOWs, so as the guy with almost a million unspecified bucks in the bank, I threw that particular dead fish on the table early just to see who would scream. The first person to wince was McFarlane himself—the imputed source of a U.S. repayment guarantee—who tabled it for later. It was my first and best indication that all the ducks had not been lined up on the American side—that the whole deal had been, perhaps, a bit impulsive and opportunistic on the part of the NSC. I began to get the sinking feeling that I had been roped into yet another "hobby-shop" operation.

To his credit, Bud quickly shot down the Iranians' high-tech ploy. In answer to Ghorbanifar's repeated requests for Phoenix and Harpoon missiles, Bud responded, "These kinds of systems are completely out of the question."

Without missing a beat, Ghorbanifar changed his tack to ask for more TOWs (5,000 of them) and perhaps more HAWKs once the misunderstanding about the last shipment was cleared up, which to my mind and among the Israeli experts, it already had been. Then came the 64-dollar question:

"What can the U.S. and Israel expect in return for these additional shipments?" Bud asked Ghorbanifar.

Gorba then launched into a detailed disquisition linking every shipment specifically to a hostage or some combination of hostages, which, in Gorbaspeak, were always referred to as "boxes," or sometimes "crates." (We good guys referred to them as "zebras"—a bit less funereal.)

"I can guarantee one box for one thousand TOWs," Ghorbanifar said in true rug-merchant fashion. "If you ship another thousand immediately, I can guarantee two boxes. I can also give you one box for some Phoenix missiles, if you deliver them immediately. If you give me one hundred Phoenix missiles, I'll give you two boxes. We may be able to come up with other approaches, but this is the one Tehran already has in mind, and I suggest we use it. After all, we have to establish trust, and this will be a good step because on a number of occasions Iran has been held hostage by the hostages. If we can clear this up, we can get on to better relations." (When he later testified before the Select Committee, Ghorbanifar would claim he never talked about hostages or arms, only strategic matters, which was hogwash!)

Bud replied in no uncertain terms that the U.S. would not deal in this fashion; it simply wasn't what *we* had in mind.

"We are desirous of establishing a dialogue with Iran, it's true," he said. "We are indeed concerned with the strategic situation—the possibility of collapse of Iran in the war and all the problems affecting Iran. But we're not going to get into a barter arrangement of this nature."

He repeated Ollie's request to both Ghorbanifar and the Israelis to arrange a high-level meeting between Iranian and American officials rather than continuing to rely on "go-betweens," which in the current framework meant arms dealers like Gorba and Nimrodi.

Ghorbanifar and Schwimmer choked on this one, and the meeting dragged on until dark, shortly after 5:30 P.M., without resolution. Bud terminated the discussion by saying, in effect, when you're ready to do something at a higher level, give us a call.

Bud, Ollie, and I flew back that night to Andrews AFB outside Washington on a Gulfstream III provided by USAF Special Missions, the same unit that operates Air Force One. The atmosphere on the plane was gloomy, and I got the impression that, whatever the full scope and grand design of the Iran Initiative had been conceptually, it was now dead as a doornail.

"I don't think I've ever talked to a more despicable character than Ghorbanifar," Bud said. He also voiced his disappointment with the Israelis and said that, after his report on all this to the President—and particularly in light of the criticisms the initiative had received during a December 7 meeting with Weinberger and Schultz, who, although they agreed with the objective, thought the political risk of vending arms to Iran was too great—he would recommend turning off the project.

This surprised me for two reasons. First, nothing Ghorbanifar had said during the entire meeting was essentially different from what Bud had heard already from Ollie and me and other sources. Why did Bud have the sudden urge to strangle in the crib what was still a potentially promising brainchild? From the Middle East perspective, the "mating dance" had hardly started. Schultz and Weinberger, formerly chief executive and head counsel, respectively, for the Bechtel corporation, a construction giant that had done business all over the region, should've known that even if McFarlane didn't.

Second, Ghorbanifar was undoubtedly pond scum, but he wasn't the most despicable character I'd ever met, not by a long shot. Who did Bud think inhabited this big, wide, wonderful world outside the White House? I think it was the jet lag talking—that and Bud's disappointment over Ghorbanifar's fixation on the arms-for-hostages aspect, which even disappointed me.

I said to Bud, "I wouldn't be too simplistic in your report to the President."

"What do you mean?" he asked.

"I'm not so sure the basic idea is so bad. It may just be the people who were involved in this go-around—guys like Ghorbanifar, Schwimmer, and Nimrodi." I gave him a quick summary of the still-classified paper I had written for Weinberger in 1982 pushing for an active intelligence capability in Iran that could then be used more easily and reliably to reestablish diplomatic relations.

"For years there's been a lot of talk in the government about regaining contact with Iran," I said, "but nothing's happened. Interagency processes among State, the White House, and the CIA have been paralyzed while we wring our hands over the march of Shia fundamentalism and how much we should tilt toward Baghdad or Tehran. And don't forget Moscow—when have they ever let a chance to do mischief in the area go by? One of the few things I ever heard from General Sharon that I agreed with was the necessity to do something about reestablishing links with Iran. It's a valid objective and one we've done very little to achieve. I think a separate U.S. assessment of the likely players in Tehran would be in order—how amenable they might be to clandestine communications and support and all of that."

Unfortunately, Bud still seemed locked on the hostages.

"They just spoil the entire issue," he said bitterly.

"Then issue a no-bones-about-it order to the CIA to find those guys and bust 'em out with our counterterrorist force," I replied. "It's inconceivable to me that the hostages can be held for so long in such a small area amid so much turbulence without a competent intelligence service, given enough resources, being able to track them down."

I still didn't realize how strongly President Reagan felt about the hostage issue. I assumed that he, like the rest of us, put the smaller-scale tragedy of the hostages and their families in perspective behind the greater strategic implications of a new rapprochement with Iran. I spent the rest of the trip writing up three or four pages of suggestions in longhand, which I gave to Bud before we landed. It was clear that Bud, however, had already made up his mind to give the President a very negative report. I only hoped his disappointment would not scuttle entirely a project that might, if handled properly, undo some of the enormous damage inflicted during the Carter years on a region that still meant a lot to our national security.

Well into January 1986, I tried, with less and less success, to keep up with the demands of my commercial business, as well as my work for the Contras. I had already hired an old joint task force compatriot, Dick Gadd, to direct on-site airlift operations, including the job of corralling the aircraft we had picked out.

Personally, I was still concerned about nailing down any loose ends regarding our sizable escalation of Contra support—particularly after the slipshod way the Iran missile deal had been handled. I discussed this with Ollie on the G-III coming back from London, and he agreed to set up a meeting between me and Bill Casey.

I had met with Casey during my Pentagon years, usually in the company of Cap Weinberger. He was a gruff, antsy guy who had been one of the founding fathers of covert operations, beginning with the OSS, the Office of Strategic Services, in its "Terry and the Pirates" days during World War II. If he remembered me as one of the CIA's critics (for their HUMINT failure in Iran and the inappropriateness of their trying to conduct an overt Contra war as a covert operation), it didn't stop him from inviting me to his office near Tyson's Corner late one dreary, drizzly winter afternoon.

After the usual hassle getting through CIA gate security, I took the director's private elevator that opened directly onto his seventh-floor office, a warmly inviting, bookish place with a view of the icy Potomac. Casey, rumpled as usual in a thick woolen suit, greeted me courteously and offered me a chair in front of his desk. He looked much older than I remembered, giving depth to the rumors of his ill health. He would last another year as director of the CIA before departing this earth with a million secrets still locked in his head—a piercing, mercurial mind whose loss depressed the people who knew and admired him, not to mention the Iran-Contra inquisitors.

I began discussing the Contra air-support program. He nodded knowingly, interjecting comments and questions until, after about five minutes, it occurred to me he was talking about *Iran* and not Central America. Oddly enough, the details of one operation matched the details of the other sufficiently for the conversation to advance on parallel tracks.

I shifted gears and gave him my views on the Iran-Iraq war, the role likely being played by the Soviets on the one side and the Israelis on the other, but I wasn't up to speed on the latest intelligence, having been out of government now for two years, and the conversation quickly degenerated into banalities.

Casey did make one very significant comment, I thought. Ollie and McFarlane had both mentioned Cap Weinberger's and George Shultz's lukewarm reaction to the President's Iran Initiative—mostly a reaction based on fear of a negative Arab backlash should the U.S. be discovered dealing secretly with a non-Arab nation embroiled in a war with their Iraqi brethren. I repeated this to Casey, to get his reaction, and it became immediately clear where his sympathies lay.

"They just don't have a good strategic appreciation for the situation," he said of Weinberger and Shultz. "This is a pretty bloody business. It's not just a game."

He went on to say that the Arabs (Saudis, Omanis, and so forth—all the Gulf Cooperation Council, or GCC, countries) were vitally concerned with the progress of the war and had their own tendrils out continuously toward Tehran.

As I tried to steer the discussion back to the Contras, which is where I had most of my concerns, Casey suddenly asked, "Do you know Mike Ledeen?"

"Sure," I said. "I met him several years ago when he was a consultant to Fred Ikle, Undersecretary of Defense."

"That's the man. I talked to Ledeen recently about Iran—a real bright guy." I said, "You know, the operation last month was a failure."

Casey grunted an acknowledgment, rolling a hand at the wrist in a dismissive gesture, so I didn't pursue it. Ledeen was a professional advisor who, like our "advisors" in the early stages of the Vietnam war, often did more than advise. I saw his fingerprints all over the Iran Initiative—as a player—at least in the early stages.

Casey's disinclination to talk about the I-HAWK fiasco allowed me to segue into my Contra support concerns. I gave him the bottom line: If the soldiers in the field were to have the kind of support everyone wanted, it would take at least another $10 million in cash, immediately. I added that I was not impressed with the Contras' political or military leadership, problems only magnified by the CIA's abrupt withdrawal (owing to the Boland Amendments) without leaving behind a logistics capability. The Contra leaders were amateurs—some well intended, some not—trying to do a job that would tax the most experienced professionals. The future for them looked bleak.

I hoped this would hook Casey's professional instincts and pry loose some information or assurances, but he just acknowledged my comments, neither agreeing nor disagreeing.

I let him know that Ollie North was regularly apprised of my efforts, and as long as the funds held out, we'd proceed with the emergency-strip construction in northwest Costa Rica and finish collecting our ragtag "Air America," to be operated in the manner of my CIA-Laos air branch—and by some of the same people. At that point I entered a personal plea:

"If we're to be successful, we'll need intelligence support. I realize we can't get financial or material aid from the Agency, but intelligence coordination should be made available. I hope we can count on the support of the senior CIA personnel in Central America."

Without access to intelligence regarding Sandinista defenses, our crews would be flying into harm's way blind as bats—low and slow over what was quickly becoming a lethal air-defense system. Despite the opposition of Casey's deputy, John McMahon, who I felt was needlessly afraid of Boland, the COS in Costa Rica and elsewhere in Latin America had already given us some basic intelligence information, as had the military group chief in San Salvador. What we lacked was a systematic and regular update on enemy troop movements, air-defense emplacements, and weather (particularly visibility) data over hostile territory. Although Casey must've done at least as much homework as I had into the legal constraints of the Boland Amendments, he again remained somewhat oblique but promised to help. Before departing, I added:

"I've also obtained a legal opinion that, as long as we don't carry troops, our Amcit [private American citizen] crew members won't violate the U.S. Neutrality Act."

The old man nodded and stood up, extending his hand.

"Thank you, Dick. That's good information. Good luck to you guys. I want you to keep in touch. The President is also very pleased with your work."

With that, the meeting was over—it had lasted about 40 minutes. Before I turned to go, I made one last statement for the record—a crucial one, as far as I was concerned, if I was ever to see government service again:

"By the way, Mr. Director, if and when the CIA gets its hunting license back from Congress, which I hope will be very soon, all the assets that we intend to create will be turned over to the Agency."

"I understand," Casey smiled. "Thank you very much."

I left the meeting reassured that Casey and the President knew and approved of North's activities, but not about much else. I thought it was significant that Casey didn't want to talk at length about the failed Iran Initiative, and that was fine with me; if McFarlane's report had torpedoed the effort, so be it. His reticence on Contra support, though, bothered me. The whole operation was grossly underfunded and, because of the heavy capital commitment required for air programs, you are either in that game or you aren't: There's no middle ground because funding has to be a long-haul proposition. I also knew, despite Ralph Quintero's great spadework, our political clout with the friendly commandantes in the countries neighboring Nicaragua was about zilch without the CIA. North knew all this, of course, and now Casey did too. We would all go into this with our eyes open, but I still felt like I was hopping, hog-tied, into a pool filled with piranha.


Around January 6, 1986, I received a request from Admiral John Poindexter, who had just succeeded Bud McFarlane as Reagan's National Security Advisor, to meet with him at the White House around 7 P.M. Our session would be brief, he promised, no more than a few minutes.

I knew Poindexter only slightly at that time, although his reputation preceded him greatly. I first met him in 1983, shortly before my retirement, when he had just joined the NSC as a brand-new rear admiral. He had astonishing credentials even in a town top-heavy with talent and expertise. He had been first in his class at Annapolis and held a Ph.D. in nuclear physics. I remembered him as a soft-spoken guy who had a way of framing his comments and questions with crystal clarity. I would gain an even deeper appreciation for John's great breadth of knowledge and scope of vision over the next few months, and would seldom leave one of our meetings without scratching my head and wondering, *Now why the hell didn't I think of that?*

It was a cold, clear evening as I drove downtown. I presented myself to White House security and was escorted to Poindexter's corner office in the West Wing—a place that had seen a lot of other famous tenants: Kissinger, Brzezinski, and most recently, Bud McFarlane, who may have found those ghosts a bit intimidating. Poindexter's legal aide, Naval Commander Paul Thompson, was present at the start of our discussion, and then drifted in and out as our "brief" meeting stretched into an hour.

John, puffing on his ever-present pipe, began by thanking me for the work I'd done to help the Contras during the last year and, most recently, in the failed Iranian project. He said the NSC had reevaluated the Iran situation and that the President had decided—in principle, if not in particulars— to go forward with a formal covert operation to achieve certain goals as soon as possible.

"What goals are those?" I asked.

Poindexter knitted his brow. "Well, the primary goal is to penetrate the outer layer of revolutionary zealots to reach the more pragmatic factions in Tehran. The President wants to start a process that would, someday, restore normal relations between the United States and Iran." He acknowledged that I was already well versed in the strategic importance of the area, and went on to describe recent intelligence about Soviet moves involving Iraq and Iran.

As far as the November weapons transfer scheme went, he conceded, "It was a mess. I'm not satisfied at all with the way the operation was handled by the Israelis. However, Ollie has been in touch recently with Israeli authorities, and they have agreed to consider a new project."

This really surprised me, since Ollie had mentioned around New Year's that the NSC was reevaluating the situation. He didn't mention any new contacts with the Israelis and sounded pessimistic. Anyway, this was the NSC's show: I had just been along for the ride—a one-time troubleshooter for the bollixed I-HAWK deal—so I just sat there and kept quiet, expecting Poindexter to move on to the Contras. He didn't.

"As I'm sure you know," he continued, relighting his pipe with a blast of blue smoke, "the President is deeply concerned about our hostages. At this point, we believe three are still alive: Southerland, Anderson, and Jacobsen. Bill Buckley, the CIA-COS in Beirut, is probably dead. Our secondary goal is to secure the release of all American hostages plus the Israeli prisoners of war. In fact, we want to clear out all Western hostages being held by the Shiite groups, particularly Hezballah, the Party of God. If we proceed, it's going to be a well-compartmentalized operation, one in which you can be of great assistance with your organization. What do you think—can you participate?"

I had heard enough by now to know that the Iranian show was at least not a North-Casey affair. In a way, it was reassuring to hear a guy like Poindexter refer to it as a rather clear-cut, run-of-the-mill covert program operating without all the hamstringing of the Boland anti-Contra provisions.

I replied, "It's no secret that I've always been interested in the establishment of an American, or at least American-controlled, intelligence operation in Iran. We've got to get a handle on the internal political situation before we can make any intelligent moves to reestablish government-to-government relations.

"However, as I'm sure you know from your talks with Bud and Ollie, I consider what I saw last November and December—the abortive weapons-delivery deal and the meetings in London—to be very unprofessional, at best. At worst, it looks like a simple ransoming operation through unscrupulous arms dealers. If that's true, and if this is just a hostage-bartering deal, then I'm not up to it. But, if we are going to truly establish a strategic relationship with a friendly faction in the Iranian government, then I'm for it—provided we use better means for achieving what you want."

I half expected Poindexter to look offended, or at least to defend "his boys," North and McFarlane, of whom I was not nearly as critical as I was of Schwimmer, Nimrodi, Ledeen (apparently), and especially Ghorbanifar. Instead, John just nodded in agreement, pulled his pipe out of his mouth, and leaned forward onto his desk.

"I know exactly what you're talking about," he said earnestly. "As a matter of fact, we're preparing a finding to address those very issues."

I was greatly relieved to hear this. As few people knew before the Iran-Contra hearings—and as almost everyone knows now—a presidential finding is a top-secret executive order directing the CIA to conduct covert operations in accordance with applicable federal law. It's like the "enabling legislation" that mandates the actions of regulatory agencies within the executive branch (the EPA, Interior Department, Commerce Department, and so on) but in the realm of covert operations. For John to say that a finding was in process meant, first of all, that presidential supervision of the project was already in place; and secondly, that the intelligence services would be involved as well—a prerequisite to the success of any such venture.

Poindexter added hastily, "The strategic objective that will dominate the project, of course, is our ability to influence the successor to the Ayatollah Khomeini. To accomplish that, we'll need to tap your expertise in clandestine operations and your knowledge of the region. Besides, everyone involved trusts you immensely; we believe that if anyone in the private sector can keep a secret, it's got to be Dick Secord."

Admittedly, I allowed myself to be swept up in the moment. It felt damn good to be doing what all my years in the service and at the Pentagon had prepared me to do. Perhaps with more valor than discretion I said, "I'll be glad to do what I can, John," and stretched out my hand. "I'm honored that you would ask me."

"That's good," Poindexter grinned, shaking my hand and walking me to the door. "Ollie will be in touch."

On January 14, 1986, I got that call from North. He wanted me to come downtown for a 6 P.M. meeting in the Situation Room in the White House basement.

When I arrived I found Clair George, the CIA's Deputy Director for Operations (DDO), who headed covert operations, along with one of his staffers; Stanley Sporkin, the CIA's general counsel; Paul Thompson, NSC general counsel who had been in and out of my meeting with Poindexter; and, of course, Ollie himself. The subject of the meeting, Ollie said, was to review the draft of the presidential finding Poindexter had described.

A rather typical, unspectacular bureaucratic interchange followed in which I had very little to say. Most of the discussion involved paring down a lot of detailed information into a few succinct, legally acceptable paragraphs. The biggest issue seemed to be the question of Congressional notification. Sporkin said more drafting was required on this problem, but it seemed to him that adequate precedents existed for notification to be legally delayed until no more lives were in jeopardy. Very little time was given to the process, spelled out in the finding, authorizing the Pentagon to sell weapons to the CIA in accordance with the Economy Act. This act simply says that the cost for interagency transfers is to be set at the lowest possible price—usually excluding markups for depreciation or inflation. The law then allows the Agency to sell them to a commercial entity (called a "cutout" by the CIA) that would, in turn, resell them immediately to another commercial entity or to nations involved in CIA programs—in this case, Israel and Iran.

This was a change from the previous plan—making shipments culled from Israeli stock and replenishing them from the U.S. through usual FMS procedures. I was actually quite pleased to see this new provision, since it meant the CIA lawyers had really done their homework in identifying the legal means for taking weapons from the U.S. inventory. FMS transfers, in my opinion, stood on shaky legal (and probably indefensible political) grounds. The new plan also meant the materiel—missiles or whatever—would be considerably cheaper, since items sold through FMS were marked up for federal overhead (including R&D) and other various and sundry expenses.

Naturally, I gave this section a pretty close reading and suggested, since it was my end of the log, that the President's intention to utilize commercial companies and "third parties" to facilitate the operation should probably be more explicit. This change was, in fact, inserted into the final document President Reagan signed. Other than that, the only issue I could spot that was relevant to me was retention of the earlier Israeli model for dealing with the Iranians, which I questioned. But at this point, mine was not to reason why, but to figure out some way to make it happen, given the constraints.

There was no discussion of the propriety of the action in light of America's own widely touted arms embargo on Iran and public designation of Iran as a terrorist state, nor did I expect any. As far as I was concerned, the executive branch made foreign policy, subject to Congressional advice and consent in specific cases, and that was that. Policy isn't law, and any chief executive who allows himself to be hamstrung by past decisions—particularly in the face of dire strategic necessity (the loss of the Shah's Iran and life-and-death hostage situations, for example)—doesn't deserve to be president. I suspect that if each congressman calling later for Reagan's resignation for covertly ignoring his own policy in the interest of a larger objective were to resign over similar differences between their own campaign rhetoric and subsequent legislative action, Washington would quickly become a ghost town.

In my view, Iran Initiative opponents' guns are better aimed at the President's bigger blunder (aided and abetted by Casey and Sporkin): the delay in notifying Congress—or at least the eight key men on the Hill—in really sensitive cases. It seemed to me this notification would be good common sense, even if the law didn't require it. One rule of covert operations is to nail down your cover. The right words to the right people can usually keep a lid on things, provided you convince them of your mutual interests, if not the larger picture. I don't know of any congressional leaders from that era who wouldn't have indulged the President on a small-scale clandestine effort to reestablish a strategic foothold in Iran and, incidentally, get the hostages released. Shutting Congress out indefinitely, though, especially after it became clear the initiative would last more than a few months, just didn't make sense. Keeping things secret when you don't have to—a kind of "government by accession list"—only convinces people you've got something to hide and makes them suspicious as well as curious. When they're politicians in the opposing party, it also makes them dangerous. This may be understandable in the post-Watergate era of paranoia and mistrust between executive and legislative branches, but that doesn't make it justifiable.

Frankly, the meeting was so routine I was a little surprised I had been invited. It was really concerned with administrative matters and had nothing to do with the nuts and bolts of the operation, about which there was *plenty* to talk about, since lots of unresolved issues remained from the previous failed attempt. I suppose North and Poindexter just wanted to introduce me to the CIA crew and let them know that their chosen commercial cutout was real, knowledgeable, and fully "on board." Perhaps they also wanted to let me know that I could consider myself part of the squad at a reasonably high working level, and that any comments I chose to make about any facet of the program wouldn't go unnoticed.

The meeting ended with North saying only one copy of the finding would be retained after the President signed it, and that copy would be held in the White House. That didn't seem to bother the CIA people and it certainly didn't bother me. I would inspect the final, signed document on January 17 and wouldn't see it again until it appeared in the press a year later—a foolish move by the government: showing our nation's enemies the proper form and format of one of our most secret documents, right down to the typeface, letterhead, and watermark, all of which can be used to spot forgeries.

Ollie and I conducted several preliminary "implementation sessions" in his office at the old EOB after the finding was signed. He had now been given the title of Director of Counterterrorism for the NSC, and had a nice corner office on the third floor overlooking the Ellipse.

During one of these meetings, Ollie told me that Amiram Nir, Israeli Chief of Counterterrorism—North's direct counterpart—had been appointed by Prime Minister Peres to represent Israel in Iranian operations. This was the "Israeli official" Poindexter alluded to, the one Ollie had been in contact with in December and January—one reason the project suddenly started to look so promising. Schwimmer and his associates were out; Ami Nir was in. The only real problem seemed to be Ghorbanifar, whom the Israelis insisted on retaining as our Iranian contact.

While I only knew Ghorbanifar from our Paris and London meetings, I found him slippery as an eel. He had apparently flunked a CIA lie detector test, which Casey himself decided to discount, based on assurances from Mike Ledeen that Ghorbanifar, as poor a choice as he might be, was still the best channel available. (This story was affirmed to me by Casey himself in a second meeting at the end of January after my Poindexter interview.)

To me, this affirmation by Casey was the knockout blow for "October Surprise" theorists. If Casey, while manager of Reagan's 1980 presidential campaign, had eluded the multinational JTF intelligence net and conducted a series of secret meetings with the appropriate factions of revolutionary Iran, why would he go through the contortions of the Ledeen-Ghorbanifar connection? Why wouldn't he simply use his own, far better contacts? It just doesn't make any sense, especially if Casey was half as clever as everyone thought. This was especially true given Gorba's reputation. He had failed a polygraph test years before and CIA headquarters had sent out a "burn notice" on him to all field stations and agents stating that he was unreliable and not to be dealt with. In Gorba's case, only the director could reverse the burn notice, which is exactly what happened. I am convinced Casey would not have done so if a better channel had been available.

Given that both the Israelis and the CIA were convinced that Ghorbanifar was the only game in town, and since the whole project was envisioned to be a very short-term thing, I had to go along. As Ledeen himself said later, "We're not running him for Congress," oddly enough, the one place old Gorba might feel at home.

Ollie and I decided that our first objective should be to set up as high a level, government-to-government meeting as possible with the Iranians—preferably in Europe. President Reagan had authorized the transfer of up to 2,000 TOW missiles (plus a small number of equivalent, less sophisticated weapons if they were needed to sweeten the pot) in order to make that first breach in the Ayatollah's crusty shell.

While North was working on this, he also set up a planning session between us and the chief of the CIA's Near East division and a ranking CIA logistics officer. During this meeting, we worked out the means by which the CIA would purchase the first 1,000 TOWs from the U.S. Army stockpile and transport them by truck to a domestic CIA facility, where they would be re-crated and their paperwork and markings "sanitized."

I asked the CIA logistician for the price, but he said he'd have to get back to me. He had to figure in not only the price the Army charged for the missiles, but the CIA's own overhead—packing, transportation, man hours (including overtime), plus a 10 percent management reserve. Although the final pricing information wouldn't come until much later, we learned in a follow-up meeting in February that the price would run between $4,000 and $5,000 per missile. The actual billing price, FOB U.S., to my enterprise was on the low end of this scale; but the CIA billed us later for an additional $300 or so per unit, bringing the final price closer to $5,000 (or $5 million for the shipment).

Our efforts had now progressed to where a planning session in Europe was worthwhile. Ollie arranged for a quick meeting between us and Ami Nir in London for January 22, 1986; and a follow-up session the next day between the three of us and Ghorbanifar. Ollie traveled separately as Mr. Goode. (I never got around to asking him the subliminal significance of his alias.) I went commercial, using my own name and passport. We checked into the Intercontinental Hotel near Hyde Park, where the meeting would be held, and waited for Nir, who arrived later that day.

Ami Nir was a small, wiry man with rugged good looks. A former television journalist, he had fought in every Arab-Israeli conflict since the Six Day War and had been wounded several times. He was extremely intelligent and very intense, despite his ready humor. He spoke English in the noncolloquial, studied manner typical of well-educated, Hebrew-speaking Israelis. He had lost an eye in a roadside accident earlier in his life and, according to his wife, hitchhiked to the hospital while holding the eyeball in his hand. Unfortunately, optical nerves can't be reattached, and he was fitted with a rather poor prosthetic that left you guessing about which eye to look at in a conversation.

Over the next year or so, the three of us became good friends. In their lighter moments, Ami and Ollie would pull up their shirttails and brag about their wounds—a game I was happily unqualified to play. Nir's Israeli code name was "Adam," Ollie's was "Paul," and mine was "Sampson." We joked about recruiting a "Delilah" but never got around to it. Nir was a bona fide war hero, and I was impressed, on several occasions walking with him around Tel Aviv, at how widely recognized and respected he was. He was helped in this, no doubt, by his wife, Judy Moses, who was the daughter of Israel's largest newspaper publisher.

If Ami had any faults, it was his love of detail; he had the soul of a scientist in a very imprecise business. It was impossible to have a short conversation with Nir on an important matter, and he always had more questions than I could answer—his journalist training, no doubt. Above everything else, though, Nir was a fighter—a warrior in the highest sense. He refused to accept defeat, or even a serious reverse, in anything—another way in which he was a lot like Ollie.

The planning session was successful in the sense that we forged some real bonds as a team—took each other's measure and knew what we could expect in a pinch—but it accomplished little else. Ollie was fixed on his one big goal: get the high-level Iranian meeting scheduled as soon as possible. As a result some topics we might have productively dealt with were allowed to slide. Nir explained that he had a little trouble cashiering Al Schwimmer because Schwimmer was a longtime friend of Shimon Peres (whom Nir had worked for as a campaign manager in the 1983 elections). Nimrodi, too, had resisted being cut out, particularly while the financial aspects were left hanging.

"But these are Israeli problems," Ami assured us. "We are still examining the financial difficulties that have been created, but that is not your problem; don't worry."

I asked him (with one eye on Ollie to gauge his reaction) if those difficulties included the $750,000 balance from the blown I-HAWK deal. To my surprise, Nir dismissed it out of hand.

"Those are your funds. Keep them. That was a commercial undertaking."

It sounded as if he meant the funds could be used as initial capital for our new ventures. A short time later, though, I would find out he was actually distancing himself from an internal investigation Israel had already launched into the transaction. The Israelis knew Ollie and I were helping the Contras and may have deduced that excess funds in Enterprise accounts were being spent on Contra aid, but we never discussed it, and, frankly, I don't think they cared one way or the other. To them, the funds were proceeds from an Iranian government purchase made in the private sector and nobody had claims on that cash except the proprietors involved.

However, in my opinion, the financial side was still unnecessarily ambiguous, and I told Nir that in the future we were going to have to handle this in a businesslike fashion. Hakim wanted to establish several companies with Swiss fiduciary accounts in order to fund the operation. Nir found this acceptable since neither the Israeli nor the U.S. government was putting a dime into the operation. I stressed that the arms would have to be paid for before they were transferred from the Pentagon to the CIA—standard practice in the weapons business, and Nir understood this, too. The current batch of 1,000 TOWs, I explained, would run around $5 million, plus shipping costs to Tel Aviv, as well as the myriad costs involved in transporting them to Iran: two round trips to Tehran in an Israeli 707, crew and communication costs, and a reserve for self-insurance, which alone would turn out to be around $4 million.

Nir then asked, rather rhetorically at this point, who would repay Israel for the 508 TOWs it had shipped to Iran in August and September under the assumption that the U.S. would replenish its stocks. I could only repeat what I had said to General Meron in Tel Aviv: There was no legal way for the U.S. Department of Defense to replace their TOWs. A more relevant question at this point, I said, was what price we would charge the Iranians for the *next* batch, since once a number was broached, it would be virtually impossible to ratchet it upward. Since we were not being bankrolled by the taxpayers, we would have to be very conservative in our pricing, and both of them agreed. From the intelligence available on the last transaction, Ghorbanifar had charged Tehran at least $14,000 per missile—almost three times our cost from the U.S. government—and was suggesting a more modest $10,500 each on this next round.

Ami now became somewhat evasive, owing again to the ongoing Israeli investigation of the August-September transaction. I think he was leery about shooting his mouth off where money was concerned, even in our company. Ghorbanifar was already bugging him about prices for the next batch, and we agreed we could respond only by saying that, as far as we knew, nobody in authority had made up his mind. We weren't even sure there would be a next batch.

The one area about which we were in unanimous agreement was that we would never totally rely on Manucher Ghorbanifar again. In the meeting with Gorba tomorrow we would tell him that if he wanted to complete another deal, he would have to convince someone in authority on the Iranian side to step out of the fog and deal face to face with a ranking American official.

As far as I was concerned, it was the first real step toward achieving America's primary goal in the initiative.

The next day the three of us met with Ghorbanifar at the Hilton Hotel off Hyde Park. Courtesy of the CIA, our discussion was recorded on video- and audiotape monitors concealed in briefcases and tote bags around the room. Gorba was a connoisseur of good, florid gestures, so he hosted us to an expensive, expansive dinner in his opulent second-floor suite. After tasting several kinds of wine (dinner for Ghorbanifar was never just a meal, but a production), he judged we were sufficiently lubricated to entertain his first demand, which was that the Israelis should refund $5.4 million to Iran for the 18 rejected I-HAWK missiles still held in Tehran.

Ami responded that he would deal with old business separately. What mattered now was the high-level meeting and what America would have to offer for sale afterward as a show of its good intentions.

Ghorbanifar agreed. The Iranians, he said, required 4,000 additional TOWs, for which he was prepared to deposit some $10 million in cash for the first 1,000 units. It was at that point that Ollie and Ami hit upon the idea of solving the Israeli problem of paying for the original batch of 508 TOWs by pricing the next 4,000-missile batch as if it contained 4,508 units. To the best of my recollection, this is the first time any sort of "creative financing" was mentioned at the front end of any deal.

The meeting concluded with North and Nir, pressing for a high-level meeting, stating for the first time that the hostages, although not the specific focus of the discussion, were an obstacle to "further progress," meaning a barrier to selling more weapons to Iran. They were also a barrier to restoring government-to-government relations. I'm sure for Gorba this reinforced his own conviction that arms and hostages went hand in hand. To my mind, our big step forward had just taken at least a half-step back.

Our next meeting took place in London on February 6 with the same people. Ami, Ollie, and I ran through our agenda: Pin down the financial details on the 1,000-TOW shipment, which the President had approved and which we had finally fixed-priced at $10 million. Unfortunately, Ghorbanifar never appeared. We tried to track him down on the phone using a dozen numbers Nir carried for that purpose—Gorba's contacts and relatives in Nice, Paris, Frankfurt, and Bonn—but with "no joy," as military pilots say when their target is not sighted.

In his absence, Nir and North tried to put together a plan to force Kangarlu, Ghorbanifar's Iranian government contact, to come to Europe for the high-level meeting we desired. I had ambivalent feelings about this. I knew that high-level meetings of any kind required plenty of staff-level preparation if they were to succeed, but none of this spadework had been done. I mentioned this a couple of times, but neither Ami nor Ollie seemed particularly concerned about it.

Back in Washington, we finally solved one of our nagging security problems. Woben Smith at the NSA issued each of us an encryption device for sending brief, secure messages over commercial telephone lines. The device, a KL-43 (made by TRW), comes in a "clandestine black" canvas case and resembles a portable typewriter. It handles about 2,000 bytes of data, enough for a two-page letter. You simply type out your message, making any corrections just like a word processor, and then transmit it all at once with the push of a button.

Typically, if I had a message for North's office, I would call his secretary, Fawn Hall, and say, "Okay, Fawn, I got one for you," and, knowing what that meant, she would set up her own KL-43 with the code of the day. After I said, "10 seconds," she'd put her phone handset on the modem. If the connection was good (international lines often aren't), one pass would be enough. Otherwise, we'd try again. The beauty of the system was that any two KLs could talk to each other—you didn't have to go through a central processor—and it even worked with a radio, making it a dandy device for field agents. Woben would be disciplined in 1988 by the NSA for "supplying KLs to operators who did not properly secure them" and "who lacked appropriate security clearances," making him one of many Iran-Contra walk-ons who were pilloried after the fact for simply doing their jobs. In truth, my top-secret clearance was still valid and the devices were designed specifically for field agents, with plenty of safeguards against reverse engineering should one fall into enemy hands.

Back on the Contra side of the ledger, I was becoming quite concerned with not only the CIA's lack of intelligence sharing in El Salvador, but also the active interference we were receiving from Alan Fiers, the head of the Agency's Central American task force. I told Ollie I wanted to meet again with Bill Casey, and he set up an appointment for me at CIA headquarters. It was now pretty clear from the way both men talked about each other and from my own observations that they were personally very close. I was in Ollie's office on numerous occasions when he got calls from Casey on both secure and commercial phone lines, and Casey once dropped in to visit North, all indicating an open and friendly—if not father-son—relationship. This was unusual, given their great difference in age, rank, and experience, but their mutual affection and respect seemed genuine.

In my February meeting, Casey was just as cordial to me as before, but much more forthcoming with information and his own views on both Contra support and the Iran Initiative. He suggested, in fact, that a CIA communications team should be positioned in Tehran as soon as arrangements could be made. Considering the halting progress we were making through Ghorbanifar, this was very bold thinking, especially coming from Casey; I could almost hear Ollie's voice behind the Director's words, another sign of the way one man influenced the other. No doubt Casey recognized in Ollie a lot of his own younger characteristics: a mover and a shaker, someone who just refused to let obstacles stand in his way. They both shared a disdain of the Washington bureaucracy, and I had the feeling Casey took a patron's interest in Ollie's career, saw his own days in government as numbered, and wanted to leave some like-minded heirs. I have no doubt that Ollie was one of those annointed few and would've gone on to higher and more critical offices had the old man's fatal illness, as well as events, not made all that academic.

My main reason for the meeting with Casey was to find out the CIA's intentions regarding our airlift operations at Ilopango. As permitted by the Boland Amendment, the CIA was supposed to provide and coordinate intelligence information while refraining from tangible or financial participation. Instead, Dick Gadd reported he had been "interrogated" at length by officials of the CIA's Central American task force, including Fiers and another CIA officer, about the source of our funds and materiel, our financial network, the people involved, and *my* role personally—in short, an investigation instead of assistance.

Even worse, the CIA agents at the Contra air base at Aguacate, as well as the senior CIA man in El Salvador, seemed openly hostile to the operation, as if this were some kind of turf war, and had made a number of disparaging remarks about us that filtered back to Gadd through the Salvadorian air force. The COS had even classified one of their field reports on our operations "confidential" (the lowest category, which is fairly widely disseminated) rather than top secret. I told Casey I considered this to be a gross breach of security.

"I don't want to waste your valuable time," I said, intentionally sounding a bit testy. "We're both too old to beat around the bush on important matters. I'm prepared to do my part to support the Contras against the enemy in Nicaragua, but I can't fight the friendlies, too."

"What do you mean by that?" Casey grumbled.

"Mr. Director, that means my problems begin with your task force chief here in Washington and extend south to your operatives in the field."

"Task force?" The old man looked surprised. "What task force?"

I reminded him about the Agency's Central American task force and gave him the name and background of Alan Fiers, the man in charge—a well-known Middle East expert before Casey reassigned him.

"Oh yes, yes, of course. *That* task force."

Between the mumbling and the bluster, it would've been easy to chalk up Casey's "forgetfulness" to senility, which I almost did, until it struck me like a ton of bricks that he had been feigning ignorance, even at the risk of embarrassment, just to see (a) how much I knew, and (b) how willing I was to tell him. It's a standard technique in this business, but somehow I didn't expect it from the Agency head; and most of all I didn't expect him to pull it on *me.*

"Mr. Director, I'll be brief and candid. At the risk of being presumptuous, I believe your task force director, Alan Fiers, is not qualified for the job. He does not know Latin America. He has no paramilitary experience. By profession, he's an Arabist. But if he's your choice, so be it. All I ask is your personal assistance in getting this guy off my back and out of my hair. I'll brook no interference in organizing and operating this project. In my opinion, the CIA's entire air branch has few real professionals. The contract officer your task force chief sent down to question Dick Gadd is a retiree I knew well in Laos. At no time in his career has he ever been an airman. The point is, if I need a loadmaster, I'll hire him. If I need some conceptual thinking, I'll do it. But, if I can't get effective intelligence and weather information—which, in my view, is perfectly legal for the U.S. government to furnish—I'll be unable to operate."

Casey dropped some of his bluster and said, "Well, Dick, I think with respect to Fiers"—he cleared his throat—"he's very sincere and absolutely dedicated to doing the job."

"Mr. Director, I'm not calling his sincerity into question. I'm simply saying that he must be kept out of my way."

The old man jotted down some notes, which surprised me a little, and said, "I'll look into it."

"That's all I came here for. I appreciate your hearing me out. I think you know me well enough to realize I wouldn't raise the issue unless I considered it extremely serious."

As I prepared to leave, I paused as I did at the end of our previous meeting to deliver the same message.

"And Mr. Director, if and when the Agency gets back into the game in Nicaragua, I promise that all the facilities, equipment, supplies, and personnel will be turned over to you if you want them. We agree that if the Contras are forced from the field during the Congressional hiatus, there's little chance they'll ever go back. That's the only reason I've gotten involved with this thing. I know it's going to be a project with a lot more grief than rewards."

"Dick, I appreciate all this." He shook my hand and I left.

The tense little meeting took no more than 10 or 12 minutes, but its effect was immediate.

The contract officer who had been harassing Dick Gadd suddenly made himself scarce—and what contact his people did have with us was much more cooperative. The rumor mill from the Salvadorian air force stopped spitting out CIA gripes, and Ollie reported that Fiers, the Central American task force chief, suddenly seemed to "find God" in their interagency meetings—no more Contra- or Secord-bashing. According to the grapevine, Casey came down hard on him, which is probably what it took. Running a bureaucracy as its politically appointed head is a lot like operating a hydraulic system in reverse; you have to push hard at one end to get even a little movement at the other, but it can really pay off.

The downside of all this was that during the summer, some newspaper stories appeared linking me with the Contras—kicked off by a lengthy television "investigation" by CBS. There was no particular way the detailed information they presented could have leaked out except through disaffected CIA contacts, aided, perhaps, by Felix Rodriguez (a.k.a.: Maximo Gomez), a Contra partisan who by now had been foiled in his attempt to take over the airlift operation from me and was rumored to be working for Ron Martin.

And cash was becoming our problem as well.

After February 1986, Albert was concerned that our business entities were becoming too well known by too many people. As a result, he completely changed the financial "wiring diagram." He created a new family of what he called operating companies: Gulf Marketing, Inc., which would do business in the Middle East; Dolmy, Inc., which was chartered to procure and operate a ship; and Hyde Park Square, Inc. and Udall Research Corporation, which were to do business in Latin America.

Lake Resources, which received Iranian arms payments and donations for the Contras, was retained as a treasury company, from which deposits to the other operating accounts would be made. This commingling of income before it was earmarked for various projects (especially those divided between the Iran project and the Contras) was a real problem and would make us look shadowy as hell after our cover was blown. I blame Albert Hakim for this, and he blames me for insisting on security measures that required our Swiss accountants (but not Bill Zucker) to be kept in the dark on the true nature of our operations. Instead, we would make periodic visits to the CSF fiduciary in Geneva and try to reconcile, after the fact, the hundreds of transactions that had been made. Many of the corrections I directed were never implemented, which left a real snarl in what would ordinarily have been a clean and easy audit trail. Documenting cash balances—money available and cash flows—was usually not a problem because the bank recorded all transactions except for securities investments made by Zucker. Accounting for sums *within each account* that were spent on the Contras or Iranian projects was a constant headache. I inevitably found expenses in support of the Contras journaled into the Middle East ledgers and vice versa. Sometimes the same expense was accounted twice between companies. It was a nightmare.

Albert always promised that he would get his bookkeeping under control, but he (and I) always thought we were on the verge of shutting down the covert operations and it never quite happened. I also knew he was sensitive to criticism about his friends at CSF, so I learned early to tread lightly in that area.

Once, however, after a particularly infuriating snafu, I told Albert, "I want to get rid of Zucker and CSF. They're an administrative nightmare, and one of these days they're going to get us into trouble. Money will be missing or we'll think it's missing, and that's the last thing we need on top of everything else!"

Albert replied, "Fine. I'll be happy to do that as soon as you suggest a better alternative," which he knew I could not without going to a whale of a lot of trouble. International finance wasn't my bag, and I couldn't see compromising security or taking the time necessary to hire a lawyer and interview "discreet" fiduciaries, although in retrospect it might have been worth the trouble. One thing about Swiss bankers: They may be dull, but they're honest. The running sore became a running joke until later in the year when the independent counsel lawyers froze our accounts, got a hold of some of the books, and made us look like fools—and worse.

In early May 1986, I was conferring with Ollie in his office when he received a call. He hung up and asked, "Can you come down the hall with me and meet with someone?"

"Sure," I said.

As we walked down the polished corridor, he added, "That was Casey. He has an office here in the EOB."

Casey's home-away-from-headquarters, one of several offices he had squirreled away in various parts of the city, was a lot less sumptuous than the one overlooking the Potomac. We entered a small reception room where the Director's security guards sat relaxing. One showed us into a small, spartan office with bookless shelves. Casey sat behind a worn desk and did not act surprised to see me.

"It's a good thing you are here, General," he greeted me.

"Mr. Director, we've got to get the Agency back into the field with the Contras," Ollie said, picking up a previous conversation about Congressional funding. "It's the only way they're going to survive. Money is very tight and it's getting worse. The $27 million in humanitarian aid is exhausted. As you know, Dick and his people have done minor miracles in stretching out the limited dollars we have. Even now they're starting to get the small air operation in gear. But these are only stopgap measures, and unless substantial funds are put into the operation in the very near future, there is no way in which this war can be continued."

Casey asked me, "How much money do you think is needed?"

"It all depends, Mr. Director—for how long a period of time?"

"Aww, well," Casey slouched in his chair. "We're gonna get Congress on board but it's not going to go as fast as they think over there." He glanced out the window, across West Executive Avenue toward the West Wing of the White House.

"Are we talking another four or five months?" I asked.

"Yeah," Casey answered.

We were about to log some big expenditures for procurements, maintenance, and personnel, so, although I didn't want to shoot numbers off the hip, I felt obliged to say something.

"Mr. Director," I said, "we need a minimum of $10 million in the very near term in order to generate a professional air operation and procure certain munitions that are in short supply. Even feeding the troops and all the refugees takes about a million a month. If we're going to sustain significant military operations against the Sandinistas, we'll need the $10 million right away."

"The only way I know to get the money that fast is from the Saudis," the Director said. Ollie had already told me Casey was planning a trip to

Saudi Arabia. Casey knew I was friendly with the Saudis and that I had asked them for a donation to the Contras in 1984 and 1985. I never knew how much they contributed, but whatever it was, it was undoubtedly substantial to the guerrillas and pocket change to Riyadh. Casey looked straight at me and added, "You can get the money from the Saudis."

"Mr. Director, I'm not a member of the government—"

"Well, I can't legally go to them," Casey interrupted.

I disagreed—I had read Boland closely and knew its legislative history as well as anyone, and I didn't believe it proscribed third-party solicitations. But this was not the time to play barracks lawyer.

Then, rather strangely, Casey said: "But George [meaning George Schultz] could do it."

"Well, damn it, Mr. Director," Ollie said in frustration, sounding a bit like me in Laos 20 years before, "*somebody* better do it or we're going to lose the war!"

"I'll talk to George," Casey made a note to himself. He was more sanguine about Schultz than I was, but if the director thought he could do it—more power to him. He then asked me for an assessment of the military situation in Nicaragua—"Nica-wawa," as he called it.

I told him, "Calero has ostensibly joined Arturo Cruz and Alfonso Robello to form an umbrella organization called UNO. As a matter of practice, though, the FDN still isn't interested in allocating significant resources to the southern front. If I were the CIA, I'd make it painfully clear to Calero and Bermudez that they don't really have any choice in the matter. If I can put my general's hat back on for a minute—and not to belabor the obvious—if the Contras can't field a small but effective fighting force in the south, then there's no hope for victory in the north, where the Sandinistas have Cuban officers and are just too strong and too well supplied. The FDN will be defeated unless the Sandinistas are compelled to stretch their resources to fight against a southern front. I also think the Contras must organize and employ some special operations units to infiltrate the population centers and attack the classical guerrilla targets: communication networks, command posts, individual leaders, public buildings and utilities, and all the rest. In short, they need some kind of urban guerrilla warfare to keep the Sandinistas off guard, worried, and spread thin. Right now, the Ortega brothers are having a free ride in Managua—life there is fairly easy going. I think that's crazy. They'll be perfectly content to fight this little brushfire war as long as it stays in the bush. The Contras also need better leadership—not in Miami, but in the field. Right now, looking at it from a cold-blooded military perpective, I'd much rather be a Sandinista. They're the ones who look like winners."

Casey agreed, but said there was not a lot he could do about it at this time. He was obviously well informed on the Contra situation, far beyond my little analysis. Then he asked:

"Are you having trouble with any of my people since our last talk?"

"No trouble," I shrugged, "but not much support."

"What's wrong?" Casey grumbled.

"We need intelligence for the air operation. It just seems like we can't get it."

"That shouldn't be too hard," he said, dismissing the whole problem with a wave of his hand. It was one of those wonderfully ambiguous Casey-style answers that could've meant anything, from "I'll take care of it" to "that shouldn't be too hard for *you* to take care of."

Casey said he was late for another appointment, and we walked him into the hall.

"Call me later and we'll talk some more about funding," he told Ollie. He turned to me and said, "Thanks, General. I appreciate what you're doing."

"Thank you, sir." I shook his hand. "But we can't do it forever."

As Ollie and I walked back to his office, he asked, "Where did you come up with $10 million?"

"It was just a WAG [a "wild-assed guess" in Pentagon slang], but I had to put some number into his head."

Ollie nodded. "It's a fair number. The thing that bothers me is that the old man [as North often referred to Casey] thinks a new bill is going to take another several months. I trust his judgment more than the legislative liaison people because he deals with the intelligence committees and is never too far from the Hill. One thing's for sure, though: The Contras will soon be bankrupt."

I laughed. "Maybe they can declare Chapter 11!"

Ollie didn't like my private-sector humor. He was counting on getting more Iranian money into the Contra account, which seemed to me wishful thinking, an Ollie North trademark. He kept hoping for big surpluses, and I often had to explain the facts of life of our little operation. The Iranian project required large capital reserves. Those "surpluses" were needed for self-insurance of our airplanes (the Israelis, for example, required a reserve of $2 million for each Israeli-registered aircraft we used), for forward payments for U.S. government–supplied materiel, and to offset our huge operating costs—the *M.V. Erria* (an oceangoing cargo ship purchased in March) alone soaked up $1,600 a day and had a nine-year maritime inspection due in early 1987 that would cost at least $300,000. Ollie knew all this, but because he was so focused on our major goals, he sometimes acted as if he didn't.

When Ghorbanifar resurfaced with some improbable explanation for his disappearance, North went over the plan to coax Kangarlu out of Tehran. Two weeks later, on February 20, Nir, North, and the CIA chief for Near East met in Frankfurt to await the Iranian. Despite a brave effort to overcome the cultural and bureaucratic barriers inevitable in any dealing with a midlevel

official like Kangarlu, the guest of honor was a no-show. When Ghorbanifar
called Iran via international telephone to find out why, Kangarlu told him
his bosses would not release him and had given him other assignments.

"Besides," he reportedly said, "Iran Air is not running properly today."

Ghorbanifar made his usual excuses, but it was obvious that North and
Nir had either the wrong mullah or the wrong intermediary—and probably
both. The meeting was rescheduled for February 24.

While this was going on, I had arrived at Tel Aviv to supervise the
clandestine shipment of the first 500 TOWs of the 1,000-TOW batch to Bandar Abbas. To show our good faith (and to make sure we got the 18 rejected
I-HAWKs back to Israel from Tehran on the return flight), we let the shipment
continue on a chartered Israeli 707.

The shipment went through as planned, although interestingly, only 17
of the rejected I-HAWK missiles were returned. The 18th had been torn down
by Iranian air force technicians to see how the so-called high-altitude components differed from the standard low-altitude configuration of the roughly
500 other HAWKs in their inventory. They found no differences, of course,
except the Star of David stenciled on a couple of interior components, which
explained the flap over "Israeli insignia" still being on the missiles.

Four days later, North, the CIA man, Nir, and I returned to the Frankfurt
Sheraton for the rescheduled meeting. This time, Kangarlu arrived as promised, along with Albert Hakim, whom I had dragooned as a translator. It was
the first meeting between Iranian and American officials outside The Hague,
where billions of dollars worth of post-revolution claims were being adju-
dicated. Albert likes to advertise himself as a hardheaded businessman, but
I think he was worried that a chance to be part of a potentially historic
breakthrough in relations between his adopted and native lands was about
to pass him by.

The 40-ish Kangarlu was slightly built and wore the revolutionary Iranian
"uniform" of a tightly buttoned shirt and unkept beard. Despite his swarthy
complexion, he did not look especially Persian. The elementary Farsi he spoke
(much of which I could understand before translation) revealed his lack of
formal education. Like many in the Ayatollah's government, he had no particular credentials for his post save circumstance and zeal.

At the beginning of the three-day meeting, Kangarlu claimed the delivery
of the 500 TOWs was no factor in his being authorized to attend, but he was
obviously pleased by it and said that feeling was reflected by his superiors.
The rest of the meeting covered previously plowed ground, but at least it was
accomplished with an Iranian official present.

Our basic plan for the high-level meeting was for me to fly the American
delegation onto Kish Island in the Gulf of Oman, using an unmarked, chartered Israeli 707. I suggested to Ollie on more than one occasion prior to the
Kangarlu meeting that our special ops forces should be pre-positioned nearby

as a contingency, but Ollie objected, thinking it would only magnify our security problems.

"They don't have to know what the mission is for," I told him. "The important thing is to get them deployed in advance."

Ideally, we would "forward-deploy" an armed force to Oman, Saudi Arabia, or Bahrain under the guise of a training mission. I wanted to use the Delta Force plus one Ranger battalion. With all the airlift and covering Naval forces in the Persian Gulf, enough man-, fire-, and airpower would be available to bust into Kish and take our people out if the Iranians tried anything funny. Our CIA counterparts supported this plan, and Ollie himself reluctantly went along with it on the condition that McFarlane and Poindexter agreed, which they eventually did.

North left Frankfurt the afternoon of the 26th, and I remained overnight to talk to Kangarlu privately on the morning of the 27th. His Iran Air flight—which was now working properly—departed that afternoon, after which I called North, who, having gotten the go-ahead from Poindexter, told me to release the second installment of 500 TOWs, completing the first batch of 1,000.

I went back to Washington and waited for Ollie to get word from Nir (through Ghorbanifar) of Kangarlu's success in Tehran: Would the Kish Island meeting come off? The answer was yes—and no. Kangarlu had convinced the mullahs to endorse a high-level meeting, but no, it would not be on Kish, but in Tehran.

I thought this change was totally unacceptable and said so to North, suggesting we make a counterproposal to hold the meeting on some neutral spot, like Switzerland or even Asia—in a place where the Iranians would feel safe, such as Tokyo, where the Iranians were doing a lot of business, and our people could not be trapped. Ollie thought this made sense and passed it through Nir back to Kangarlu, who turned it down. To get the kind of Iranian delegation you want, he said, the meeting will have to be in Tehran.

After the February transaction, we had a balance in the various accounts of about $5 million—$2 million of which had been set aside as self-insurance for one aircraft, another $1.7 million earmarked for the procurement and operation of the *Erria* (registered in Denmark), and a few other miscellaneous expenses. That left a balance of approximately $1 million (or minus $1 million, if an additional reserve of $2 million was needed to self-insure a second aircraft), an amount that Ollie immediately dubbed "surplus": the funds we would have available to continue the enterprise.

This attitude, plus the pressure of time as events unfolded, only aggravated the lax financial controls that allowed funds from various sources and intended for certain projects—Contra or Iranian—to become commingled. Albert later maintained that he viewed the "surplus" used to help the Contras as a cash advance from us in expectation of reimbursement from Ollie's donations. We probably should've clarified those expectations then.

Using the term "diversion" for such residuals or cash advances caused most of our future problems. It was first mentioned publicly by Ed Meese in his notorious press conference of November 25, 1986. It implies a deliberate change in course from an existing or proper path. (Ollie, in his famous memo that led to Meese's press conference, had used the term casually, not legalistically as Meese did.) If money were truly "diverted" in the legal sense, it was from the proprietors' pocketbooks into operational reserves or Contra assistance—a fact Albert Hakim pointed out with justifiable concern. He wasn't crazy about the idea of shipping money that ostensibly belonged to the Enterprise south of the border. But Albert didn't control this operation— I did. I started it, directed it, and implemented its various functions. Maybe, had we been a public corporation, the shareholders might've complained about management giving away its assets—but we were a private group of companies, all controlled by me, so there was really no debate.

Around March 7, North, Nir, the CIA Near East chief, and George Cave, a new member of the team, met with Ghorbanifar in Paris.

Cave was a retired CIA officer (and Middle East expert) rehired by Bill Casey on contract. He was an old Iran hand, going back to the late 1950s, and spoke Farsi and Arabic fluently. George was soft-spoken and analytical; he gave the rough-and-tumble North-Nir duo a cosmopolitan touch with his debonair moustache and grey temples. An expert on moving money, he immediately felt bad vibes about Ghorbanifar and recommended privately that we drop Gorba like a bad habit.

During the meeting, Ghorbanifar repeated the Iranians' insistence that the proposed high-level meeting not take place on Kish because "the facilities are not suitable." It had to be held in Tehran. He also said that Kangarlu had brought the Iranian military, specifically the air force, in on the discussions, and the shopping list had changed. Instead of more TOWs, they now wanted spares for their existing stock of I-HAWKs, although he could not be specific. (The list was transmitted later that month.)

These demands went down poorly with the team for obvious reasons. Sending a high-level representative into Tehran during a major war and while the Shiites had declared open season on hostage taking was pure lunacy. Also, the system for obtaining materiel from the U.S. inventory was not set up to accommodate HAWK or other higher-tech components. The proposition spelled nothing but trouble.

After Ghorbanifar left, the team decided that these latest problems were more a function of poor advocacy than Iranian intransigence. The Americans returned to Washington after convincing a reluctant Nir that a concerted effort should be made to find another channel to congenial Iranian ministers.

That was fine in the long run, but it didn't solve the immediate problem of finding an acceptable location for the meeting. Something would have to give.

A week or two later, Ollie informed me that the Israeli investigation into the original 508-TOW transaction in August–September was nearing a climax. Nir and his compatriots were getting very nervous about the replenishment of the TOWs that McFarlane had promised, so we devised a complicated, pro-rata system to gradually pay for $2 million in replacements beginning with an $822,000 reserve I told Albert to establish as a separate account. In concert with the President's January 17 finding, we made all pricing assumptions based on the Economy Act rather than FMS methods, which meant that we might eventually face a shortfall for all the extra FMS markups once replacements were actually shipped, and for which the Israelis would actually be billed. But the language of the finding really left us no choice. Had we followed the more expensive FMS route to replace the 508 TOWs, the Israelis might claim (and with some merit) that we were ripping them off for the difference; and, in all fairness, our pricing method *was* different from the handshake deal used by McFarlane to launch the original batch. He had promised the Israelis essentially free replacements, which he was not in a position to deliver. Bud's later desire to skirt that issue after our cover was blown by altering the chronologies in Casey's testimony to the House Intelligence Committee was, in my view, the place where Iran-Contra stopped being an "operation" and started to become an "affair."

Although it doesn't excuse Bud's action, part of the responsibility for it lies with Israel's handling of the costs of the original batch of 508 TOWs. It would've been a small matter for them to eat the cost, which would've got McFarlane off the hook and eliminated his need to rewrite history in the Casey talking paper. It would also have stopped us from ever thinking in terms of having to create residuals for use elsewhere. (Remember, other than the self-insurance reserves, our main goal was to "save" enough money to repay Israel for the TOWs, period.) If I had it to do over again, I would probably insist that Israel bankroll the whole operation—they knew better than anyone how much the Iranian connection was worth, and how to make it pay.

On April 3, Ghorbanifar came to Washington for a two-day meeting with North and the CIA, which I didn't attend. Ollie said the agenda was "next steps," namely, the list of desired I-HAWK spare parts Iran supposedly wanted, and more definitive planning for the high-level meeting. McFarlane and Poindexter had reluctantly agreed to holding the meeting in Tehran, now targeted for May.

Unfortunately, Gorba was still hawking wares he really didn't possess. For example, he promised that Rafsanjani, at the time Speaker of the Majlis (the Iranian Parliament), would attend the meeting in April 1986. When he was polygraphed by the CIA for the second time on that very matter (among others), though, he flunked miserably. Still, Gorba was left in the loop.

I had already talked to Ami Nir by phone about the logistics for the trip to Tehran: an epic voyage (not through Turkey, but over the Gulf of Aqaba and the Red Sea, around the southern part of the Saudi peninsula and on to the Sea of Oman, and thence into Iran) that would tax our picayune capabilities to the limit. If the parts and the people had to be moved at the same time, we would need two or three aircraft, preferably equipped with fuel-efficient fanjet engines for a long-range (at least nine-hour) circuitous over-water flight, and a corresponding amount of insurance—up to $4 million. We would also need a fail-safe communications system, not only between Tehran and the command post in Tel Aviv (where I would be stationed), but between the command post and the aircraft at any point on their flight. This eliminated the use of CIA aircraft, since they lacked these longer-range aircraft.

We had other problems as well. Ollie said Ghorbanifar was beginning to complain about financial problems, which was hard to accept since we assumed the Iranians were bankrolling him with advanced payments for future deals. We assumed Kangarlu had simply tightened the financial controls used to keep Ghorbanifar on his leash, which certainly made sense. But, as we would eventually find out, that was not the case at all.

We also had a logistics problem. By the end of April, the CIA had located and priced only 226 of the 240 items on the I-HAWK spares list and didn't seem particularly anxious to speed up the glacially slow bureaucratic wheels to support our little sideshow. On the other hand, the clock was running out on the Iranian side, and we still faced risks giving them "guesstimate" prices, and then having to bump them up later. It was an environment where any mistakes would inevitably be viewed as deception—another reason that Ollie's tendency to leave things to the last minute (at least where I was involved) really made my stomach churn.

I got around this little crisis by pricing the material myself in such a way that we'd be safe on the HAWK spares costs and solve the McFarlane/Israeli TOW replenishment problem all at once. I simply took the latest CIA price list and doubled it, adding $1.2 million that the Israelis had promised to contribute, which, when added to the $822,000 reserve Albert had already established, paid to restock Israel's original 508 TOWs. The grand total—the price the Iranians would have to pay—came out to $14.7 million, which was still in the ballpark they expected to see.

On May 12, after a long, item-by-item pricing session in North's office, Ollie's assistant, Robert Earl, gave the complete spares list and their prices over the commercial phone line to Nir in Tel Aviv. The final, scrubbed price bumped Israel's contribution up to $1.5 million, which Ami bitched about a little, but in the end he approved.

Critics claim the I-HAWK spares, not to mention the TOWs, gave Iran an advantage in the Iran-Iraq war, but that's nonsense. The antitank TOWs were of marginal value because most of the war was fought via static defenses, a war of attrition like World War I—not a war of maneuver like World War II or America's armored thrust in Desert Storm. Regarding the HAWK spares, I'm always amused when some journalist or congressman stands up and lectures me about a system I crafted, installed, and verified in Iran. Suffice it to say that from the first time I eyed the list, I knew the Iranians were in deep yogurt militarily—through a lack of technical competence and knowledgeable leadership. The list itself was meaningless.

For example, they asked for 10 "high-value" electrical generators even though the country was and is full of this type of equipment and it could be obtained easily from their own internal market. They also asked for printed circuit boards, simple cable connectors (by the dozen), and an oscilloscope—Radio Shack stuff that had little or nothing to do with the HAWK's mission-peculiar systems. As soon as I saw the list, in fact, I told my colleagues and the U.S. intelligence community that Iran was in bad shape because they didn't even know what they should be asking for. Any military expert would've expected Iran to ask for spares for their more mundane but workhorse equipment—transport and attack fighter aircraft, as well as replacement artillery "tubes" (barrels) and hard-to-get parts for armored vehicles. Only when this aspect of the war was under control would it make sense to go for the high-tech stuff, but the Iranians and their intermediaries invariably got it backward.

The people who really helped Iran in their war effort were the Israelis, beginning as early as 1981. As Deputy Assistant Security of Defense for Near East, Africa, and East Asia, I saw intelligence reports documenting enormous shipments of war materials of all types from Israel to Iran, from the well-publicized F-4 spares of 1981 to 700,000 *tons* of artillery shells delivered by Danish vessels in 1986. All this was done with the full knowledge of the U.S. intelligence community and a wink from the President and Congressional oversight committees. Compared to this, the equipment shipped in the Iran Initiative was a drop in the ocean, which may explain why it was so difficult for us to get the attention of targeted Iranian officials, especially through a low-quality, high-attenuation intermediary like Ghorbanifar.


While my pricing exercise was going on, Ollie and George Cave met with Ghorbanifar in London about the upcoming meeting in Tehran. The session included a conference call between Cave and Ghorbanifar and Kangarlu in Tehran. I never heard the details of this conversation, but Cave was reportedly satisfied with the arrangements Kangarlu had made. The proof would have to be in the pudding, which for me was a terrifying prospect.

The new plan was to have the American delegation, led by Bud McFarlane, arrive in Tehran with half the HAWK parts. (Although he was no longer a government employee, as a handpicked Presidential envoy who had been the penultimate national security man—as well as a guy the Iranians recognized and knew better than someone like Poindexter—he was probably an acceptable choice for a pathfinding mission like this; the "portfolioed ministers" would come later.) McFarlane and his delegation would be greeted by government officials and taken to a secure facility where they would be made comfortable and concealed from the general population. Talks would then commence with Prime Minister Mushavi (and officials from his office) and Speaker Rafsanjani. Once Tehran had reciprocated the gesture of trust by causing the hostages to be released in Lebanon, the remaining HAWK parts would be dispatched from Tel Aviv.

We built some latitude into this plan by assuming the second plane could be recalled at any time in case something went wrong, or looked like it was going wrong. Contrary to later media reports, the second plane was not something Ollie dreamed up while Bud was asleep at the Tehran Hilton. It was a reasonable contingency that everyone, including Nir and McFarlane, agreed upon well before the fact.

We discussed the possibility of my going with Bud, Ollie, and Ami to Tehran but finally decided against it, mainly because I'd be needed to explain things to the rest of the world if they all got busted. The fact also remained that my face was still too well known around Tehran. Americans weren't the most popular people in Iran at the time, especially those who had been closely connected with the Shah and his generals. I was also pretty pessimistic about the whole idea—not just its chances for diplomatic success, but also its odds of getting everyone back in one piece. Like a good soldier, I gave the team the reasons for my concerns, and then sat back and shut up. These reasons were as follows:

1. Even if George Cave was convinced the arrangements (security and otherwise) were satisfactory, they were still made through Ghorbanifar, which, as far as I was concerned, made them immediately suspect.
2. It's foolish to let so important and seminal an event as the first post-revolution, high-level U.S.-Iranian meeting take place without complete and thorough preparation at the staff level, which meant a face-to-face meeting between someone like North and his counterpart in the Foreign Ministry on substantive, as well as logistical, matters. I knew better than anyone that the Iranians, even in prerevolutionary Iran, weren't as efficient as the West in these matters, and the margins for mistakes and misunderstandings, let alone duplicity, were enormous. Plus, everything so far—even agenda items—were still being discussed through intermediaries. This was a recipe for disaster, not just disappointment.

3. How *in the name of God* can a recent National Security Advisor, who still carries a lot of important secrets in his head, put himself into the hands of a hostile power without U.S.-backed security being in place? To my mind, that alone was grounds to seriously rethink or cancel the mission. The only rationale I could think of was that Bud had somehow let his own vanity or the rush of events get ahead of him. I think he saw himself as something of a latter-day Henry Kissinger, opening Islamic Iran the way Kissinger opened Communist China. Even so, an enormous amount of preparation through informal channels and high-ranking intermediaries had anticipated the 1971 Kissinger trip. In this case, similar reliable channels just weren't available—only Ghorbanifar.

On May 15, just as Ghorbanifar was depositing the $15 million we had asked for, the CIA came through with the rest of their detailed pricing for the earlier shipment of TOW missiles. Their not-so-apologetic message was, "Oops! We underpriced the February delivery; you owe us $240,000 right now. And, of course, these errors carry over to the prices we gave you for the next batch, too."

This really put me in a box. The Iranians had just paid what we asked and the Israelis had grudgingly ponied up with their $1.5 million, and neither was in a mood to go back to the well because someone with a green eyeshade in the bowels of the CIA had used the wrong price catalog. I was worried that, at minimum, this would create a "float" (a traveling shortfall) between the pricing, payment, and delivery phases of each batch that would haunt us for the rest of the program. As it turned out, my "fudge factor" (doubling the CIA's prices) saved our bacon and actually delivered a small operating surplus, although in the middle of May, that outcome was far from certain. Critics of Iran-Contra have never credited us with paying this government cost overrun—something any other commercial vendor would've argued cats-and-dogs about. If nothing else, it illustrates how careful we were to make sure that not one U.S. government dollar was spent on either program.

By this time, too, we had remitted $6.5 million to the U.S. government for the I-HAWK parts and Israel's original 508 TOWs. Transportation crews and miscellaneous expenses cost us another $1.2 million plus $900,000 set aside for Israel to pay back the $1 million that they had put in for TOW replenishment. We decided that $900,000 was a good pro-rata share (this being the second transaction), leaving $8.1 to $7.9 million after subtracting all costs and set-asides. From this $7.9 million, we set aside $4 million for future self-insurance, leaving $3.9 million. If we kept a million of that for continuing Iran Initiative operations, that left about $3 million, which met Ollie's definition of "surplus."

Albert wanted to allocate this money toward our targeted $7 million aircraft procurement and operations fund. If we added the $2 million aircraft operation cost to the $3 million surplus, we realized we would have $5 million available for short-term or forward financing and thereby eliminate Ghorbanifar, who, as conduit for the Iranians, had bankrolled the operation.

We had several good reasons for wanting to do this. As a money man, Ghorbanifar was notorious for giving us bad checks. For example, the last $15 million deposit to Lake Resources was made in three installments. The first $5 million check was pure rubber, drawn on the now-famous BCCI Bank of Monte Carlo and made by "tested" telex—but the telex had the wrong coding and wording on it. After a day or so, the Swiss bankers informed us that something suspicious was afoot; apparently Ghorbanifar was not aware that our Credit Suisse bankers (the same Swiss bank as Gorba's) were giving Albert a blow-by-blow description of each transaction in Monaco and its follow-up investigation. I called Ghorbanifar and he swore it was just an administrative screwup, which launched four or five days of great confusion and totally wasted time and energy. After listening to one too many of Gorba's fish stories on the phone, I finally told him:

"You are a deceitful liar. I'm not going to tolerate you any further."

Ghorbanifar sputtered, "No one can talk to me like that!"

"Someone *is* talking to you like that!" I snapped. "I simply won't deal with a liar. I am recommending that you be terminated," I said and hung up the phone.

I sat there fuming a few minutes, reflecting on the fact that since my first meeting with Ghorbanifar in Paris, he had proven himself to be a pathological liar. I had read numerous intelligence reports on discussions between Ghorbanifar and Kangarlu in which Gorba repeatedly claimed to have offers from the United States for various high-tech weapons like Phoenix missiles, which had been roundly rejected by the U.S. at every juncture. His obvious motive was to entice Kangarlu to put ever-increasing amounts (as much as $50 million, at one point) in Ghorbanifar's Credit Suisse account in Geneva on the prospect of swinging these high-tech deals. With the stakes now greater than ever, I decided we just couldn't afford to go on with this guy.

I called Nir and told him of my acrimonious exchange with Ghorbanifar and said I was recommending to the American side that he be "burned" once again.

Nir got very upset and said, "But Gorba is the only channel we have! We need to hang onto him!"

"A bad channel is worse than no channel at all," I said, and suggested Nir take up the matter with North.

Ami did, in fact, call Ollie, mostly to complain about my heavy-handed way of dealing with his boy. He said that, just after my call and before he contacted North, Ghorbanifar had called Nir sounding close to a nervous breakdown—completely unstrung.

"Copp is about to have me killed!" Gorba cried into the phone. "You've got to do something!"

Ollie and I had a good laugh when he relayed Nir's story. Ghorbanifar obviously interpreted my use of the word "terminate" to mean "terminate with extreme prejudice": the Hollywood term, ascribed to the CIA, for assassinating a traitor. I meant, of course, that I wanted Ollie and Ami to terminate Gorba's business relationship, nothing else. But I'm glad his guilty conscience finally gave him a bad few minutes.

Nonetheless, that little exchange led Ollie to a series of poor decisions that would eventually torpedo the operation. Since North couldn't really fire Ghorbanifar, who was an Israeli operative, he told Ami to handle all contact with Gorba himself, since I henceforth refused to deal with him. Instead of removing Ghorbanifar from the project, though, this only drove him closer to the Israelis and had the net effect of putting more cards in his hands, since there were now even fewer cross-checks on his self-dealing.

In any event, the main problem with Albert's $7 million goal was that it ran counter to our desire to support the Contras on a continuing basis. Fortunately, once we reached that goal, $2 million of that would be instantly released since our self-insurance requirement would drop from $4 million to $2 million. However, even without this clash in priorities (helping the Contras versus deep-sixing Ghorbanifar), we never had at this time more than $3 million of Iranian receipts that could have been spent on the Contras.

Of course, funds from private contributions, conservative political groups, foundations, foreign countries, and the like also came in at this time, but they never amounted to more than $2 million to $2.5 million. If the healthy donations attributed to the Saudis and Taiwanese and certain other wealthy individuals and groups by the Tower Commission actually materialized, I never saw them. Even Ollie had no clear idea of how much money the Contras *may* have received during this period, since he had no control over those accounts. Both of us could only go by what we were told by donors (who sometimes had reasons to exaggerate or diminish the real amounts) or heard through the grapevine. From these, we tried to make educated guesses based on what we saw versus what we expected to see in terms of Contra assets, equippage, and effectiveness.

The main point is, the enterprise was not the only source of Contra funds during the Boland cutoff period, and may not even have been the biggest.

The date for the Tehran meeting was finally set for May 25. Gorba deposited the $15 million in the middle of the month, and then told Nir the Iranians would want two more I-HAWK radars after the meeting—but that was the least of my worries.

On May 22 and 23, the Southern Air Transport (SAT) 707s arrived in Tel Aviv from Texas with the I-HAWK spares and 508 replacement TOWs for Israel. I arrived on the 23rd along with two handpicked SAT crews I had hired to fly the chartered, unmarked Israeli 707s to Tehran.

Captain of the McFarlane plane was to be Paul Gilcrist, SAT's chief pilot and a man who seemed born for aerial heroics, right down to his blond hair and Nordic movie-star good looks. His deputy, Lyn Toodle, a former Air Force pilot, was just as gifted at the controls and would skipper the second plane. Between them, they astounded their Israeli check pilots with their airmanship as they test-flew the birds in preparation for the mission.

Bud, Ollie, Cave, and Teicher, plus two CIA communications technicians and their gear, arrived from Ramstein AFB, Germany, on the 24th. They were in good spirits, all things considered, and, I think, tended to look at the trip as another form of combat mission, with all the risks and skills that demanded.

After a quiet dinner at a seaside restaurant chaperoned by an Israeli security detachment, I took the delegation back to the Carlton Hotel, where (except for one CIA technician who would remain with me to monitor the flight) they prepared for a midnight departure.

I chatted with Ollie in his room while he got ready to "move out." Before we left, he said:

"Oh, by the way, there are a few small things I need your help with while I'm in Tehran."

He then told me about a separate attempt to find the Lebanese hostages being held by Hezballah using Drug Enforcement Agency operatives working out of Cyprus and a Lebanese agent. Ollie said he needed two things from me to support the ongoing effort. First, he wanted me to provide $30,000 for the Lebanese agent to carry into the country; Ollie had already dispatched a DEA agent to Geneva to pick up the cash from Albert. Second, he needed a small ship to stand offshore and pick up the hostages should the operation be successful.

I sent a message to Hakim to get the money ready for the agent and to contact the ship, the *Erria*, which was in the Mediterranean at the time, through our agent in Denmark. The captain was told to proceed to Cyprus, where he would receive further instructions.

I asked Ollie, "Who are you working with—the Druze or Israelis or just who, exactly?"

"I don't know, exactly, who or what group the DEA people are working with, but they have a lot of knowledge of the area in Lebanon, and I have some confidence in them. The CIA completely fucked up the rescue of Kilburn." He was referring to the American University librarian kidnapped in Beirut in December 1984. In April 1985, the CIA followed up a ransom offer by staging a rescue attempt through some friendly foreign agents using money that would chemically self-destruct after the payoff. The scheme had dragged on for months with no results, and then Kilburn was "bought" by Libyan intelligence agents three days after the bombing of Libya and killed by them in retribution. The CIA moved too slowly for Ollie, and I couldn't fault his desire to try another agency—although it would've paid him, I think, to check out the arrangements more thoroughly before committing to the plot. But that was Ollie. I told him I'd do the best I could while he was gone.

I shook the delegation down for "pocket litter," any personal effects that would give away their identity or nationality, and at a quarter after 11 took them with another Israeli security detail to the plane. Satellite photos of the intended route of flight looked good, and Paul reported that the aircraft was shipshape. I tried to think of even one good reason to scrub the mission, but everyone was spring-loaded to the "go" position, so I could only wish them well and walk down the stairs chewing my lip, as the loadmaster "buttoned up" the aircraft behind me.

I watched the 707 start its engines, taxi out, and take off. I asked myself the same question I had asked a thousand times before on other dangerous missions: Had I done everything that *could* be done to ensure our men had the best possible chance of coming back?

Then, as now, only time would provide the answer.

# —14—

# Bear Any Burden . . .

After launching Bud, Ollie, Ami, and their group, I went to our Tel Aviv command post in the Carlton Hotel to monitor communications. Throughout the night, in-flight aborts or diversions to Oman, Saudi Arabia, South Yemen, Ethiopia, and Somalia would be a constant possibility. Rest was out of the question. In some ways it was worse than a combat mission, since we had all the tension of war without the release of action. It would be a very long night.

Communications got especially touchy when the plane overflew elements of the Soviet fleet stationed off the Saudi peninsula. Our "fail-safe" go/no-go code system, similar to the one SAC once used, ensured that, unless authority to proceed was received at specific waypoints, the plane would automatically return to Tel Aviv or land at an approved diversion base. In case of an in-flight emergency, such as an engine fire, they'd have to land as soon as possible, so my job then would be to activate our external legal and diplomatic mechanisms to get the VIP passengers out, first and foremost; then the aircrew if the plane was detained; then the plane if the cargo was impounded. Depending on how big a media splash the plane made when it set down, I would then run damage control in cooperation with Poindexter and whoever else he saw fit to bring into the game. As always, we were dealing with various shades of risk, a dozen interlocking contingencies, and a hundred things that could go wrong—and those were just the ones we knew about.

Our planning, however, paid off. The winds were true and the luck of the dice was with us. Nine hours later, at 9:30 A.M. Tehran time on May 25, the plane landed safely at Mehrabad Airport.

As Bud and Ollie would later tell the story, they parked on the military side of the airport and were greeted by officials that nobody, including Nir, recognized—more than a little disconcerting. Under armed escort, the delegation was taken to the old Hilton Hotel where they were isolated in one wing. At first, the aircrew stayed with the bird, as instructed, and the Iranians initially had no problem with that. Our crew's job now was to keep the cargo and aircraft secure and superintend the plane's servicing for the trip home.

That night, however, the crew was forcibly taken to the hotel, and the Iranians refused to refuel the plane—perhaps to discourage an unauthorized departure, but more likely because of poor communication on the Iranian side. (Aircraft are normally refueled immediately after flight to prevent condensation from forming in the fuel tanks—an important safety precaution.) Our pilot in command made a stink about this, but there was nothing he could do. The plane was eventually refueled, but after a two-day delay.

Soon after his arrival at the hotel, North called me on the CIA's special secure-scrambled satellite communications gear, which also allowed us to talk directly with Agency headquarters at Langley. It was a big relief to hear his voice. Other than an "all's well—for the moment" he didn't have much to say. I got the impression that he was a little bewildered by their reception and that Bud, as usual, was playing his cards very close to the vest—being aloof and dignified in a way that comes very naturally to him, playing the statesman's role to the hilt.

On the second day, May 26, Ollie called again on the secure line and asked about the DEA operation in Cyprus. Ollie had been in touch with his assistant, Bob Earl, in Washington, who reported that Hakim had delivered the money successfully in Geneva and that the agent had gone on into Lebanon. It turned out this $30K was only earnest money or for lower-level bribes among the Hezballah. The real cash, $1 million (I later learned the amount was actually twice that much) was being delivered by a courier, Jay Coburn, on behalf of H. Ross Perot. Coburn was scheduled to arrive by Lear jet in Cyprus and stand by to ransom one or more hostages when notified by our man in Lebanon. This was specifically the kind of ransom operation I'd told Poindexter I didn't want to be involved with, let alone one connected to a high-profile civilian like Perot, who had a reputation in Washington for muddying up the operational waters.

But Ollie was concerned that the logistics were getting too large for the DEA to handle, and asked if I would send a reliable man to assist. Naturally, Tom Clines was the first name that popped into my head for this kind of work, and I immediately phoned Albert and asked him to get Tom on a plane to Cyprus, via Geneva, ASAP. All my communications with Albert were by means of KL-43, so both time and the capacity of the machine limited the details I could relay. That was one reason I wanted Tom routed through Geneva, so Albert could brief him personally before he went in.

Tom arrived in Cyprus on May 27, the third day of the Tehran trip. He had no trouble linking up with the DEA people, assessed the situation, and the next day reported to me using brevity codes on a commercial line. He said planning had been poor and gave the scheme only a 20 to 30 percent chance of success. The weakest link in the chain was the DEA's Lebanese agent, who, although a very brave fellow, had never been tested in this type of action.

That day I heard from our pilot in Tehran, who said that sometime while the crew was being detained at the hotel, the single pallet of I-HAWK spare parts accompanying the delegation had been off-loaded by the Iranians. This was done without his knowledge or permission—in fact, it ran contrary to McFarlane's instructions to the Iranian reception committee. This concerned me a great deal, since it indicated either a breakdown in communications and confusion among the Iranians, or the possibility that the Iranians no longer cared what the American delegation chief thought or said, neither of which was a good sign.

Over the next couple of days, I heard periodically from McFarlane and Poindexter on the status of the deputation—a typical good news/bad news situation. The good news was, the situation seemed stable. The bad news was, it was so stable that no change or headway was being made in the discussions. In fact, nothing much was happening at all.

Late on the fourth day, however, things seemed to be breaking loose. Shortly after midnight on the 28th, I received a message to launch Lyn Toodle with the second aircraft (filled with 12 pallets of the remaining I-HAWK spares) toward Tehran, but to "be ready to turn it around on command." Four hours into the flight—about the time the aircraft had just about finished traversing the length of the Red Sea—I received instructions to do just that.

Even the recall caused us a few anxious moments. Our initial coded radio messages for the plane to return all went unanswered. For 30 minutes we tried to raise the aircraft, but to no avail.

We checked our transmitter and verified that everything was working fine, and then tried again. Fortunately, we knew they had a fail-safe waypoint at the southern end of the Red Sea. What happened then would answer our primary question: Were they still in the air?

To our great relief, the pilot soon checked in with a laconic message that he was "returning to the barn." Subsequent troubleshooting showed that the 707's SelCal system (short for "selective calling" radio receiver, a device widely used by airlines that allows pilots to receive transmissions from their company while screening out the radio chatter of other aircraft) had malfunctioned over the Red Sea, causing it to block our abort signal. Since the pilot had not received confirmation to continue, he followed his instructions and returned to Tel Aviv, where he landed without incident.

At the time, I had no idea why Bud requested, then aborted, the second plane. Worst case, of course, was that the Iranians had tricked him into ordering the remaining parts and then clapped the whole delegation in irons. However, I got another message later in the morning, after sunup, that the delegation was coming home. The mission had failed.

The group's 9:00 A.M. departure from Tehran was apparently pretty hairy—not because of the Iranians, but because of the physical factors surrounding the takeoff. The airplane was completely "grossed out" (fueled to its gross weight limit) because of forecast head winds on the long flight back to Israel. When this high-weight factor was added to Mehrabad's high field elevation—about 4,000 feet, where the air is noticeably thinner than at sea level—and the fact that the plane was equipped with older-style straight turbojet engines rather than higher-thrust fans, the ingredients were in place for a major accident should an engine fail on takeoff.

Although they used nearly every inch of the runway's 13,000 feet to get airborne and dragged their tail around Tehran while clawing for altitude, they made their getaway with everyone on board. Their luck held during the return flight, which was a bit shorter than expected. The forecast adverse winds never materialized.

I met the delegation on the ramp as they disembarked, looking tired, disheveled, and disappointed. Although nobody seemed anxious to talk, McFarlane gave me a quick rundown on events right there by the plane, including the reason for the second ship's abort.

As a negotiating ploy, Bud decided to launch the second bird so as to create a tangible deadline for the Iranians to release the hostages: the second plane's arrival time in Tehran. Unfortunately, this strategy backfired when the Iranians (earnestly, in my view) told him they simply couldn't pull the long-distance strings in Lebanon that fast. Although the Ayatollah wielded considerable influence over Hezballah, it was in no way a "solid-line" political, military, or even paramilitary relationship. Even worse, neither Prime Minister Mushavi nor Speaker Rafsanjani had appeared at the conference, which quickly degenerated into a glorified bargaining session for more arms. When it was apparent that his high-ranking counterparts were not going to show and his rather theatrical deadline was meaningless, McFarlane ordered the second plane to turn around and told his troops to prepare to pull out. I got the feeling his personal, as well as professional, pride had been wounded by the Iranian snub. Things like this never happened to Henry Kissinger. Somehow, being ignored seemed worse than being arrested.

Bud called Poindexter from planeside using the portable sat-comm gear, gave him the bad news, and then went immediately to the Lear jet I had chartered for the return trip to Washington.

I stayed an extra day to arrange storage for the undelivered I-HAWK parts, and then caught a commercial flight to Geneva.

Diplomatically, the mission had been a disaster. Not only did it *not* advance U.S.-Iranian relations in general, it actually set back the rapport-building process because of the slap in the face delivered to the U.S. by the failure of the promised high-level Iranian delegation to appear.

Even from an arms-for-hostages angle it was a bust. A partial load of I-HAWK parts had been delivered, and the U.S.-Israeli team got nothing in return. However, Ollie, Nir, and George Cave put as bright a face on things as they could. They maintained (as Bud's representatives after he quit the talks) that substantive issues were discussed and progress was made and that these facts would certainly be made known to the Ayatollah's inner circle as well as the moderate factions. Ami Nir was especially adamant on this point. Like me, he felt Bud's demands for an "instant" hostage release to match the transit schedule of the second plane was simply unrealistic. As I had done, Nir had also pressed for a preparatory meeting before sending McFarlane, and was not surprised that the Iranians were unprepared to take advantage of the team's appearance in Tehran.

All in all, the diplomatic side of the mission had been handled in an amateurish fashion. The Israelis attributed most of this to McFarlane's "unstatesmanlike conduct," but there was plenty of blame to go around. We all agreed, however, that our disappointment over the failed opportunity was partially offset by our relief that everyone was able to get home safely to bitch about it in their old age.

I arrived in Geneva on May 30 and immediately called Tom Clines in Cyprus to see what had happened in the DEA-hostages deal. Tom said he had not heard from the Lebanese agent for several days and was holding the *Erria* off the coast on the outside chance that something would break. He did not sound optimistic.

"Unless there's something I can do to help, Tom," I said, "I'm going to go back to Washington."

"Adios, señor," Tom replied. "I think we've got a dry hole here."

It turned out he was right. After 10 more days without hearing a word from the Lebanese agent, Tom and the DEA representatives returned to the United States. Perot's man Coburn took the $2 million back to Europe. I notified Ollie that the whole operation had been wound back to its starting point and that the Lebanese agent was either (a) lighting his cigars with $20 bills at the *Casino du Liban* or (b) stuffed in some trash can in Beirut. Either way, we were unlikely to see him or the money again.

Several weeks later the DEA agents came back to Tom with an improbable story that closed the case. According to them, the Lebanese man had a couple of close calls and just managed to escape with his life—*without* the $30,000, naturally. Tom said the whole operation seemed to him like a colossal waste of time—real Keystone Cops stuff—which told me mainly how much pressure Ollie must've been under to get the remaining hostages (by now, Reed, Ciccipio, Anderson, and Jacobsen) out. According to John Poindexter, "the old man" (military slang for the commanding officer; in his case, the President) asked on an almost daily basis, "Why can't we do more? Why can't we get them out?" This gave new significance to what McFarlane had told me earlier about the August–September TOW shipments.

"He wants to get the job done," McFarlane said, paraphrasing the President. "He wants to get those hostages out!"

As time went on, it became clear to me who was driving the "arms-for-hostages" aspect of the Iran Initiative.

It wasn't Ollie, who always did his damnedest to implement whatever orders he'd been given. It wasn't McFarlane, a far less passionate guy, who by nature and experience understood the logic of subordinating a handful of lives to larger strategic interests. It wasn't even Poindexter, who more than any of us grasped both the big geopolitical picture and small nuances of the problem and its players.

It was President Reagan himself—the man who, more than anyone else in government at that time, loved to personify state problems and opportunities in the form of individuals. He had made great issue of (and got great mileage from) the Iranian hostage crisis in the campaign against Jimmy Carter and now felt vulnerable to his own criticisms. He followed the career of hostage Terry Anderson's sister, Peggy Say, who took potshots at the administration regularly in the media for its inability to gain Anderson's release. He had mandated the CIA, State, and Defense departments (and just about everyone else in government) to find the hostages and spring them, no questions asked, but nobody came up with anything. Reagan apparently suffered acutely when Peter Kilburn was murdered in revenge for the Libyan bombing, which was supposed to punish and discourage such terrorism. The failure of Reagan's reconstituted military, diplomatic, and intelligence apparatus to make even the *slightest* dent in the hostage situation was worse than frustrating to the President—it was bewildering, embarrassing, and, in his mind, I believe, a tangible threat to his presidency.

Two National Security Advisors, McFarlane and Poindexter, and the chief assistant to both, Oliver North, not to mention their civilian technician—me—and CIA director Casey saw the Iran Initiative in its larger perspective. Unbelievably, it was the Chief Executive himself who stood those priorities on their head, who viewed the effort to achieve high-level rapprochement as primarily another tool for releasing the hostages. It was tremendously shortsighted for a president who was otherwise credited (at least by a majority of voters, who continued to rank him high in presidential polls all through the 1980s) with the vision to reverse America's previous economic and military decline. I believe the historic and strategically significant Iran Initiative was resuscitated by Reagan after its 1985 failure chiefly to relieve himself of the hostage issue. As much as we on the operations end sympathized with the American hostages and their families, we were all disheartened to see this misplaced emphasis, and I, for one, believed that incorporating it so heavily into our negotiating posture carried with it the seeds of almost certain failure.

First, it gave Iran and Hezballah an inordinately powerful bargaining chip. Once they looked past the rhetoric of the President's men to see the attitudes of the President himself, their motivation to deal substantively with U.S.-Iranian strategic issues would evaporate. The Iranian leadership did not sabotage McFarlane's Tehran trip half as badly as his own boss, President Reagan, did.

Second, the President's overriding concern for the hostages came at a time when Tehran's influence with the Lebanese Shia was declining. This gave Iran a perfect (and perfectly valid) excuse for not delivering on hostage-related promises while keeping, or attempting to keep, the pipeline full of American war materiel.

Finally, it demoted the *real* American agenda—a new U.S.-Iranian relationship, sorely needed since 1979—to the role of a surrogate issue. How could we expect the Iranians to give the initiative its proper weight if the U.S. President *himself* refused to see it in perspective?

I expressed these concerns to Poindexter and North many times after the Tehran trip and each time they commiserated with me, but, loyal servicemen and good federal employees that they were, they had to shrug them off. They defended the President by saying he knew, and wanted the Iranians to know, that the hostages represented a real political barrier to rapprochement. Well, one man's barrier is another man's bulwark—a tool for attaining his objectives while foiling the goals of his opponent. History shows *that's* how the Iranians actually perceived and played the Lebanese hostage issue during these crucial months.

And, sadly, that's why they won.

In early June I returned to Washington and met several times with North. Because of the recent disappointments, he said, the President had decided that all the hostages had to be released as a precondition to a further dialogue. That "all-or-nothing" proposition didn't look likely, so the Iran Initiative was moved to the back burner, and Contra support (and the possibility of renewed Congressional funding) returned to the fore.

The administration was promoting a $100 million Contra-aid appropriations bill in Congress along with a restoration of the CIA to its pre-Boland role as mentors and managers of the effort. This activity was a real tonic to our flagging spirits—not just because of the bad news from Iran, but also because it seemed to justify our belief that our whole Central American enterprise was temporary and something we could soon take out of our active files and put into our résumés and scrapbooks.

But that was not to be. Although the House approved the funding on June 25, our troubles were far from over.

Bob Dutton, the retired Air Force colonel with a strong background in special ops I had hired to straighten out the mess in Ilopango, now turned in his first report on Contra air operations. The bottom line was that the program was still plagued by a lack of money, poor personnel and maintenance, weak coordination between air and ground ops, and faulty communication with just about everyone else.

I had tried to adopt a hands-off policy in the day-to-day management of our Central American operation, but even with a capable man like Dutton, it was impossible to really succeed without strong institutional backing. Our best allies in this regard turned out to be the Salvadorian air force commander, General Bustillo, and Enrique Bermudez, commander of the FDN operating out of Honduras. On our side, Ralph Quintero continued to work miracles gathering hard intelligence and forging or patching up alliances with the American or local powers-that-be, but even these dedicated guys could do only so much.

A surprise blow came in May, when President Oscar Arias's new government in Costa Rica reversed course and threw all kinds of roadblocks in the way of our using the emergency airstrip at Santa Elena, now nearing the end of construction. Elliott Abrams, assistant Secretary of State for inter-America affairs, and Ambassador Lewis Tambs, who knew about our project, did what they could, but Arias would not be persuaded to follow his predecessor's example.

The biggest obstacles seemed to be created by Felix Rodriguez (a.k.a. Maximo Gomez, a legendary Cuban hero), General Bustillo's close friend. It would not be unfair to categorize Rodriguez as the "Ghorbanifar of the Contras." He had worked with Tom Clines after the Bay of Pigs, on and off with the CIA in Cuba, and with the U.S. Army in Vietnam. His own best promoter, Rodriguez loved guns and gadgetry and was intimately involved in the pursuit (and some say the assassination) of Che Guevara in Bolivia. It would be hard to say which Felix hated more—Communism in general, or Fidel Castro in particular. His grand passion was to create a kind of unified command for anti-Communist operations for all of Central America: El Salvador, Guatemala, Honduras, Costa Rica—and the Contras in Nicaragua. Fortunately, the Communist movement in the region seems to have self-destructed, robbing Felix of his chance to become a latter-day El Cid.

Rodriguez's contact with the administration was through Don Gregg, then Vice President Bush's national security advisor. Gregg and Rodriguez had worked together in Vietnam and Gregg had introduced Felix, under the name of Gomez, to General Bustillo. Felix helped organize helicopter operations to support Salvadorian paratroopers—and actually took some lessons in a Hughes 500 (shades of Iranian General Tadayon) to try to become the pilot he always claimed to be.

I first met Felix in the early 1970s the same way I met a number of CIA people, including Edwin Wilson: casually, through Tom Clines. Until I saw Felix on the ramp at Ilopango in April 1986, I hadn't seen him in over a decade.

Ollie and I had gone south for a one-day review of our faltering air program with military group chief Colonel Jim Steele, Ralph Quintero, Enrique Bermudez (and his air chief), and Dick Gadd. We had flown via SAT Jetstar into Ilopango, and after the meeting, Felix volunteered to chopper us across town to the U.S. Embassy, where we would meet with the ambassador.

My first mistake was to sit in the rear of the helicopter. By the extreme yawing and rolling of the little bird, I could tell our pilot was pretty hamhanded and inexperienced—and possibly dangerous. On the return flight, I sat in the left front seat (in most helicopters, the pilot in command sits on the right, the exact opposite of the way it works in fixed-wing aircraft), where I could be within a split-second's reach of the controls. I gave Felix a little tutorial in fling-wing piloting technique, which he seemed to appreciate—particularly since we were on headset and intercom and nobody else could hear us. To his credit, Felix admitted he was a novice who was barely qualified to fly solo. Nevertheless, he had put his macho image ahead of good judgment in volunteering to ferry visiting VIPs around without supervision.

By June 1986 Felix had switched from a booster of the airlift project to its biggest critic and detractor. Despite his later statements to the contrary, Felix was paid by our enterprise about $3,000 a month from February until the Hasenfus shoot-down in October—and we have plenty of testimony to prove it. He liked to portray himself as a great patriot (and to the extent that he hated Castro and wanted to help people get rid of their Communist masters, he was), but his real goal was to run the Contra air force. To that end, he seemed intent on making sure our air operation at least appeared to be unsuccessful, sabotaging us administratively and politically, hoping that if things got bad enough, our supervisors would appoint him to command.

For example, during the summer of 1986, he insisted that our two C-123s not be allowed to make air drops into Nicaragua in formation—that is, as a mutually supporting team. Since Felix was against this and had become good friends with General Bustillo, the Salvadorian commandante forbade it, which he could do under the operational agreement that allowed us to use Ilopango.

This may not seem like much of a problem, but it cut to the heart of the airlift philosophy I had put in place—tactics developed and verified in Laos and Vietnam in over 10 years of jungle warfare. With formation drops, you improved command and control over aircraft on the mission, ensured more reliable navigation (owing to the redundancy of crews and equipment), and vastly increased the chances of rescue should one of the ships go down (the other could loiter in the area; act as spotter; or, at minimum, ensure that emergency communication was made). It also permitted a larger volume of cargo to be delivered on each mission, reducing risks caused by bad weather, enemy troop movements, and other imponderables.

Instead, Felix (still basically a nonflier) dictated aerial drop tactics to our Provider pilots, William Cooper (the project manager, who had 29,000 hours of flight time) and his deputy, an ex–Air America jock who had logged 19,000 hours of his own, much of it under combat conditions. When these veterans objected, Felix reminded them that he was a personal friend of Vice President Bush (which may or may not have been true) and talked frequently on the phone to "Bush's office," meaning Gregg (which was true enough). Felix's real power, though, came through his rapport with General Bustillo. As a result, our guys just saluted and did the best they could, complaining to Dutton and me behind Felix's back.

In August 1986, North called Rodriguez to Washington to try to moderate his behavior—give him something to do that would keep him away from the flight crews. We were also beginning to sense that Felix posed a growing security threat. He tended to piss people off, and angry, disgruntled people always talk more than they should. Felix was also known to shoot off his mouth about the project whenever VIPs were in town. He even brought the mayor of West Miami to Ilopango! On several occasions, too, according to Ralph Quintero, Felix briefed Mario Del Amico, one of Ron Martin's agents, on the operation. Martin by now was determined to add the Salvadorian side of the arms business to his monopoly in Honduras, despite the decision to make all Contra arms purchases through me. Martin came to view me as his chief competition in the area, which was untrue because our enterprise dealt only with the Contras and the Iranians and nobody else. In truth, I was looking for ways to get *out* of the arms business, not further into it. But according to Felix, *we* were the source of all problems. Something had to be done.

The first thing Felix did when he got to Washington was to call up Don Gregg and make an appointment to see his *patrone* George Bush (ostensibly to report how things were going in Central America) right after his meeting with North, where Bob Dutton was also present.

At the first meeting, Bob and Ollie tried to convince Felix that he was driving me out of the operation by publicizing my role too much. This, they said, was not in the best interest of the Contra project and other projects of national interest (meaning the Iran Initiative, which had generated some funds for the Contras as well), and was against the express instructions of the National Security Advisor and the wishes of the President himself.

Felix took all this in stride without arguing much. But in his next meeting with Bush and Gregg (at least according to Gregg), he produced notes and photographs that supposedly proved the shoddy nature of the arms and air operation being run by the "Secord enterprise." He claimed we were selling the Contras poor-quality ordnance and defective grenades (probably the faulty Brazilian hand grenades Calero had purchased before I got on the program), and were overpricing substandard machine guns and ammunition. Part of this story seemed to be that most of the materiel we provided was old and unreliable, including the aircraft Dick Gadd had purchased, which he claimed had been overpriced to inflate our purchase commission. In short, he said ours was an "enterprise" intended not to help the Contras but to make ourselves as rich as possible before Congress restored government aid and the NSC took away our charter.

Interestingly enough, despite all the misinformation and innuendo, we can only assume that Rodriguez did brief Bush fairly accurately on our general organization and operation at Ilopango. Any subsequent claims by Gregg, and presumably George Bush, that they were uninformed about the interim resupply airlift should be viewed very skeptically. In fact, Don Gregg went through all these so-called problems again immediately afterward in a meeting with North.

What makes Rodriguez's claims so outlandish, of course, is that since late 1985, the Contras had nothing to do with the private finances that kept them in the field. They didn't pay one dime for any of the equipment or munitions they received. In effect, Felix was claiming "the enterprise is ripping itself off" because our financial network in Europe supplied both the money and the provisions. Who, exactly, did he think was being cheated?

Beneath the surface, Felix's plea was really "Get Secord out of the loop so that money can get back into the hands of Calero and his lieutenants—and thereby into the hands of Ron Martin et al." And, without me around, Rodriguez would be the ideal person to run the air operation from Ilopango.

Rodriguez's allegations raised a fairly big stink, which Felix took as a sign that he had succeeded. However, it was all about to boomerang on him severely. Immediately upon his return to El Salvador, he briefed General Bustillo on his "success." Understandably, Bustillo was so outraged at us that he stormed down to the operation's warehouse, where the faulty munitions were supposedly being stored, and demanded to see samples drawn at random from various crates: H&K machine guns, 7.62 ammunition, 81 mm mortar rounds, 60 mm mortar tubes, and M26 hand grenades. Moreover, the general insisted that selected samples be tested in his presence.

Laboriously, the crates were randomly selected and transported to a military weapons range, where they were uncrated and samples chosen and fired. To Felix's consternation and the general's relief, all weapons and explosives (in addition to obviously being new) functioned flawlessly.

How the general dealt in private with his "good friend" after this fiasco is unknown, but everyone said Rodriguez suffered immediate loss of face with the Salvadorian military and Calero's lieutenants.

Dutton and I reported the whole episode to Ollie, and he took it at once to Gregg in the Vice President's office. Rodriguez's accusations and any questions about quality or serviceability of the materials we supplied were never raised again—at least until the old stories were trotted out for the Select Committee hearings after the Iran-Contra story broke.

All through June I had two overriding goals: one, to improve the Contra airlift, per Bob Dutton's recommendations, and get ready to go out of business down there as soon as Congress allowed the U.S. government to get back into the ring; and two, to see what I could do to drop Ghorbanifar by opening a second channel to the moderate factions in Iran.

Throughout 1986 Ralph Quintero reported that Joe Fernandez (a.k.a. Thomas Castillo), CIA's Costa Rican chief of station, had been helping with the airlift. Castillo had been given a KL-43, and he supplied intelligence information to Ilopango by telephone on a regular basis. It was only because of this information, in fact, that we were able to locate and successfully resupply Contra forces on the southern front—American military and civilian officials in El Salvador were still needlessly paralyzed by "Bolanditis." (The one exception was Colonel Jim Steele, the El Salvador military group chief, who cheered us on and offered a lot of good advice but stopped short of the tangible aid prohibited by Boland.)

At least the CIA campaign of harassment against Gadd had stopped. In my judgment, Fernandez acted well within the Boland strictures, and I think Casey agreed with that, too. Why this information was never transmitted to the San Salvador CIA in the form of a directive I'll never know, but the "disciplinary action" Fernandez received after Casey stepped down because of illness (the brain tumor that finally killed him) was more for public than internal CIA consumption. It was a product of the "running-scared syndrome" that becomes pandemic in the bureaucracy whenever there's a clash between Congressional and executive wills. Presidential vacillation only makes it worse.

Fernandez's messages included limited but vital information on the Sandinistas' order of battle, radar locations, fortifications, recent troop movements, and basic weather data. Still, we were never able to obtain the full range of intelligence and weather information a truly professional operation demanded. It is a great credit to the skill and dedication of Contra commanders and troops in the field that favorable results started showing up almost as soon as the airlift began. Ollie periodically told me about the numerous clash reports coming in from the south—an area that had been quiet for months.

In late August 1986, for example, one southern Contra group raided a Sandinista stronghold near the Atlantic coast. It was a bold move that surprised Managua and made everyone in our operation very excited; for once, it seemed as if the long-sought southern front was becoming a reality. The success allowed Fernandez and his opposite number in Honduras, another good CIA man, to pressure the FDN to make more supplies available to the south. Our enterprise was able to add about $1 million worth of small arms and ammunition, and together they proved just enough to keep the southern fighters going.

About the time of McFarlane's May trip to Tehran, I received the clearest signal yet that the airlift was truly becoming a threat to the Sandinistas. A civil lawsuit was filed in federal district court, Miami, naming me and 30 other U.S. and Latin American citizens (some of them Cuban-Americans living in Florida) as co-conspirators in a plot to violate U.S. arms export regulations. In addition to charging actual violation of some of those regulations, it also accused us of complicity in the attempted assassination of Nicaraguan leader Eden Pastora (a.k.a. Commander Zero) in a bombing attack in southern Nicaragua in May of 1984.

This remarkable legal "counterattack" was filed on behalf of two expatriate American journalists living in Costa Rica as husband and wife: Tony Avrignan and Martha Honey. The plaintiffs' attorney was Daniel Sheehan, a well-known anti-establishment lawyer who gained fame in the Karen Silkwood suits against Kerr-McGee and class action suits following the accident at the Three Mile Island nuclear power plant.

I received the documents in this suit with a combination of amusement, outrage, and curiosity.

I was amused because my first connection of any sort with the Contras began with the phone call from Ollie in late June or early July 1984. In May of that year, two months earlier, I didn't even know how to spell "Contra," let alone mastermind assassination plots against their leaders. The suit was an obvious setup based on half-truths and wishful thinking. I was in no danger from the facts, and the straws my accusers were grasping at would have been laughable had the suit not also represented a possibly serious security risk to ongoing operations.

My anger stemmed from having to carve yet more hours and dollars from an already too short workday and too thin budget to respond to these fanciful charges. It also irritated me that people with absolutely no connection with the project were being involved—a great inconvenience to them and more security headaches for me.

The agenda of the plaintiffs was clear, but my curiosity was piqued by who, on our side, could have supplied them with enough information to convince a federal judge that the lawsuit might have merit. I decided it would be important not only to my own defense but to operational security to conduct our own investigation.

I discussed the matter with Albert and we decided to hire Glenn Robinette, a retired CIA officer and well-known security consultant for many large corporations. We asked him to run a background check on our accusers and to follow up any leads that might take him to the heart of the matter: who was behind them, and why.

Glenn's investigators—a team of ex–law enforcement people, mostly retired FBI—uncovered some dramatic facts. Avrignan had a long and checkered past as a "stringer," a free-lance journalist who seemed to specialize in anti-American articles, including one called "From Hanoi with Love" written during the Vietnam War. He later showed up with the Cubans in Angola and covered the Soviet invasion of Afghanistan from the safety of Mozambique. His wife, Martha Honey, also claimed to be a journalist but had no publishing history. Her role seemed mainly to provide support for her husband. Both were frequent travelers to Managua, Nicaragua, after the Sandinistas came to power.

The crux of the lawsuit was a claim that Avrignan had been "grievously wounded" during the Pastora assassination attempt, an account disputed by the statements of the attending physician in Costa Rica where the victims from this incident were transferred. More intriguing, the physician received a phone call from the Nicaraguan embassy *before* any word of the incident had been received, asking if any "casualties from a bombing" had been brought in. As if by magic, he stated, Ms. Honey appeared at the hospital as soon as her husband arrived to have "superficial scratches" treated. The doctor concluded that the Nicaraguans, as well as Honey, knew about the assassination attempt before it occurred.

Robinette also obtained five depositions from British and American citizens being detained in Costa Rica in 1984, stating that Avrignan, Honey, and a representative from a U.S. Senator's office had visited them in jail and offered them cash and a "green card" if they would falsely claim to be mercenaries working for the CIA in support of the Contras. One of these five accepted the proposition, but later recanted.

In sum, the suit seemed to be the end product of a concerted effort to undermine post-Boland U.S. Contra support, with roots in the Congressional opposition and possible assistance from foreign intelligence services—perhaps the KGB, but more likely the DGI, the Cuban intelligence arm.

Sideshows like this made it almost a relief to get back to the Iranian side of the tracks.

After the McFarlane trip, it was obvious that the Ghorbanifar channel was actually hurting our effort to establish a high-level contact in Iran since it reinforced President Reagan's proclivities to turn the whole operation into an arms-for-hostages deal.

Because the Israelis still wanted to use Gorba, I tried to come up with a scheme to keep Gorba on the squad but out of the game. I realized that Ghorbanifar, in addition to being in business primarily for himself, was really an agent for the Israel-Iran connection, not a U.S.-Iran connection. Once his role was viewed from this perspective, his many failings seemed more manageable. The key would be to keep some arms deals (preferably from Israel) flowing in his direction while shifting the diplomatic effort onto a second channel. This was the only way I could see us making any progress on the strategic issues and, just as important, keeping Israel happy and Ghorbanifar quiet.

I discussed this approach with Ollie and he agreed at once in principle, although the old fire in his eyes seemed a bit dimmer. I think he was starting to feel the strain from all the pressure to show immediate results with the hostages. As I've said before, Ollie is a good man to have on tap, but not on top, in a clutch situation. He's one of those guys, so beloved in the military, that you point at the enemy and say, "Take that hill!" and that's just what he does, come hell or high water. Like an Army mule, his bosses load him up with more and more burdens until they break his back—then they eat him.

In this case, I think Ollie was too preoccupied with the hostages—President Reagan's top priority—to wade too deeply into other diplomatic waters, however sensible that may have been even from the hostage perspective. He also may have doubted my ability, as a private citizen, to come up with a second channel, which I could understand.

I went back to Hakim and repeated what I had told Ollie: "Albert, we've got to get off this Ghorbanifar kick and get us a dog that can hunt. If we don't, we're really going to look like fools."

Albert agreed. Fortunately, he was quite knowledgeable about events and personalities in postrevolutionary Iran. We discussed a couple of potential contacts, the most promising of which seemed to be a man we had both heard about: a close relative of Speaker Rafsanjani. Albert also had a friend, an ex-Savak agent of considerable talent named Hossein, then living in England, who had known "the Relative" (as we began to call him) for quite some time. I had met Hossein during my postrevolution tour at the Pentagon and agreed he was an excellent choice—a "high-fidelity" reporter who knew the playing field and the players as well as the rules of the game.

Albert hired Hossein to contact the Relative in Tehran and let him know that intermediaries in the West were interested in establishing high-level communications between the U.S. and Iranian governments. Results, if any, would be agonizingly slow, but at least the courtship had begun.

While this was going on, I put on my STTGI hat and tried to tend to the other commercial business ventures that were supposed to be paying the bills. It wasn't long, though, before Ollie called with "another small problem." I hadn't talked to North in about 10 days, which seemed like 10 months, so

I invited him to stop by my house that evening after work—always the best time to get Ollie's full and undivided attention.

North told me that evening that he and George Cave would soon be meeting with Gorba and Nir. From what Ami reported, he thought the next deal would involve air delivery of the remaining HAWK parts to Tehran and sea delivery of two bulky HAWK-related ground radars. The quid pro quo for this "gesture of sincerity" was to be the release of another American hostage, supposedly within the next few days. North asked if I would get the shipment ready.

I put my other business on hold and alerted Southern Air Transport for a short-notice return to Tel Aviv. This time I decided to take Bob Dutton with me and introduce him to our personnel and procedures so that if anything happened to me, the project wouldn't grind to a halt.

On July 26, American hostage Father Lawrence Jenco was released in the Bekka Valley and was immediately taken by Syrian troops to Damascus. The Syrians tried to take credit for the release, which didn't bother me since it muddied the U.S.-Iranian connection and helped improve our cover.

Three days after Jenko's release, North arranged to have Ami Nir visit then Vice President George Bush in his suite at the King David Hotel during a visit to Jerusalem. With Bush's chief of staff, Craig Fuller, taking copious notes, Nir briefed the Vice President (an ex–CIA director) on the history of the Iran Initiative and reviewed our current situation and options, which I knew would include a heartfelt Israeli plea to abandon the current American hard line on an "all-or-nothing" hostage release. How heartfelt a plea it had been and how soft that American hard line really was, I would not discover until a couple of days later, when I visited Ami in his Tel Aviv apartment to begin organizing the delivery of the remaining HAWK spares.

"Things couldn't have turned out better!" Nir grinned, his good eye twinkling like the glass one that stared disconcertingly over the rim of his coffee mug. "Mister Bush was very attentive, very interested in everything—a very quick study. You know, you can't always count on a good audience with foreign politicians—"

*Or even most domestic ones,* I thought; but I knew what Ami meant. In the handful of times I'd worked with Bush in meetings, I found him to be an active listener and good executive; not a grandstander, but a team player who knew what his boss needed to know and made sure those facts were developed and passed along. I also knew that even half an hour with the intense Ami Nir was like half a day with anyone else.

"We covered all the bases," Ami continued proudly. "I went over our latest intelligence, including reliable information regarding contacts between Hezballah headquarters in the Bekka Valley and the Iranian Revolutionary Guards in Tehran. I told Mister Bush about our latest dealings with Gorba and gave him a quick rundown on Bud McFarlane's trip—although he seemed up to speed on all of that."

"Did you give him your pitch for sequential release?" I asked. It was a rhetorical question. The Israelis viewed the briefing as an opportunity to make sure that first, they were credited for their past contributions and still considered part of the team at the highest levels within the Reagan administration, and second, that American "intransigence" on the hostage issue might be mollified in such a way that Ghorbanifar could be kept in the game. That meant linking the release of specific hostages with reciprocal shipments of American arms—as far as I was concerned, an approach that was anathema to the whole project.

"Of course! But I assured the Vice President that it was a tactical maneuver only. The strategic aspect—development of high-level contacts so that we are well-positioned when Iranian leadership changes—I think that interested him most."

"I wish you had asked him to have the President go public—to jettison the whole shooting match and start over through a better channel."

Nir shook his head. I could see the stubborn warrior taking over from the diplomat inside him. "No. Absolutely not. Not yet, anyway. We can't let Gorba go, and when you have Gorba, you're going to be trading zebras for trucks. Look, my friend, we're in hot pursuit of our objective. I'm not asking you to trust Ghorbanifar, eh? Just trust me. I know that's the way Ollie wants it, and now, I think, the Vice President, too."

The last remark surprised me a little, since Ami went out of his way to say that Bush, however attentive to details, was noncommittal in his response after the half-hour meeting. He indicated only that he would take the proposal for sequential release back to President Reagan for final judgment.

We went on to other business—arranging details for the next shipment of HAWK parts, to be launched in another day or so—but the briefing and its aftermath bothered me. After my visit with Ami, I went back to the Carlton Hotel where I was registered under what had now become, at the direction of the Israeli security people, the official pseudonym for everyone traveling incognito on the project while inside Israel: Moshe Dor. We signed the name to everything, including restaurant bills. The aircrews had a lot of fun with that, greeting each other, "Good morning, Moshe," and replying, "Oh hi, Moshe, how are you?" At times we must've had a half-dozen Moshe Dors running around the Carlton, but that's the way the vaunted Israeli security service wanted it, so we complied.

Back in my room I telephoned Ollie in Washington. He was almost as upbeat as Nir, despite what had now become the ritual opening of our conversations: complaints about Ghorbanifar. North confirmed everything Ami said, and more. The vibes coming from the Oval Office were positive—a big change over the last few days—owing in large part, I assumed, to the Jenko release. The big news was, of course, that the day after Bush relayed the Israeli proposal to President Reagan, the all-or-nothing policy had been dumped in favor of sequential release. Since the President had been so adamant before, Nir's briefing must have been a doozy, moving Bush from note taker to advocate, but that appears to be what happened. Thanks to Nir, Israeli stock was high in Washington, increasing White House confidence in the project, which always made Ollie happy.

I wish I had been able to share Ollie's joy, but I couldn't. To me, this piecemeal approach was nothing more than a codification of the initiative's de facto modus operandi from the start. It didn't matter to me, from an operational perspective, if the hostages were released en masse or one at a time, provided they were removed as a barrier to the initiative's larger objective. Frankly, I thought it was poor judgment for the U.S. head of state to worry about tactical details like this, but the hostages obviously weighed heavily on the President. On the strength of Nir's argument, Bush's apparent endorsement, and his own frequently articulated desires to get the hostages home, the President decided to deliver to Iran the remaining 12 pallets of I-HAWK spares, which were still in storage in Israel.

On August 3, Dutton and I launched another "false flag" 707—disguised as an Irish airliner—from Ben Gurion Airport in Tel Aviv for Bandar Abbas in Iran. I sent Ollie the mission profile, route, and communications protocols via KL-43 so that our intelligence community could monitor the flight. This was the message the 1987 Tower Commission later declassified—to me, an irresponsible disclosure to foreign powers of the covert command and control procedures used by the CIA and other security agencies, including Israel.

The mission went smoothly in every respect—a good exercise for Bob Dutton to cut his teeth on. The plane returned to Israel on August 4. After a few days, though, it was clear that no more hostages would be released as a result. My worst fears (short of blowing security) seemed to be coming true: The "sequential release" plan was only leading us deeper into the arms-for-hostages swamp. It was exactly the game Ghorbanifar wanted the U.S. to play.

In my view, a second channel was now a lot more than a good idea; it was an absolute necessity.

Fortunately, after several months of diligent effort and a number of false starts, our agent, Hossein, arranged for an exploratory meeting between the Relative and me in Europe.

Iran had already been stung by a great number of shady arms dealers. Albert's man said we should be prepared to show them some pretty impressive bona fides. I suggested to Albert that the best way to do that, now, would be to give them our real names so that the Iranians could check up on us themselves in Tehran. Lord knows, my name was on thousands of Iranian documents, and my face was well known, too. Albert was less traceable, but he wasn't exactly obscure. With this as a starting point, Hossein was able to schedule a meeting in Brussels for the third week in August 1986.

Meanwhile, Ghorbanifar's latest shenanigans made our efforts to sideline him even more imperative. Beginning right after the McFarlane visit and continuing well into July, he raised hell with Nir and North about Kangarlu's complaints that the HAWK spares were greatly overpriced. To support this he produced a microfiche price list somehow obtained from Raytheon, the HAWK's manufacturer, showing lower costs for HAWK-related parts. After we analyzed the list, however, we discovered it was fragmentary and presented only Raytheon's internal production costs, known in the trade as COM or cost of manufacture data. They were completely unrelated to Pentagon prices or even to Raytheon's own sales prices, since they excluded cost increments for overhead, G&A (general and administrative expenses), cost of capital, transportation expenses, economic escalation factor, and Raytheon's own profit. It became obvious that the list was a device used by Kangarlu to avoid paying Ghorbanifar the balance owed after the May 1986 transaction—the remaining four-fifths of the HAWK parts shipment, which had already been paid for. I reminded them that Bud had aborted the shipment en route because the Iranians had failed to deliver the hostages—as much a contingency of the deal as the cash, at least in McFarlane's mind.

This pricing tiff led everyone to look a little closer into the project's financial status, which led us to discover a real bombshell: Ghorbanifar was not acting alone.

Although he led us to believe he was using Iranian money, his forward purchases and bridge deposits were actually being bankrolled by Adnan Khashoggi, a well-known Saudi financier, as well as one or two others. Reportedly $10 million of the last $15 million deposit had been provided by Khashoggi—a bit of information that, all by itself, would've caused me to slam on the brakes and stop the transaction for security reasons, making the debate over McFarlane's trip academic. Ghorbanifar undoubtedly realized this, which is why he went to so much trouble (via his Monte Carlo bank, which Khashoggi owned a good piece of) to keep it from us. The worst of it was, Ami Nir knew about it all along and said nothing.

This revelation astonished me, since our intelligence from previous transactions showed Ghorbanifar had drawn directly on Iranian government accounts at Bank Melli in London and Credit Suisse in Geneva, giving us no reason to suspect he was conducting bridge financing with third parties. It was also more than a little unsettling, because it multiplied our risks almost exponentially. (Perhaps we should've suspected it anyway, no matter what our intelligence showed. The Iranians mistrusted Gorba, too, and what better way could Kangarlu show his displeasure than by withholding advance payments, forcing Gorba to "put up or shut up" when it came to his extravagant promises?)

I also wondered if there was anything else the Israelis had neglected to tell us, and Ollie did, too. Nir would later say, contritely, that he kept it secret because he knew it would blow the deal, and his government had instructed him to keep Ghorbanifar in the picture no matter what. He was caught between a rock and a hard place, and although I really felt he let us down on that one, it's tough to blame a guy for being patriotic.

While we had been prospecting the second channel, in fact, Nir and Gorba had been putting together a deal for more TOWs and, as usual, the much-promised meeting with high-level Iranian officials and delivery of more hostages. According to Ami, Gorba had accumulated about $4 million, about half the amount needed for the 500 TOWs required by the Iranians. Ghorbanifar's method for bridging this shortfall was to go back to Khashoggi.

Khashoggi had an on-and-off relationship with Israel for many years and evidently had been in the loop as Ghorbanifar's backer from the very beginning. This put even more pressure on Gorba for a big Iranian markup, since Khashoggi claimed he owed a consortium of Canadian businessmen who provided *him* with the money a return of 20 percent for one month's use of their funds. (Khashoggi recanted his "Canadian businessman" story in 1988, but that didn't help us in 1986.)

Khashoggi and Ghorbanifar would later testify that they never made a penny from these deals, but the Senate Committee concluded, using methods of their own, that Gorba's profit margin was 60 percent—the actual figure will probably never be known. In the end, Gorba got the poetic justice he deserved. His explanations regarding the busted I-HAWK deal were now so convoluted and inconsistent that his credibility was completely shot, even with the Israelis. Although he would never be completely out of the loop, his freewheeling days were numbered.

Unfortunately, this only made him more reckless—and dangerous to us.

In mid-July, I had met with Ollie (first in his office, and then later in my home over a beer) and said that I had a gut feeling the Iran Initiative was about to blow and the President should begin thinking about making a public statement (a press conference or nationally televised speech, in consultation with Congress) to preempt the inevitable adverse publicity that would accompany a third-party leak—especially of the type that someone like Gorba would make.

I said that if the President focused on his continual efforts to open a dialogue with Iran—a former ally that had been foolishly lost, and one that also had the power to influence the release of our hostages—he would steal the thunder from his detractors and ensure that the ensuing debate stuck to relevant issues. The last thing any of us wanted was for the inevitable public dialogue to get sidetracked by those who would depict the operation strictly as an arms-for-hostages trade that, although technically legal, would've been tough for a law-and-order politician like Ronald Reagan to defend.

Understandably, perhaps, but to my mild disappointment (and later major regret), Ollie reacted coolly to this plan.

He said the White House did not want to go public but wanted to keep moving forward on the hostage issue. I could tell from the way he talked (a bit formally, which was not the way we usually hammered out these problems in private) that Ollie was under *one ton* of pressure to show results. He was being crushed by a daily grind—attending endless interagency meetings, drafting papers, writing explicatory memos—and the fatigue factor was starting to show.

I dropped the issue and suggested we move ahead quietly with a new Iranian connection. I would try to "vet" the Relative (check his credentials and intentions) and find a way to deal with the hostages expeditiously, but in due course. I reminded Ollie that nobody knew about our second channel—not even Nir. I had been in this business long enough to realize what a squall this revelation would raise in the press and among the President's opponents in Congress. Even the State Department and DoD, which McFarlane, Poindexter, and Ollie all reported were never on board, would join the chorus of snide comments about "amateur diplomats" and "private profiteers." Among Washington veterans, this would be translated into just what it was: the "not invented here" syndrome—sour grapes for not participating in a game they chose to avoid.

But it would be *nothing* compared to the fire storm of protest ignited if either the press or Congress stumbled upon the initiative on their own. I felt that if the President took the high road, showed the American people he had been trying hard to bring something good from a tragic human (and strategically very dangerous) situation and stated firmly that he would *never* give up until the American and Iranian people had again reasserted their traditional friendship and the hostages were home, we could weather the storm and protect our new connection with Tehran. In fact, such an announcement by the President might actually have reinforced that connection, since it would have confirmed to everyone that we were jettisoning the old, unsuccessful, and unpopular intermediary.

But if the story cracked with Ghorbanifar? Well, I was afraid to contemplate the results.

Whatever happened, I told Ollie, the press and Congressional opponents must not be allowed to represent the Iran Initiative as an arms-for-hostages deal. Despite the President's pressure in that direction, the operation's own history so far worked against that interpretation. Credit for the Jenko release was claimed by the Syrians, and McFarlane's Tehran "summit" didn't result in anything.

The only case administration opponents could really make was that shipping even small amounts of defense materiel to Iran constituted a blatant disregard for our own counterterrorist policy. If the President took the initiative and made the first announcement, however, the word "blatant" could at least be replaced by "judicious," which is what the policy was all about. From this perspective, Reagan's Iran Initiative was simply an extension of long-standing U.S. policy going back to the 1950s.

However, I was afraid that if the President *didn't* take this initiative, to the word blatant would be added "illegal," "foolish," "idiotic," and any other epithet the administration's opponents could think of. The basic story, in my view, was too hot to keep secret indefinitely because far too many people (especially Ghorbanifar, now that he was complaining about "financial trouble") were already involved, and some of those were completely untrustworthy.

Ollie and I hashed this over for hours. The longer we talked, the more depressed I became. When I agreed to help Ollie in 1985, it was with the clear understanding that I would do so as a technician. I didn't view myself as a political advisor and kept my mouth shut when most policy questions came up.

Moreover, I was no expert on the provisions of the Hughes-Ryan Act, which was ambiguous about the President's duty to inform Congress on covert operations. The White House had relied on Stanley Sporkin's (the CIA's general counsel) judgment that an earlier opinion by the Attorney General could be used to delay notification indefinitely. However, I was now deeply concerned about Congressional reaction to all of that. Even if the letter of Hughes-Ryan had been met, they would feel its spirit had been evaded. And if that was the case, Congress (and the media) might get out the legal ropes for yet another Presidential lynching.

No, Ollie insisted, it will never come to that. "We only need to hang on a little longer," he said, "and work a little harder."

If there were 40 hours in a day, he might have been right.

# — 15 —

# ... Oppose Any Foe

For two days and two nights in August 1986, Albert and I at last met with four representatives of the Iranian government at the Sheraton Hotel in Brussels. Two of them spoke English well, but the Relative and his assistant did not. Fortunately, Albert (a native-born Iranian) speaks Farsi and I understand it a little, having been tutored while I lived in Iran. Both sides soon worked out a system for making clear what each wanted to say and concealing what was best said in private.

The relative of Speaker Rafsanjani was a young man in his late 20s who obviously had an excellent education, as revealed by his immaculate Farsi and broad knowledge of world affairs. Albert and I felt at once that this was someone we might deal with.

The first sessions were a fencing match to find out who knew what; that much was expected. What surprised us was the method the Iranians used to establish their credentials—swiftly and dramatically. They said they knew all about the Ghorbanifar-Kangarlu connection and its troubled history over the past year, including the magnificent failure of the McFarlane trip. This didn't convey their feelings on those matters, or even if they were in a position to do better than the previous team. It merely showed they were insiders, and for the moment that was good enough.

As we talked, they revealed more of their knowledge of the Iran-Iraq war: names and details involved with verifiable events and the status of the armed forces and Revolutionary Guard. It was clear from the tenor of the exchange (mostly the Iranians' focus on the issues we ourselves held paramount: Soviet adventurism and Iraqi aid, and so on) that they and the officials they represented truly, if cautiously, wanted to reestablish some durable link with the United States.

U.S. intelligence sources believed that in the ever-shifting mosaic of Iranian politics, the Islamic Republican Party, or IRP (a coalition of pragmatists led by Rafsanjani), was becoming increasingly dominant. Ghorbanifar never referred to this ascending group and failed also to mention the formation of the Supreme War Council, a powerful ad hoc group established in 1986 and headed by Rafsanjani; or the Pasdaran, the group of Revolutionary Guards that had recently given Rafsanjani its full support. Our second channel reps were quite familiar with these entities.

Despite his youth, the Relative brought some much-needed maturity and vision to the Iranian side of the table. Although he said he regarded Ghorbanifar as "a crook," he believed that neither Gorba nor Kangarlu should be punished because, despite the greed of the one and the ineptness of the other, they had blazed a trail that had, at least, resulted in our current meeting. As I said, such high-mindedness was a refreshing change.

I closed the meeting by telling them that I would relay their comments to the U.S. government and would need a way to communicate directly with them in Iran. The Relative gave us two telephone numbers, both in Tehran, but said they would prefer to communicate as much as possible through our intermediary, Hossein, or a commercial arms buyer in London whose calls would raise much less suspicion. I gave them a short brevity code for these unsecure contacts and said we would be in touch.

After the Iran-Contra story broke, I was criticized in *The Washington Post* for making U.S. foreign policy as a private citizen by promising during this meeting that the U.S. would fight the Russians if they invaded Iran. What I *actually* said was that the U.S. had already spent millions of dollars to deter the Soviets from invading Iran and had established the Central Command (the very organization employed so successfully five years later in Desert Storm) specifically for that purpose. These were facts known to any serious student of the Middle East and had been supported in public statements by many presidents, including President Reagan. If people have a problem with "citizen diplomats" embarked on covert presidential missions, I suggest they pick up any number of history books detailing the travels of Harry Hopkins, a private commissionaire from FDR's "kitchen cabinet" whom he launched on some of the most sensitive missions of his administration. Like Hopkins, everything I did was supervised by duly appointed foreign policy officials in the White House and reported to the President himself. Nobody seemed surprised by it except *The Washington Post* and the Democrats on the Select Committees.

I wrote a report on the meeting, which was sent to Washington via KL-43 and later presented, in an expanded version, to North, who discussed it with Poindexter and the CIA. The consensus that came back was that, although the Israeli (Nir and Gorba) connection would not be abandoned, the second channel looked so promising that we should take a rather bold step to accelerate progress by inviting the Relative to Washington. I was also permitted to brief Nir on the second channel during my next trip to Israel, on September 10, although I did not mention the Relative's anticipated Washington visit, which still hadn't been scheduled and did not involve the Israelis.

We presented this plan to the Relative on the unsecure phone numbers I'd been given. After several weeks of follow-up calls, the Relative—mostly on the strength of my reputation in Tehran, he said—agreed to come to America if I could guarantee that the visit would be secret. I told him that only God can guarantee such things, but we would do our best.

Now we had to make it happen.

(During this period, we also got some good news from another quarter. At the end of August, Congress amended the Contra aid bill and appropriated $100 million in aid, although it would not be implemented until the end of October, which, as things turned out, would be about one month too late.)

Our plan for the Relative's visit called for him and his assistant to fly to Istanbul posing as Iranian businessmen, since such travelers didn't need a Turkish visa. From there, they would be exfiltrated to a friendly facility where we could guarantee secure transportation to Washington. The Iranians were quite adamant about making the entire trip without getting their passports stamped, which seemed to be a real "scarlet letter" to the revolutionary regime.

I handed the whole project over to North, who passed it on to the CIA, where it languished for two weeks. Finally, the Agency said it could not come up with false documentation or a company airplane in time, and so suggested the Iranians simply fly commercially under assumed names. This meant the CIA would have to inform Customs and Immigration, and also the Justice Department, that they were bringing in foreigners under private circumstances, and to please not make waves.

I found this simplistic and risky approach a little disheartening—it certainly wasn't the CIA I remembered—and also disquieting. Telling so many other agencies just a little, but not too much, about what we were doing was also bound to pique their curiosity. In short, the CIA "solution" would likely create more problems than it solved.

This plan percolated through the system until the very day the Iranians were scheduled to depart, when my conscience and good judgment got the best of me. I phoned Ollie and told him to call off the CIA. *I* would get the Iranians here myself.

I leased a private Lear jet from Aero Leasing, Inc., in Geneva, and had it pick up the Iranians in Istanbul. We still hadn't received any documentation from the CIA, so we had to get through Turkish customs using the assets we had.

Fortunately, Albert's London-based Irani had a U.S. entry visa in his passport, so I sent him a telex, using very officious language, inviting him and the Relative to visit our firm, Stanford Technology Trading Group International, for the purpose of concluding a countertrade transaction. We then told our London agent to use this telex, plus his own entry visa, to convince anyone who asked at the Istanbul General Aviation Terminal that the Iranian nationals were authorized to visit the United States. If anybody balked, he should just show them the long-range private jet waiting on the ramp, engines idling, with its U.S.-bound flight plan properly filed.

The flight transited Switzerland, Ireland, and Iceland without incident and landed at Dulles. The CIA helped with immigration and got the Iranians in without a visa. We put them up in three rooms at the new Sheraton Hotel in Tyson's Corner. We asked the CIA to bug the rooms and especially the telephones, which was the Iranian instrument of choice for divulging state secrets. Here, too, however, I ran into problems with the "new CIA."

In order to tap domestic phones, permission is needed from the Justice Department, which was understandable. What was *not* understandable was the Justice Department's insistence that only *one* of the three phones could be tapped. What was the point—to make it a shell game? It was incredible.

I raised hell with everyone over this inanity and almost resigned from the whole project. But the bureaucrats wouldn't budge. As it turned out, we lost several important calls to Tehran from those untapped phones, and captured some pretty silly conversations on the other. The most famous recordings, perhaps, were those of the 40-odd calls made on the second night of their visit trying to locate an escort service that would make house calls after midnight. Fortunately for them, this was D.C., virtue capital of the world, and they eventually hit a winner.

George Cave and I picked them up the next morning and took them to Ollie North's office in the old EOB, arriving around 10, where we worked off and on for 12 hours. The agenda was nothing less than a complete review of U.S.-Iranian relations since the revolution, focusing eventually on the current situation in their war with Iraq. To my delight, our Iranian guests were the first to express concerns over Soviet designs in the area (the Russians had an even bigger problem with the Ayatollah Khomeini than we did; the last thing they wanted was fundamentalist unrest in their enormous Muslim population). They said very little about the hostages, and didn't even mention them until Ollie brought it up.

"The hostages are obstacles to the strategic process," North said. "They are not currency to trade with. Rather, they are political obstacles to practical progress on our very important agenda."

The Relative agreed, and then repeated Ghorbanifar's favorite line about the Iranians being hostages of the hostages themselves. They conceded the Ayatollah had some influence with Hezballah, but not with every faction within that umbrella group, which is something Gorba had never admitted, but the CIA had suspected for some time.

At lunchtime, we took the Iranians to the Tap Room of the Hay Adams, by Lafayette Park across from the White House. We interpreted the menu for them, and they became very concerned about eating meat that hadn't been properly slaughtered and bled, so we all ordered fish. At the end of the evening session, Ollie took them on a tour of the White House, including the Oval Office. (President Reagan happened to be at Camp David.) After that, they returned to the Sheraton and dined alone.

The next day's meeting convened in my office near Tyson's Corner. North, Cave, and Charlie Allen, the national intelligence officer for counter-terrorism, represented the U.S. The discussion continued until late in the afternoon, when Ollie took a break to attend to a couple of matters at his office. Actually, he used the recess to consult with Poindexter about the status of the meeting.

By the end of the session that evening, the Iranians had given us an eight-point list of war materials they wanted. This list, they said, represented their highest-priority needs once firm government-to-government relations had been reestablished. It was notably clear of Ghorbanifar's or Kangarlu's influence: no "Star Wars" gadgetry—Phoenix or Harpoon missiles or the like. Instead, it mentioned 10,000 rounds of 175 mm extended-range artillery ammunition, several 175 mm replacement barrels, 5,000 rounds of 155 mm ammunition, more TOW antitank missiles, and a maritime navigation radar. This last item surprised me a bit, since it was readily available on the Japanese market, which was, and had always been, accessible to Iran.

"All of this is very interesting," North said. "The President will be informed of our exchange of views."

He then made some recommendations for the future. First, he suggested that we schedule a high-level meeting as soon as possible in Europe. We did not expect the location to be a particular problem given the face slap McFarlane had received in May—even the Ayatollah wouldn't expect the Great Satan to slip on the same banana peel twice. He also repeated Casey's advice that we be permitted to establish a secure communications post in Tehran and thus eliminate the need for both our London connection and the unsecure phone lines we'd been using to date.

North said that if progress was made in these areas and a satisfactory relationship was established, the U.S. would be willing to share intelligence information with Iran concerning the Soviets and the war—including information about recent high-level visits between officials from Moscow and Baghdad, the substantial increase in Soviet military aid that was beginning to flow into Iraq, and increased KGB activity in Iran. Ollie concluded by saying that, provided the hostage obstacle was removed and a series of government-to-government meetings could be held at the appropriate level, all things seemed possible in the military-supply relationship.

Before the Iranians left, we arranged for an expanded list of telephone brevity codes. Cave and I took them back to Dulles, where the chartered Lear jet returned them by the original route.

Although the visit represented a very positive beginning, everyone recognized more groundwork would be necessary before we reached a level of activity comparable to the Ghorbanifar connection—a fact that was not lost on Gorba himself, who had heard about our connection from Kangarlu in Tehran and refused to take our offer lying down. He complained about our second channel and did all he could to make the Israelis, who were uncertain of our ability to deliver anyway, worry even more about losing the connection they had.

Ever since the Nir-Bush briefing, Israeli credibility had been high at the White House—the revelations about Khashoggi's bridge financing notwithstanding. Now that a reliable second channel had been vetted and was at the starting gate, North and Poindexter drafted a letter for President Reagan's signature reassuring the Israelis that they were still full partners in the venture, although the U.S. would necessarily be calling more of the shots. Because I was the guy who pioneered the second channel and knew more about it than anyone, North asked me to stop by his office at the EOB, supposedly to review and comment on the letter. As soon as I got there, though, my role changed considerably. He slapped an envelope into my hand.

"*Vaya con dios, compadre*," he said. "We'd like you to hand deliver this to Shimon Peres [the lame-duck Israeli Prime Minister] and answer any questions he may have."

No new shipments were planned, and I hadn't really thought about going back across the pond so quickly, particularly with the backlog of commercial business that was waiting on my desk. Still, I was at the moment as much a part of the second channel as the Relative. Opting out as the President's personal representative and courier would've been more than bad form; it would've meant negating the very alternative to Gorba I had been demanding for so long.

I opened the envelope and read the letter silently. Except for a misspelling of Ami Nir's name (they left the "i" out of Amiram, and I had to wait while Ollie got the whole thing retyped and back on the President's signature pad), the letter was accurate and, as far as I could see, worthwhile. In essence it read:

*So far, things have been difficult for all of us. Your man, Amiram Nir, has distinguished himself as a hero and we believe his efforts have been invaluable to our common cause. As I mentioned when you last visited Washington, Mr. Prime Minister, we are actively exploring a second channel, but we still regard this as a joint venture. You will be fully apprised of all developments. If we collaborate in the future as we have in the past, our initiative can end only in success.*

The letter was accompanied by a talking paper expanding on these points, including a bit of intelligence that was a real poke in Ghorbanifar's eye—and therefore indirectly in Israeli eyes, too: information showing that Kangarlu had been indirectly involved with the taking of three additional hostages in Lebanon in September.

"Good!" I told Ollie, stabbing the paragraph with a finger. "That stunt was a gross breach of the operational ground rules. There were supposed to be no anti-U.S. actions anywhere in Iran's sphere of influence while negotiations were taking place. I agree, Israel should stay in the loop, but if they stick with the Gorba-Kangarlu connection after this, they're absolutely nuts."

North agreed we could augment the letter's ceremonial language with that kind of twist orally. After the note was retyped and signed, I was on the next commercial flight to Paris, and thence to Tel Aviv.

Ami Nir met me at the airport, as always. He knew, generally, what the letter said and was consequently in a good mood. While he shepherded me around customs, we joked about my being reduced in status to a courier, but we were both happy this high-level affirmation of the program was finally taking place between our two governments.

It was the Jewish sabbath, so rather than going to the Israeli ministries, Ami took me to his house in the suburbs. I had been authorized to let him read the letter before sealing it for Peres, so that's what he did as soon as we arrived. Unexpectedly, Ami's ruggedly handsome face turned dark.

"What's this?" he said. "Oh no, we can't let Peres read this!"

"What are you talking about?" I asked, concerned that John's and Ollie's painfully correct diplomatic language might have somehow inadvertently committed a faux pas.

"Here," Ami pointed to a paragraph describing his role in the initiative, "President Reagan calls me *a rare man.* And over here, he says I am *one who serves well our common cause.* They'll think I'm a toady—too self-serving. It's embarrassing. It's too much."

I laughed. "Damnit, Ami, they mean every word of it. More than that, you deserve it. You're just going to have to learn how to shut up and take a compliment."

Nir sat back, finished the letter, and read through the talking papers. His face got even cloudier when he got to the revelations about Kangarlu's role in seizing the most recent batch of hostages. Because Israel's technical intelligence was less sophisticated than ours, we periodically dropped these bombshells on them. This news was a particularly painful blow for Ami (not to mention ironic, given the flowery letter), since he liked Gorba no better than the rest of us and put up with him only at the direction of the Israeli government.

"Well," he said finally, "I'm happy the second channel is bearing fruit for you. Maybe this will be the key to putting Gorba on the sidelines, although my people will still want to keep him around just in case. If Poindexter agrees, we should tell Ghorbanifar that your second channel is trying to solve his money problem with Kangarlu. That would shut Gorba up, at least for a little while."

I grunted, "That seems like a pretty heavy rock to throw in the Relative's knapsack just now, but I see your point. I'll relay your suggestion to Ollie."

Nir glanced through the package again and shook his head. "Maybe we can't change the letter, but we should revise these briefing points. They look like they were prepared for Ronald Reagan, not Shimon Peres. I've worked for Peres a long time. He likes more detail—the facts behind the facts—like your Vice President Bush. No, these won't do at all."

I borrowed a typewriter and, at the seaside hotel where I spent the night, wrote an expanded version of the talking points, making it clear that the additional verbiage was attributable solely to me. The key message we both felt had to be transmitted loud and clear was that the U.S. still viewed this as a joint venture, although America was compelled at this juncture to take the lead because Israel historically cannot deal directly with Iran. I added that the President still desired Nir to be part of the team, and would allow him to attend second-channel meetings in Europe under cover as an American.

Because Prime Minister Peres couldn't schedule a meeting with me until late the next day, Ami recommended that I deliver this material to Peres's military aide, a General Doron, as soon as possible so that the PM could at least have a chance to read it and, if he desired, present it at his last formal Cabinet meeting before turning power over to his replacement from the Likud party, Yitzhak Shamir, two days hence. I agreed.

We drove to Jerusalem late Saturday night and went directly to General Doron's small, tidy apartment in the western part of town. Although we Americans pride ourselves on our informality, it's nothing compared to the "frontier casualness" of the Israelis—Cabinet ministers and legislators go to work in open collars and shirtsleeves—and General Doron had no problem at all receiving an American presidential envoy at midnight over a strong cup of coffee.

I explained the basic talking points, as well as my supplementary letter, and suggested that the PM might appreciate having the opportunity to disclose their contents to his inner Cabinet, particularly on the eve of his departure.

General Doron agreed and thought the letter would materially assist the transition since it showed the new Shamir government that the President of the United States continued to fully support the Iran Initiative and appreciated Israel's role in bringing it about. From Washington's perspective, there would be no significant differences between the Labor and Likud government's approach to Iran.

That same new government would be enormously shocked when, a mere six weeks later, the U.S. Attorney General, Ed Meese, would publicly disavow any knowledge of the initiative—without giving Israeli officials so much as an hour's advance warning by telephone—and try to lay blame for any hypothetical misdeeds squarely at Israel's feet.

Even Ghorbanifar hadn't been as despicable as that.

I left Israel for Frankfurt on October 5 for the first of a series of post-Washington meetings with the Relative and his party. I met Ollie at the airport Sheraton and gave him a copy of the expanded talking points I had prepared for Peres. He then used my KL-43 to report the results of my Israeli mission to Poindexter.

The sky was dark and rainy—weather reflecting the dour events transpiring halfway around the world in Nicaragua. Shortly before we spoke, one of our C-123s on an extended-range route to resupply the southern front had been brought down by a Sandinista surface-to-air missile, killing pilots William Cooper and Buzz Sawyer and a Spanish translator who also doubled as a security man. The loadmaster, Eugene Hasenfus, was captured.

I first got the bad news via KL-43 from Dutton while Ollie was en route.

"We have an aircraft missing," said the terse, cold letters.

The next day we got the details about the way the aircraft had been brought down, the casualties, and the prisoner. There was nothing either of us could do about it now, especially with a critical meeting coming up, except to stay informed and pray our local people could keep the thing contained. We had to wait for the rest of our party—Albert Hakim and Tom Clincs—and the Iranians (the Relative and two Revolutionary Guard officers, including a senior official, nicknamed "Ayub," who had attended McFarlane's meeting in Tehran) to show up, which they did at noon on October 6. Everybody on the American side used their real names except George Cave, whose alias was Sam O'Neil. At North's request, the meeting room had been outfitted with recording devices, compliments of the CIA.

Although Ayub's presence showed that the second channel was being taken seriously in Iran and receiving top-level coordination, Ayub himself was a real pain in the neck to deal with—the stereotypical Iranian radical. Thin, dark-complected, and sporting a full, wiry beard, he was as volatile as a vial of nitro: pleasant one minute, hysterical the next. He looked about 40, going on 70, and claimed to have been imprisoned for seven years by the Shah, which apparently gave him license to act as he pleased toward Westerners.

His religious zeal seemed genuine. He would eat only appropriate foods—fish or lamb that was properly bled. He prayed five times a day in the Islamic tradition, and on several occasions asked me the direction of Mecca, which I noted by drawing an arrow on a piece of scratch paper—from Frankfurt, to the southeast. (Hotel rooms in Islamic countries have an arrow on the nightstand showing this direction.) He would then go into another room or into the corner of the meeting room if necessary and make his devotions. He was fond of spouting revolutionary clichés, liked to shock us with outlandish demands, and had no apparent understanding of, or concern for, the logistical problems of covert operations. He was Godzilla to the Relative's Bambi. In fact, the two of them played the classic "good-cop/bad-cop" routine to the hilt, and not without success. During one break, we gave him a code name: the Monster. It stuck for the remainder of our dealings.

Ollie opened the meeting by reciprocating the gift to President Reagan of a Holy Koran from Rafsanjani, made during the September Washington visit. He gave the Relative a New Testament Bible, which my wife, Jo Ann, had purchased for Rafsanjani, inscribed by the President with a quote from Galatians: "And the Scripture, foreseeing that God would justify the Gentiles by faith, preached the gospel beforehand to Abraham, saying, 'All the nations shall be blessed in you.'"

The Iranians were pleased with the gift (even the Monster) and thought it was wonderfully appropriate. Students of Islam know there is great respect for the Bible in the Muslim world and—fools and extremists aside—that respect is generally shared among Christians for the Koran.

The meeting thus started on a positive note. Ollie said the President was most interested in working through this new channel toward mutually beneficial ends. He said President Reagan desired to see the Iran-Iraq war end on an honorable basis, preserving the integrity of Iran as a state, and thereby helping to safeguard U.S. interests in the region, particularly in the Persian Gulf.

By citing the inscription as proof that President Reagan was a man of God, Ollie embellished, perhaps, our Chief Executive's religious ardor, just as the Iranians frequently exaggerated their own. He went on to say that the President had prayed one whole weekend before concluding that the God of Abraham's words should be enough to show that the path of peace between America and Iran was the right one to take. It was a bit of "show biz" that was perfectly acceptable in context but, like an earlier statement Ollie made about being at Camp David to discuss the Iranian's September request, was easy to misrepresent (as it was in the Tower Commission report) and lampoon (as it was by the press). It is significant that neither the Tower Commission nor our major media saw fit to quote further from the literally hours and hours of recordings that showed Ollie sticking very close to his written instructions and talking points.

In reply, the Iranians stated flatly that, other than David Jacobsen, they did not have control of the remaining American hostages. They told us William Buckley, the CIA station chief, was dead, but that they could soon obtain the release of "one-and-a-half" additional hostages—their way of saying "Jacobsen for sure, maybe another if we're lucky," but only if everything else goes right. These assertions were made on the strength of a recent trip to Lebanon that Ayub claimed to have made himself.

The "thing that had to go right" to secure Jacobsen's release was mostly the delivery of 500 TOWs. The Iranians said he would be released in West Beirut, which was our preference, but possibly somewhere in the Bekka Valley, which we dreaded. The last hostage to be released into Syrian custody, Father Jenko, was taken to Damascus and used ruthlessly as a propaganda tool by President Hafez al-Assad before he was released. Our real worries, though, were operational. Relations between the U.S. and Syria were at an all-time low, owing to the Hindawi-Murphy terrorist incident. A young Palestinian, Nezar Mansour Hindawi, living in London, placed thin sheets of PETN, a plastic explosive, at the bottom of an airline carry-on bag and rigged a detonator for it in the form of a hand-held electronic calculator. He then gave the bag to his pregnant Irish girlfriend, Anne Marion Murphy, and promised to meet her at the "Ramallah Hilton on the West Bank," where they would be married.

Murphy attempted to board El Al flight 16, bound from London to Tel Aviv with a stop in Munich. When the Israeli security guards heard her tell a fellow passenger of her plans to be married at the "Ramallah Hilton," they became suspicious—there is no Hilton in Ramallah—and took her into a search facility where they discovered the bomb. Hindawi was convicted in a British court, and Margaret Thatcher broke diplomatic relations with Syria, the source of the explosive. She asked her allies to do the same, and the U.S. recalled its ambassador.

We had now inherited the Hindawi-Murphy situation and faced a very adverse political climate in Syria. The last thing we wanted was a run-in with the Syrians that would jeopardize the safety of the hostage. The Iranians seemed sympathetic and once again promised to see what they could do.

North introduced a new seven-point plan (basically the Nir "piecemeal" plan, his main agenda) and raised the stakes by offering 1,000 more TOWs, shipped in two batches, and additional HAWK spare parts. The core of this plan was the sequential release of all three remaining American hostages— Terry Anderson, David Jacobsen, and James Southerland—plus return of the body of William Buckley, after which both countries would participate in a high-level meeting in Europe. If that meeting went well, the U.S. would provide price and availability information on the Iranians' previous eight-point list and send a team to Tehran to establish a secure communications facility.

Assuming each government endorsed these arrangements, actual shipment of goods on the Iranian list could commence in six or seven months— a surprisingly long time, considering Iran's war needs. I never learned precisely where such a lead time originated, but that was the U.S. position. Ultimately, the plan called for a meeting at the "highest possible level," which under the circumstances meant between the U.S. Secretary of State and Iran's Minister of Foreign Affairs.

Not surprisingly, the Iranians rejected North's offer. They liked the prospect of more TOWs; were ambivalent about the HAWK spares; were very negative about the delay in implementation of their war-materials list; and said once again that the commitment to release all the hostages was clearly beyond their compass, although they were working hard on the matter. Ayub added, in his typical, acerbic way, that the two new hostages, Frank Reed and Joseph Ciccipio, had been grabbed by factions specifically at odds with the Tehran regime. Furthermore, the three previous hostages, Jacobsen, Southerland, and Anderson, were being held in two different locations, implying difficulty in communicating and coordinating any release.

Instead, the Iranians suggested another—and essentially retrogressive—plan that hinged mainly on a certain type and quantity of arms for a specific hostage. All of us sagged in our chairs. It was as if Ghorbanifar had suddenly crashed the party. We wrangled about this step backward for the rest of the day.

The next morning, October 7, North told the Iranians their proposal was absolutely unacceptable, reframed his original proposal to reemphasize its government-to-government aspects, and then suggested that the Iranians go back to Tehran and reconsider their approach. As for himself, he had a seat on the afternoon Pan Am clipper for Washington and would be taking George Cave with him. The meeting, in other words, was over.

The Iranians looked surprised—even a little stunned—at Ollie's reaction. They urged him to stay, but refused to say whether that meant they had any "new ideas" regarding their previous proposal.

I went to the airport with George and Ollie and walked them to the gate. We spent about half an hour discussing the situation.

"Do you mind if I take another shot at them at the Steigenberger?" I asked, referring to the new hotel they had moved to for security reasons. They were afraid of being recognized by the other Iranians transiting Frankfurt, a major European port of entry. They had tossed the place looking for wiretaps—removed pictures, opened wall vents, and inspected all the drapes and fixtures for bugs—but found nothing, so any discussions we'd have would be sans CIA. I figured I'd need Ollie's permission for that.

North replied, "I have no objection as long as you don't give them the impression the U.S. would give in on a tit-for-tat exchange. I've got no authority to depart from the seven-point plan. You've got until I get back to Washington to get this train back on the tracks or we're going to bail out."

"Hey—I've been ready to bail out all along!" I replied, a little miffed. Between the Hasenfus shoot-down and the son-of-Ghorbanifar now raising its head, tempers were getting short. I took a deep breath: "But I'll give it a whirl."

I took a cab to the Steigenberger and met Albert, the Relative, and Ayub in a corner of the lobby. Speaking through Hakim, the Monster began to grouse about the meeting—how North had been irrational and abrupt, demanded too much, and didn't understand the constraints on Iranian influence over the hostages. "You were at all the sessions," he said, waving his arms at me. "Don't you agree?"

Despite Ayub's bluster, or maybe because of it, I sensed a certain amount of fear in his voice—and it was obvious in his face. I knew enough about Iranian culture to know they were very apprehensive about returning with nothing to show for their efforts. They had underestimated American impatience and overplayed their hand—behaved like rug merchants in a bazaar and were startled when Ollie decided he would no longer play the game.

From their perspective, the haggling over little details as well as big issues was a way of sealing the bargain. In the Middle East, when a negotiation is hard, both parties come away from it with a stronger incentive to make the deal work—a sense of shared accomplishment and a personal bond forged in the crucible of "ceremonial combat," which is what bargaining is for them. North had, like a typical Westerner, broken off the ceremony "just when it was getting good," at least in their eyes.

I decided to renew the game on their terms. I was a lot more experienced at it than Ollie, and we really had nothing to lose. My plan was to adopt their own strategy, become the "bad Copp" for Ollie's "good cop," the Dutch Uncle for Mr. Clean Marine who departed in a huff because nobody bought his wares. I told Albert to translate my words as literally as possible.

"Since you have asked for my opinion," I said, "I will tell you. Speaking very frankly, you have behaved like fools. When you were in Washington, you told us how bad Ghorbanifar was and how ineffective Kangarlu was as a representative for your government. Now, you present to the American side proposals that are identical to theirs and to which you *know* the American President can never agree. We have told you this before, but you do not listen. You remind me of a bunch of uneducated Arabs."

Albert winced as I said this, but knew I understood enough Farsi to keep his translation honest.

"In my opinion," I continued, "you have missed an historic opportunity to do something good for your country. I am afraid that opportunity has now passed. This makes me personally very unhappy because it was mainly due to me that our discussions so far, in Washington and here in Frankfurt, have taken place. When the President hears how you performed today, he will think me a fool for recommending that we continue dealing with you."

Ayub started to answer, but the Relative, saucer-eyed and pale, touched his forearm to silence him and replied, "Colonel North behaved too much like a military man in these discussions. He is not a diplomat like you."

Surprisingly, the Monster grunted in agreement. In one of those electric moments when two minds connect, Albert and I smiled—almost giggled—at each other. In fact, Ollie had been unusually polite and soft-spoken, even when he broke off the meeting—nothing like the usual, hard-driving, ebullient "military man" they had come to know. Now, I verbally pistol-whip them and suddenly *I'm* the diplomat! It was a typically Middle Eastern paradox, and Albert and I saw instantly that a corner had been turned.

"Is there anything we can do to keep the dialogue going and make progress in any way at all?" the Relative asked.

"Unless, in the next few hours," I said gravely, "we come up with something sensible, something the President can live with, then it seems to me that North's suggestion to return home while we are still friends and think about it some more would be the best one."

I then excused myself for a moment, saying I had to change my own reservations for an earlier-than-planned departure, which really made them squirm. When we reconvened, still in the lobby, the Relative said:

"We came up with a nine-point plan last night but decided not to present it because North was showing no flexibility." In Middle East logic, this meant: *The haggling had not gone on long enough to present our backup plan, you silly people!*

"Nine points?" I acted noncommittal. "I thought seven were too many. After all, we don't want to confuse our superiors!"

They laughed with us, and some of the tension melted away. Instantly we were "back at the table."

The Relative produced two pages of handwritten notes, which Albert quickly translated. The nine-point plan was actually quite similar to Ollie's seven-point plan, with two major exceptions.

First, Ollie had the release of two hostages, then one, followed by the delivery of 1,000 TOW missiles in anticipation of the high-level meeting. The nine-point plan showed one hostage coming out, then two, *after* the delivery of the 1,000 TOWs.

The other major difference involved the U.S. using its influence with the Kuwaitis to gain the release of the Dawa 17 (17 convicted terrorists being held in Kuwait City), an action the U.S. had publicly opposed for a long time.

We debated these new points for an hour or so, arriving at a nine-point plan that featured delivery of 500 TOWs and release of "one-and-a-half" American hostages—the Relative's shorthand for saying, "one for sure; if we can't get two, we'll give you a complete explanation why not." Ayub added that he would go again personally to Lebanon and press for two. As far as the Dawa prisoners went, I told them:

"Just like your own leaders, the American leadership cannot instantly reverse a major public policy. Instead, I will suggest that the American government recommend a plan to both Iran and Kuwait for bilaterally resolving this problem with a phased release of all 17 prisoners over a period of time." I said I thought the U.S. would be agreeable to mediating the views of the parties, including the Saudis, against whom the terrorist attacks had been aimed. As far as the nine-point plan went, I said, "This plan would be presented for Iran's consideration immediately after step two, the release of the American hostages."

They accepted this, and we wrote up the new nine-point plan in longhand in both English and Farsi, stipulating on each that it was subject to approval by the U.S. President and Iranian central authorities. I retained a copy in Farsi for later presentation to George Cave.

Thus was born the famous nine-point plan that so shocked Secretary of State George Schultz in the Iran-Contra hearings. It shouldn't have shocked anybody, least of all an experienced diplomat. The President of the United States, in the finding of January 17, had authorized "third parties" to facilitate the initiative, and I was that duly designated third party. The nine points were drawn up and proposed "ad ref," or ad referendum, which, as any State Department sophomore knows, means the offer was contingent upon executive approval. I'm willing to bet a steak dinner at Washington prices that Schultz himself and literally dozens of detailed CIA and State Department officials acting in a similar capacity have done exactly the same thing on many, many occasions.

I then went to my hotel room and typed a KL-43 message to North's secretary, Fawn Hall, describing these events and transmitting the nine-point plan verbatim, including my recommendation that the President accept it. Fawn said she would print out the message and deliver it to Ollie as soon as he got off the plane. From North, the plan went to Poindexter, who took it to the President.

That evening, Albert and I had dinner with the two Iranians and learned a lot more about life in revolutionary Iran, including a few war stories from the Relative that curled our hair. He had served on the infamous southern and central fronts as a platoon leader and, later, a company commander. War ages men rapidly, and the Relative, although a very young man, had matured well into middle age.

We each departed for our respective capitals the next day. I met with Cave as soon as I arrived in Washington and gave him the originals of the plan. His initial reaction was that this was, indeed, a breakthrough, although he wasn't sure if the CIA would be able to come up with a plan for the Dawa prisoners in a reasonable amount of time.

"Never mind," I told him. "I'll write the damn plan myself and give it to the White House. If we wait for the bureaucracy, we'll never get this canoe in the water."

From October 10 through 20, Ollie and I met more or less continuously at his office, during the workday, or at my house in the evening, to discuss fast-breaking events in Iran and Central America. The Hasenfus affair was scorching the television airwaves, and everyone with a press pass seemed to be in Honduras, Costa Rica, or El Salvador trying to track down leads on the airlift and otherwise make our lives miserable.

Fortunately, the nine-point plan was finding allies within the administration. Poindexter approved it and, according to Ollie, had briefed the President and Casey. The CIA was willing to go along with my Kuwait/Dawa prisoners idea, and if the Relative and Ayub were having half our luck, both countries were well on their way to putting the hostage mess behind us.

Israel, however, created a new wrinkle.

The 508 TOWs delivered in May to replenish the first shipment from the previous year were rejected by the Israeli Defense Force as too old—earlier versions of the missile that were near the end of their shelf life. This had no particular bearing on the overall U.S.-Iran Initiative except that it created a flap between Ollie and the CIA logistics people that demanded time for bureaucratic wrangling that he just didn't have to spare. They finally agreed that the older, replacement TOWs would be held in secure storage in Israel as a contingency against another Iranian shipment. This pleased the CIA, I think, even more than it did me and Ollie, since tapping government supplies is like pulling Kleenex from a box: It's a lot easier to take things out than put them back, which just messes up the system.

Throughout October, Cave and Hakim were in telephone contact with the Relative and Ayub in Tehran. Our brevity code had now swollen to 230 words plus a special alphabet, but it allowed us the real-time communications with our Iranian counterparts—something unheard of in the Ghorbanifar era. Although the Iranians had agreed in principle to establishing a secure CIA communication facility in Tehran, we all realized that, practically speaking, such an installation was months away at best. As an interim solution, we equipped them with a $121,000 secure suitcase telephone system purchased by Ami Nir from an Italian firm. This system, used widely by private corporations to thwart industrial spies, simply scrambles the voice signal using standard commercial lines. Our main concern during this interim period was hostile intercepts by the Soviet Union, who had a definite interest in the failure of the Initiative.

As it turned out, the KGB may have had more to do with Iran-Contra unraveling than most of the so-called experts currently believe.

On October 19, the Iranians confirmed that the Rafsanjani crowd had accepted the nine-point plan and had agreed to meet as soon as possible in Europe, preferably Frankfurt (where they felt most secure), to discuss implementation.

Ollie and I left Washington via TWA and arrived at Frankfurt, by way of Geneva, the morning of the 21st. We went immediately from the airport to the Intercontinental Hotel for a meeting with Ami Nir, whom we updated on our remarkable and long-overdue success. We told Ami that another shipment of 500 TOWs was imminent, provided he could clear it with Israeli authorities, which he did that same day.

On the 22nd, Nir took possession of the suitcase scrambler and gave Ollie and me a little tutorial on how to use it. Five units would be in place: one at Ollie's office, one for me, one at Nir's office, and one in his home, with one going to the Relative (a sixth was also to go to Iran, but was never delivered because the project was shut down). Ironically, we learned the Iranian unit was installed at the Revolutionary Guard's headquarters: the old American Embassy in Tehran.

Nir told us he was becoming very concerned over Ghorbanifar's constant bleating about his financial problems. Gorba's position was that Kangarlu was refusing to pay him because of our "price gouging" and poor quality of the I-HAWK spare parts. This didn't carry any weight with Khashoggi, Gorba's financier, who was leaning on him heavily for return of $10 million, plus interest, ostensibly for his Canadian backers.

We didn't shed many tears for Kangarlu or Ghorbanifar, naturally, but the Canadians were another matter. According to Nir, Khashoggi said they were on the verge of filing a lawsuit in the United States and knew enough about Gorba's intended use of the funds to leak some very intriguing statements to the press.

Ollie took all this phlegmatically (maybe he was just tired), but it really pissed me off. I raked Ami over the coals for what had to be the world's worst security on the Israeli side—Ghorbanifar was the Typhoid Mary of covert operations, and it made absolutely no sense for the Israelis to cling to him with the second channel performing so well.

"This thing is completely out of control!" I barked. "It strains any kind of logic that you would still be attached to Gorba—and now we've got a band of unnamed Canadians threatening to take us to court!"

Ollie tried to smooth things over, but my patience had finally snapped. This whole thing with Ghorbanifar had gone on way, way too long.

"Look," I continued, "this is an official, top-secret, compartmentalized covert action of the United States. The President has taken a big political risk to keep Congress out of the loop and now the press—Jack Anderson, no less—is breathing down our necks."

Anderson's man, Dale Van Ata, had called Noel Koch, the Pentagon's deputy assistant secretary for international security affairs in charge of counterterrorism, as well as the NSC, and asked for comments on a rumor about the U.S. transferring weapons to Iran in exchange for hostages. To Koch's credit *and* Anderson's, the story was shelved, at least temporarily, because lives were at stake (as well as the fact that, as Koch pointed out, much of Van Ata's information was wrong)—but the story wouldn't wait forever.

Nir went back to his old refrain. "We need to get the Relative—the second channel—to help Ghorbanifar. Get him paid and the problem will go away, I promise you."

"Sure, we can ask the second channel to help, but that's not the real point," I answered. "The point is: How in the name of God could we have gotten ourselves into such a position to begin with? It's a miracle that the whole operation hasn't blown sky-high already!" I was mainly concerned with Ghorbanifar's *next* surprise, not just the current problem. When would these guys get the message?

Nir shook his head. "Ollie was aware of Khashoggi's involvement. I personally tried to help Khashoggi—"

This was news to Ollie, and his surprise showed on his face. Ami was a little rattled and was confusing his commonwealth businessmen. In truth, Nir had tried to raise money from *British* businessman Tiny Rowland, and another Khashoggi/Canadian intermediary, Roy Furmark. Furmark was the guy Ollie knew about, not Rowland or Khashoggi. Furmark had contacted Casey on October 7 and told him about the Canadian connection, which was how the news got to North. George Cave and Charlie Allen went to New York to follow up on the matter with Furmark, to impress upon him, no doubt, how important it was to keep the lid on things while Ghorbanifar's various dealings were sorted out.

I must admit, although part of my anger stemmed from the extra back flips we'd all have to do to appease these Canadians, whoever they were, a lot of it came from my deep disappointment in Nir and the Israelis—and even Ollie. Their willingness to trust and indulge Ghorbanifar surpassed all understanding. If I'd had my way, Gorba would've been history that summer. To quote Hienie Aderholt once more, "You can get away with anything— once." Well, Gorba had had his chance—and a second, third, and fourth. The easier you tried to make things for him, to gently shunt him onto a siding, the more desperate he got and the bigger the crater he was prepared to leave behind. Now, we would have to use up a lot of goodwill we had laboriously created with the second channel in order to neutralize all the radiation left behind by Gorba's self-destruction. How much wiser it would have been to use that goodwill in pursuit of our mutual objectives.

"You're upset about nothing," Ami tried to charm me. "Nothing is out of control. It's only a matter of paying Gorba what is owed him."

"He's a damned snake who can't be trusted, and the situation is far from under control. It can blow up at any moment."

Ollie and Ami obviously wanted to move on to a more immediate topic— getting ready for the next transfer—and I felt like one of Custer's scouts, raving and pointing to all the hoofprints, and being roundly ignored. As it had been on the eve of the McFarlane trip, everything about the project suddenly felt all wrong.

Ollie and I moved on to Frankfurt for a tactical meeting with the Relative's representatives (he would not be coming). We felt it would be inappropriate for Nir to be there, but promised him a seat at the next policy-level discussion. He accepted this gracefully and returned to Israel.

The Monster and his aide (who had been at the earlier meetings) were already at the Steigenberger and had been meeting with Hakim while Ollie and I were talking with Nir. We arrived on the 24th and were lucky to obtain rooms at the Steigenberger—Frankfurt was full due to the international book fair.

As soon as we stepped off the plane, Albert took me aside. The way things stood now, he said, one hostage would be released after the first 500 TOWs were delivered. Ayub said he tried hard for a second "box," but could only guarantee one.

This information did nothing to brighten my already lousy mood. We immediately went to North's room for our first session. Without the Relative and only Ayub, the atmosphere was grim.

Ollie finally began to show he was as upset as I was with all the recent bad news. Two hostages had been the caveat to the nine-point plan, and, as far as North was concerned, the Iranians already seemed to be welshing on the deal. Ayub counterattacked by criticizing our plan for the Dawa prisoners. He maintained (with a straight face and despite the fact that his own Farsi version of the agreement said otherwise) that the U.S. had promised to *intercede* with the Kuwaitis rather than mediate the conflicting claims. That "misunderstanding" happened to be a line item right out of the Iranians' previous seven-point plan—a step backward and a bald-faced lie. This completely exhausted our patience. We now demanded that the Relative fly up for the meeting, or they could forget about the TOW delivery.

Ayub responded predictably, saying the Relative could not come up because "It is an insult to me!"

"It is no insult," Ollie said. "He has been presented as the representative of Speaker Rafsanjani. It seems as if serious problems are preventing us from implementing step one. We need to have an emergency meeting."

Albert worked the Relative's aide skillfully, and after numerous phone calls back and forth, the Relative agreed the next day to join us.

On the strength of this positive sign, I called Bob Dutton via KL-43 and asked him to proceed to Tel Aviv, link up with Nir, and prepare to ship an installment of 500 TOW missiles—the first transaction undertaken through the second channel. Ollie considered going back to Washington, which I thought was a bad move. After discussions with Poindexter, he agreed to wait while George Cave flew over to join us.

The evening of the 25th, I told Albert that he would have to attend to a small chore.

"I know what it is," he said, rolling his eyes in disgust. "You are going to make me have dinner with the Monster again."

I clapped him on the shoulder. "You are both so beloved by everyone, you have a lot in common. Besides, my Farsi is so bad I would only cause more trouble."

"Your Farsi is like Gorba's English," Albert teased. "Sometimes excellent, sometimes you can't speak it at all. Why is that?"

"Senility," I joked, although between the Hasenfus crisis and Ghorbanifar's complications, the whole project had aged me a dozen years already. Albert knew I was out of patience with Ayub, and knew too that we needed him and really couldn't risk offending him needlessly. Besides, despite his awful personality, he was at least an earnest guy—tough and nasty, but sincere. The more we learned about Ayub, in fact, the more our grudging respect turned into affection. Despite all our handicaps, woes, and constraints, both sides really and truly wanted the relationship to work and to blossom into some kind of healthy government-to-government understanding. That's what diplomacy is all about. That's why all of us stayed in the ring.

George Cave arrived the morning of the 26th, and at noon we picked up the Relative at the Frankfurt airport and drove directly to Mainz, about 30 minutes away. The hotel situation had gotten worse in Frankfurt, and the CIA had "arranged" (meaning bugged) some rooms at the Mainz Hilton. We did not want to preempt the discussion, but during the drive we mentioned how hard the Monster was to talk to in isolation.

The Relative shrugged and said, "Ayub is very doctrinaire and can be hardheaded at times. I knew there would be trouble sending him to deal directly with you. We will have to carefully review the nine-point plan to make sure that there are no further misunderstandings."

The talks began as soon as we arrived. We summed up the "emergency," at least from the American perspective, as follows: Two points of the nine-point plan had already been violated. Ayub had offered no compelling reason why two hostages could not be released instead of one, and was misrepresenting American obligations with respect to the Dawa prisoners—obligations clearly spelled out in the original Farsi translation.

The Relative sided with Ayub on the question of the hostages, stating that only one release was feasible "so long as you are anxious to get it done in the next few days—before the election." This was a gentle dig at what he supposed was our political preoccupation with the off-year Congressional elections. Perhaps he supposed that, like parliamentary systems, our chief executive served at the pleasure of the ruling majority party. Each of us had, in various ways, informed the Iranians that the election had no bearing whatsoever on the project.

"This isn't France," I told him. "It makes little difference if the American hostages are released before, during, or after the election—the President is not up for reelection this year or any other," and explained that the President was already halfway through the second of a constitutional maximum of two terms. "The point is, we want to get them all out, to get this obstacle behind us and move on with the relationship."

Ollie expanded on this by saying that, unless we could get the nine-point plan in motion to our mutual benefit without these acrimonious, after-the-fact lapses of faith, it would be best for both sides to table the program—at least until more meaningful talks could be held between our two governments. I thought Ollie was soft-pedaling what was really a fish-or-cut-bait issue, so I asked Albert to translate—again, verbatim:

"During the years I was in Iran," I said, "especially in the later years as a senior U.S. official, when I myself had communication difficulties with my counterparts in the Iranian air force or even with the Shah, I always said what I had to say as plainly as possible without the Persian embellishments—no poetry, no songs and dances, just the way we do it in the U.S. military. I found it to be very effective, and the people I dealt with seemed to appreciate that approach. That's what I think we should be doing now." I then repeated a proposal I had made several times in the past—that if the Iranians really wanted to rid themselves of the burden of the hostages, they should simply tell us where they were and let us do the rest—and relieve themselves of *all* political risks.

The Relative took this as an invitation to be candid, so he was. He said we really didn't understand the difficulties he and Ayub were having in Tehran with their end of the program and that, far from ignoring the problems of the hostages in Lebanon, the Iranian government was giving it a lot of attention. "Believe it or not," he said, "we are trying ourselves to locate the two additional hostages, Reed and Ciccipio, but we have been unable to find them."

This would've been unbelievable coming from Ayub—that the Iranians were not only unable to pull the Shia's strings, but they weren't even privy to key information like hostage location—but from the Relative, it was credible, and actually jibed with Cave's information from the CIA.

The rest of our discussions, up through the morning of the 27th, followed this tack. The hang-up with the Dawa-Kuwait plan was that it required ambassadorial-level communication between Iran and the Foreign Minister of Kuwait, with assurances that Iran wouldn't sponsor any attacks against the Kuwaiti royal family or any of the foreign missions located there—basically an extension of the U.S.-Iran terrorist moratorium to include Kuwait while the Dawa question was being negotiated. Eventually the Relative agreed that the Kuwait plan was acceptable as written and would be taken seriously in Tehran.

"But we simply cannot release more than one Lebanese hostage in the near term, and that one will probably be Jacobsen," the Relative said. "I am willing to go back and wait and work some more. Rafsanjani has personally made phone calls regarding the hostages and the Revolutionary Guards have sent an officer to Lebanon, but it still does not look like they will get more than one released in the near term. Once the plan is implemented and Iran can tell the Shia in Lebanon that the Dawa prisoner issue is being addressed in a positive fashion and Iran is in a position to promise something—a gesture by Kuwait, for example, on Muhammad's birthday [which was coming soon]—then the whole thing will break loose."

We then discussed terms, and the Iranians arranged for $3.6 million to be deposited to the account of Lake Resources in Credit Suisse. This was not as much as we wanted, but it was sufficient to finance the procurement and delivery of missiles at about $7,200 each—considerably cheaper than the previous tab of $10,000 per unit. We might've been able to finagle a higher price (I could see the gleam in Albert's eye), but I knew the shipment would be older missiles, and a suitable "discount" would go a long way toward disarming the inevitable complaints that would greet them on the other end.

I also thought it would be wise to offer the second channel some kind of tangible benefit, partly to enhance their standing among Iranian officials, and partly to give Kangarlu (who had been accused of profiteering) and Ghorbanifar a black eye. In any event, of the $3.6 million, $2.4 million was spent on the missiles, of which $2,037,000 went to the CIA and $400,000 went for transportation, including the cost of picking up the released hostage, and so on. (I took no salary from Iranian payments, and although some of my expenses were picked up by the enterprise, the others I paid myself, being very sensitive to any future accusations of profiteering. Some of these additional expenses were paid by STTGI, for which I planned to seek reimbursement later but was prevented from doing so when our accounts were frozen in December 1986.) We had calculated that it would take about $1.5 million to buy a 707 (Southern Air Transport had located one for us in Jordan) and about half a million to pay for operations and maintenance. In addition, we had set a goal of $5 million to be used as front-end money to finance these new transactions—to offset the cost of middlemen and avoid any hidden surprises (like Khashoggi and his Canadians) or security breaches caused solely by the lack of adequate funding.

This Iranian payment, therefore, fell a little short of what we needed to be truly self-sufficient: to buy CIA materiel, and then ship it on a case-by-case basis, rewarding Iranian progress toward the Initiative's larger goals. The Relative kept our attention by mentioning a $50 million revolving fund they wanted to establish to support ongoing decisions of the joint U.S.-Iranian "committee"—a higher-level government-to-government team that would reduce dependency on privateers like me, which was music to my ears. In the meantime, both sides would depend on me to keep the pipeline open.

One incident now occurred that is worth detailing here. After the meeting, I flew to London, where I had been invited to address the International Special Operations Symposium later in the week. Before the Relative and Ayub went back to Iran, they took Albert to the Frankfurt branch of the Credit Suisse to make sure he was satisfied that the $3.6 million had been properly credited. During their meeting with the banker, Ayub offered, out of the blue, to transfer another $40 million from Iran's Credit Suisse account into Lake Resources "in order to improve the atmosphere, show our good faith, and set the stage for the next steps."

Albert was understandably startled by this offer, especially considering who it came from, and called me in London. He felt he needed a witness, and I agreed. I spoke to the banker in German, and although he was very guarded, he confirmed that a very large transfer between accounts was discussed.

In the end, Albert and I decided that it would not be wise to accept so large a deposit at this time because it might be construed as committing the U.S. government to some of the later, more extensive aid mentioned in the nine-point plan. To maintain the "spirit of goodwill," if that was in fact the Iranian intent, we decided that Albert would tell them we preferred for the money to be deposited into an account jointly controlled by the U.S. and Iran rather than a private party like Lake Resources. In short, neither Albert nor I wanted to be "held hostage" by this big deposit. As things turned out, around $8.2 million of Lake Resources money would, in fact, be impounded by the Swiss as the Iran-Contra story broke and federal investigators turned the screws on the Credit Suisse. You can imagine the media and political frenzy that would've occurred if the balance of that account had been $48 million!

After the session at the bank, the Iranians returned to Tehran and Ollie returned to Washington. After reviewing the program's status with Poindexter, North authorized me to go ahead and ship the next batch of TOWs, which we decided would be the warehoused TOWs the Israelis had rejected. The destination this time, though, was the airport at Bandar Abbas, a port city on the Strait of Hormuz at the entrance to the Persian Gulf, since it was 90 minutes' flying time closer than Tehran and controlled by the Revolutionary Guard and Iranian air force (important factors given the power struggle going on in Tehran). It was also, at that time anyway, just out of range of most Iraqi fighters.

Almost immediately, Ollie and I got word in Frankfurt that hostage David Jacobsen was about to be released in West Beirut.

Unfortunately, this good news was tempered with some practical concerns. West Beirut was a very dangerous place at that time. If Jacobsen were to be released in a manner similar to that of Reverend Weir (who had been pushed out of a moving car at night in front of the British Embassy—a gangster-style maneuver that almost drew gunfire from the edgy embassy sentries), his chances for injury or death would be incalculable. Ollie and I agreed that we would do just about anything to ensure that didn't happen.

Coincidentally, at this time the U.S. chargé d'affaires in Damascus, David Ransom, and the U.S. ambassador in Beirut, John Kelly, had both worked for me as State Department exchange officers during my stint at the Pentagon (Kelly in the Southeast Asia branch of ISA from 1972 to 1973; Ransom had been my deputy when I ran ISA's directorate for Middle East, Africa, and South Asia from 1981 to 1983). North obtained permission from Poindexter for us both to go to Beirut and brief the embassy staff on the upcoming release so they would be in a position to react quickly and responsibly when our "zebra" was delivered.

Poindexter cabled (via back channel) Kelly and Ransom, outlining our basic plan, identifying Ollie and me by our true names, and giving our ETA at Beirut. George Schultz would later complain about this, claiming the chain of command from President to Secretary of State to Assistant Secretary for the region had been usurped. This was nonsense. As Schultz well knew, every U.S. ambassador in the world—under law—works *directly* for the President. Back-channel messages are not only legal and proper, they are used all the time for security and intelligence reasons. Schultz obviously used the incident to try to make a much bigger point: that the Secretary of State is somehow empowered or mandated to exercise ironclad control over every aspect of foreign policy, which isn't, wasn't, and never will be true. Al Haig had made the same mistake three years earlier and found it didn't work. After Iran-Contra broke, Schultz came closer than any Secretary in modern history to making this dream of centralized State Department power come true. When Meese and Reagan managed to turn an unfortunate incident into a major scandal, the NSC took the hits and Schultz stepped in, made his opposition (disloyalty, some say) to the President look like a virtue, and picked up most of the marbles. In my view, it was a truly remarkable performance.

While Poindexter paved the way, Ollie called Terry Waite, an Anglican Church official who was at the time a highly visible hostage intermediary (and soon-to-be hostage himself), in London and asked him to join us in Frankfurt immediately for the final leg into Beirut.

Terry is a very dedicated man. He sensed in the hostage release a payoff to his labors as well as a share of headlines and dropped what he was doing to join us. He arrived with no bags, just a big, bearded grin and the clothes on his back. We then boarded our Lear jet, leased by the enterprise, and departed for Larnica Airport in Cyprus.

We arrived about 11 P.M. on a balmy night. We went directly from the Lear to a U.S. Army H-60 Blackhawk helicopter for the 50 or so minute flight to Beirut. Blacked out as if for combat (Beirut was a regular war zone—intelligence suspected Hezballah, Syrian, and Palestinian groups might be packing aircraft-killing SAM-7s), we broke out of the clouds and zeroed in on the helicopter landing zone near the American Embassy. As we approached, the landing lights popped on and we dropped in fast—Ollie must've thought he was back in Vietnam. As we ducked under the spinning rotors to greet the security team sent to meet us, I glanced at my watch. It was exactly midnight, Beirut time.

We went by car to the embassy where John Kelly was waiting in his office with Terry McNamara, his deputy chief of mission (a classmate of mine from the Naval War College), the senior CIA officer, and the defense attaché. The embassy building only reinforced the impression of a war zone: It was segmented and bunkered like an artillery command post. Ollie and I briefed Kelly and his people on the situation; Terry Waite, who had been exposed to none of this beforehand, was allowed to listen only to the unclassified parts. For our discussion of more sensitive information, he was escorted from the room, and then returned.

First, we confirmed that the release of hostage David Jacobsen seemed imminent. We added that the release of a second hostage—either Anderson or Southerland—although unlikely, wasn't out of the question, so we should be prepared for two. We said the location would probably be West Beirut, but we couldn't be sure, so we had to be ready to handle any one of several scenarios. We concluded that the safety of the hostage or hostages was a major concern and that our response, whatever it was, should not exacerbate an already dangerous situation.

While Kelly relayed this information to Ransom on a secure line, I made a long-distance commercial call in another room to Bob Dutton at the Carlton Hotel in Tel Aviv and got an update on the TOW shipment via KL-43. At that moment, things were going smoothly. The TOW delivery aircraft was airborne and estimated arrival at Bandar Abbas at 7:30 A.M. local time in Iran.

We convened again, and Ollie and I answered what questions we could about the nature of the Iranian information. Kelly ordered his hostage reception staff and security personnel to prepare to go into West Beirut, reminding them to exercise extreme caution. We left Terry Waite with Kelly and boarded the chopper for the return flight to Cyprus, having been on the ground about three hours. There was no point remaining in Beirut. Kelly was well prepared to handle the situation, and our continued presence might only draw unwelcome attention to ourselves rather than to Jacobsen when the world's media descended on the place to cover the release. Besides, we hadn't slept in about three days, and no problem looks solvable when you're seeing it in double.

Back in Larnica, we checked into the Sun Hotel on the beach and slept from about 5:00 A.M. until 10 that morning, and then took the Lear back to Geneva. Ollie returned to Washington and I joined Albert at the Intercontinental Hotel to follow developments. About midnight our time, Ollie called from D.C. to say that arrangements had been made to move the hostage (or hostages) to Damascus should the release take place other than in Beirut. Since U.S. relations with Syria were still severely strained, we decided to move the Lear back to Cyprus in case a U.S. military aircraft could not be cleared into Damascus.

In the meantime, Dutton advised me that the TOWs had arrived safely at Bandar Abbas. I told him, "Well done!" and asked him to proceed directly to Milan, Italy, to join me for a meeting with Italian businessmen on an STTGI commercial project—an industrial waste disposal system.

While I was preparing to leave Geneva, Ollie called and said he was coming back to Europe to participate in the hostage debriefing. I thought this was an unnecessary drain on his time and energy (he looked like a zombie by this time) and told him so; but Ollie had a big emotional investment in the release and would've left his deathbed to be there. I was also concerned about stretching our resources, like the Lear, too thin just when we'd need them most. Having Ollie (or any of us) fly commercial in these hot spots was just too big a security risk to take at the time.

I flew to Milan on the Lear, where I met Bob and Ralph Quintero, whom I'd asked to come to Europe to lend a hand. Ralph was at his best at moments like this: an utterly reliable agent who was at home, faceless, and effective just about anywhere, particularly in a dangerous, short-fused situation. Ollie arrived soon after we did and brought us up to date. The NSC was beginning to worry that, because of political tensions with the U.S., Syrian President Assad would try to pull some stunt should the hostage(s) be released in Syria. He might impound our rescue aircraft or sequester its crew, since it was impossible to obtain visas for lawful entry into Syria. Our Syrian ambassador had been withdrawn, leaving only chargé David Ransom, who could be diplomatically ignored, to handle official affairs. Things could quickly turn sour, despite our best plans and Iran's best intentions.

Bob and Ralph took the Lear from Milan to Cyprus. North arrived separately and went to the U.S. embassy to wait out the situation while Dutton and Quintero went to the Sun to stand by. This was when the famous snapshot was taken of Ollie getting into a CIA car at the Larnica airport—the sort of security breach I thought increasingly likely as the media homed in on the story. Ollie's familiar face, and to a lesser extent, mine, were the last things we needed in the eastern Mediterranean during those final hours of the countdown.

The next day, November 2, Jacobsen was released—by the grace of God, in West Beirut instead of Syria. He was taken to within a block or so of the old U.S. Embassy building and told to "start walking." Unfortunately, he was disoriented and began walking the wrong way. Instead of suspecting some kind of setup and shooting him, which was a real possibility when something unexpected like that happens, one kidnapper just walked up and turned him around. While this was going on, another captor called an intermediary, who phoned the U.S. Embassy. Within half an hour, Terry McNamara, along with U.S. and Lebanese security forces, had punched across the so-called Green Line separating Christian from Moslem sections of Beirut, snatched Jacobsen, and whisked him back to the Embassy.

Jacobsen was immediately debriefed by Kelly's people—mostly for information on the location of other hostages and the movement of the terrorists who might be momentarily vulnerable for a rescue or other action. (Dutton had choppered in from Cyprus to be present for the debriefing.) We had especially high hopes in Jacobsen's case, since he was the brightest and most helpful of the hostages after his release. The two clerics previously released were either unable (too shell-shocked) or unwilling (because of the "Stockholm syndrome"—identification with their captors—or previous political beliefs) to be of much help. It was quickly apparent, though, that Jacobsen had been pretty well isolated by the kidnappers. His information was helpful in reconstructing and understanding how the hostages were being handled— he had been kept, shackled and unclothed, in the dark and often beaten—but better use could've been made of his tactical intelligence. Had a more detailed analysis of his lengthy debriefing been made by our security people, the place where he had been held could have been deduced with some precision. For example, he mentioned hearing "departing aircraft" flying in certain patterns at a certain time of day. This, plus other physical clues, may have been enough to mount a raid. As it was, our "zebra herd" would consist of "one box" only.

I had been continuing with my business meeting in Milan all this time, following events on television and ducking out to send or receive KL-43 messages. I was elated when confirmation was received that Jacobsen was safe in Amercian hands. His release was one less brick in the barrier erected by the President against our strategic objective and my own happy exit from the project.

The next day, Jacobsen, Waite, and Dutton took an Army helicopter to Larnica Airport, where our Lear jetted the "official party" (everyone but Dulton and Quintero) nonstop to the U.S. Air Force hospital at Wiesbaden, Germany—the customary reception area for returning hostages. Before a thousand flashing cameras, Waite and North took Jacobsen off the plane, and the Lear returned to Geneva.

Speculation arose then, and later, that North used Waite as a tool or cover for Iran-Contra operations. To the extent that Waite, already a known hostage negotiator, drew press attention to himself instead of us in this instance, I suppose that accusation has some superficial appeal. To the extent that such theories link Waite to the enterprises and the negotiations with Iran, I know for a fact that they are false. To my knowledge, the reverse is also true. Waite was very closemouthed in private about his dealings with various Lebanese militia groups and the Hezballah, and I doubt that he shared much if any of his inside knowledge with North. I know he shared none of it with me, as helpful as it might have been. Ours was a union of convenience, nothing more.

Not long after David Jacobsen's release, another two-day meeting was scheduled for Germany, with the same Iranian team and myself, North, Cave, and Hakim. We took a hotel room in Mainz, which the CIA set up for surveillance before we arrived.

From late September through October, the hostage situation had not gone well, Jacobsen notwithstanding. Three additional hostages had been taken in Lebanon by a group identifying itself as Islamic Justice, a radical splinter group. A big debate was waged between the State Department's Intelligence and Research (INR) Bureau and the CIA about whether this was an attempt by ultraradicals to spoil Reagan's Iran Initiative (the CIA's view) or if Iran had orchestrated the kidnappings to gain more bargaining chips (INR's pet theory). Of course, the State Department had never been "on board" the Iran Initiative and based their conclusion on their own dictum that "everything that happened in Iran's sphere of influence was Iran's fault." To the Iranians' credit, of course, was the fact that, aside from these new kidnappings, there had not been one terrorist act—bombing, abduction, or assassination—aimed at U.S. interests since the secret initiative began almost 18 months before, a fact the NSC and CIA never tired of telling their critics. From State's point of view, though, they couldn't have it both ways: Either Iran had the influence or it didn't.

The Iranians began by telling us they were beginning to feel the heat from putting Ghorbanifar, Kangarlu, and their faction on the back burner. Rafsanjani's people had apparently just arrested Mehdi Hashemi, the son-in-law of the Ayatollah Montazari (Khomeini's designated successor), and 17 of his followers for various crimes against the state, and Montazari's supporters were looking for ammunition to shoot back at Rafsanjani.

At first, we were heartened by this development (which we had the CIA confirm during the course of the meeting). Mehdi Hashemi was known to be the head of a very radical, terrorist-oriented group operating out of Iran, with tendrils deep in Lebanon. His followers had tried to smuggle explosives into Saudi Arabia during the Haj (the holy pilgrimage to Mecca), causing the Saudis to protest formally to Iran. Even more, the Saudis gave the Iranian government information from their interrogation of the suspects, which led to the Hashemi arrests and discovery of incriminating evidence in his compound—including a large cache of weapons and documents linking him to the assassinations of Mujahdeen, Afghan guerrilla leaders. They also discovered his plans for terrorist attacks in Saudi Arabia, Bahrain, Kuwait, Egypt, and Europe.

Anyway you sliced it, this was good news: a die-hard terrorist and his cabal had been taken off the streets, and Rafsanjani's pragmatists, strongly supported by the Revolutionary Guard (who made the arrests) led by Mohsen Resaii (the Monster's boss), were finally showing their moderate colors by acting like responsible officials.

Unfortunately, Montazari (who was either voluntarily or involuntarily under house arrest) decided to strike back. Helped by details that could only have been revealed by Ghorbanifar or Kangarlu, Montazari papered the Tehran University campus with leaflets (over *five million* were printed!) "exposing" the May 1986 McFarlane visit. It was their way of smearing Rafsanjani, who appeared to be dangerously close to a breakthrough with the Great Satan—namely, us. According to the leaflet, which we never saw, the U.S. had sent McFarlane and his party "to come begging" into Iran with false passports. They had been arrested upon arrival, the leaflet claimed, and expelled after a few days.

Against this dramatic backdrop, which really took our breath away (we flashed the information to the CIA and NSC immediately), the Iranians proceeded to sweeten the nine-point deal. Since September they had alluded to the possibility of delivering a top-of-the-line, Soviet-made T-72 tank to Western intelligence operatives. Now, they showed us Polaroid snapshots of just such a tank and offered to give it to us unconditionally—as a show of trust and gesture of goodwill.

"Send your ship to Bandar Abbas in two weeks," the spokesman said, "and the T-72 will be yours."

They already knew about the *Erria* (which, coincidentally, was in Haifa, Israel, taking on board a small container of AK-47 rifles and ammunition, plus 400 rifles and 15,000 rounds of ammunition captured by the Israelis from a Palestinian boat, for the Contras). We immediately worked out an ETA for Bandar Abbas, and agreed on a time when radio and shore contact instructions would be delivered.

(As a footnote to this episode, the *Erria* did proceed to Bandar Abbas via the Red Sea and stood offshore until the end of November, but never received the tank. By that time, the Iran-Contra story had broken in the press, and nobody in Iran was willing to brave the resulting hail of publicity to complete the transaction. As American success against the T-72 in Desert Storm later proved, the loss was not as great as the tank experts imagined at the time.)

In a reciprocal gesture, as well as to further our plan to establish a secure communication base in Tehran, I procured some special, portable telephone equipment from the Israelis for $100,000 and trained two of the Iranians in its use. In October, this equipment was taken to Tehran and used almost exclusively for our subsequent communications right up to the time of President Reagan's and Ed Meese's famous press conference on November 25, 1986, "exposing" the operation.


Obviously, five million pieces of paper floating around with the details of a top-secret visit by a high-level U.S. emissary *on Iranian soil* was a major security disaster. At least that's the way I saw it. Ollie wasn't so sure.

"We're going to be demolished by this," I told him somberly after we returned to Washington. "Just demolished!"

"Well, I don't know," Ollie replied. "I've got to go to a meeting. After that, let's talk about it some more."

Ollie was always running off in the middle of things for one meeting or another, most of them trivial. I guess he'd never been on the business end of an avalanche before.

"Forget about your damn meetings for a moment," I said, completely frustrated. "For Christ's sake, Ollie—let's focus on this. *This* is going to burn us down!"

Ollie didn't exactly ignore the problem, but I think in retrospect that something deep inside him just didn't want to deal with it—like a scientist who works tirelessly on a research project and then finds some anomalous bit of data. Subconsciously, perhaps, he just couldn't accept the fact that maybe—just *maybe*—his whole project was about to go up in smoke; so he tabled it, or rationalized it away. To be fair, Ollie had never shown any tendencies to do this before. On the contrary, he was a workaholic to whom no detail was too minor to merit his full attention. At worst, he was like a computer you could load up with data—register everything in perfect order; but if you forgot to hit the "memory" button, it would all evaporate. I truly believed he would take this to Poindexter and some considered damage-control plan would come back through channels: hopefully, the candid, courageous speech by Reagan I had already suggested, plus a lot of backing and filling among the people who were counting on us, namely the Israelis and second-channel Iranians, but that was not to be. If I'd had even an *inkling* that the administration was about to let the whole matter slide into the graveyard of inaction, I'd have made the circuit banging on desks, beginning with Poindexter's and Casey's—but, to my great regret, that circuit, too, was never made.

So, while President Reagan basked in the momentary sunshine of David Jacobsen's return, the rest of us hunkered down and waited for the tornado to hit.

On November 3, the day after Jacobsen's release, it did.

A little-known and lightly read Shiite weekly magazine published in Beirut, *Al-Shiraa*, ran a story that read as if it might have been printed from a revolutionary leaflet. In intriguing detail, it recounted a bizarre tale of a high American official's clandestine flight to Tehran on a mission to trade arms for hostages.

Within 36 hours, it had been picked up by every major news service on earth.

# —16—

# No Good Deed Goes Unpunished

Despite the rising waters from the *Al-Shiraa* leak pooling around our ankles, and then our knees, life went on. The next meeting with the Iranians was scheduled for November 9 in Geneva, and we determined to make the most of it.

I was still dissatisfied with the Relative's explanation (or lack of explanation) for why Jacobsen was the only hostage released, and before leaving London for the meeting, I told the aide (who spoke English well and had been meeting with Albert) to contact the Relative and let him know that reviewing my complaint would be first on our agenda.

The aide replied that Ayub, and possibly the Relative, if he could attend, would be willing to discuss it again at Geneva, but that everything that could be done had been done. The aide and I went back and forth on this issue until he finally relapsed into revolutionary jingo. In frustration, I raised my hand and cut him off.

"We are trying in good faith to move this deal forward and to get our respective governments into meaningful talks," I said. "This kind of rhetoric is not helpful. I only want to deal with the facts."

I then went back to my hotel room.

According to Albert, after I left, the aide said, "That Secord is a real bastard!" We had a good laugh about that: The Monster meets his match in the Bastard. But the message got through.

Albert and I arrived in Geneva about the time the first reports on the *Al-Shiraa* article were appearing in the Western press. The details were still sketchy and the articles were filled with lots of conjecture and misinterpretation, but Albert and I read the same thing in each other's faces: This was the beginning of the end. Years later, we would learn through the efforts of journalist Morgan Strong, a Middle East expert, that the roots of the *Al-Shiraa* "hit piece" apparently went much deeper than the Hashemi-Rafsanjani contretemps.

It seems the story of the McFarlane trip had been offered to, and rejected by, the two major Lebanese dailies before it was presented to the editor of *Al-Shiraa*, a Shiite weekly with limited circulation. The editor said he was approached by two men claiming to be Iranians (the editor recognized them as Syrian military intelligence agents) twice before receiving what was clearly a death threat to print the piece, which he did out of fear for his life. A couple of weeks later the editor was, in fact, shot by persons unknown, but survived.

According to Strong, the information had to have been fed to the Syrians by the KGB in an attempt to spoil the U.S.-Iranian rapprochement they saw developing to the detriment of their own designs in the region. The last thing Moscow wanted to see was Uncle Sam cozying up again with Tehran. The commissars probably fell off their *dacha* bar stools laughing with glee when word of the leaflets arrived. Since officials in Iran wanted to keep news of the U.S. overtures secret, it had fallen to Moscow to make sure incriminating evidence made its way to Baghdad or Damascus, and from there to a location, like Lebanon, where it would do the most damage. If true, this amounted to one of the KGB's last hurrahs of the Cold War. We were not tickled to be its target.

Ollie arrived on November 5, and the first thing I asked him about was the damage-control plan for the *Al-Shiraa* piece: specifically, when the President was going to make his "buck stops here" television speech or hold a news conference. Ollie said he didn't know for sure, but that Poindexter and Casey were working on the problem. Ex-hostage David Jacobsen had visited the White House and ended a Presidential photo-op, which was disrupted as usual with provocative questions from the media, with a heartfelt plea to the journalists: "In the name of God, would you please just be responsible and back off?" Needless to say, they did not.

On November 6, President Reagan made his first public statement in response to the brouhaha. It was not the hard-hitting mea culpa I'd been pressing North and Poindexter for, but a rather lame pronouncement that the claims of an Iranian-U.S. connection had "no foundation." Obviously, the buck was not ready to stop. The best the President and his men could come up with apparently was another "Operation Ostrich"—stick their heads in the sand and hope that the whirlwind would blow over.

On November 9, Ayub and the Relative's aide arrived in Geneva. According to the Monster, the Relative was lying low because the *Al-Shiraa* piece had raised his profile a little too high in Tehran's political shooting gallery. In some of his messages, the Relative sounded a lot like Jacobsen: "For God's sake, this is blowing all over the area. You are going to get us killed!"

However, Ayub assured us that both the Relative and Rafsanjani were anxious to continue with the plan, although we should expect to hear some anti-American propagandizing to appease the opposition. He reminded us that Mehdi Hashemi was still in custody and the Ayatollah Khomeini himself had stated that he should be "tried for his crimes," which in the parlance of the revolution meant execution.

Ollie replied that everyone on our side was keenly disappointed about getting only Jacobsen out, particularly since the others, Anderson and Southerland, had been held so long. He then gamely tried to turn this to our advantage, suggesting that the criticism accumulating against the President and militating against the nine-point plan could be quickly diffused if Iran caused the others to be released at once. Ayub wouldn't buy it.

Nir now arrived as well, but we kept him under wraps since he had been seen and photographed in Tehran during the McFarlane trip, and it did not seem wise to tell the Iranians that Israel—still vilified for its ties to the first channel—was somehow involved in the second. Consequently, we adjourned our working session with Ayub and went to brief Nir and get the Israeli input before reconvening with the Iranians.

Interestingly enough, Nir's concerns were almost identical to the Relative's. He was worried about maintaining clear communications and keeping the operation alive, no matter what storms might rage in the media and political arenas. With the new criticism arising in Tehran about contact with the West, Ami was more concerned than ever about getting Gorba his due. One public revelation had a way of inviting more revelations, and pretty soon everybody and his brother, the Canadians included, we supposed, would be crawling out of the woodwork claiming to have special knowledge of President Reagan's "secret arms for hostages deal."

He was not far off. In Washington, the crisis was growing by leaps and bounds. The Hasenfus shoot-down was still in the news, and reporters were beginning to notice how the tendrils of both the Iran-hostage deals and off-line Contra support seemed to be converging at the White House. Jack Singlaub had even been approached by the press (his visibility as a pro-Contra spokesman having always been high) and asked if he had been involved. He correctly answered that he had not, but used the opportunity to criticize the people who had shut him out of the Contra air resupply business as "amateurs"—and this coming from a walking security violation who doesn't know a barrel roll from a Cuban eight.

Anyway, Poindexter got on the horn to Geneva: We want Ollie back. Before North left, I told him:

"For God's sake, Ollie, let's get off our rear ends and get the President in gear—have him make a firm speech, or at least call a press conference and lay out the strategy, stake out his goals and position, and assure the American people that he's still got the ball and is running with it."

Ollie agreed and said he would do what he could—as he always did—but he looked worse than ever when he left: tired, deflated, distracted. From accounts in the newspapers, chief of staff Don Regan was "taking charge" for the President and was stonewalling all inquiries on the grounds that responding to them would endanger the hostages. I categorically rejected this strategy, since our plan didn't rely, and had never relied, on the public utterances of either head of state. We had agreed at the working level that the propaganda "shot and shell" from both sides could fly over our heads; it didn't matter one whit to the strategic aspects of the initiative. Regan would later breach his stonewall and allow the President to put out a partial and misleading story in a speech on November 13, which would wind up doing more harm than good, since it made the President look wounded and weak— the first of many such mistakes by his handlers.

After Ollie left, I spent the morning of November 10 training Ayub on our secure communications device—"the briefcase," which encodes a conversation on a public phone line. We also spent a couple of hours the next day with him candidly reviewing the situation: the Monster and the Bastard having a *tête-à-tête* through the civilizing offices of Albert Hakim.

"I'm afraid all our efforts are going to blow up because the newsmen will have our leaders running scared," I told Ayub. "From the beginning we didn't want to make this a relationship that focused only on the hostages. I feel Ollie is right when he said the only way to quickly defuse this matter is to get our remaining hostages out of Lebanon right now—or at least the two who have been there so long. If your organization can at least give us the locations of the hostages, we'll deal with the matter ourselves."

I purposely did not—and never had—used the word "rescue" or "raid" since no honorable soldier would ever ask another to condemn a comrade to death. I intentionally left the rhetoric open enough to suggest bribery or direct negotiations as a means of getting the hostages back, and the Iranians seemed to understand this. It was a way for them to get off the hot seat without losing face.

Ayub answered, "You are wrong. You do not understand the situation in Lebanon. I've spent a lot of time there. The Hezballah do not blindly follow the Ayatollah. Our influence is very limited. It's going to take time."

"But we have evidence that the three Americans seized in October were abducted at the direction of certain elements in Iran and that the Islamic Justice Organization is just another cover name for Hezballah."

Ayub, tears welling in his eyes, replied angrily, "I would rather die than report a conversation like this back to my superiors! It is exactly the kind of attitude that drove us to our revolution! You obviously know nothing about the revolutionary spirit in Iran! Your insistence on dealing with the hostages is offensive and is not going to benefit either side!"

Albert said in English that he was having difficulty translating a conversation like this and lapsed into Farsi for several minutes trying to calm the Monster down.

I said in as calm and firm a tone as I could, "Albert, tell him he is not the only soldier in this room. I take the most serious exception to his comments about me—a person who has spent four-and-a-half years in Iran working for the Iranian people and the Iranian nation. These radical outbursts will do nothing but keep Iran isolated and open to the Soviet Union—and certainly will not help it in its war with Iraq. I do not think further discussion between the two of us is warranted at this time. I am returning to Washington."

As I stood up and turned to go, Ayub rushed across the floor and blocked my path. I half-raised my hands, not knowing what the hell to expect, and he took one of them and shook it heartily; then leaned over and gave me a ceremonial kiss on each cheek.

In a fraction of a second, his eyes communicated reams of information—about himself, his country, his situation—that he could and would never put into words.

Ayub obviously identified with my "tough Copp" role and wanted to acknowledge it. The last thing he wanted was to go back to his masters with the message that he had failed to placate the Great Satan's running dog on this tedious hostage issue. But now—in fact, weeks before—I had concluded that the Relative and Ayub were probably right: We were asking for something they just couldn't provide, at least as easily as we could provide our own tokens of good faith—ministers and missiles. But they sure as hell could try a little harder, which was the reason I rode roughshod over Ayub. As far as I was concerned, the ball was still in Rafsanjani's court, and time was quickly running out.

I bid Ayub a safe trip home and got back to business myself.


Over the next 10 days Ollie and I spoke from the secure communications set in North's office to the Relative, his aide, and Ayub in Tehran. They told us they were working hard on "the obstacles" (the hostages), but that the necessity of having to keep a low profile "while the storm blew over" was slowing things down.

"Can't you get them to pipe down?" the Iranians asked. "Can't you control your own press?" With their experience under the Shah as well as the Ayatollah, they just couldn't conceive of an independent media.

Still, we saw no indication that the Iranians were trying to pull away from us.

Firm evidence of Iran's continuing commitment to the plan came on December 10, when Ayub refused to meet with Charles Dunbar, George Schultz's State Department representative (a midlevel official from the Middle East bureau) in Frankfurt—one of the higher-level meetings the plan called for—unless Albert Hakim was present.

In this bizarre meeting, which George Cave also attended, Albert arranged to have his lawyer, Richard Janis, present, since he had reason to believe that Dunbar was commissioned not to support the initiative, but to torpedo it in the interests of keeping the State Department's institutional skirts clean. The first sign of this came during Dunbar's prep session with Hakim, during which Albert noticed the State Department man had no talking papers to work from—no agenda, only a vague desire to get the Iranian representative to tell him all he could about the Iran Initiative; in other words, to get information, but decline any substantive discussion; to *interrogate* Ayub, not to negotiate.

Albert immediately told Dunbar he could not participate under those conditions, which was basically a misrepresentation of the meeting to the Iranian delegation, and called me. He swore at Schultz like a sailor, which was just extraordinary for Albert, ordinarily one of the most self-possessed, civil-tongued men I ever knew.

Dunbar and Cave went ahead with the session, and the first thing Ayub said was that the Iranians intended to proceed with the nine-point plan, the one Schultz later expressed such shock about hearing of via his representative Dunbar. Schultz also claimed to be surprised and angered to learn that the CIA rep, George Cave, had met with Ayub separately after the meeting with Dunbar. Although I can understand Schultz's desire to backpedal, given the incredible heat everyone was taking at that time, I can't condone him for doing it. The plain facts are as follows:

- The nine points were negotiated ad ref, subject to executive approval, and subsequently had been approved by Schultz's own boss, President Reagan, standard operating procedure even in the State Department.
- The separate meeting between Cave and Ayub was entirely proper, given the negotiating history of the initiative.
- The history of the initiative was available to the State Department from the CIA and had been discussed in detail prior to the Dunbar-Ayub meeting.

In short, Schultz's reaction was the product of a politician's survival instinct directly at odds with his duties as secretary of state. The Iranians—facing firing squads, not just fiery editorials—showed a lot more courage than their American counterparts in sticking with the program they knew to be the official policy of the president of the United States. In that respect, they proved to be a lot more loyal to the American president and faithful to our national interests than some of our own administration teammates. A strong president would never have permitted such actions by a Cabinet officer—

another sign that the Iran-Contra contraption was now lurching monstrously out of control.

Reagan's handlers advised him to play ball with the press and release certain details on a piecemeal basis. Rather than satisfying the media's appetite, whetted by the whiff of scandal, it only excited them to a feeding frenzy. Reagan was assailed by increasingly belligerent and pointed questions everywhere he went: on the White House lawn, entering or leaving a public event, during photo ops with foreign and domestic dignitaries—the media had only one thing on its mind, and, by inference, so did the American people. In the end, the President and his advisors decided he should address the nation on November 13.

Cave and I were in North's office on November 12 talking to Ayub on the secure communications device when Ollie mentioned the speech and what he thought would be in it. Although he was sketchy on details, he thought the President would take a "real hard line" on his decision to open a dialogue with Iran, his role in supervising the initiative, and his decision to delay notifying Congress as long as American lives were at risk—namely, the remaining Lebanese hostages. (Congressional leaders had, by this time, been briefed, at least minimally, by the White House and CIA.)

I asked what Ollie thought an example of this "hard line" might be, and he produced a copy of the speech outline. In one place, the President was supposed to explain how the arms shipment was so small that it could fit on a single airplane—implying that it was mostly symbolic, but sounding very defensive. His basic approach, apparently, was that "We didn't do anything wrong, and by the way, it wasn't a very big mistake."

"This is the biggest bunch of watered-down drivel I've ever seen," I said. "Why not talk to the point? The President needs to make a hard-hitting speech showing he is fully in control. He needs to explain the strategic importance of this undertaking and point out that although it had not completely succeeded yet, it had not completely failed, either. There's still the potential for positive results; he should tell them he's going to continue the initiative as long as it holds out the promise of success."

Ollie gave me that pained, "Yeah, but—" look we had grown accustomed to giving each other over the last few months. He said, "Yeah, I agree with you personally, but I'm not the speech writer and I don't have the final word anyway."

"Who does? Don Regan?" I grunted.

"You betcha," Ollie said.

"Look, Ollie," I said as I slapped my knees and got up. "I'm going back to my office, and I'll draft the goddamned speech for the President. Maybe words on paper will convince you guys. I'm no longer in my commercial role, see? I'm putting on my old hat. As near as I can tell there is not a goddamned general within a mile of this place, and there has to be one because we're all going down the tubes!"

"Yes, sir!" North saluted with a grin.

"I tell you, this is an emergency, Ollie! Reagan's got to go out there and say, 'In 1980 you guys elected me by a substantial majority and in 1984 you reelected me by one of the biggest landslides in American electoral history. I regard that as a mandate to lead this country where I think it ought to go in foreign policy and in accordance with the Constitution.' He's got to act like Harry Truman and say, 'The buck stops here. These aren't easy choices. Sometimes you've got to make hard choices.' He should remind them that the Iran-Iraq war is a great opportunity for Soviet mischief in the area—say something like, 'We've had this clandestine project under way for some time to gain rapprochement with pragmatic factions within Iran that will help solve these problems, including the hostage situation. Unfortunately, it appears that attempt has failed for the time being—but we're not going to give up.' *That's* the speech he should be giving. I'll send a draft to you on the KL-43. I want your promise you'll take it to John Poindexter and voice my concerns to him, okay?"

"Sure, Dick. I can do that," Ollie said.

If Ollie honored his word and my two-page draft—more or less reflecting the above—made it to Poindexter, its spirit and text certainly was not approved up the chain of command. The President's November 13 speech was worse than disappointing; it was destructive. Ronald Reagan came across as fearful and uninformed—no comfort to our Iranian or Israeli counterparts, even though they were prepared for a propaganda broadside.

Even as propaganda, the speech propagated the wrong message. Reagan was vague on salient program details that had already been disclosed in the press and ignored completely the strategic aspects, the foundation of the initiative. It occurred to me that what I was seeing, perhaps, was a man whose obsession with the hostages had, in fact, turned the initiative upside-down even in his own mind—and he understandably felt guilty and threatened by it. It was the kind of response I would have expected with Regan and Schultz calling the shots on the President's response instead of Poindexter, who was obviously being distanced from the President. The speech was poorly received even by those not privy to inside information—and rightly so. It was awful.

I watched the speech on television at home, cursing the screen like a sailor. My oldest daughter Julie was married and out of the house, and the twins were tuned to whatever teenagers listen to through those earphones, but even they weren't ignorant—from television and friends—that their dad's world once again seemed to be crumbling around him.

After the speech, I thought the only thing that could make the situation worse would be a fumble at the press conference, which is exactly what happened. The newspeople seemed a hell of a lot better informed than our President on the whole affair, and by the time it was over I realized for the first time what a vacuum existed at the upper reaches of the White House when it came to practical statecraft. I don't mean just Ronald Reagan, but his band of advisors who misdiagnosed a blown covert operation as another Watergate. I literally felt sick to my stomach.

Part of my rage and disgust was with the politicians, but most of it came from a sense of betrayal—that hollow feeling of impending, inescapable doom. Heightening all this was my acute personal disappointment at seeing what I had hoped would be my entrée back into government service, to complete a career I had trained for all my life, vanish in a puff of smoke.

This was no reprise of the Edwin Wilson smear job. This was ground zero at Hiroshima—and there wasn't a damn thing I could do about it!

After the press conference, I called Ollie, and we decided to warn the Relative and Nir immediately. Albert was our spearhead on this, communicating a great deal of sensitive, nuanced information from English into Farsi and back again. Everybody tried to figure out just what might happen next and how to prepare for it.

The media piranha now sensed the President's thrashing, and their attacks on the administration went from merely rude and sensational to vicious. The House and Senate began scheduling briefings with virtually any government agency they thought might've had anything to do with Iran or the Contras. For all intents and purposes, the U.S. government stopped.

William Casey was called to appear on November 21 before the House Select Committee on Intelligence, which I thought was a much-needed opportunity to start addressing all the far-out rumors that whirled up like waterspouts over the ocean of unfathomable "facts." Cave and North began preparing chronologies and narrations from the tangle of records, personal notebooks, and individual recollections—good as far as it went, but it would later allow the usual honest mistakes and variations among perceptions to be misconstrued as dark conspiracies to deceive the public. The Iran Initiative and Contra support plan had officially become "affairs" and were beginning to take on lives of their own.

On the morning of November 18, Ollie asked me to come by his office and meet with his assistant, Bob Earl, another aide, and Howard Teicher—the chronology team. I had already seen some of their preliminary drafts and contributed what I could from my own notes and memory, but until that morning I had not reviewed the completed talking papers.

As far as I could see, the CIA's version was the least accurate, which was understandable. They had not been present at many of the negotiating and planning sessions, so Casey's House briefing materials, if that was all he used, were going to be incomplete and subject to revision later. This could cause a real problem, since revisions to a previous story would only undermine his credibility. To their credit, Ollie and his people were genuinely trying to untangle a real plate of spaghetti and arrive at a historically accurate record of the Iran Initiative rather than a set of "defensible positions" aimed at defusing political criticism. Unfortunately, the director was going up on Capitol Hill in only two days, so a final draft had to be coordinated with the relevant honchos and put into Casey's hands almost immediately, which left precious little time for fact checking and revision.

The biggest mistake I found—and I immediately called it to North's and Teicher's attention—was a statement that the President was upset with the Israelis over the August–September 1985 TOW deliveries and that McFarlane and the rest of the NSC staff did not know the true nature of the Israeli I-HAWK delivery that November. This assertion was a lot different from the earlier draft I had seen and was at variance with the facts, as I understood them. Both Ollie and Bud had told me a year before that the President had approved the Israeli TOW shipment as early as July 1985; and I *knew* Bud and Ollie were both aware that the content of the November shipment was not "oil-drilling equipment," the official cover, but I-HAWKs.

When I mentioned this to Ollie, expecting him to say something like, "Oh yeah, you're right!" and get out his red pencil, he just gave me a funny look and shrugged.

"Bud rewrote that last night," he said.

I gave him a blank stare. "Yeah? So? Bud rewrote it wrong. If the director doesn't want to address the issue, then the director should just leave it out. But we've got to have the correct facts down on paper. This is a nonissue. Who cares?"

Ollie broke eye contact and stared at the ceiling, just like a miniature Casey, and said, "It will be a problem with the lawyers. Remember—Sporkin had a problem with it earlier."

I was unaware that Stanley Sporkin, general counsel to the CIA, "had a problem with it," and replied, "Still, it's a matter of very little importance at most because whether the President approved it before or after the fact, he *approved* it."

Ollie nodded and went back to his paperwork. I got the chilling feeling that whether or not he agreed with me, the new, phony version would stand.

"Well," I sighed, "I guess I get the picture, now. I'll get out of your hair. I'm not going to be a part of this anymore," and I got up and left.

I went back to my office feeling a thousand years old. *Why* would Bud get so fussy about misrepresenting two such minor points—and cow Ollie into going along with him—particularly when the rest of the paper contained stuff I found to be a lot more explosive politically—namely, all the quid pro quos for missiles and "boxes" that, retrospectively, could be construed as strictly arms-for-hostages deals? Something fishy was going on, but at the time, with all the shouting, I just couldn't see the larger picture these smaller fragments were beginning to form. If somebody wanted to cover things up and fabricate evidence, to represent the initiative as something other than what it was, there were a lot better ways to do it.

The real agenda, of course, was to begin spinning a web of lies that, while remaining more or less faithful to the actual story, tried to isolate the President from that story. This focused on what the politicians (as opposed to the statesmen) in both camps viewed as the "real issue," what the President knew and when he knew it, and the media sniffed it out like sharks on the trail of blood. It was a self-inflicted wound that would only get wider, deeper, and more infected as time went by. Ultimately, the debate would ignore the main questions: Was postrevolutionary Iran vital to U.S. interests? Were the Contras worth supporting? Were the methods chosen to do both in conformity to legal and historical precedents? In their rush to prevent another Watergate, the cover-up artists managed to convey exactly the wrong message.

As always, the characters who play this game think their trump card— "I was only trying to protect the President"—will excuse them, which was eventually the position Bud took. How an experienced guy like that can conclude that sidetracking major security issues and promoting nonissues into major debacles actually helps anyone, especially the President, is beyond me. Their real concerns should have been: "We were treading dangerously close to an arms-for-hostages deal; how can we convince Congress and the people that our intentions were honorable and not in contravention of our overall antiterrorist policies? How can we convince our Arab friends that our partnership with Israel in this important endeavor was to their best interests, too? How can we convince Congress that our delay in notifying them of the President's covert action finding was not an intent to break the law but one of several unfortunate side effects resulting from a string of delays that we believed day by day, month by month, we were always on the verge of overcoming?"

All this was nothing new. These were the same concerns Cap Weinberger had raised a year earlier. The simple fact is, *public* public policy debate in this country does not happen on that plane. It focuses on who the "public champion" is and if he's got cracks in his armor—period. That's *politics*— and on the morning of November 18 that's how the Iran Initiative and Contra support effort got demoted from matters of state security to a scandal.

Unfortunately, if Reagan's waffly speech and press conference threw scraps to a scandal-hungry media, Casey's less-than-candid Congressional briefing served up a banquet. Nothing starts the opposition salivating in Washington like the whiff of weakness, and nothing signals weakness more than fear—and "all the President's men," especially at the highest echelons, were now giving Congress and the media a snootful.

The administration's political enemies wasted no time in responding.

As soon as Casey's "secret" briefing was over, House Speaker Jim Wright justified every concern the White House had about forwarding the January 17 finding to Congress by immediately disclosing everything he'd heard to the press. This created a tornado inside a hurricane, and the reporters went absolutely crazy. By November 21, media pressure was so intense that President Reagan, Don Regan, and Ed Meese decided that Meese should conduct a showcase internal investigation to convince the nation that (a) all Iran-related actions had been legal and proper, and (b) the President didn't know much about them anyway.

On Saturday, November 22, I talked to Ollie on the phone about the investigation and suggested he might want to meet with my attorney, Tom Green, immediately, if not sooner.

At first, Ollie couldn't understand why I would make this suggestion. Like me when the Edwin Wilson scandal erupted, he naively assumed the Justice Department was there to do just that: to pursue justice, to bear any burden and oppose any foe—just like us—in the name of truth, freedom, and the American way. That's nice work if you can get it, but that's not what political prosecutions are about. I convinced him that talking to a lawyer wouldn't hurt, and that's what we did later in the day.

The inquiry began with Justice Department and FBI agents scouring the files at North's office, a search that continued through the weekend. They got more than they bargained for. Among Ollie's already partially sanitized files they found an unsigned think-piece dating from April 1986, written by him presumably to Poindexter, outlining where the Iran Initiative stood, its prospects for the next month, and an offhand comment that if everything happened as planned with Ghorbanifar and the Iranians, as much as $12 million could be "diverted to the Contras."

These couple of lines in an otherwise bland and routine memo galvanized the investigation and, with only the words and none of the music that went with them, gave free rein to scurrilous imaginations: Whose money are we spending here, Mr. North? And didn't Mr. Boland's amendment say something about keeping the U.S. wallet shut?

Meese personally interviewed Ollie on Sunday, November 23. North didn't know the investigators had this paper and was absolutely stunned to see it in Meese's hand. Although it dealt with a speculative action that never came to fruition, it raised one of those "Have you stopped beating your wife?" kinds of questions. No, Ollie answered, that "diversion" did not take place; but yes, some "diversions" had occurred, although he did not know to what extent. Meese, apparently, did not question him further on this crucial point.

The next day, Meese discussed the paper with the President and Don Regan, and later, separately, with Poindexter.

On Tuesday, Meese was back in the White House, white-faced. In essence, he said, this was the infamous smoking gun, the Son-of-Watergate. Congress and the media would be talking impeachment as soon as this got out; they'd be in no mood to discuss the distinctions between private and public funds. All they would see is an NSC internal document that referred to proceeds from one unpopular covert program somehow being "diverted" to fuel another that the media (but by no means the American people) had labeled politically incorrect. The court of public opinion, let alone Congressional hearings, would have no patience for arguing tedious facts and technicalities. Nobody drawing a U.S. government paycheck is supposed to even *think* the word Contra, even if the law was set up specifically to exclude certain agencies, like the NSC, from that prohibition. The game just isn't played like that—especially on television.

Through their own actions, though, the President's mishandlers had just guaranteed that it would.


On Tuesday just before Meese and the President went on television, I heard that Poindexter was resigning. I couldn't believe it and immediately called John, but his aide—a Commander Thompson—refused to put me through. John's ideas about the presidency and government in general were more utopian than mine. Maybe that was because his insight and optimism allowed him to see the glass half-full whereas the scars from my own bruising years in the lower echelons caused me to see it as half empty—I don't know. I also didn't know why John wasn't taking my calls. He may have been ordered to do so by the President or advised by counsel to avoid me—but I couldn't believe he really thought that crawling into our own little bunkers would make things better.

I told Commander Thompson in no uncertain terms to put me through or I would come down to his office, put my size nines through the seat of his pants, and make the connection myself.

After a pause, a familiar voice came on the line. "Hello, Dick. This is John."

"John—what in the name of God is going on down there? Meese is running around like an idiot! This whole thing is going to wipe us out unless somebody stops the avalanche."

Poindexter—reflective, stoic, philosophical—explained that he was going to step down, ostensibly to save the President.

"The hell you are!" I said. "Stay at your post, Admiral. Force the President to step up to the plate and take responsibility for his actions, like Truman, Eisenhower, Kennedy. Even Nixon and Carter did that!"

"Meese was just in here."

"I don't give a damn about Meese!"

"You don't understand, Dick. He's going on the air. He's going to have a press conference."

Now smoke was coming out of my ears. I told Poindexter, "I would like to talk to the President."

"It's too late," he said. "They're building a wall around him."

"That's no good, John. Somebody with some brains has got to talk to the President."

"Dick, the tragedy is that guys like you, who should get medals, will be condemned—"

It was as if he didn't hear me. The Admiral's ship had been torpedoed, the bow had slipped below the waves, and he was already making wistful speeches on the poop deck. Nuts to that.

I rang off and got ready for another meeting with North and Tom Green.

Having had the experience of the Wilson affair, Tom was no virgin when it came to politically inspired assaults, yet even he had paled visibly when Ollie first told him his story. He sensed a political disaster of Biblical proportions in the making, and had gone on Monday to see Bradford Reynolds, Meese's point man during the weekend investigation.

Reynolds, an assistant attorney general for civil rights and Meese's own, if unsuccessful, candidate for deputy attorney general, was his boss's longtime friend and troubleshooter. Although Tom was laboring under the most cursory briefing by me and Ollie, he tried valiantly to explain to Reynolds the true nature of the President's Iran Initiative and interim Contra support plan.

That evening, he consulted again with Ollie and me and went back to Reynolds's office on Tuesday, November 25, 1986. His message was simple: Let's not do anything hasty that will turn this brushfire into a major conflagration. His main point was that going public with the "diversion" aspect would create more heat than light. The principals expected a diplomatic breakthrough on the Iranian front, and a repeal of the Boland Amendment had already taken place. There were no "diversions," but instead donations or cash advances from a private commercial undertaking—for God's sake, let's use our heads and get all the facts. As an example of the need for deliberation, Tom pointed out that Ollie couldn't even testify for sure that Contra-related payouts from Iranian profits ever *had* taken place—that simply wasn't his end of the log. Only Secord, Hakim, and Zucker had definitive knowledge in this area.

So, Tom said, the whole money issue was a red herring because according to the presidential finding these funds were private-sector. The fact that the private parties involved *also* had nonmonetary reasons to assist the U.S. government in its policy objectives was neither here nor there. As long as the proper rules, regulations, and public laws were observed, our critics were out of luck.

Tom's intention was to prove to Reynolds that North had no real working knowledge of the finances in either project and that no public disclosures should be made until *accurate* statements could be prepared. In these areas Green appeared to be successful.

Reynolds agreed, just moments before Meese's national television appearance, that the Justice Department would make no public announcement of the so-called diversion until a more deliberate and comprehensive investigation would be made. He therefore must have been floored, like the rest of us, when his boss went ahead on national television and announced, after being introduced by President Reagan himself, that John Poindexter was resigning and Oliver North had been dismissed. Further, Meese "estimated" that some $10 to $30 million had been "diverted from Iran arms sales to the Contras."

Tom Green heard the speech on a taxicab radio returning to his office; I saw it on television. I said aloud, "Meese is dead wrong. How could he have come to such conclusions after a weekend investigation?" It was a stunning event—yet another betrayal by our own government.

When the speech was over, I called Ami Nir in Tel Aviv, where it was just about 9 P.M. I told him about the broadcast and how the top U.S. leadership had apparently made up its mind to ignore "the plan." Nir couldn't believe it and neither could I. The Israelis had agreed to say they had shipped the arms to Iran, which, in essence, was true since that's where all the flights originated. Plus, they were an approved "end user" that could buy things the Iranians wanted from CIA stock. They were ready to take the political heat, since nobody was going to vote anybody out of office in Jerusalem for playing up to the Iranians; it had been a cornerstone of Israeli foreign policy for years. And, as everyone also knew, Israel had a great many friends in Congress. Most representatives would much rather tackle the President than "America's trustiest Middle East ally." Israel could weather the storm and so would the administration.

Yet Meese had ignored even this escape valve. Worse, he didn't even have enough sense to call the Israeli Prime Minister in advance. Instead, without consultation, he said the Israelis were responsible for funding the Contras.

Nir called Prime Minister Shamir, and Shamir called an emergency Cabinet meeting for 2:00 A.M. that same morning. Both Shimon Peres and Shamir called Meese and complained bitterly about the American betrayal of the joint venture. Later, George Shultz joined the conference call. Nir, who was in the room with Peres and Shamir, later told me he had never seen them so upset.

Referring to Meese's allegation that Israel funded the Contras with supposedly U.S.-owned money, Nir said, "Your people have done the one thing that we cannot accept, and that is to pit us against the Congress. You can never put us in that position. We won't accept it."

Nir later thanked me for tipping them off at least a few hours before word of Meese's "revelations" could hit Israeli newsstands.

"M Day," as I have come to refer to Meese's November 25 speech, had two immediate consequences, neither of which Reagan's handlers anticipated in their headlong panic.

First, it sounded the "abandon ship" bell to everyone involved in either operation, within or outside the United States. It was now every man for himself. A Chinese wall was snugly in place around the Chief Executive—nobody but the inner circle would ever again be allowed to penetrate it.

Second, in one fell swoop it changed the entire debate from presidential leadership and difficult policy choices to criminal conspiracy, which was absolute lunacy.

Unless the last two years had been one long hallucination, the facts were these: I had been asked by bona fide representatives of the President, two national security advisors and their chief counterterrorist aide, to help the President in a delicate covert foreign policy initiative. I had, with the blessing and encouragement of these same people, developed a second, more reliable channel to accomplish our national objectives in Iran. These same people, in addition to the director of the CIA—on three separate occasions—reinforced this program and the President's commitment to it on a regular basis with information and encouragement.

Yet, on the strength of a politically inspired and amateurish weekend investigation, and despite agreement from the principal investigator that such disclosures were premature, and without any prior notice or coordination with Israel, our chief ally in the project, *all* these facts were disregarded. In their place came the fiction of "rogue advisors" and "opportunistic profiteers" running an illegal guns-for-hostages scam to skim profits from a trusting President (and a heroic but uninformed Congress) to support the Contra strongmen in Central America.

That was now the official story.

Amazingly, all sides found this false scenario much more appealing than the truth. Reagan's inner circle liked it because painting the operatives as criminals and brigands further distanced them from the "Teflon" president. Democratic Congressional investigators liked it because it held a lot more potential for impeaching or at least neutralizing a popular president of the opposite party. The media liked it because it was a delicious scandal that played better on prime time than tedious legal and policy debates.

The afternoon following the Reagan-Meese follies, North (who had just become the first man in history to get fired on national television) and Tom Green met me in a hotel room at the Sheraton in Tyson's Corner to try to figure out what it all meant and what we were going to do to protect ourselves. Tom had just left the room for a moment when Ollie got a call from Vice

President Bush. Bush praised him as a hero, one for whom he had the highest regard. After the call was over and Ollie relayed this information, I asked him:

"If that was the Vice President, why in the name of God didn't you explain things to him?"

"Like what?" Ollie asked.

"Well, for starters, they didn't even give you the courtesy of informing you in advance that they were going to depict you as a criminal, fire you, and throw you to the wolves. I would've told old George exactly what was going on!"

"Well," Ollie demurred, as he does very easily when authority figures are involved, "Bush didn't know a whole lot about it."

That may have been true of the cover-up, but it sure didn't apply to the initiative. Bush was no figurehead vice president, and he knew what combat was like. He could've and should've done something to save his men.

About two hours later, after Tom Green had returned, President Reagan called Ollie. Despite all that had happened, North actually came to attention when he picked up the phone—a completely spontaneous, touching, and, I think, telling gesture on Ollie's part. Colonel Chauvin, say goodbye to the Gipper.

The President told North he was "a national hero."

"Well, Mr. President," Ollie answered, "I'm just sorry that my attempts to serve you have turned out as they have."

"Let me talk to him," I asked.

Ollie glanced at me but continued listening to the President.

"Let me talk to him!" I said loudly, hoping to be heard on the other end. It was not a request.

Ollie hung up looking proud and drained.

*Jesus,* I thought. I was so mad I could hardly speak. All the President had to do was make one ceremonial, hypocritical phone call and Ollie was floating on cloud nine.

Tom took my arm and said, "Okay, Dick. Forget about it. We've got a war on our hands. We've got to get Ollie his own lawyer."

He was right, of course, and the next day he did. I think it took a while for the enormity of it all to really sink in for Ollie—for it to register as a problem that he was "authorized" to do something about. As far as he was concerned, we were all still team members—the President, Meese, me, himself, Poindexter—who were just playing different roles now. A dyed-in-the-wool military man, Ollie knows you don't whine when the artillery rounds streak in. You just hunker down and take it. He didn't realize, though, that we were the only guys left in the foxhole. I couldn't really blame him. He hadn't had the same experience I'd had in the Edwin Wilson affair. I must've sounded pretty bitter, if not paranoid, to Ollie back then, although later we'd be singing in perfect harmony.

Ollie would later say that he as much as told Reagan on several occasions that if the going got tough, he'd do everything he could to save the President; however, if he, North, ended up in trouble, he would expect a Presidential pardon. He certainly didn't talk that way during the phone call, so I have no way of knowing if it is true, but it's something that sounds plausible: North to stick up for his rights and the President to ignore them.

So, Ollie went his way with his lawyer, and I went my way with mine. Except for a few loose ends (and a number of subsequent secret meetings I would have with Nir), the Iran Initiative and the Contra support effort were essentially over for both of us. As far as the Iranians were concerned, Meese's injudicious remarks only reinforced their need to be discreet—a fact we certainly appreciated, particularly since their opposition mullahs were now crowing about how pure-hearted Iran had once again beaten us black-hearted Westerners at our own vile game. This was the beginning of the Ayatollah's "entrapment" theory, which held that the whole arms exchange had been an Iranian sting operation. It was a silly Persian fable, but it at least allowed the second channel to stay open a few months longer than it might have had the Iranians come down as hard on its own people as the administration came down on us.

After being at sea for eight months and waiting offshore for six weeks after the November 25 Meese announcement, the *Erria*, on orders from me after consultation with Ami Nir, returned the container of rifles and some medical stores to Haifa, where they were transferred to the Israeli Defense Force, and sailed for its home port in Denmark, which it reached on January 10, 1987. It was impounded at once because of liens placed against it by the shipping agent, whom we owed upwards of $200,000. We suspected we could never pay them because the U.S. government had asked Switzerland to freeze our accounts (which included our reserves for self-insurance and other costs) in the interim, which they did. As a result, the shipper could only take his place in a long line of creditors.

In Central America, the enterprise's equipment and facilities were essentially quarantined—unused even by the CIA when it took over Contra support after the Boland Amendments were repealed in August 1986. I took this as a personal insult, since I had made clear to Bill Casey several times that the assets would be his when we withdrew. Instead, the CIA publicly refused to touch the assets because they were, as they put it, "tainted." They feared that if they took over our operation and folded it back into theirs, people would claim they had been running it all along in violation of the Boland injunctions. All the blood, sweat, and money that went into building the airlift operation (we had successfully dropped over a hundred tons of small arms and ammunition up to that time) were ignored. After the Wilson smear five years earlier, I probably should have understood the CIA's attitude better, but at the time it really stung.

On December 19, 1986, President Reagan appointed the now-infamous independent counsel, special prosecutor Judge Lawrence Walsh, a senseless and desperate act that would only obscure and prolong the investigation and end up destroying the lives of all the principals involved. When it was clear that our Swiss accounts had been targeted, CSF took the initiative and began liquidating the stocks and bonds where the money was parked. The total estimated cash balance at the end of the operation was around $8.2 million, with unpaid bills amounting to approximately $1.5 million, against which another several million dollars in legal fees would be added over the next six years.

Had I known that the Iran-Contra adventure would end with everybody getting out their lawyers, I would've liquidated the entire enterprise in the summer of 1986. At minimum, I would've made sure some sort of legal defense fund was set aside in a safe haven. As it was, I would soon find myself in even worse financial shape than I had been in 1983.

In a way, I envied Ollie the luxury of his continued sense of devotion—his blind loyalty to the administration. I went into the operation with both eyes open, hoping not only to help the Contras and advance our national interest in Iran, but to win back my political reputation and a chance to serve again in a high-level official capacity, one for which I had trained and prepared all my life. Now that seemed gone forever. Although the sunshine patriots and fair-weather sailors had once again revealed themselves for what they were, I had nobody to blame but myself. Nobody said it was going to be fair.

I had been shocked many times by the amateurism, incompetence, and plain bad judgment of "our team," but I always hung in there—tried to repair what I could and work around what I couldn't. I'd tell myself: This funny business won't last forever. If someone had slipped the front page of the November 26, 1986 *Washington Post* into a time machine and had me read it, say, in the middle of the previous April, I wouldn't have believed it. After the Wilson fiasco, I vowed I would never again be washed down the political gutter.

But here I was. Go figure.

The next several years of my life belonged to the media and the lawyers.

When you become notorious, you and your family lose your civil rights—or even the right to civil treatment. Reporters, stringers, and photographers from several nations swarmed over us, literally like flies. They trespassed on our property, stuck cameras in our windows, shouted bellicose questions whenever we came within earshot, and chased our cars wherever we went.

Our appeals for relief went unheeded. Everyone presumed I must be guilty of *something*, and, tacitly or intentionally, the media played along with the prosecutors, hoping that unrelenting pressure would make me crack and thereby crack the case. It was a war of nerves, a siege, in which all the resources were on one side. Had it not been for loyal friends like Jim Ahmann, Bob Dutton, Bill Cox, and Hienie Aderholt, as well as letters of support from a great many of my West Point classmates, their "head games" might have succeeded—if not against me, then against my family. Just as the rules of law give more latitude to the prosecution than the defense (in power of discovery, subpoena, and so on), so does the unremitting media pressure sap a defendant's strength when he needs it most.

One of the reasons I was not too concerned about not taking a profit from our Iran-Contra transactions was my belief that if an appointive, higher-level government job did not materialize when the projects were over, I would still be well placed commercially to earn a good living—perhaps, as Albert was hoping, through contacts pioneered through the second channel. He saw a big future in Iranian civil sector countertrade—food, clothing, minerals (a long list), for oil. He curried his commercial contacts for several months after M Day (he even met a few times with Ayub), trading medical equipment (wheelchairs, prosthetics, and the like) for Persian carpets, which he resold in Europe and the U.S., trying gamely to restore his commercial life. The last thing either of us expected was a total shutdown of *all* our options following abandonment by our government, the Congressional inquisition, and our vilification in the press, but that's essentially what happened.

From December 1986 through April 1987, I refused on Tom's advice to make any on-the-record comments, including giving testimony to the Tower Commission (a Presidential fact-finding task force led by Senators John Tower and Edmund Muskie, and presidential advisor Brent Scowcroft). Although the Commission did a good job under the circumstances, their real agenda seemed to be fending off criticism of President Reagan, which, in my opinion, was incompatible with the facts. What amazes me is not the gaps and inaccuracies in its report, published in late February 1987, of which there are many, but that they were able to assemble as cogent a picture as they did.

In early 1987, Albert and I were served subpoenas by John Kecker, a lead attorney for the special prosecutor and one who reported directly to Judge Walsh, to appear at the federal district courthouse on a variety of occasions.

On March 25, 1987, our motion to reconsider Judge Aubrey Robinson's order to deliver all records of Stanford Technology Trading Group, Inc. was rejected. However, negotiations did narrow the scope of the subpoena to permit the special prosecutor's agents to come into my office, inspect the records, and physically remove any documents they wanted for copying—at their expense—and return them after a few days. This was at least a small improvement over having to provide the usual (and mostly useless) carload of data that characterizes most discovery phases.

The next issue was what the prosecutors were really interested in—delivery of all the records related to our foreign corporations: Energy Resources, Inc.; Lake Resources, Inc.; the Udall Research Corp.; and so forth, all Panamanian companies. I took the witness stand and Tom asked, "Do you have in your possession or control any of these records for any of these foreign companies?" and I answered, "No."

The judge said, "Thank you very much. You are dismissed."

This surprised Kecker, who was unprepared for my response and lost his opportunity to cross-examine me. It set up an informal exchange that was to prove typical of many we would have with representatives of the special prosecutor and house counsel.

With Tom Green and me out on the street after the session, Kecker asked, "Is there no way you can exert control over these companies?"

"That's what I just said under oath, Mr. Kecker," and added, "if it weren't for the special prosecutor, nobody would've taken the Fifth Amendment, and the story would've been out months ago. If you want a villain for this piece, go see Ed Meese. He circumscribed this whole mess by raising the question of criminality. He's not concerned with the interests of the country. He just wants to protect the President, but he's doing it in a very shortsighted way. Now, you're an attorney. Tell me what you'd do if you were suddenly made the subject of a criminal investigation about a series of international activities you undertook at the behest of the President."

"I understand," he said, "but you should trust us. If you haven't done anything wrong, there will be no problems."

Tom Green, who had held my hand through a similar speech by Ted Greenberg in the Edwin Wilson investigation, recognized this offer at once as a cruel joke, and interjected, "We *don't* trust you. You are here to indict."

Kecker smiled, and we agreed to disagree.

Also in March 1987, *U.S. News and World Report* ran a cover story in which Iran claimed the entire U.S.-Israeli operation had been the result of a plot devised by the Ayatollah Khomeini two years earlier to stimulate factionalism and disunity in the Iranian government, flush out his opponents, and thus draw the U.S. into a sophisticated trap that would provide both arms for the Iran-Iraq war and give the Ayatollah yet another opportunity to humiliate the Great Satan.

This "sting story" was the source of great amusement for those of us who had been there. Not only had Iran failed to get any significant arms out of the deal, but the project exploded at precisely the point when a breakthrough was possible and substantial aid *might* have been available from the U.S. Also, the factionalism within the Tehran government needed no stimulation and was anything but a source of comfort to the Ayatollah.

In February 1987, Green and I met with John Nields, chief counsel for the House Select Committee that had been created in early January (along with a Senate Select Committee) to investigate and report on what had now become universally known as the Iran-Contra scandal. As is customary prior to any Congressional hearing, witnesses are located and their potential "contribution" is carefully screened by attorneys and Congressional staff.

After an early bit of toe-dancing, the slim, long-haired Nields said that his main interest lay in two "special areas," and if I had knowledge (and was cooperative) in those areas, I would probably be granted immunity—despite the defamatory articles about me circulating in the press at the time.

I replied that I was indifferent to immunity (North, Poindexter, and Hakim would later be granted limited immunity in areas Nields felt would have minimal impact on the special prosecutor). Tom was more adamant, immediately affirming that I was guilty of no misconduct and that much of the information in the press was just plain wrong, as well as scurrilous.

I was less concerned about being pilloried in the press than being maligned even further in official circles, which was bound to happen if the investigators didn't start off with (a) a few straight facts, which they weren't getting from the White House, and (b) a true picture of the overall operation regarding both the Iranians and the Contras. I had no illusions; these guys were here to put people out of business, if not in jail, and beat up on the President any way they could, and I didn't want to volunteer more than was strictly necessary, since after the Wilson affair I knew how such witch-hunts worked.

Nields's first area of concern involved relationships among U.S. government officials: Who met with whom, and what did they say and do? The second had to do with money—the main agenda of Arthur Liman, the Senate Committee's Wall Street attorney who seemed to believe the world was composed of people out only to make a fast buck, like Michael Milken, whom he later defended. By his own admission, any other motivations—patriotism, personal loyalty, belief in certain ideals—just didn't register for him. As a consequence, the investigation tended to mold itself in Liman's image: "Follow the money."

Nields too wondered about the money. I told him that I knew about the money in a macro sense, like any chief operating officer knows about budgets and reserves, but little about its micro details: exactly how, when, and how much people got paid, how and when money was collected and disbursed, and so on. In short, I was the enterprise's operations and chief executive officer, not its treasurer or comptroller. Those duties were up to Albert Hakim and Bill Zucker.

"Very well," Nields said. "How much money is left?"

"A lot," Tom said.

"How much is a lot?" Nields looked at me.

"A bunch," I smiled, and he smiled back. We had now established, at least, the difference between the operations officer and the comptroller.

"Did you have much contact with senior U.S. government officials outside of Ollie North?" Nields asked.

"Of course I did."

"With whom, for instance?"

"Bud McFarlane on several occasions; John Poindexter, of course. And both of North's assistants, as well as Howard Teicher and other officials at the CIA—including two Central American chiefs of station, and the director himself on several occasions. At State, I was in contact with U.S. Ambassador Robert Corr in El Salvador and the CIA station chief in Costa Rica. From the Pentagon, I worked with the military group chief in El Salvador."

Nields and his Republican minority counsel took copious notes.

"Let's go back to November 1985. Just what was the U.S. government doing at the time of the abortive HAWK shipment to Iran through Portugal? How much do you know about this activity?"

"I think I know more about it than anyone else."

"Why is that?"

"Because I'm the guy they sent in at the last minute to unravel the snarl in logistics—"

"We're not interested in logistics," Nields said. "We know about that."

"Then I was asked to go to Israel and investigate to get to the bottom of the story—which I did, and reported it to the White House."

Tom Green got real antsy at this point—we were getting into details he didn't know about—but I knew exactly why Nields was interested. Nields was aware of the changing versions of Casey's story prepared by the NSC before he testified on November 21, 1986, before the House Intelligence Committee: when and how the President had approved the Israeli TOW and I-HAWK missile transactions. McFarlane had told the Tower Commission he made certain changes in the draft testimony to protect the President. The problem was that Nields and the other investigators ascribed dark and nefarious motivations to this change. They couldn't accept the fact that it arose from a simple, stupid blunder on McFarlane's part—a misguided desire to shield the President from responsibilities that most certainly had been his.

I relayed to Nields the story of my visit to Portugal and subsequent investigation in Israel during which the Israeli Ministry of Defense, thinking I knew about the earlier TOW transactions, confronted me with the problem of their replenishment—and, specifically, *who* was going to pay for them. I told Nields that General Meron in Tel Aviv mentioned that McFarlane had assured Defense Minister Rabin that he, McFarlane, would "take care of that problem," an approximately $3 million problem that, as far as I knew, the Pentagon had no legal way to pay for. I felt at the time there was some misunderstanding on this point between Bud and Rabin—and perhaps in Bud's mind as well—that needed to be resolved. It was a significant blunder on Bud's part to promise the Israelis that the 508 TOWs would be replaced at no cost to them. It was an error the CIA general counsel, Stanley Sporkin, picked up in December 1985, when the CIA was trying to decide how to protect the President with a written, after-the-fact finding (different from the January 17, 1986 finding) covering the preceding transactions.

"So," I told Nields, "there were really two problems with the President's oral approval of the TOW and I-HAWK deals. One was a political problem that McFarlane created by talking through his hat about who would pick up the tab. The other was the practical problem of who would pony up the $3 million or so, which haunted us for a long time."

As I had guessed, the House Committee was completely in the dark on this and was also unaware that I had gone to the White House twice in mid-November 1986, to review the various versions of the draft testimony being prepared for Casey. I gave Nields the names of the people who had been in North's office and felt certain at least one or two of them would recall my taking exception to McFarlane's creative editing of the final version. I said both sides seemed to be making a federal case (literally) out of a nonproblem by focusing on how and when the President approved the transfers. I blamed the investigators far less for this than I blamed McFarlane, who had a fixation on creating a fairy story to give "plausible deniability" to a President who didn't need it. I even told Ollie at the time, "The Israelis will never sit still for such a story—and if you come up with a yarn they can't or won't backstop, it will unravel quickly. These guys aren't fools. Since the President approved it in July or August of 1985 and we all knew he approved it, why not say so and get on to bigger issues?"

Plausible deniability is and always will be an important tool for covert operations, but it has to be built into the plan. You can't jury-rig something after the fact, which was simply an extension of the irritating amateurism that affected the whole Iran Initiative. I was doubly upset about this now, with Congressional hearings looming, and really ticked at McFarlane and disappointed in Ollie for going along with him because we were no longer fussing with talking papers, but giving testimony under oath to Congress. There is a *big* difference between peddling disinformation as a cover story and committing perjury. When the project goes south and you're caught in the spotlight, you simply refuse to discuss what you don't want to discuss; you don't lie about it and create phony evidence. Nields understood this, which was why I gave him the facts.

Nields and I met again a few days later in Tom Green's office. He said he was preparing an outline, or rather *gaps* in an outline—holes in the overall story he thought I would be able to analyze and fill in, particularly about CIA involvement, which was more extensive than any investigator realized with both Iran and the Contras. For his part, Tom thought I was crazy, giving up my Fifth Amendment rights to cooperate so freely and openly with people

342 Honored and Betrayed

who admitted they were out for scalps. Yet I understood what Nields was up against. "Talking to them [the special prosecutor and his people] is like talking to the wall," Nields said once in disgust. I also knew I was about the only guy around who could or would help. I guess, like Ollie, I've got my own blind spots. In the end, Nields was at least fair, which is more than I can say for the special prosecutor's people.

When the Select Committees began gearing up for the hearings in the spring and summer of 1987, they faced a number of practical problems, not the least of which was choosing a lead witness. Since the whole thing was viewed as a referendum on the Reagan administration, a televised gladiatorial event in which the trappings of trial, if not its substance, were going to be present, the first few sessions would set the tone for the whole public portion of the investigation. I was concerned that the tone be as high-minded and substantive as possible.

Naturally, Bud McFarlane and Ollie North were the leading candidates to face the committees first. Tom and I had a pretty good working relationship with Nields by this time, and we felt that either would be a bad choice.

Ollie's attorney was being very hard-line with everyone, especially Liman, who was adversarial to begin with. The Committees realized that by compelling North's testimony, they'd have to grant him Congressional immunity, which at the time was being negotiated and was something the investigators weren't ready to concede. Consequently, the special prosecutor, Lawrence Walsh, had asked the committees to hold off on North.

Bud was their next choice, but I think Nields convinced them from his discussions with me that McFarlane was too far removed from the details to know very much of the story. Besides, Bud had bought into the stonewall, disinformation plan Meese and the administration's inner circle had adopted to defend the President. Between his lack of real knowledge and motivation to dissemble (not to mention his affinity for dense, compound-complex answers), starting with him would likely have only confused the issue.

That left me.

Testifying before the Iran-Contra Committee was the most intimidating experience of my life—and that includes my share of physical as well as bureaucratic battles. At least when you're dodging bullets, a television camera isn't taped to your face recording every grunt and grimace for instant replay on the nightly news. Oddly enough, my main impediment to doing the job I came to do for the Committee was a clear conscience and my belief in a system that had already let me down—even as I continued to serve it.

Ever since Meese's in-house investigation had put two and two together and come up with 22, the Chinese wall around President Reagan was stronger than ever, insulating him not only from his critics, who smelled impeachment, but, I think, from his own better instincts to step up to the firing line and defend his actions. In the absence of such leadership, all the opportunistic

congressmen, bureaucrats, special prosecutors, and reporters outside that wall
scrambled like acrobats to exploit any hole, real or imagined, for their own
purposes. That was how the hearings of the Select Committees began, although it was not how they would end.

The Iran-Contra hearings were never about presidential prerogatives or
a "runaway" White House staff. They were never about Congressional oversight of critical national and international affairs. They were never even about
the fundamental balance of power among branches of government under the
Constitution. They *were* about bare-knuckles politics of the dirtiest sort.

First, the ground rules changed from the orderly process Nields promised
to a media circus. The day before I was to testify I sat down with the Select
Committees' staff to go over chronologies and other relevant details. I was
handed a set of so-called financial ledgers obtained without my knowledge
from Albert Hakim through a grant of immunity. After only an hour or two
with these complex and voluminous records, I was asked to comment on a
number of flaming irregularities. The books looked like Greek to me, and I
said so. The reason they were unfamiliar is that they had been doctored,
without my knowledge, by the Swiss fiduciary agent who was supposed to
be helping Albert keep our records straight. As it turned out, these were only
a fraction of the documents the Committees had obtained under such
circumstances.

I realized then that they didn't want witnesses in an investigation; they
wanted Christians to throw to the lions.

Second, I felt Congressional Democrats (and a couple of like-minded
Republican senators) believed that "Irangate," as they now reveled in calling
it, represented the opportunity they had been seeking since Watergate to
return the White House to Democratic control. (Outsider Jimmy Carter and
his largely failed administration didn't really count. This time they were going
to do it right, and the Meese/Reagan stonewall played wonderfully into their
hands.)

Third, certain Republicans (Warren Rudman, William Cohen, and Paul
Trible) came up with the "cancer theory" of an out-of-control staff as variations on the Meese strategy to shield the President. Under this scenario
(fortified by phony exhibits introduced by Rudman), well-intended "rogue
elephants" at the NSC (North and Poindexter, principally, aided and abetted
by "greedy contractors" like me), and a "CIA-within-the-CIA" led by Bill
Casey conspired to implement their own foreign policy against the express
wishes of Congress and the President. This ever-expanding "cancer" within
the administration, which could be surgically excised by heroic Congressional
hearings, was seen as a preferable and more bankable alternative to the out-
and-out stonewall defense created by Reagan's inner circle.

So into the hearings I went. I thought I knew what risks were worth
taking and how to do the right thing. Instead, I was shattered by the cross

fire. I went to give answers and explanations to substantive questions about what we did and why we did it—about policy and strategic issues. Instead, I became a sitting duck in the political shooting gallery. I received a crash course in democracy, Congressional-style. The country I pledged to serve, honor, and protect with my West Point commission and in over three decades of service—a good deal of it not only out of the public eye but deep in the trenches of its dirtiest little wars—no longer existed, if indeed it ever had.

In place of the civics-book America I grew up believing in, I discovered a government dedicated to perpetuating itself and promoting the agendas of its paymasters—and I don't mean the American taxpayer.

I led the inquisition without immunity because, after lengthy discussions with my lawyer, I concluded that I hadn't broken any laws and had performed in good faith every step of the way. I had kept silent during one character assassination attempt before—the Wilson scandal—and I was in no mood to do it again. Predictably, lots of red herrings were raised to create an environment of suspicion and conspiracy that had absolutely nothing to do with Iran-Contra other than they occurred during the same span of time.

One example is the famous used Porsche I purchased in 1986. The inquisitors wanted it to appear as if I funded the car from Iranian proceeds and then lied about it. In fact, I funded the car by borrowing the $31,000 from Albert, which is how I have had to finance my personal expenses on a number of occasions. He also lent me money in 1983 for my Wilson affair attorney's fees, but nobody seems to care about that.

Another was the infamous security system for Ollie's home, installed about the time of the 1986 McFarlane trip. The inquisitors wanted it to appear as if it had been some kind of illegal gratuity for a public official. In fact, Ollie and his family had received credible death threats from the master terrorist Abu Nidal and had been informed that his status was "just below" the cutoff point for government-provided security. To make matters worse, he couldn't locate a private security contractor who could install even a minimal system before he left on the trip. (By the way, Ollie didn't volunteer these facts; I was concerned about his security and asked him what he was doing to protect himself and his family.)

Fortunately, Glenn Robinette was working for me at the time on the Honey-Avrignan case, so I told him to meet with North and his family and see what could be done. Glenn did not add the cost into his ongoing invoices and thus did not get paid. After the lawyers got involved, Ollie apparently got goosey about the fact that he had never reimbursed Glenn for the system and backdated some correspondence to match Glenn's backdated invoices. It was a silly thing to do, especially since the special prosecutor knew the fence issue was a red herring. Nonetheless, he continued to beat Ollie and me over the head with it, like one of Hilter's Big Lies, since the superficial details seemed so wonderfully incriminating, at least to the press.

All this notwithstanding, my three days on the stand were sheer hell.

John Nields opened the proceedings with some pro forma questions about events and chronologies, as expected—the real purpose and value of my appearance. Things took an ominous turn, though, when Arthur Liman picked up the cudgel and used it. As I had said when I first looked over the doctored financial records Albert had delivered, I could scarcely recognize a thing—not impressive testimony from a man who claimed to have nothing to hide. Things went downhill from there.

Of all the Congressmen, Representatives Michael Dewine and Louis Stokes had done their homework (had joined the Saturday and Sunday debriefings of the Joint Committee staffs) and so were prepared with relevant and, I think, helpful questions. Not so David Boren, designated axman for the Senate. He proceeded to try to grill me in a most prosecutorial way, leading to such "illuminating" exchanges as this:

"General Secord, have you ever read the Constitution?"

"Yes, and I've fought for it, too!"

If I'd done *my* homework about the Senator, I would've asked, "Have you?" The answer would've edified the audience.

Senator George Mitchell traded off with Boren in the role of "bad cop/worse cop" and fared a little better. Boren was clumsy and abusive and piqued my combative instincts, which, according to public reaction, at least, allowed me to score some hits of my own, which I wasn't really there to do. Mitchell was a bit more polished and didn't alienate as many people. In his later book, *Men of Zeal*, coauthored with Republican Cohen, one of the first in the growing library of ill-informed Iran-Contra literature, Mitchell tried to preserve and extend that tone, particularly his attacks on me, which subsequent history has pretty much debunked.

Senator Daniel Inouye (D-Hawaii) showed his colors by praising the Israelis for "being so forthcoming" with relevant information when they actually stonewalled the whole investigation, prohibiting their key agent, Ami Nir, from ever visiting the United States, even after he left Israeli government service, lest he fall into the clutches of the Select Committees, the special prosecutor, or, worse, the press.

Most irritating of all were Republicans Rudman, Cohen, and Trible, originators of the cancer theory. Even if it had not been coordinated and rehearsed with the White House, it fit the Meese plan well—although the "Republican Cancer Society's" goal was to save the party, not just (or especially) the President. Their theory sold like hotcakes to the media, but not without a price. Senator Trible was effectively ruined as a politician by his insinuations and sarcasm in the hearings. He stepped down from the Senate a year later to run for governor of Virginia and didn't even make it through the state's primary, so incensed were his constituents.

Overall, the House committeemen seemed a lot better prepared and took their charge more seriously than the Senators, who came only for a lynching. My three-and-a-half days of agony helped set the themes for the rest of the hearings: witnesses trying to keep the discussion on track; the inquisitors trying to derail it with innuendo and minutiae about money.

Later on, I was disappointed by Bud McFarlane's testimony, of course, as was just about everyone else. On February 8, the eve of his third session with the Tower Commission, he had taken an overdose of Valium. This apparent suicide attempt left him muddled and obtuse—he certainly wasn't the man I'd known and worked with for almost 15 years.

I don't think Albert Hakim did us any favors either, although his heart was in the right place. Under immunity, he probably volunteered more than was necessary and wound up raising more questions than he answered. Most of these were inconsequential, but I think they deflected the Committees from their work.

John Poindexter's professorial style came off as too aloof for some people and may have made him appear smug to prime-time audiences. I didn't put up with a lot of crap, which people seemed to appreciate, and Ollie's *performance* (and I use that word with its highest and most positive connotations) was simply brilliant. Sandwiched in between, during the seventh-inning stretch, so to speak, was poor John, and I think the media, in his case, really obscured his message, which, for those who really listened, was insightful and succinct.

Worst of all, any vestige of public-spirited truth seeking went out the window of the hearing chamber when the first television cameras rolled through the door. Congressional procedures and rules of evidence quickly gave way to political harangues and attempts to depict covert operations as conspiracies, and mistakes as crimes. Justice and public policy discourse was never the agenda of the Iran-Contra hearings. Partisanship and public scape-goating was never off the docket.

As I said, my family suffered a lot during the Iran-Contra hearings and afterward. I suspect they still jump when the phone rings and can't open a door without half-expecting some jerk with a minicam to climb in their face. My daughter Julia was harassed even though she was married and no longer living at home. Laura had to drop out of college so that her dad could use the money to pay his lawyers—something I will *never* forgive my tormentors for.

My son John had problems, too. Still a teenager while the story broke, he had a tough time with his peers in high school, from taunting to fistfights—the sad spectacle of kids in a schoolyard drawing blood over something neither side really understood. As I complete this book, John is serving as a paratrooper in the 82nd Airborne. He used to feel his dad would be ashamed of him because he wasn't an officer and didn't go to West Point. I think he realized how untrue that was when I appeared with a big grin and a Bible at his enlistment to administer the serviceman's oath.

Ollie's testimony at the hearings merits a brief discussion all its own. As far as I'm concerned, it was one of those epiphanies of modern history—at least in the age of mass communications.

One of the problems plaguing media manipulators these days is that they can't undo what people witness on live television. Try as they may (and believe me, many journalists and Congressmen have tried *very* hard) to diminish or dismiss the phenomenon that happened during North's five days of testimony, his performance (especially in contrast to the performance of his inquisitors) personified much that is wrong with America's legislative system. An "archetypal American hero" stood his ground against a cabal of venal, hypocritical bullies, and that spectacle burned itself into the American psyche. No one since has been able to erase it. It began a tidal wave of anti-incumbent feelings that is only now beginning to crest.

Judging from the many tens of thousands of supportive cards, letters, and telegrams I received—and the many *hundreds* of thousands Ollie got—during that period, our nation was searching for something to express its own growing dissatisfaction with that system. In my opinion, Ollie North did less to create his own mystique than to come along at the right time to give an existing, unpersonified force a name, face, and voice.

Congress was and is quick to equate Congressional agreement with public consensus; the two are not the same. The more Congress lost touch with the American people, the bigger that gap became. During the Iran-Contra hearings, the gap got so big that even Congress and the media could no longer ignore it.

But the vendetta didn't end for some of us, as it did for the Joint Committee, when the television lights switched off.

North and Poindexter went on to a series of show trials during which those accusations that weren't thrown out in court were eventually reversed in appeal—John's being the last, in November 1991. Ollie's memoir, *Under Fire*, hit the best-seller list about that time, reflecting the great popularity he's found as a speaker and champion of conservative causes. What Congress and the politicians took away, the American people were willing to give back.

I pleaded guilty on November 8, 1989, to one count of "making a false statement to Congress" and received a $50 fine and two years probation. The circumstances of this plea are illuminating. The statement in question had to do with an answer I gave in a Congressional staff deposition (no members of Congress were involved) to the question, "Did Oliver North get any money from the enterprise?" I answered, "No, except maybe airline tickets." I did not mention the security fence because it had been paid for by Glenn Robinette, a fact substantiated by Robinette's own income tax return. However, by November 1989 I had already been billed for over $1 million in legal fees, and rather than fight the charge in yet another lengthy trial, the plea bargain made more sense. At the sentencing, the chief judge of the District of Columbia Federal Court was very terse with the prosecution for pressing this insignificant matter and suspended the imposition of sentence. Instead, he pointedly imposed a $50 fee, the *minimum* required by federal law, and dealt the special prosecutors a sharp rebuke from the bench.

In 1988, Southern Air Transport and I were sued by Eugene Hasenfus (a 10-year veteran of Air America in Southeast Asia) for "grievous damages and pain" resulting from his bailout of the downed Contra supply plane in 1986. They alleged the aircraft was unsafe due to improper maintenance and inadequate navigation systems—a fishing expedition of charges cooked up by lawyers, not pilots or experts who knew either the aircraft or the situation. I expected the suit to be dismissed, but it finally went to trial in 1990. After five weeks, the case went to the jury, who found in my favor. No damages were awarded. At this writing, however, the plaintiff has appealed the case in the 11th Circuit Court. My lawyer in the Hasenfus case was Miami attorney Tom Spencer, the same man who so ably defended against the nuisance suits of the Christics.

Also in 1988, I launched a defamation suit against Leslie Cockburn, author of *Out of Control*, a 1987 book that simply regurgitated all the specious allegations of the Christics. After two years in a D.C. court, my suit was dismissed because we were unable to demonstrate that the lies and misstatements were the product of malicious intent, and not just bad journalism. I have since been subpoenaed to testify in a variety of criminal and civil cases arising from our country's affairs in Central America, including the trial of General Manuel Noriega, which (as both prosecutors and defenders soon realized) I knew absolutely nothing about. Such are the wages of notoriety.

Bud McFarlane pleaded guilty on March 11, 1988, to four counts of withholding information from Congress and was given a $20,000 fine, 200 hours of community service work, and two years' probation.

Albert Hakim pleaded guilty to a misdemeanor count of supplementing Ollie's salary, for which he received a $5,000 fine and two years' probation. Lake Resources was ordered dissolved for its role in "diverting" proceeds from Iranian arms sales to the Contras—a rather gratuitous insult to injury since the company was already defunct.

Tom Clines was convicted on September 18, 1990, of four counts of underreporting his income to the IRS and denying his foreign financial accounts, for which he was sentenced to 16 months in prison and $40,000 in fines—both of which are currently on appeal. Unfortunately, Tom's motion to delay the imposition of sentence pending the outcome of his appeal was denied in May 1992, and he has begun serving that sentence, what I believe to be a complete travesty of justice.

My friend Ami Nir came to an even unhappier end. Five times in 1987 and 1988, we met in secret (usually all-day and all-night meetings at places like a hotel on Lake Konstanz in the *Bodensee* in Switzerland) to compare chronologies and prepare an accurate narrative of events—one reason these points were so clear in my mind when I testified. This was without the knowledge of the Israeli government, which had commissioned its own nominal investigation, headed by an IDF logistics general rather than an intelligence specialist as one might expect (so much for Senator Inouye's lavish praise of Israeli "candidness"). Although Ami had resigned his government post in May 1987 in disgust over both U.S. and Israeli stonewalling (he had been prohibited from visiting the United States by Israel for "security reasons") and was working for a European food conglomerate, he had lost neither his loyalty to his friends nor his taste for justice. He once spoke to Tom Green for two hours on the phone and, at our last meeting, offered to come to the U.S., despite his government's prohibition, and testify on my behalf if it was needed. I was deeply touched that he made this offer only for me, and not for Ollie, whom he faulted (and I believe unfairly) for going along with Meese's strategy. However, his trip to America never materialized. In late 1988, Nir was reported killed in a light airplane crash in Mexico. Few details were offered about how the chartered Cessna went down, and his body was quickly shipped back to Israel for burial.

Before his death, however, Nir informed his wife, Judy Moses, and his sister that he had numerous tape recordings and notes concerning activities in his long and varied government career and that these should be inventoried and safeguarded. In the summer of 1991, Judy complained to me that the Israeli government was pressuring her to surrender the tapes and documents on the grounds that they pertained to national security matters. In October 1991, she reported a burglary of the Tel Aviv apartment where these materials were stored. Some, but not all, of these records were apparently taken. I planned to go to Israel to help her identify and catalogue the remaining records, but she was quite apprehensive and later that month canceled the invitation. Not long thereafter, the rest were removed from her custody.

I can think of no better tribute to Ami and the principles for which he stood than for the Israeli government, with the backing and encouragement of the U.S. Congress, to reveal the contents of this material and so put to rest many lingering questions about the Iran-Contra affair that still trouble the people of our two great nations. Sadly, this is unlikely to happen without strong pressure from pro-Israeli senators, like Daniel Inouye, who winked at Israel's earlier intransigence.

A more satisfying postscript to the affair was written in December 1991, eight months after the end of Desert Storm and the beginning of a new era of hope in the Middle East:

The last American hostage, Terry Anderson, finally regained his freedom in Beirut.

For a covert program that, by our most optimistic accounting, transferred in a perfectly legal manner perhaps $4.5 million from Iran arms sales to Contra support, Special Prosecutor Walsh has spent over *$40 million* in taxpayer funds (matched by $60 million in additional government costs) to further the longest, most tortuous, wasteful, misleading, and iniquitous political vendettas in the history of American jurisprudence. As of this writing, his office is still in business, six years after the fact, charging U.S. taxpayers $30,000 a day in rent, salaries, and other expenses, despite the fact that no judge or jury has seen fit to ratify his major accusations.

In the summer of 1990, Congressman William Broomfield of Michigan asked U.S. Attorney General Dick Thornburgh to terminate Mr. Walsh's office and assume responsibility for any remaining investigations, but was turned down because the action would have been "politically difficult." Congressman Broomfield then introduced the "Independent Counsel Sunset Act of 1991," which would place a two-year limit on current and future independent counsel investigations. The bill is still languishing in Jack Brooks's (D-Texas) Judiciary Committee.

Perhaps a ruling by the Swiss made in early 1992 will accelerate this process and put to rest the issue that had, rightly or wrongly, become the crux of the Iran-Contra affair.

On January 3, 1992, the Ministry of Justice and Police in Switzerland formally rejected Walsh's claim that the enterprise's residual working funds, frozen since the Iran-Contra story broke, belonged to the U.S. government. Long after the 60-day appeal period for this ruling expired, Walsh petitioned for, and was granted, another hearing on this issue before the Swiss supreme court. Since the success of his appeal seems doubtful, he has, as insurance, turned his guns against Cap Weinberger, one of the most able Defense Secretaries in U.S. history, whom he indicted in late June 1992, as this book goes to press, on five counts of allegedly misleading investigators and making false statements to Congress—a feeble offensive against a fine public servant that smacks more of desperation than the search for justice. In response to this travesty, I went on national television to express my outrage and dismay and to urge the American people to flood the White House with demands for Walsh's swift and long-overdue dismissal.

Despite the public outcry, however, the wheels of injustice grind on.

The Swiss have agreed to "consult" further with the U.S. while Walsh's appeal runs its course, so the ultimate disposition of these funds, and the many claims against them—including the spiraling legal expenses incurred by many Iran-Contra participants—still is unclear. In April, 1992, Albert and I returned to Switzerland to arrange for an independent audit of the account and the eventual release of remaining cash so that bona fide claimants may be paid if and when the Swiss ruling takes effect. If "Irangate" was, in fact, a "follow the money" affair, as the witch hunters have claimed, then that long-awaited day will surely mark the end of their trail—but who can be certain as long as new headlines and more public funding can be had?

As I have maintained throughout my life, war and politics are not about technology or money, but people, and that certainly was true in Iran-Contra. Although it is encouraging to note that the Democrat-controlled Congress seems unwilling to renew the so-called Ethics in Government Act that spawned the special prosecutor's office (and thereby suffer the heated debate and public inquiry into Walsh's activities and tactics that such a decision would inspire), the terrible monster the act created will never truly die until its extraordinary, imperial powers are repudiated as well as rescinded.

Until then, no matter how much we've bled or long to heal as a nation, the story will not be over.

# — Epilogue —

To err is human, and, as you've seen, I've made my share of mistakes traversing the high and low corridors of life. Still, one should not be burdened with more grief than is one's due. With this in mind, I want to discuss in these last few pages some issues concerning me, Iran-Contra, and the lamentable state into which our nation has declined in the 40-odd years since I first began to serve her.

Critics have accused Iran-Contra principals of everything from breaking laws and usurping the government's chain of command to ignoring, with malicious zeal, the Constitution itself. At their most charitable, our accusers charge us with grave improprieties in which the rules of covert operations, let alone good judgment, were violated daily. In short, the Iran-Contra episode has been represented as one of America's darkest hours: one that points the way toward imperial presidents and unaccountable, arbitrary governments-within-a-government that threaten to subvert the state.

Many of these allegations have already been dealt with in this book. I want to now put the whole thing in perspective, since the unobstructed picture—the long view—seems to be what our persecutors understand least and fear the most.

Legal problems began when the Iran-Contra story broke and certain politicians within the administration scrambled to "protect" the President. As far as I was concerned, once our cover was blown, there was no point in hiding the significant details of our operation—at least those that did not compromise other covert programs or give away technical secrets to the enemy. Despite all the hollering to the contrary, we had done everything properly, albeit "off line" from the Congressional viewpoint, and there was nothing special about that. As confirmed by a recently declassified U.S. Army Intelligence report, there's not a dime's worth of difference between the way Iran-Contra was organized—as a commercial venture operating covertly at the direction of the President and within the confines of the law—and the way President Franklin Roosevelt ran Claire Chennault's Flying Tigers despite a Congressional ban on American aid to nationalist China before World War II. As Robert Schriebman, attorney for the Flying Tigers survivors (who won belated veterans' benefits from the DoD), told the *Los Angeles Times* in July 1991, FDR's clandestine China operation "makes the Iran-Contra affair look like a small-scale operation," which, indeed, it was.

In an episode of PBS-TV's "Frontline" series called "High Crimes and Misdemeanors," Bill Moyers, dean of television's moralizers and former press secretary for Lyndon Johnson, likened Iran-Contra to President Johnson or Nixon conducting the Vietnam War by proxy had Congress ordered military appropriations cut-off—something FDR (and his Flying Tigers) and Jimmy Carter, who issued a secret 1979 finding authorizing aid to the Contras while publicly backing the Sandinistas, could've instructed Moyers about. In fact, as John Prados points out in his history of the National Security Council from Truman to Bush, *Keeper of the Keys*, it was under not Reagan, but Lyndon Johnson himself that the NSC first took on an operational as well as advisory role. Since that happened on Mr. Moyers's watch, I'm surprised it wasn't mentioned in his show.

Yet even before modern times, Congress was regularly bypassed by executive order. Abraham Lincoln raised troops, expropriated previously *un*appropriated money from the Treasury, suspended habeas corpus, and made war against the Confederacy—all without Congressional blessing, which he received only after the fact. In World War I, President Wilson's request to arm merchant ships was filibustered to death in the Senate, so he armed them on his own by Executive Order, and even sent troops without Congressional approval to support the Czar in 1918. And these are not isolated examples.

The source of cash for such operations is another red herring, particularly when the criticism comes from practicing politicians. The Select Committees, in their majority report, said, ". . . allowing foreign policy to be conducted by funds supplied by private parties and foreign governments is likely to create the expectation by the donor nations that they can expect something in return for their largesse." Of course they can. That's also what domestic corporate and PAC contributions to Congressional and presidential candidates—as well as U.S. foreign aid, which Congress regularly approves—are all about.

What continues to languish are the real constitutional issues.

The Tower Commission concluded that the NSC was, is, and must be "the President's creature," which I agree with; but the Constitution says nothing about the NSC, or the CIA, or the FBI, or Social Security—well-institutionalized sacred cows few people, inside or outside of government, seem inclined to put out to pasture. It doesn't even say there has to be a

State Department or Defense Department—ministries our critics say were "unconstitutionally" cut out of the policy-implementation process.

The lesson here is that anyone who wishes to join the debate about the "constitutionality" of issues raised in Iran-Contra ought to read the document they're worried about. Out of the hundreds (and perhaps thousands) of references made to the Constitution by the Select Committees during televised hearings and in their voluminous written report, they seldom if ever *quote* that document—a tactic I find quite illuminating. Congress today has become what the U.S. high command was during the Vietnam era: "hep" from on high too busy pursuing its own agenda to discharge the true business of the republic, or even to show much common sense. Similarly, White House paranoia, born of Watergate, that believes any inquiry into a lawful covert action must be stonewalled at any cost only compounds the problem.

Whether or not Iran-Contra started out or became a cowboy operation conducted by rogues and charlatans I will leave for you to decide. I can only say that America's interest in Iran goes back through eight administrations to before World War II, and one thing that *all* these disparate presidents—despite their differences on defense, domestic, and economic policies—seemed to agree on was that the nation-state of Iran was vital to U.S. interests. The continuity and coherence of U.S. foreign policy toward Iran (prior to Jimmy Carter's presidency, at least) was exceptional in U.S. history. From this perspective, President Reagan's original decision to recoup influence with a nation we should never have "lost" was hardly ill conceived or reckless; it was in keeping with mainstream American strategy going back more than 40 years.

It seems to me, though, that these surrogate issues represent the symptoms of a larger "disease" caused by Iran's revolution. A major buffer state was suddenly removed from the U.S. sphere of influence in one of the most economically and geopolitically vital regions of the world, and we simply did not know how to handle it. This basic problem was compounded when the Imams resorted to an ancient tactic for that part of the world—the taking of hostages.

We in the West were so incensed by this that we allowed it to cloud our view of our own best interests. Other great nations—the Soviet bloc, Japan, South Korea, Israel, Brazil, and virtually every NATO nation—looked past the terrorists and kidnappers to reestablish commercial and military ties with the postrevolutionary regime. Even the Arab states like Saudi Arabia, Kuwait, and Egypt decided to quietly reestablish some sort of relations. Turkey and Pakistan tried repeatedly to act as intermediaries for us, but we refused to play on any terms whatsoever until the Iran Initiative began under U.S. supervision in February 1986. In this we did not seem to me to act like impulsive cowboys, but rather like people who finally woke up and smelled the coffee.

As far as kidnappers go, I don't know of one police department or one country, including Israel, that does not have a "no negotiation" policy with respect to hostages and has not violated that policy countless times. Back when Iran was Persia and we Westerners spoke Latin, you solved a political hostage problem by grabbing hostages yourself or, even more usual, exchanging hostages formally to ensure each side's good behavior. I'm not recommending we go back to that system, but we should remember that some societies have never given it up.

None of us involved ever gave the Iran Initiative more than a 50–50 chance of succeeding—bad odds for surgery, but pretty good for a covert operation. Compared to other clandestine operations I had been involved with, the U.S. had very little in the way of material to risk (some surplus missiles and obsolete spare parts), and even the human stakes were manageable considering the tremendous amount we had to gain.

One thing I can attest to with certainty is that we Iran-Contra players at the working level all assumed that, if the initiative failed, our leaders and their top advisors would act professionally. The "scandal" of Iran-Contra occurred not when the initiative began, but when the operation ended—when the President's advisors set up their Chinese Wall and began lying needlessly to investigators and falsifying evidence.

Unfortunately, throughout the initiative, time was working against us. In addition to disarray at the State Department, the postrevolutionary government in Iran was in chaos. The groups we'd identified in that government as potential working partners wanted assistance and were willing to build relationships with anyone who could help them advance and consolidate their power. You always run the risk of backing the wrong racehorse in such situations, but if you don't place your bet, you'll never win. I will say this: I believe we managed to open a valid second channel much more quickly than any government agency I have ever worked with could've done it. Sadly, things were just beginning to break loose when the plug was pulled.

Unlike Ghorbanifar, the second channel representatives never viewed the Lebanese hostages as their *raison d'être*—a way to "blackmail" Uncle Sam—but as an appendix to the larger strategic issues. Their two main agendas at every meeting from Brussels to Washington to Germany to Geneva were a high-level rapprochement with the U.S. government and for the U.S. to be more forthcoming in adjudicating the billion dollars' worth of claims being contested in the International Court at The Hague. (They said U.S. negotiators there were being intransigent about technical matters, such as accounting details, and they were probably right—although the Iranians tended to overestimate how quickly the U.S. could move on any particular issue.) The hostages were seldom mentioned at any meeting until *we* brought them up.

On the Contra side of the hyphen, the use of surplus Iranian payments, about $4 million from November 1985 to November 1986, donated by the enterprise to support the guerrillas in Nicaragua seems to offend Sandinista apologists and foes of the Reagan political agenda far more than it has offended a long line of federal judges and the Swiss Ministry of Justice and Police, which ruled, in January 1992, that those funds were, indeed, private property. Although it has been largely ignored by the media, *no* Iran-Contra player has been convicted for misappropriating funds because that crime simply did not occur, despite numerous, futile attempts by the special prosecutor to make it appear as if it did. Yet the myth of criminal wrongdoing remains, as most man-in-the-street interviews will probably attest. It's a very frustrating experience, and an impression the major media seems in no hurry to correct. We Iran-Contra principals still twist in the wind because of a cowardly President Reagan and a Congressional/justice system that seems broken beyond repair—at least by the current cast of characters.

By and large, the Israelis kept much better tabs on the Iran Initiative than top-level White House officials—or even Ollie North, who was spread incredibly thin during this time. Iran was terribly important to Israel's foreign policy, and both Peres and Shamir insisted on a continuous, clear, and comprehensive view of the program in all its aspects. The Israelis knew our pockets were pretty shallow for Contra "diversions" or anything else. Most of the time we didn't know how much margin we'd have, if any, between U.S. government prices (which were usually delivered at the last minute) and our European or Israeli costs, which varied for each transaction. Every month or so we'd run a new financial fire drill, figuring we'd have to procure new commercial coding gear or long-range radios or have to place and support a team in one or more remote outposts—let alone buy and operate and insure airplanes and ships. In such an environment, "profit" was a word as foreign as "vacation."

In short, the whole private-versus-public funds issue was a political stalking horse—hardly of constitutional import. The bitter pill is: As poorly administered as much of the Iran-Contra project was, it was always legal and well within the framework of the Constitution as President Reagan found it. Perhaps, if we'd had a few of the clever criminal, conspiratorial minds attributed to us by the media, Congress, and Lawrence Walsh, we'd have come out of it much better off, but we didn't.

As far as the Central American "theater" went, I still do not consider myself an expert in that region, though I certainly became more informed about it than most Americans because of my Contra support duties. After a few months of observing the situation and working with experts like Tom Clines and Ralph Quintero, I became convinced that the Contras could not win militarily—and Clines was even more pessimistic about them than I was. Our penny-ante support operation could postpone their defeat, but that was about it. I told that to North and Casey many times and my opinion didn't change throughout the operation. But Ollie had not signed me on to give policy advice. Although the Contras were small potatoes in the field, they exerted enough pressure to hasten the collapse of the Sandinistas whose true undoing, history shows, was through their own corrupt and arbitrary rule and the alienation it caused the Nicaraguan people.

One of the big problems with both the Iran Initiative and the Contra support operation is that neither had what Albert or I came later to term, "a general." Ollie was a good field officer, and like all good field officers, he was totally absorbed with turning his orders from on high into reality. He did not think too much about the advisability of those orders. When he disagreed with them, he would say so or write another of his now-famous electronic memos, then he would shut up and do the best he could. He responded and coordinated wonderfully, but he never took the projects by the horns and said, "Here's what's got to be done to get this thing accomplished," then made sure that's what happened.

That's what a general does, and with only a couple of exceptions, that never happened.

McFarlane didn't do it, partly because of his temperament and experience, and partly because he was out of government during the final year and generally deferred to Poindexter.

Poindexter didn't do it because he had other irons in the fire and had confidence in Ollie. People forget, there was a lot going on in the world from 1984 through 1986. Iran-Contra wasn't the biggest game in town, which is why so many high-level officials let it languish without adequate resources or attention.

Other administrations had a Kissinger or a Brzezinski or a Melvin Laird to supervise such important "off-line" projects.

We had Ollie North.

Today, international security affairs are far different than those that dominated most of my three decades of government service. To the extent that a rival superpower no longer exists to challenge us in third-world wars by proxy or threaten us with nuclear annihilation, the world is a safer place for America. However, the very end to that "balance of terror" has left a world of confusion in its wake. Regional conditions are more complex and volatile than ever, from religious and national fanaticism to proliferation of nuclear/ biological/chemical (NBC) weapons and the beginning of true global economic competition. World affairs will now be defined more by the kinds of geopolitical issues that characterized the pre–World War I era than the ideological competition that followed World War II.

Unfortunately, we Americans have shown a great penchant for disarming ourselves when we perceive a war to be won, a threat to be over. We did this after both world wars, and to a lesser extent after Korea and Vietnam. If we follow this pattern into what President Bush has termed the new world order, we could quickly find ourselves in mortal danger, let alone thwarted in achieving our significant national goals, when these new alliances exert their power.

In many ways, the new world order may reflect American *political* values the way the world already reflects many of the cultural and economic trends we started after World War II. "Democracy" will flourish to the extent that totalitarianism, on the left or the right, retreats. Our military preeminence and our huge consumer markets will insulate us awhile from the effects of our declining economic prowess, but they can't do it forever. Our problems with basic education, lack of strong religious or family focus, dependency on entitlements (from subsidized or protected big businesses to welfare recipients), and friction between races and among economic classes will have to be addressed—not just by those at the top, but by the citizens whose lives are most affected by those forces and values.

Nobody can predict the future, but we can all think long and hard about the kind of nation we want and the kind of government that's most likely to achieve it. The country can ill afford more Congressional star chamber coup attempts against the executive any more than it can tolerate endless interbranch civil war via battalions of special prosecutors. Right now, I see our bloated executive branch as too fearful of a venal, imperial Congress to lead our nation to the economic and political renaissance we'll need to prevail in the 1990s, let alone the 21st century. Because the "incumbocrats" in Congress have become more concerned with self-perpetuation and expansion of their power—to look after the special interests that sustain them instead of the common good—we will likely see ourselves weakened in the planetwide race for markets and resources. Even worse, this stalemate in our system of checks and balances has left most citizens confused, cynical, and disengaged. They know things must change, but they haven't a clue about how to get there from here, especially using a system that constantly lets them down.

There are ways out of this morass.

First, we must realize that the system of government we've inherited is not the one we started out with, nor is it the one we were promised. Whether or not it's the one we *deserve* will be determined only by what we do about it.

Politicians and pundits talk a lot these days about "Congressional reform" or "governmental reform," but what we really need, I think, is *voter* reform. Until we revitalize our system of representation by rejecting and uprooting our entrenched, professional rulers—not once, but over and over—we will only perpetuate a machine that governs, but is not governed *by*, the people.

Thus, my appeal to all thinking Americans is simple: Don't just *throw the rascals out*; do so again and again until they—and we—get it right.

Throughout my life, one theme seems to have dominated all others: the idea that if something happens "off-line" or occurs without the scrutiny of some well-intended public agency, it is automatically suspect. I believe we've learned this reflex from the gradual and massive intrusion of political authority into every aspect of our lives—if it's not overseen by the government, we just can't believe it's legitimate, or worthwhile.

I suppose this reflects the traditional tension between liberty and freedom that has always troubled Americans: What's not explicitly permitted is assumed to be prohibited. That appears to be our mind-set in late 20th-century America, and I can't think of anything that has quashed individual initiative and responsibility more effectively in our people. If you want to find the general source of many of our problems, from drug abuse to a flagging economy to failing families and smoldering rage that erupts into burning cities, that would be a good place to start.

Freedom, however, is an "off-line" activity. It assumes that what's not explicitly prohibited is permitted. Freedom, equality, and independence for the founding fathers, it seems to me, meant not being subjected to the will of others. It meant people were personally and psychologically equal, particularly under the law, and did not imply that they had to live the same way or enjoy the same incomes or think the same thoughts.

Those were revolutionary ideas in 1776 and 1787 and continued to be in 1917 and 1991. If the breakup of the Soviet Union and the rejection of Marxism and Leninism around the world symbolized anything, it was the salute of one revolutionary movement, whose ideas had failed, to another whose principles were at least in better tune with human nature.

To me, the future of our country lies not in the futile effort to "expand our liberties" by granting bigger and better benefits to selected groups, but to recapture and defend *all* our individual and collective freedoms. America was founded by men who had had their fill of King George's "liberties" and found them wanting.

If America is to begin her third century the way she began her first, she needs to remember what it felt like to take the future in her own hands: to deal with those who would dominate her, to create the best life she could with the resources she had been given. And to remember how good that freedom feels.

# APPENDIXES

I.   Letter from Thomas C. Green to the Chairmen of the Select Committees in response to the Congressional testimony of Richard V. Secord

II.  Letter from Thomas C. Green to John W. Nields, Counsel to the U.S. House Select Committee, concerning the purchase of assets for the Contras

III. The Memorandum of Conversation between Amiram Nir and Vice President George Bush, July 29, 1986, on the status of the Iran Initiative, recorded by Craig Fuller, the Vice President's Chief of Staff

IV.  Service Awards and Decorations, Major General Richard V. Secord, USAF (Retired)

LAW OFFICES

## SHARP, GREEN & LANKFORD

1800 MASSACHUSETTS AVENUE, N. W.
WASHINGTON, D.C. 20036

JAMES E. SHARP
THOMAS C. GREEN
V. THOMAS LANKFORD, JR.
STEVEN M. JOHNSON
BARBARA STRAUGHN HARRIS
MARK M. KATZ •
ROBERT L. VOGEL †

• MEMBER OF PA BAR ONLY
† MEMBER OF NY & NJ BAR ONLY

August 20, 1987

TELEPHONE
(202) 659-2400
TELECOPIER (202)296-1249
TELEX 697 4605 SGLDC

HAND DELIVERED

The Honorable Lee H. Hamilton
Permanent Select Committee on
   International Affairs
U.S. House of Representatives
United States Capitol
Room H405
Washington, DC    20515

The Honorable Daniel K. Inouye
Chairman, U.S. Senate Select
   Committee on Secret Military
   Assistance to Iran and the
   Nicaraguan Opposition
901 Hart Senate Office Building
Washington, DC    20515

Gentlemen:

On behalf of Richard V. Secord, I am writing to correct and comment on certain testimony taken before the Select Committees and to respond to certain statements made by various members of the Committees which misrepresent the facts and portray my client and his conduct in a false and underserved light. In view of the effort undertaken by various members of the Committees to discredit General Secord and the attempts to impeach portions of his testimony, we feel it fair and appropriate that this letter and the accompanying exhibits be made a part of the official record of investigation; and we formally request such relief.

General Secord was the first witness called to give public testimony. His appearance before the Committees followed countless hours of debriefing during which he patiently and with great accuracy recited the facts and

SHARP, GREEN & LANKFORD

The Honorable Lee H. Hamilton and
   Daniel K. Inouye
August 20, 1987
Page 2

circumstances surrounding the operational details of the Contra supply operation and the Iranian initiative. It is only fair for the Committees to acknowledge that the information provided by General Secord was of critical importance and of invaluable assistance to the progress of the investigation. It should also be noted that General Secord ultimately succumbed to the entreaties of both Chief Counsel who largely induced his voluntary testimony by appeals to General Secord's sense of duty, service and responsibility to his country and the Congress.

General Secord was prepared for tough questions and tough criticism. But in light of the way his testimony was procured, we were not prepared for unfair criticism or for the technique employed by some interrogators of using false information to prompt derogatory comments about General Secord from other witnesses. When, from time to time, we contacted the staff to tender correct information and corroborating data we were usually thanked, but never vindicated. All the misinformation has been permitted to linger, and the record requires and deserves correction.

Several Senators were effusive in their use of the term "profiteer" when making reference to General Secord. We start from the rather basic proposition that every man is entitled to make a living. General Secord devoted two years to the Iran/Contra projects at the expense of virtually all other

SHARP, GREEN & LANKFORD

The Honorable Lee H. Hamilton and
    Daniel K. Inouye
August 20, 1987
Page 3

business pursuits.    During that time he received a salary of

$6000 per month.    The amount is hardly excessive.

        Albert Hakim acknowledged in his testimony on June 3,

1987, that he accumulated profits from arms sales for the

benefit of General Secord in an account known as Korel Assets

even though General Secord forswore any such remuneration.

None of the accumulated profits were ever distributed to

General Secord, a fact confirmed by House Counsel, Mr. Nields,

when he stated publicly on June 3rd that:

> I think the record should reflect that
> unlike some of these other accounts, we
> have been able to determine no withdrawals
> from the Korel Assets account as of this
> date.

        A great deal of time and attention was devoted by

members of the Committees in examining the profit earned on

arms transactions.    The frenzy to portray these sales as

generating exhorbitant profit came close to overshadowing what

should have been the more important issues.    General Secord

testified that the gross profit on arms sales ranged from

between 20 percent to 30 percent.    That markup was and is

extremely reasonable, and the merchandise delivered was

unquestionably of high quality.    When General Singlaub appeared

some members again attempted to use his testimony to criticize

General Secord's efforts through a supposed comparison of the

prices charged by each.    The comparison was nonsense and the

equivalent of an apple and orange exercise.    We demonstrated

SHARP, GREEN & LANKFORD

The Honorable Lee H. Hamilton and
   Daniel K. Inouye
August 20, 1987
Page 4

all of this in a letter I wrote to the Committees on May 26,
1987. A copy of my letter is attached hereto for your
convenience. Additionally, we supplied the staff with an "Arms
Sales Profit Analysis" memo which was nothing more than an
exercise in basic arithmetic confirming the profit margins
testified to. A copy of this document is also attached. It is
our belief that the staff has now been able to confirm the
basic accuracy of our figures. Finally, I note the testimony
of General Secord's customer, Mr. Calero, who acknowledged in
his testimony on May 20, 1987, that General Secord's prices for
ammunition and FAL type rifles were extremely reasonable and
about 50 percent less than what this government was charging
the witness for the same items.

Although General Secord never withdrew money from his
so-called profit account and although he attempted no movement
or secreting of funds during the days when these operations
were on the brink of public disclosure, the notion was born and
nurtured by several members of the Committees that the residual
funds were accumulated and preserved principally because of
devious profit motives, all of which worked to the unfortunate
detriment of the Contras. This is a pernicious and
particularly offensive allegation.

Funds were on hand when these transactions terminated
simply because the ongoing operations were aborted. General
Secord was saddled with the responsibility to preserve and

SHARP, GREEN & LANKFORD

The Honorable Lee H. Hamilton and
    Daniel K. Inouye
August 20, 1987
Page 5

allocate funds in response to a number of real and anticipated needs. This required a continuing assessment of priorities and the need to reserve against contingencies known and unknown. General Secord delivered to the Committees long ago most of his original, contemporaneous worksheets which reflect his decisional process. None of this material was contrived, and no one has been silly enough to suggest otherwise. Even a cursory review of this material will demonstrate that General Secord intended that the residual funds were to be devoted to operations.

Rather than burden this letter with a detailed summary of General Secord's testmony, I have included an extrapolation from the documents he provided, which is essentially a series of "snapshots" which capture the process of allocation over time in 1986.

## FUNDS AVAILABLE AND ANTICIPATED DISBURSEMENTS

A.    Early February, 1986 -- $87,000 available. Several million dollars required to carry through with the Central American airlift project.

SHARP, GREEN & LANKFORD

The Honorable Lee H. Hamilton and
   Daniel K. Inouye
August 20, 1987
Page 6

B.          Early March, 1986 -- $6 million available. $2-4 million required for aircraft hull self-insurance per Israeli demand.[*]

C.          <u>Estimated</u> disbursements for March and April, 1986, included the following:

| | |
|---|---|
| Israeli Air Force | $ 150,000 |
| Costa Rica Air Strip | |
|    Project (Contra) | 150,000 |
| Defex (Contra) | 2,360,000 |
| Aircraft Procurement (Contra) | 1,000,000 |
| Salaries (Contra) | 50,000 |
| Contra Medical Expenses | 50,000 |
| Initial Blowpipe | |
|    Procurement (Contra) | 200,000 |
| Fenced Insurance | |
|    Fund (Contra) | <u>200,000</u> |
| | $4,160,000[**] |

---

[*]We are confident that the Israelis will confirm this requirement.

[**]Does not include what by this time is a $4 million hull insurance fund.

SHARP, GREEN & LANKFORD

The Honorable Lee H. Hamilton and
    Daniel K. Inouye
August 20, 1987
Page 7

D.          April 1, 1986 -- $5 million available. <u>Estimated</u>

            disbursements   for   April,   May   and   June,   1986,

            included:


            Aircraft Operations and

                Maintenance (Contra)      $  650,000

            Israeli Air Force               150,000

            Communications Procurement

                (Contra)                    100,000

            Initial Blowpipe Procurement

                (Contra)                    350,000

            Medical Supplies and Local

                Operations at Il Pango

                (Contra)                     45,000

            Southern Air Transport

                (Contra)                    120,000

            Salaries (Contra)                72,000

            Defex (Contra)                2,200,000

            Israeli TOW's                 <u>  822,000</u>

                                         $4,509,000[*]

_____

    [*]Does not include what by this time is a $4 million
hull insurance fund.

SHARP, GREEN & LANKFORD

The Honorable Lee H. Hamilton and
    Daniel K. Inouye
August 20, 1987
Page 8

E.          End April -- $4 million available.  $4 million needed

            for hull insurance reserve.  Estimated disbursements

            through June included:


            Defex (Contra)              $  280,000

            Aircraft Operations and

                Maintenance (Contra)       650,000

            Three British Air Crewmen

                (Contra)                   110,000

            Blowpipe Procurement (Contra)1,000,000

            Salaries (Contra)               72,000

            Israeli TOW's                  822,000

            Costa Rica Air Field (Contra)   60,000

            SAT (Contra)                    55,000

            Insurance Fund Fenced (Contra) 200,000

            C123 Spare Parts (Contra)      200,000

            Israeli Air Force              185,000

                                        $3,634,000*

---

*Does not include what by this time is a $4 million
hull insurance fund.

SHARP, GREEN & LANKFORD

The Honorable Lee H. Hamilton and
    Daniel K. Inouye
August 20, 1987
Page 9

F.          Early June, 1986 -- Hull insurance requirement still

            in effect.     $13    million    available.     Estimated

            disbursements through July, 1986, included:


            Refund demanded by

                Ghorbanifar                $15,000,000

            Airlift Operations and

                Maintenance through

                July (Contra)                   500,000

            Salaries through July (Contra)    90,000

            Israeli Air Force                 240,000

            Costa Rica Airfield Completion  100,000

            Shipload of Munitions (Contra -

                for delivery in August     3,300,000

            Insurance Fund Fenced (Contra)   200,000

            Aircraft Procurement

                (Contra)                    __500,000__

                                           $19,930,000[*]


G.          July 1, 1986 -- $12 million available.    $2 million

            still needed for hull insurance.    Ghorbanifar claims

---

    [*]Does not include what by this time is a $4 million
hull insurance fund.

$10 million owed to him. <u>Estimated</u> disbursements
through August, 1986, included:

| | |
|---|---|
| Refund demanded by | |
|     Ghorbanifar | $10,000,000 |
| Airlift Operation and | |
|     Maintenance, July and | |
|     August (Contra) | 500,000 |
| Salaries, July and August | |
|     (Contra) | 90,000 |
| Insurance Fund Fenced (Contra) | 200,000 |
| Secure Communications | |
|     Equipment (Iran) | 120,000 |
| Ship, Erria, Operations | |
|     (Contra) | 150,000 |
| Shipload Munitions (Contra) | 2,200,000 |
| | $13,260,000* |

H.      Early August, 1986 -- $9 million available.
Ghorbanifar still claims $10 million owed to him and
threatens to expose the operation unless paid.

---

*Does not include what by this time is a $2 million
hull insurance fund.

SHARP, GREEN & LANKFORD

The Honorable Lee H. Hamilton and
    Daniel K. Inouye
August 20, 1987
Page 11

> Estimated disbursements through September, 1986,
>
> included:

| | |
|---|---|
| Refund to Ghorbanifar | $10,000,000 |
| Airlift Operations and | |
|     Maintenance, August and | |
|     September (Contra) | 400,000 |
| Salaries, August and | |
|     September (Contra) | 90,000 |
| Shipping, Erria, Expenses | |
|     (Contra) | 90,000 |
| Insurance Fund Fenced | |
|     (Contra) | 200,000 |
| | $10,780,000* |

Although at the time these operations were disclosed
in November, 1986, approximately $8 million was available,
Ghorbanifar still continued to press his claim. During this
period General Secord contemplated the purchase of a 707
aircraft and spare parts in connection with implementing the

----

*Does not include what by this time is a $4 million
hull insurance fund.

SHARP, GREEN & LANKFORD

The Honorable Lee H. Hamilton and
　　Daniel K. Inouye
August 20, 1987
Page 12

second channel ($2-2.5 million), and roughly a million dollars
were owed or obligated on account of the following:

> Danish ship agent ($300,000+); Southern Air Transport
> ($100,000); death benefits ($200,000); Swiss Air
> charter ($50,000); Salvador bills ($100,000); Costa
> Rica real estate bill ($100,000+) and $100,000
> miscellaneous (including continued funding for the
> ship Erria).

> Planning for the establishment and funding of a
permanent European joint venture company to support
U.S./Iranian commercial transactions over a several-year period
(until such time as the two governments could deal directly
with one another) was terminated when these operations were
exposed. Israel had concurred in this venture, and it was
contemplated that Iran would donate $20-40 million to the new
venture to make it viable. This would include sufficient funds
to "forward finance" procurements from the U.S. and from Europe
after agreement by U.S. and Iranian government officials as
envisioned in the nine-point plan.

> The allocation exercise periodically undertaken by
General Secord was admittedly based on estimates, but it is
against this background of competing claims and demands that he
made his decisions to fund the Contras at whatever level
circumstances would permit. Ghorbanifar's claims were serious,

SHARP, GREEN & LANKFORD

The Honorable Lee H. Hamilton and
    Daniel K. Inouye
August 20, 1987
Page 13

and they presented a credible threat to the continuation of operations (although not in General Secord's view in any meaningful legal sense). Contrary to the picture painted at times at the hearings that abundant excess money was available to fund the Contras, funds were expended to support their operations almost always with consequent risk to the continuation of the Iranian operation and to General Secord personally. Had the Contra airlift project not been deemed so vital by General Secord, it might have been suspended or stopped any number of times as a result of other funding requirements.

In the final analysis over $4 million from the Iranian operation was expended for the benefit of the Contras as a result of General Secord's juggling of his priorities. In view of the fact that General Secord devoted two years of around-the-clock effort to making these projects work, we think it hardly fair to engage in an after-the-fact review of his priority decisions. He was after all, despite contentions to the contrary, acting in furtherance of the policies of this government and with its blessing.

There are a couple of other "money" issues which have been exaggerated to grotesque proportions. In October, 1985, well before the Iran initiative began, General Secord purchased a 1973 Seneca airplane for the approximate sum of $35,000. The money used to buy the aircraft came from a consulting fee and

SHARP, GREEN & LANKFORD

The Honorable Lee H. Hamilton and
   Daniel K. Inouye
August 20, 1987
Page 14

was reported as income on General Secord's 1985 tax return. In
1986 General Secord purchased a Porsche automobile for $31,000.
(Porsche never got so much free publicity). General Secord
insists that the money to buy the car was borrowed from Albert
Hakim, consistent with a pattern of loans made to him in
accordance with a 1983 business agreement, which includes yet
another loan of $32,000 for legal fees made by Hakim in
February of this year.

     We, of course, are not familiar with the personal
purchases of members of Congress. It would be interesting
(perhaps) to know all about them. But what is so unwholesome
or sinister (or of national importance) about buying a Porsche
and a 15 year old airplane, and if you insist on linking these
acquisitions to the Iran/Contra projects: "where's the beef?"
If you add up every dime that found its way to General Secord's
pockets which is in any way arguably related to the Iran/Contra
projects (even without regard to what it represents), you never
get above $225,000.00. That is hardly an extraordinary sum for
two years of work, and it is clearly unworthy of the
exploitation attempted by some members of the Committees.

     Certain members of the Committees chose (we think
deliberately) to ignore confirmed facts in an effort to
embarrass General Secord and serve their personal, political
agenda. For example, General Secord was accused of using
donated funds to purchase Maule aircraft for himself, a

SHARP, GREEN & LANKFORD

The Honorable Lee H. Hamilton and
    Daniel K. Inouye
August 20, 1987
Page 15

supposed fact which astonished several of the donors during

their public testimony and which was presumably designed to

elicit similar emotions from the listening audience.  The truth

is simply that all Maule aircraft were transferred to the

Contras; the Committees know that and knew it at the time this

charade was played out in public.

Toying with the facts is unbecoming during a

congressional investigation, yet it occurred frequently.  In

interrogating another witness, a Senator asserted that General

Secord and Albert Hakim were the owners of East Inc., a company

which contracted to provide operations and maintenance services

in Central America.  The claim is false.  Even worse was the

Senator's use and manipulation of documents to make it appear

that General Secord was charging excessive profits on aircrew

salaries.  The facts are that the documents used by the Senator

did not relate to aircrew salaries and, even more

significantly, the documents were not records of any company

owned or controlled by General Secord.  The language used by

the Senator to make his point was downright ugly, and the whole

episode was outrageous.

Other members attempted to dance on General Secord's

back by asserting that he had no security clearance.  Again,

the truth is that General Secord held the highest level DOD

security clearance until January of 1987.  When Felix Rodriguez

was called to testify, he was fed a series of leading questions

SHARP, GREEN & LANKFORD

The Honorable Lee H. Hamilton and
    Daniel K. Inouye
August 20, 1987
Page 16

(in reality the answers) in an attempt to taint General Secord
with the sins of convicted felon Edwin Wilson. Although
Rodriguez denied any association with Wilson, it is he, not
General Secord, who worked with and for Wilson over an extended
period of time. Moreover, when Rodriguez was prompted to
criticize the military supplies furnished by General Secord to
the Contras, someone was kind enough to expose the fact that
Rodriguez's hearsay was based on information from Mario Del
Amico, a competitor in the arms supply business.

        The attempt by certain members to seize opportunities
to link General Secord to Edwin Wilson evolved rather quickly
into blatant character assassination. General Secord did know
Edwin Wilson long before the time Wilson's legal problems
arose. Allegations first raised in 1982 that General Secord
(and others) might have been involved in business transactions
with Wilson were exhaustively investigated by the Department of
Justice for over two years. The investigation of General
Secord was ultimately terminated and formally closed for lack
of any evidence -- a fact never mentioned by any member during
the hearings.

        General Secord and his colleagues were also
criticized for departing from or misrepresenting United States
foreign policy. This claim is absolutely baseless. His
dialogue with the Iranians tracked established policy and was
based on approved proposals. As the tapes would demonstrate,

SHARP, GREEN & LANKFORD

The Honorable Lee H. Hamilton and
   Daniel K. Inouye
August 20, 1987
Page 17

General Secord never committed the United States to fighting the Russians in defense of Iran. General Secord knew about, and was qualified to explain, United States policy in regard to a possible Soviet invasion of Iran. As all members should know, the United States government has expended billions over the past six years creating a United States Central Command to respond to this contingency in accordance with established policy.

Although other portions of the record are deserving of comment, it is impossible to examine each and every distortion or inaccuracy in a letter such as this. What is important to emphasize is that General Secord was made to pay a very high price for voluntarily coming forward, without immunity, to assist the Congress in its investigation, and, for sure, he is not inclined to answer the phone if his government calls again.

Certain of the immunized witnesses were actually praised for their courage to testify, in contrast to General Secord, whose reputation and integrity were attacked for obvious, partisan purposes. Although this entire experience has been more than slightly bitter for General Secord, he reamins confident that he acted appropriately and honestly in the service of his country.

Whether by its treatment of General Secord the Congress has hampered its ability to entice and receive

SHARP, GREEN & LANKFORD

The Honorable Lee H. Hamilton and
    Daniel K. Inouye
August 20, 1987
Page 18

voluntary testimony from important witnesses is a separate
question. Certainly the treatment accorded General Secord
could not have been designed to enhance the image of Congress
as an impartial and fair investigator.

On behalf of Richard V. Secord, I respectfully
request that this letter be entered in the official record of
the Committees' investigation.

Sincerely yours,

Thomas C. Green

TCG:jme

attachments

LAW OFFICES
## SHARP, GREEN & LANKFORD
1800 MASSACHUSETTS AVENUE, N. W.
WASHINGTON, D.C. 20036

JAMES E. SHARP
THOMAS C. GREEN
V. THOMAS LANKFORD, JR.
STEVEN M. JOHNSON
BARBARA STRAUGHN HARRIS
MARK M. KATZ •
ROBERT L. VOGEL †

• MEMBER OF PA BAR ONLY
† MEMBER OF NY & NJ BAR ONLY

May 26, 1987

TELEPHONE
(202) 659-2400
TELECOPIER (202)296-1249
TELEX 697 4605 SGLDC

John W. Nields, Jr. Esq.
Counsel to U.S. House Select
  Committee to Investigate Covert
  Arms Transactions with Iran
Room H419
United States Capitol
Washington, DC

Dear Messers. Liman and Nields:

I am writing to clear up some confusion which has arisen with respect to the purchase of certain assets for the benefit of the Contras. Three Maule aircraft were tranferred to the Contras in 1985 at the direction of Mr.Secord. The first aircraft, tail number N5657H, was titled to NRAF, Inc., 52 Y el Vira Mendez, Panama, RP, in approximately July or August of 1985. This aircraft was previously owned by Mr. Secord and several colleagues. The Contras purchased the aircraft by wire transferring an amount equivalent to the outstanding indebtedness on the plane.

Maule aircraft tail numbers N56611 and N5661J were titled in the name of NRAF, Inc. on September 10, 1985, and on October 29, 1985, respectively. These aircraft were bought at cost from Maule Air, Inc. All three of these aircraft are owned exclusively by the Contras. Mr. Secord has no interest, direct or indirect, in any of these planes.

During the interrogation of General Singlaub, he was led to confirm that he could have bought twice the quantity of munitions at the prices charged by Mr. Secord. This conclusion is absolutely without merit. Only four items were purchased by both General Singlaub and Mr. Secord.

General Singlaub sold 10,000 AK-47's, folding stock model, at $135.00 per rifle. Mr. Secord sold 3,000 AK-47's, wooden stock model, at $217.00 per rifle. The wooden stock rifles were purchased for a cost of approximately $180.00 per rifle, and they were sold at a 20% mark up to the Contras.

General Singlaub sold 15,000,000 rounds of 7.62 x 39 at a price of $110.00 per thousand. Mr. Secord sold 7,500,000 rounds at an average price of $136.00 per thousand. Including mark up, Mr. Secord's price equates to 2.5¢ per round on one-half the quantity.

SHARP, GREEN & LANKFORD

General Singlaub sold 200 RPG-7's at $1,650.00 per launcher. Mr. Secord sold 80 RPG-7's at $1900.00 per launcher. Mr. Secord's price was 15% higher than General Singlaub's price on less than one-half the size of Singlaub's order.

General Singlaub sold 5,000 RPG-7 rounds at $185.00 per round. Mr. Secord sold 3,000 such rounds at $225.00 per round. This presents a 21.6% mark up over General Singlaub's price on little more than half the quantity supplied by General Singlaub.

General Singlaub shipped 348 tons of material and charged the Contras approximately $300,000.00 for shipping. Mr. Secord shipped over 600 tons and charged the Contras $150,000.00 for shipping.

If Mr. Secord had dealt in quantities comparable to those purchased by General Singlaub, the resulting price differential would have been de minimus, which means, in effect, that Mr. Secord was buying at substantially better prices.

Sincerely yours,

Thomas C. Green
Attorney for
Richard V. Secord

TCG:ddd

ARMS SALES PROFIT ANALYSIS

PREPARED BY RICHARD V. SECORD

1985-1986


Phase I (Airlift February 1985; Sealift April 1985)

      Sell   $2,346,175

      Costs   1,634,901

      Profit   711,274 or 30.3% gross (43.5% of cost)


Phase II (Airlift March 1985)

      Sell   $1,235,596

      Costs     924,756

      Profit   310,840 or 25.1% gross (33.6% of cost)


Phase III (Sealift June 1985)

      Sell   $6,407,512

      Costs   5,190,512

      Profit 1,217,000 or 18.99% gross (23.45% of cost)


Phase IV (Airlift November 1985)

      Sell   $2,255,200

      Costs   2,003,200

      Profit   252,000 or 11% gross (12.78% of cost)

-2-

Phase V (Airlift March 1986)

       Sell   $504,140

       Costs  _354,140_

       Profit 150,000 or 29.7% gross (42.3% of cost)


Phase VI (Airlift April 1986)

       Sell   $441,640

       Costs  _353,337_

       Profit  88,303 or 19.99% gross (25% of cost)


Phase VII (2 airlifts May 1986)

       Sell   $938,635

       Costs  _637,467_

       Profit 301,168 or 32% gross (47.2% of cost)


       GRAND TOTALS

       Sell   $14,128,898

       Costs  _11,101,313_

       Profit  3,027,585 or 21% gross (27.3% of cost)


Note:   Sealift July/August 1986 aborted

       Costs about $2,400,000

       Sold CIA      1,500,000

       Returned to Enterprise - 1,200,000 (300,000 brokers

                             fee to DEFEX)

-3-

TOTALS OF TRANSACTIONS PRICED EXCLUSIVELY BY SECORD

Sell   $11,782,723

Costs    9,466,412

Profit   2,316,311 or 19.65% gross (24.5% of cost)

The Vice President's Chief of Staff, Craig Fuller, attended the meeting and memorialized it:

THE VICE PRESIDENT'S MEETING WITH MR. NIR—7/29/86 0735–0805
PARTICIPANTS: The Vice President, Mr. Nir, Craig Fuller
DATE/TIME: 7/29/86 0735–0805
LOCATION: Vice President's suite/King David Hotel, Jerusalem

1. SUMMARY. Mr. Nir indicated that he had briefed Prime Minister Peres and had been asked to brief the VP by his White House contacts. He described the details of the efforts from last year through the current period to gain the release of the U.S. hostages. He reviewed what had been learned which was essentially that the radical group was the group that could deliver. He reviewed the issues to be considered—namely that there needed to be ad [sic] decision as to whether the items requested would be delivered in separate shipments or whether we would continue to press for the release of the hostages prior to delivering the items in an amount agreed to previously.

2. The VP's 25 minute meeting was arranged after Mr. Nir called Craig Fuller and requested the meeting and after it was discussed with the VP by Fuller and North. Only Fuller was aware of the meeting and no other member of the VP's staff or traveling party has been advised about the meeting. No cables were generated nor was there other reporting except a brief phone call between Fuller and North to advise that "no requests were made."

3. Nir began by indicating that Peres had asked him to brief the VP. In addition, Nir's White House contacts with whom he had recent discussions asked him to brief the VP.

4. Nir began by providing an historical perspective from his vantage point. He stated that the effort began last summer. This early phase he said "didn't work well." There were more discussions in November and in January "we thought we had a better approach with the Iranian side," said Nir. He said, "Poindexter accepted the decision."

5. He characterized the decision as "having two layers — tactical and strategic." The tactical layer was described as an effort "to get the hostages out." The strategic layer was designed "to build better contact with Iran and to insure we are better prepared when a change (in leadership) occurs." "Working through our Iranian contact, we used the hostage problem and efforts there as a test," suggested Nir. He seemed to suggest the test was to determine how best to establish relationships that worked with various Iranian factions.

6. Nir described Israel's role in the effort by saying, "we activated the channel; we gave a front to the operation; provided a physical base; provided aircraft." All this to "make sure the U.S. will not be involved in logistical

aspects." Nir indicated that in the early phase they "began moving things over there."[84]

7. Before a second phase a meeting was desired. Nir indicated a February meeting took place with "the Prime Minister on the other side." Nir did not make it clear who else attended the meeting. He said the meeting was "dramatic and interesting." He said "an agreement was made on 4,000 units— 1,000 first and then 3,000." The agreement was made on the basis that we would get the group," Nir said. "The whole package for a fixed price," he said.

8. Although there was agreement the other side changed their minds and "then they asked for the other items," according to Nir. "We were pleased because these were defensive items and we got to work with the military," said Nir. He continued, "there were 240 items on the list we were provided and we agreed to it."

9. A meeting was organized for mid May in Tehran to finalize the operation. The VP asked Nir if he attended the meeting and Nir indicated he did attend. Nir said, "two mistakes were made during this phase." "Two people were to be sent to prepare for the meeting but the U.S. had concerns about McFarlane," according to Nir. He described the meetings as "more difficult—total frustration because we didn't prepare." And he said, "their top level was not prepared adequately." During the meeting in Tehran the other side kept reminding the group that "in 1982 there was a meeting which leaked and the Prime Minister was thrown out of office." Nir said that at the end of the May meeting, "they began to see the light." "McFarlane was making it clear that we wanted all hostages released," Nir reported and, "at the last moment the other side suggested two would be released if those at the meeting stayed six more hours." According to Nir, "the Deputy Prime Minister delivered the request (to delay departure) and when the group said 'no,' they all departed without anything."

10. According to Nir, "the reason for delay is to squeeze as much as possible as long as they have assets. They don't believe that we want overall strategic cooperation to be better in the future. If they believed us they would have not bothered so much with the price right now." Further, according to Nir, "there are serious struggles now within the Iran power groups. Three leaders share the view that we should go ahead but each wants to prove his own toughness."

11. Turning to what Nir said was the final or most recent phase, he reported, "we felt things would just die if we didn't push forward to see what

---

[84] Charles Allen told the board that he remembered the memorandum as reporting Nir to have talked about the Israelis initiating, taking the initiative, proposing this, sort of directing this, I think probably overstated my understanding of the situation.

Indeed, I think they were proposing it and pressing it on the United States, but based on my understanding and all the memoranda that I have put together is that Mr. McFarlane saw a real strategic need to pursue this effort.

And also, an ancillary aspect was to solve the hostage problem in order to move to broader relationships.

(C. Allen (2) 13–14)

could be delivered. They asked for four sequences, but we said no to talks until they showed something."

12. According to Nir, he told them about 10 days ago he would cancel the deal. Then nine days ago their Prime Minister called saying that they were taking steps to release one—the Priest. The second one to be released would be Jacobsen. The Prime Minister also said that one would be released and then "we should give some equipment." Nir indicated to the VP that the bottom line on the items to be delivered was understood to be the same or even less but it was not the way the deal was originally made. The items involved spares for Hawks and TOWs. No denial or approval was given according to Nir. Nir said he made it clear that no deal would be discussed unless evidence is seen of a release.

13. On Tuesday or Wednesday a message was intercepted between Tehran and the guards according to Nir. On Friday, three hostages were taken out and on Saturday Janco [sic] was taken out, put into a trunk and driven to a village in the Bakka [sic] Valley. Nir then described what Janco reported with regard to the conditions under which he was held and what he knew of the other hostages including Buckley. (I assume we have detailed briefing already.) The VP asked Nir if he had briefed Peres on all of this and he indicated that he had.

14. Nir described some of the lessons learned: "we are dealing with the most radical elements. The Deputy Prime Minister is an emissary. They can deliver . . . that's for sure. They were called yesterday and thanked and today more phone calls. This is good because we've learned they can deliver and the moderates can't. We should think about diversity and establish other contacts with other factions. We have started to establish contact with some success and now more success is expected since if these groups feel if the extremes are in contact with us then it is less risky for the other groups—nothing operational is being done . . . this is contact only."

15. Nir described some of the problems and choices: "Should we accept sequencing? What are alternatives to sequencing? They fear if they give all hostages they won't get anything from us. If we do want to move along these lines we'd have to move quickly. It would be a matter still of several weeks not several days, in part because they have to move the hostages every time one is released."

16. Nir concluded with the following points: "The bottom line is that we won't give them more than previously agreed to. It is important that we have assets there 2 to 3 years out when change occurs. We have no real choice than to proceed."

17. The VP made no commitments nor did he give any direction to Nir. The VP expressed his appreciation for the briefing and thanked Nir for having pursued this effort despite doubts and reservations throughout the process.

BY: CRAIG L. FULLER [initialed:] "CF 8/6/86"

HONORED & BETRAYED, Appendices (4/30/92)

The Service Awards and Decorations of

Major General Richard V. Secord, USAF (Retired)

<u>Award</u>                          <u>Number</u> <u>of</u> <u>Times</u> <u>Presented</u>


Defense Distinguished Service Medal, DDSM          2

USAF Distinguished Service Medal, DSM              1

Distinguished Flying Cross, DFC                    1

Legion of Merit, LOM                               1

Air Medal, AM                                      3

Meritorious Service Medal, MSM                     1

Most Exhaulted Order of White Elephant, Thailand   1

Foreign and U.S. Unit Citations                Numerous

Vietnamese Campaign Ribbon                 8 Battle Stars

Rating at Retirement: USAF Command Pilot with in excess of 7,000

flying hours

# — Acknowledgments —

My life has been filled with people whose heroic contributions to their nation, friends, and comrades-in-arms are seldom acknowledged in public.

I owe much of my career, and much of what I learned about leadership, to Brigadier General Harry C. (Hiene) Aderholt, USAF (Ret.), a legend to those who know him. My greatest respect and professional debt also go to Theodore Shackley, CIA (Ret.), the best intelligence officer I've ever seen; and to William (Bill) Lair, CIA (Ret.) and Lloyd (Pat) Landry, CIA (Ret.), bosses and mentors, patriots and pros; all who knew them will remember what they accomplished.

My thanks and admiration go, too, to Rear Admiral John Poindexter, USN (Ret.), one of the best and brightest men I've served with; to Lieutenant Colonel William (Bill) Cox, USAF (Ret.), combat pilot and longtime supporter, a friend and wingman who was always there when I needed him; and to Lt. Colonel and Mrs. James ("Kit") Carson, USAF (Ret.) for their 30 years of friendship and support. Likewise, for three decades of close support in campaigns around the globe, my heartfelt gratitude to Colonel and Mrs. Bill Prim, USAF (Ret.).

To Lieutenant General James H. Ahmann, USAF (Ret.) and his wife, and to Colonel and Mrs. Bob Dutton, USAF (Ret.), who gave us comfort and unwavering moral support during the "dark ages" of 1986 through 1990, I give in return my deepest gratitude. I also give my profound thanks to Major General Leroy Swendson, USAF (Ret.) for his similar, continuing support.

To Thomas Green, a great lawyer who became a great friend, and to Thomas Spencer, my brilliant Miami attorney and supporter without whom I would have been eaten alive by the Christic ants and similar insects infesting the American justice system, I give my heartfelt thanks. Between the two of you, my faith in our legal system has been partially restored.

For help and support from an unexpected quarter, I thank Buffy Sainte-Marie, militant pacifist and stellar performer, and her Nashville manager, Fred Kewley, a super friend indeed.

To Thomas G. Clines, CIA (Ret.)—one of my closest friends and a combat comrade—I offer my prayers that justice will prevail. You have not survived so much only to end up a notch on the venal special prosecutor's pistol.

Closer to home, the steadfast support of my wife, Jo Ann, and my children, Julia, Laura, and John, has been my backbone during a lifetime of hard campaigns, especially during the endless night of the Iran-Contra fiasco. I also wish to thank my stepmother, Mildred Secord, and my father, Lowell, and mother, Wahneta Decker, for their heroic preparations for, and faithful support of, my chosen career—with its soaring heights and distressing lows; and all our friends in the "Northern Neck" of Virginia—including especially Bill and Nancy Loporto, Ron and Vi Shivak, and Hank and Judy Rovan—who have stood with us since 1988; as well as the thousands upon thousands of people from all over America who came to our assistance with their checkbooks, letters, and prayers from the beginning of the 1987 Congressional hearings through the Long March of the Lawrence Walsh persecutions. We are all bloodied fighters in a different sort of war.

Finally, I must recognize and honor all the Special Operations warriors with whom it was my distinct privilege to serve during the Southeast Asian conflict and afterwards. May this book bring old friends together and a few old memories back to life.

# — Index —

A-37B Dragonfly, 98–99
Abrams, Elliott, 272
AC-130, 83
Accession List, 106
Aderholt, Harry C. (Hienie), 57, 64–65, 70, 96–
   97, 102, 148, 304, 337
   as CIA detailee, 53
   command style of, 52
Afghanistan, 131–34, 139, 194–95
Agamemnon, 95
Ahmann, James H., 110, 168–69, 337
AIPAC. See American-Israel Public Affairs
   Committee
Air America, 54, 56, 61, 69–70, 223
   and the Battle for Site 85, 79–80, 83, 87
Airborn Warning and Control System (AWACS),
   132
Aircraft
   in support of Contras, 215
   and developmental strategy of the U.S. Air
      Force, 98–99
   formation drops of, 273–74
   in Iran against Kurdish insurgents, 49–50
   manufacturers base price of, 142–43
   refueling of, 266
   in Vietnam, 29–30, 37
   See also individual aircraft
Air Force, U.S.
   aircraft development of, 98–99
   in Cuban missile crisis, 44–46
   Dr Pepper strikes in Vietnam, 62
   flight school training of, 17–22
   in Laos, 97
   and Project Jungle Jim, 24–29
   and protocol for making command
      assignments, 115–16
   and recruitment of instructors for Air Force
      Academy, 22
   secret missions to Vietnam, 27–43
   Battle at Site 85, 78, 96–97
   The Fall of Site 85, 78
   and the post-Vietnam syndrome, 154

Air Force International Programs, 142–47
Al-Assad, Hafez, 297, 312
Allen, Charles, 291, 304, 388n
Allen, Colonel, 155
Allen, Lew, 148, 170
Allen, Richard, 171, 173, 216
Allison, Robert, 30
Al-Shiraa, 316–19
American-Israel Public Affairs Committee
   (AIPAC), 168, 172–73, 183, 193–95
Amico, Mario Del, 274, 378
Amin, Idi, 31
Anderson, Jack, 303
Anderson, Terry, 237, 269, 270, 297–98, 311,
   320, 350
Antonelli, Brigadier General, 71–72
Arias, Oscar, 272
Arms Export Control Act, 171, 207, 216
AT-28 (Trojan), 30, 44–46
Avrignan, Tony, 277–78, 344
AWACS Sale to Saudia Arabia, 166–74, 183–84,
   189, 192–93, 211, 216
"Ayub" and Iranian Arms Sales, 295–96, 298–
   302, 305–7
Azhari, General, 48, 51

Baathists, 47, 123
Baghdad Pact, 123
Baker, James, 192
Bakhtiar, Shahpur, 147
Bandar, Prince, 168–69
Bank Melli, 283
Barzani, Ben Bella Mustafa, 47, 50–51
Bay of Pigs, 25, 44–46, 57, 59, 207, 272
BCCI Bank, 261
Bechtel Corporation, 232
Beckman, Rod, 131
Beckwith, Charlie, 156–58
Begin, Menachem, 145, 167, 191
Bermudez, Enrique, 211–12, 215, 251, 272–73
Bigley, Tom, 105–6
Bishop, Charlie, 138, 159

Blake, Bob, 56, 58
Boeing Corporation, 127
Boland Amendments, 219, 237, 262, 329,
    allows private aid to Contras, 203–4, 210–11,
        251
    and CIA, 214, 235, 246, 271, 276, 335
    repeal of, 331
Bolsheviks, 226
Boren, David, 345
Bradley, Omar, 15
Bradley, Pat, 97
Brezhnev, Leonid, 125
Brooks, Jack, 350
Broomfield, William, 350
Brown, Harold, 166
    and Iranian hostage rescue missions, 16, 148–
        50, 152–53, 159
    and sale of AWACS to Saudia Arabia, 168–69
Brzezinski, Zbigniew, 163, 169, 236
Buckley, James, 171–73
Buckley, William, 220, 237, 296–98
Bush, George
    and briefings on the Iran Initiative, 280–82,
        292, 294
    and conversation with Amiram Nir, 387–89
    and covert U.S. air support for the Contras,
        272, 274–76
    described, 191
    and praise for Oliver North, 333–34
    and release of the Iranian hostages, 164–65
    and sale of AWACS to Saudia Arabia, 174
    and the Iran Initiative, 334
Bustillo, General, 272–75
Byron, Lord, 24

Calero, Adolfo, 251
    and covert air support for the Contras, 211–
        13, 215, 218, 366
    described, 206
    meetings with Richard Secord, 204–6
    and private arms sales to the Contras, 207–11,
        275
Calero, Mario, 210, 212
Cambodia, 58, 98, 103
Carlucci, Frank, 170, 175–76, 189–90, 198
Carter, Jimmy, 129, 183, 330, 343
    and sale of AWACS to Saudia Arabia, 167–69
    and the CIA, 184
    supports Contras, 354
    Iranian policy of, 139–41, 233
    and the Iranian hostage crisis, 147–50, 159,
        162–64, 230, 270
    and Middle East peace accords, 145, 167
    and the Sandinista government in Nicaragua,
        203, 354
    South Korean policy of, 204
    and Soviet intervention in Afghanistan, 134
Casey, William, 114, 158, 198, 204, 214, 215,
        357
    and covert support for the Contras, 216–17,
        235–36, 246–52, 276, 335
    described, 191
    and Oliver North, 246, 300
    release of the Iranian hostages, 164–65, 241

the Iran Initiative, 24, 233–35, 237, 240–41
Castillo, Thomas, 215, 276
Castro, Fidel, 25, 46, 59, 207, 272–73
Cavaco, Silva, 219
Cave, George
    and Iran Initiative, 255, 258–59, 263, 280
    mission to Tehran of, 2–5, 269
CBS
    "The CBS Evening News," 184, 188, 195–97
    and covert air support for the Contras, 248
    and the Edwin Wilson affair, 19, 184–85, 188–
        89, 191
Central Intelligence Agency
    and covert aid to Afghanistan, 194–95
    and American hostages in Lebanon, 233, 263
    bans homosexuals, 54
    and the Carter administration, 184
    and Commando Club at Site 85, 75–92
    and support of the Contras, 27, 203–8, 210–
        17, 235–36, 246–52, 271, 335–36
    detailees in, 53
    field command hierarchy of, 56–57, 59
    and Project IBEX, 131–32, 134
    Iranian involvement of under the Shah, 120
    and the Iranian hostage crisis, 158–59, 162–63,
        165, 266
    and the Iran Initiative, 239–44, 246, 252, 254–
        55, 306–8, 311–12, 314–15
    in Korean War, 53
    covert mission to support Kurds, 123
    in Laos, 56–92
    screening process for secret operatives by, 53–
        54
    and discovery of Soviet missiles in Cuba, 44
    and obtaining Soviet weapons from Israel,
        176–77
    Vietnam involvement of, 53–92
Chancellor, John, 101
Chappel, Dickie, 40
China
    and arms sales to the Contras, 209–10
    and arms sales to Iran, 228
    and the sale of F-16s to Pakistan, 194
Ciccipio, Joseph, 269, 298, 307
Clapp, Archie, 40–41
Clark, William, 216
Clines, Thomas G., 59–60, 67, 70, 95, 97, 272–
        73, 357
    and Commando Club on Site 85, 8, 75, 77,
        81–84, 86–87
    and arms sales to Contras, 207–8, 210
    conviction of, 348–49
    and covert air support for the Contras, 211–13
    and arms sales to Iran, 219, 295
    and ransom money for hostages, 266–67, 269
    training of at the Naval War College, 101
    and Edwin Wilson, 185–88
Coburn, Jay, 266, 269
Cockburn, Leslie, 348
Cogan, Chuck, 194
Cohen, William, 343, 345
Colby, William, 56
Cold War
    and influence on U.S. strategy in Vietnam,
        104, 106–7

and the Cuban missile crisis, 45–46
and the Iran Initiative, 319
in the Third World, 48
Colonialism, 47
Commando Club, 75–92
Communism, 47, 134–36
*Compagne des Services Fiduciare* (CSF), 200–201, 249, 336
Congress, U.S., 358
  and foreign arms sales, 199–200
  and arms sales to Iran, 132
  and Israeli arms sales to Iran, 258
  letter to chairs of select committee on international affairs, 363–80
  and sale of F–16s to Pakistan, 193–95
  and sale of AWACS to Saudia Arabia, 168–69, 171–74, 183
  and support for the Contras, 2, 203–4, 206–8, 210–11, 248, 250, 252, 271, 275
  and the Iran Initiative, 239–40, 284–86, 324, 326, 328–30, 332–33
Connally, Gene, 30, 40, 95–96
Contras
  corruption within, 211–12
  covert support for, 203–19, 211–18, 233, 235–37, 243, 246–52, 354, 363–80
  diversion of Iranian funds for, 254–55
  formation of, 203
  leadership of, 235
  strategy for, 251
  weaponry of, 207, 209
  *See also* Congress, U.S., and support for the Contras
Cooper, William, 274, 295
"Copp," 206, 219
Corr, Robert, 340
Costa Rica, 213–15, 235, 272, 276, 340, 368, 370, 371, 374
Counterterrorist Command, 164
Cover and Deception (C&D), 156, 160
Cox, William (Bill), 30, 34–36, 337
Craig, Arnold R., 84
Credit Suisse, 261, 283, 308–9
Creighton, Harold (Punchy), 14
Crockett, Davy, 81
Cronkite, Walter, 42
Cruz, Arturo, 251
Cuba
  and aid to Nicaragua, 203, 206
  and aid to the Sandinistas, 251
  and backing of foreign wars, 174
  Caribbean encroachment of, 199
  Missile Crisis, 44–46, 57
  *See also* Bay of Pigs

Dalai Lama, 226
Daoud, Mohammed, 125, 131
Dawa 17, 300–302, 305–8
Dayan, Moshe, 113, 130
Deaver, Michael, 192
Defense Communications Planning Group (DCPG), 70–72
Defense Security Assistance Agency (DSAA), 112–13

Desert One, 147–52, 154–58
Desert Shield, 164, 174
Desert Storm, 91, 164, 174, 257, 288, 315, 349
  aftermath of, 50
  bombing missions in, 108
  and media coverage of the Kurds, 46
  and restoration of military pride, 110
  strategy in, 71
Detachment Two Alpha, 27, 30, 37, 42, 95
DeWine, Michael, 345
Diem, Ngo Dinh, 47
Dine, Thomas A., 172–73
*Doctor Zhivago*, 48
Dolmy, Inc., 249
Doolin, Dennis, 102, 105–6
Dor, Moshe, 281
Doron, General, 294
Douglas Skyraiders, 29–30
Dr Pepper Strikes, 62
Duc, Ngo Quang, 47
Dudley, Richard, 176–77
Dunbar, Charles, 322–23
Dutton, Bob, 156, 162, 272, 274, 276, 280, 282, 295, 305, 311–13, 337

Earl, Robert, 257, 266, 326
Egypt, 113, 145–47, 185–88, 355
Egyptian American Transport and Services Corporation (EATSCO), 185–88, 207
Eisenhower, Dwight D., 15, 330
Eliot, T. S., 22
El Salvador
  and support for the Contras, 213–15, 235, 246–48, 272, 274–76, 340, 374
  and Sandinistas, 203
Enders, Rudy, 159, 162
Energy Resources, Inc., 209, 212, 214–15, 220, 338
Eureka Briefing, 163–64
Expandtrade, 200

F–100 Super Sabre, 44–46
F–86 Sabre, 19
Fahd, King, 211
*The Fall of Site 85*, 78
Fernandez, Joe, 215, 276–77
Fiers, Alan, 246–48
Finney, David, 23–24
Fish, Howard, 113–19
Flying Tigers, 354
Ford, Gerald, 125, 183
Foreign Military Sales (FMS), 142–47
Fosmier, Tom, 246–47
Fox, Brigadier General, 117–18
France, 228
"From Hanoi with Love" (Tony Avrignan), 278
"Frontline," 354
Fuller, Craig, 280, 387–89
Furmark, Roy, 304

Gadd, Richard, 214, 233, 246–48, 273, 275, 276
Garth, Jeff, 211
Gary, Sergeant, 84–87
Gast, Philip, 120

Gates, Robert, 191
General Dynamics, 127
General Electric, 127
General Motors, 142
George, Clair, 239
Gephardt, Don, 30
Germany, West, 228
Ghorbanifar, Manucher
    and the Iran Initiative, 2–4, 24, 220–32, 238,
        241–42, 290–95, 298–99, 302–4, 356, 371,
        372, 373
    described, 224–25
Gilcrist, Paul, 2–4, 262–64
Glenn, John, 29, 194
Gomez, Maximo, 248, 272
"Goode," 206
Green, Thomas C., 189–90, 196, 329, 331–34,
    337, 338–45, 349, 363–80, 381–85
Greenberg, Ted, 188, 190, 338
Gregg, Don, 272, 274–76
Grenada, 164, 199
Grumman International Corporation, 122
Guevara, Che, 272
Gulf Marketing, Inc., 248–49
Gulf of Tonkin Resolution, 53

H–53 Helicopter, 151–55
Habib, Philip, 178
Haig, Alexander, 100–101, 176, 191, 216, 310
    and sale of AWACS to Saudia Arabia, 169
    military career of, 16
Haiphong Harbor, 101, 103, 203
Hakim, Albert, 142, 225, 263, 277
    and arms sales to Iran, 243, 253, 256–57, 260–
        61, 279, 282–83, 287, 289, 295, 298–302,
        305–9, 311–12
    guilty plea of, 348
    and Iran-Contra investigation, 337, 339, 343–
        45, 346, 350–55
    and diversion of Iranian funds to the Contras,
        254–55, 331, 365, 376, 377
    and partnership with Richard Secord, 200–
        202, 206–9, 248–49
    and ransom money for hostages, 266
Hall, Fawn, 245, 301
Halleck, Richard, 127
Hamilton, Lee H., 363–80
Hark 1, 60, 71–72
Harkins, Paul, 31
Harper, I.W., 196
Harriman, Averell, 133
Harris, Hunter, 74
Hart, John, 120
Hasenfus, Eugene, 273, 295, 298, 302, 306, 320,
    348
Hashemi, General, 223
Hashemi, Mehdi, 314, 318–20
Helicopters, 151–55
Helms, Richard, 90, 120, 125, 132, 186, 196–97
Hill, James, 144
Hindawi, Nezar Mansour, 297
Hindenburg, Paul von, 113
Hitler, Adolf, 344
Ho Chi Minh Trail, 110–11

attacks along, 84
CIA attempts to disrupt, 57–58, 60–61, 70–73
Operation Lam Son 713, 103
POWs held near, 66–67, 69–70
Holloway Board of Inquiry, 150–52, 156
Homosexuals and the CIA, 54
Honduras and the Contras, 210, 213, 215, 235,
    274, 277
Honey, Martha, 277–78, 344
Hopkins, Harry, 288
Hossein, 279, 282–83, 288
Hostages
    and arms sales to Iran, 3, 220, 224, 226–28,
        230–33, 290–91, 293, 296–303
    ransom money for, 266–67, 269
Hughes-Ryan Act, 286
Humphries, General, 127
Hurlburt Field, 26–27
Hussein, Saddam, 123, 228
Huyser, Dutch, 134–36, 139, 153
Hyde Park Square, Inc., 249

I-HAWK Missile, 127–28, 131–32
Ikle, Fred, 235
Imperial Iranian Air Force, 138–39
Imperial Iranian Army, 126
Infil/exfil Missions, 60–61, 68
Inouye, Daniel, 345, 349, 363–80
International Court, 356
Iran
    American companies in, 200
    and arms for American hostages in Lebanon,
        3, 220, 224, 226–28, 230–33, 290–91, 293,
        296–303
    anti-government demonstrations in, 139
    arms embargo against, 218, 239
    attacks against Americans in, 134–36
    covert missions to, 1–5, 28, 254–69, 271, 277–
        78, 315–17, 319–20, 344
    and Dawa 17, 300–302, 305–8
    fall of Shah, 147, 193
    government corruption in, 122–23, 139
    importance of to U.S. interests, 355
    political factions in, 225–27, 287–88, 314–15,
        338
    Project Peace Crown and, 114, 118
    Richard Secord as MAAG chief in, 119–38
    response to Soviet intervention in
        Afghanistan, 131, 133–34, 139
    threats to from the Soviet Union, 227
    U.S. arms sales to, 126, 132, 186–87, 217–46,
        249, 252–64, 269–71, 274, 276, 278–317
    and war against the Kurds, 47–53
    war with Iraq, 1, 163, 167, 192, 207, 222–23,
        228–29, 234, 257–58, 287–88, 290–91, 296–
        98, 309, 322, 325, 338
    weaponry of, 227
    White Revolution in, 121
Iran-Contra, 189
    critics of, 260
    and death of William Casey, 234
    constitutionality of, 354–55, 357
    funding for, 363–80
    impounding of Lake Resources funds, 309

international arms sales to Iran, 228
justification of, 353–59
and KGB, 302
KL–43 transmitting devices, 246
media coverage of, 33, 321, 324–26, 328–30, 357
Oliver North proposes funding scheme for, 229
presidential finding on Iran Initiative, 238
Saudia Arabian arms sales to Contras, 211
and George Schultz, 310
and Terry Waite, 313–14
*Washington Post* criticism of Richard Secord, 288
Iran-Contra Hearings, 34, 301, 326–27, 328–30, 333, 337–39, 354–55
and Khashoggi-Ghorbanifar arms sales financing, 284
and the quality of arms sold to the Contras, 276
Robert McFarlane's testimony at, 256
Iranian Hostage Crisis, 139–41, 241, 270
rescue attempts during, 147–65, 202
Iran Initiative, 217–46, 249, 252–64, 269–71, 274, 276, 278–317, 356–57
White House coverup of, 326–35, 337–43, 345, 357
Iraq
defeat in Desert Storm, 71
and the Kurds, 47–53, 123
intelligence gathering of, 229
invades Kuwait, 108
Soviet influence in, 123
war with Iran, 1, 163, 167, 192, 207, 222–23, 228–29, 234, 257–58, 287–88, 290–91, 296–98, 309, 322, 325, 338
weaponry of, 175
Islamic Republican Party (IRP), 287–88
Israel
and CIA aid for Kurds, 123
contacts with the post-revolutionary Iranian government, 165
covert mission to Iran of, 1–5, 28, 254–69, 271, 277–78, 315–17, 319–20, 344
and Iran-Contra investigation, 345, 349
and Iran Initiative, 217–46, 249, 252–64, 269–71, 274, 276, 278–317, 357, 368, 369, 370, 371, 374
and Iran Initiative coverup, 332–33, 341
and Iran-Iraq war, 234
invades Lebanon, 174–79, 192
and occupied territories, 183
and rejection of the "President's Peace Initiative," 191
and sale of AWACS to Saudia Arabia, 166–74, 183–84, 189, 192–93
and support for the Contras, 243, 332
and sale of F–16s to Pakistan, 193–95
and Yom Kippur War, 112–13
Israeli Defense Force, 113

Jack, Chet, 27
Jacobsen, David, 237, 269, 296–98, 307, 309–14, 316, 318–20

Janis, Richard, 323
Japan, 291
Jenko, Lawrence, 280–82, 285, 297
Johnson, Lyndon Baines, 51, 53, 103, 354
decides not to seek reelection, 90
and U.S. tactics in the Vietnam War, 90, 111
Joint Chiefs of Staff
blamed for losing the Vietnam War, 111
and Nixon's Christmas bombings, 105–8
Jones, David, 116, 118, 175–76
and Iranian hostage rescue missions, 148–50, 153, 162–64
and sale of AWACS to Saudia Arabia, 168–69
Jones, Mick, 24
Jordan, 175, 228

Kangarlu, Mosen, 30, 221, 224, 245, 252–55, 287–88, 291–94, 299
"Kangaroo," 221
Karubi, Ayatollah, 226
Kecker, John, 337–38
*Keeper of the Keys* (John Prados), 354
Kelly, John, 102, 310–11, 313
Kennedy, John Fitzgerald, 25, 111, 330
assassination of, 47
and Cuban missile crisis, 44, 46, 57
and Operation Farmgate, 29
and U.S. involvement in Vietnam, 32
Kennedy, Robert, 91
Kertez, George, 138
KGB, 302, 319
Khashoggi, Adnan, 283–84, 292, 303–4, 308
Khatemi, General, 121, 124
Khomeini, Ayatollah, 122, 139, 141, 147, 161–62, 192, 238, 241, 253, 290–91, 314, 320–22
theory of entrapment by, 335, 338
and American hostages in Lebanon, 268
and Israel, 223
and U.S. covert mission to Tehran, 269
Khrushchev, Nikita, 46
Kilburn, Peter, 263, 270
Kimche, David, 22, 220–21, 223–24, 226
King, Ben, 27, 46
King, Martin Luther, Jr., 91
Kirk, Tom, 116
Kissinger, Henry, 133, 216, 236, 260, 268
negotiations to end Vietnam War, 103, 104, 105, 108–9
KL–43, 245–46
Koch, Noel, 170, 303
Korea, South, 228
Korean War, 11–12, 19–20, 53, 109
Korel Assets, 365
Kurdistan, 46
Kurds
and aid from the CIA, 123
description of, 46
insurgency into Iran by, 47–53
Kuwait, 355
and Dawa 17, 300–302, 305–8
invaded by Iraq, 108
liberated in Desert Storm, 109
Ky, Nguyen Cao, 29, 55

Lair, William (Bill), 57, 59–60, 63, 65, 71–72, 97

and Commando Club at Site 85, 74–75, 82, 87–88, 92
Laird, Melvin, 102–7, 109
Lake Resources, Inc., 220, 249, 261, 308–9, 338, 348
Landry, Lloyd (Pat), 57, 59–60, 67–68, 70–72
and the Battle for Site 85, 82–86, 89, 92
Laos
  CIA in, 56–92
  escalation of war in, 75
  POWs rescued in, 65–70
  U.S. military in, 97
  See also Pathet Lao
Lapidot, Amos, 221
Laredo, Tex., 20–22
Lebanon
  American hostages in, 3, 220, 224, 226–28, 230–33, 266–67, 269, 290–91, 293, 296–303
  Islamic revolutionaries in, 224
  Israelis invade, 174–79, 192
  U.S. Marines in, 177–79, 199
  weaponry of, 175
Ledeen, Michael, 23, 223–24, 226–27, 230
LeMay, Curtis, 31
Lenahan, Rod, 158, 162
Lennon, John, 52
Lewis, Sam, 175–76, 178
Libya, 270
Lilac, Bob, 202
Liman, Arthur, 339, 342, 345, 381–85
Lincoln, Abraham, 354
Linebacker One Campaign, 103
Linebacker II, 106–8, 109–10
"Line One," 225–26
"Line Two," 225–26, 227
"Line Three," 225–26
Litton, 127
Lockheed, 127
Los Angeles Times, 354
Lubbock, Tex., 159–60
Ludendorff, Erich, 113

MacArthur, Douglas, 109
McBride, General, 118
McDonald, Don, 105
McDonnell Douglas, 143–45
McFarlane, Robert, 165
  and American hostages in Lebanon, 230–33
  and covert air support for the Contras, 216–17
  covert mission to Tehran of, 1–5, 27, 259–63, 265–69, 271, 319–20, 344, 388, 388n
  guilty plea of, 348
  Iran-Contra testimony of, 346
  and Iran Initiative, 23, 218–19, 223, 229–31, 232–33, 270–71, 283, 285, 340–44
  and Iran Initiative coverup, 327–28, 340–42
  and pressure from Ronald Reagan to free hostages, 270
  suicide attempt of, 346
McGovern, George, 105
McMahon, John, 158–59, 164, 235
McNamara, Robert, 58, 70–72, 89
McNamara, Terry, 311, 313
Madrid, 222

Mahabad Republic, 47
Marcos, Ferdinand, 133
Marines, U.S.
  in Iranian hostage rescue attempt, 151–52
  in Lebanon, 177–79, 199
  in Vietnam, 40–42, 53
Martin, Ron, 210, 212, 248, 274–75
Marwais Corporation, 202
Media
  and American hostages in Lebanon, 270, 311–13
  and arms for hostages, 316–20
  and arms sales to Iran, 257–58
  and coverage of the Iranian hostage rescue attempt, 148
  and coverage of the Kurds during Desert Storm, 46
  and coverage of U.S. support for the Contras, 204
  and covert air support for the Contras, 216, 248
  and ideology of Ronald Reagan, 171
  and Iran-Contra, 33, 288, 296, 303, 315–16, 321, 324–26, 328–30, 357
  and Iran Initiative, 284–86
  and Israeli invasion of Lebanon, 176
  publishing secret documents by, 240
  and Saudia Arabian arms sales to the Contras, 211
  and sale of AWACS to Saudi Arabia, 183–84, 189, 192–93
  and Vietnam War, 42, 108, 110, 183–84
  and Watergate, 183–84
  and Edwin Wilson affair, 19, 187–88, 190–91, 193
Meese, Edwin, 192, 254–55, 310, 315–16
  and disavowal of the Iran Initiative, 294–95
  and Iran Initiative coverup, 329–35, 338, 342–43, 345, 349
Meir, Golda, 113
Men of Zeal (George Mitchell and William Cohen), 345
Meo, 75, 77–78, 80–82, 85–87, 91
"Merchant," 220
Meron, Mendy, 176–77, 221, 223, 244, 340
MiG-21, 145–46
Miles, Ken, 120
Milken, Michael, 339
Minh, Ho Chi, 58
Mitchell, George, 345
Momyer, General, 84–85, 91
Montazari, Ayatollah, 314–15
Moses, Judy, 242, 349
Motorola of Israel, 200
Mountbatten, Lord, 31
Moyers, Bill, 354
Mubarak, Hosni, 147
Mundell, Major General, 24–25, 52, 147
Murphy, Anne Marion, 297
Mushavi, Prime Minister, 224, 259, 268
Muskie, Edmund, 337

NASA, 117
Nasser, Gamal Abdul, 101, 145, 147

National Security Council, 354
Naval War College, 100–101
Navy, U.S., 58
Neutrality Act, 216, 235–36
*New York Times*, 211
Nicaragua and support for Contras, 203–19, 233, 235–37, 243, 246–52
Nicaraguan Democratic Force (FDN), 204, 215, 251, 272, 277
Nields, John, 338–45, 365, 381–85
Nimrodi, Yakov, 220–32, 238, 243
Nir, Amiram
  covert mission to Tehran of, 1–5, 265, 269, 387–89
  death of, 349
  and Iran-Contra investigation, 332–33, 335, 345, 349
  and Iran Initiative, 26, 241–45, 252–57, 259, 320, 326
Nitze, Paul, 66
Nixon, Richard M., 125, 183, 330
  and Cambodian offensive, 98
  visits China, 101
  reelection of, 102, 105
  resignation of, 117
  and Vietnam War, 97, 102–10
Noriega, Manuel, 348
North, Oliver, 165
  and William Casey, 246
  and covert air support for the Contras, 211–14, 216–17, 233, 235–36, 243, 246
  covert mission to Tehran of, 1–5, 259–63, 265–66, 269
  dismissal of, 332–34
  home security system of, 344, 347–48
  and Iran-Contra investigation, 33, 324–27, 329, 331–36
  Iran-Contra testimony of, 346–47
  and Iran Initiative, 2, 217–20, 222–26, 227–29, 270–71, 279–86, 288–305, 357
  and ransom money for hostages, 266, 269
  and sale of AWACS to Saudia Arabia, 173, 202
  solicits military support for the Contras, 202–11
  trial of, 347
  *Under Fire*, 347
Northrop, 127
North Vietnamese Army (NVA), 28, 103–4
  air strike of, 79–81
  and Ho Chi Minh Trail, 57, 60–61, 70–73
  in Laos, 62–73
  Dr Pepper strikes against, 62
  and Site 85, 75–92
  strategy of, 76
  Tet offensive of, 78, 81–82, 89, 91, 103
  weapons of, 33

Odom, William, 158
O'Donnell, Ed, 166
Oil Embargo, 113, 183
Oman Access Accords, 174
O'Neil, Sam, 295
OPEC, 183
Operation Farmgate, 29–43

Operation Jungle Jim, 24–29, 147, 166
Operation Lam Son 713, 103
*Out of Control* (Leslie Cockburn), 348

Pahlevi, Ashraf, 122
Pahlevi, Farah, 125
Pahlevi, Muhammad Reza Shah, 47–51, 147, 153, 186, 228, 240, 259, 295, 307, 322
  death of, 161
  and MAAG operations in Iran, 119–41
  and Project Peace Crown, 114
Pahlevi, Reza, 136–38, 141, 159
Pakistan, 193–95, 355
Palestinian Liberation Organization (PLO), 177–79
Panama, 50, 164
Pao, Vang, 61–65, 83, 85, 87, 90
Pasdaran, 288
Pastora, Eden, 215, 277–78
Pathet Lao, 31, 61, 66–67, 77. *See also* Laos
Patton, Boggs & Blow, 216
Patton, George, 13, 109
Peace Sun, 143
Peet, Ray, 112–14, 127
Pentagon
  and the Iranian hostage rescue attempt, 148, 150
  budget lobbying of, 101–2
  command structure at, 101
  rejects Vietnam cease fire, 103–5
Peres, Shimon, 2, 221, 230, 241, 243, 387
  and arms sales to Iran, 292–95
  and Iran Initiative coverup, 332, 357
Perot, H. Ross, 266, 269
Pershing, John, 150
Phoenix Missile, 126
Phouma, Souvanna, 88
Piper Cub, 17, 19
Piza, Ben, 214
Pizzy, Alan, 184–85, 188–89, 196
Plank, Bill, 88
Poe, Tony, 92
Poindexter, John
  covert mission to Tehran, 265, 267–68, 387
  and ransom money for hostages, 266, 269
  and Iran-Contra investigation 326–29, 339–40, 340–41, 343
  Iran-Contra testimony of, 346
  and Iran Initiative, 32, 236–41, 254, 256, 258, 309–10, 316, 319–20
  resignation of, 330–32
  trial of, 347
Poland, 209
Portugal, 207, 218–19, 221–22, 228, 340
Powers, Francis Gary, 29, 227
Prados, John, 354
"President's Peace Initiative," 191
Price, Theodore (Doc), 194–95
Prisoners of War, 65–70, 109
Project IBEX, 131–32, 134
Project Peace Crown, 114, 118
Project Tipped Kettle, 177, 218
Prostitution, 55
*Pueblo*, U.S.S., 81

Qaddafi, Muammar, 184
Quintero, Rafael (Ralph), 207–8, 210, 211–14,
    236, 272–74, 276, 312–13, 357

Rabbii, General, 129–30, 136–38, 141, 147, 186
Rabin, Yitzhak, 218, 230, 340
Race Riots in United States Cities, 54–55
Rafsanjani, Hashemi
    and the Iran Initiative, 226, 256, 259, 268,
        279, 296, 302, 305, 308, 319–20, 322
    in Iranian politics, 287–88, 314–15
Ransom, David, 310–12
Rate-Aided Manually Initiated Tracking
    (RAMIT), 127
Rather, Dan, 184, 196
Raytheon, 283
Reagan, Ronald, 16, 193, 216, 229
    appoints Iran-Contra special prosecutor, 336
    and covert air support for Contras, 236, 250,
        274, 276
    described, 191–92
    inauguration of, 166
    and denial of Iran Initiative, 319, 321, 323–26
    and Iranian hostage crisis, 163–65, 241, 270
    and Iran Initiative coverup, 328–35, 337–43,
        345
    Iran Initiative of, 1–5, 33, 165, 232, 234, 237,
        238–41, 245, 288, 291–94, 296, 299–317,
        319–21, 323–25, 327, 355
    and policy in Lebanon, 178
    media coverage of, 184
    and "President's Peace Initiative," 191
    praises Oliver North, 334
    and pressure to free hostages, 230, 233, 237,
        269–70
    and sale of AWACS to Saudia Arabia, 169–74,
        183
    supports Contras, 203–4, 207
    and terrorism, 217
Red Teams, 128
Reed, Frank, 269, 298, 307
Reese Air Force Base, 159–60
Regan, Don, 321, 324, 329
"The Relative," 279, 282–83, 285
    and arms sales to Iran, 3, 287–90, 292, 294–
        96, 298–309, 318–20, 322
Rennenkampf, General, 113
Resaii, Mohsen, 315
Reynolds, Bradford, 331–32
Rheault, Colonel, 48
Ri, Bac, 63, 65
Riots in United States Cities, 54–55
Robello, Alfonso, 251
Roberts, John, 137
Robinette, Glenn, 277–78, 344, 347–48
Robinson, Aubrey, 337
Rodriguez, Felix, 248, 272–76, 377, 378
Roosevelt, Franklin D., 288, 354
Route 602, 78–79, 86, 91
Rowland, Tiny, 304
Royal Laotian Air Force (RLAF), 62. See also
    Laos
Rudman, Warren, 343, 345
Runways in Vietnam, 33–34, 38–39

Sadat, Anwar, 101, 145, 147, 167
Saderholm, Pete, 85
Saigon, 55, 117
Samsonov, General, 113
Sandinistas
    and infiltration of the Contras, 211
    seize power in Nicaragua, 203
    war with Contras, 212, 215, 251, 276–77
Sandino, Augusto, 203
Saudi Arabia, 355
    and arms sales to the Contras, 211
    and support for Contras, 250–51, 262
    sale of AWACS to, 166–74, 183–84, 189, 192–
        93
    sale of F–15s to, 143–45, 193
    terrorism in, 314
    terrorist attacks against, 301
    weaponry of, 175
Sawyer, Buzz, 295
Say, Peggy, 270
Schlachter, Douglas, 184–85, 196–97
Schlesinger, James, 112–15, 127, 173
Schriebman, Robert, 354
Schultz, George, 198
    and Iran-Contra, 310
    and nine-point plan with Iran, 323
    and Iran Initiative, 232, 234, 301, 322–23,
        325, 332
    relationship of with Israel, 191
    and Saudi Arabian support for Contras, 251
Schwarzkopf, Norman, 71, 109
Schwimmer, Al, 219–24, 226, 228, 230–33
Scowcroft, Brent, 337
Seaman, Tom, 158
Secord, Jim, 9
Secord, Jo Ann, 23–27, 29, 44, 46, 54, 96, 116,
    119, 122, 138–39, 192, 199, 296
Secord, John, 97, 119, 199, 346–47
Secord, Julia, 46, 54, 96, 119, 199, 325, 346
Secord, Laura, 9, 97, 119, 199, 346
Secord, Lowell, 9–11, 14, 138
Secord, Mack, 102
Secord, Richard
    at Air Command and Staff College, 53
    as Air Force flight instructor, 20–23
    Air Force flight school training of, 17–20
    at Air Force International Programs, 142–49,
        163, 166
    on George Bush, 191, 280
    meetings with Adolfo Calero, 204–6
    on William Casey, 191
    childhood of, 9–12
    as CIA detailee in Laos, 53–92
    code name of, 206
    and command of the 603rd Special Operations
        Squadron, 98–100
    and Commando Club at Site 85, 74–92
    and covert air support for Contras, 206–11,
        211–18, 233, 235–37, 243, 246–52
    and covert mission to Tehran, 1–5, 28, 254–
        69, 271, 277–78, 315–17, 319–20, 344, 387–
        89
    criticism of role in Iran-Contra, 288
    defamation suit against Leslie Cockburn, 348

at Defense Security Assistance Agency, 112–16, 118
as deputy assistant secretary of defense, 170–97
as deputy commander of the 29th Flying Training Wing, 116–19
diversion of Iranian funds to the Contras, 331
education at George Washington University, 101
education at the University of Oklahoma, 22–24
education at West Point, 12–16, 22, 26, 39, 52
on *The Fall of Site 85*, 78
on Manucher Ghorbanifar, 224–25
partnership with Albert Hakim, 199–202, 206–9, 248–49, 365, 377
and investigation of Project Peace Crown in Iran, 114, 118
and Iranian hostage rescue missions, 148–65
and Iran-Contra investigation, 336–51
Iran-Contra testimony of, 342–46
Iranian military mission of, 48–51
and Iran Initiative, 217–46, 249, 252–64, 269–71, 274, 276, 278–317
service in Laos, 4
and lawsuit charging illegal activities with the Contras, 277–78
letters defending, 363–80, 381–85
as MAAG chief in Iran, 119–38
on Robert McFarlane, 216
marriage of, 26
military decorations of, 42, 92, 195
on Yakov Nimrodi, 225
and Nixon's Christmas bombings, 102–10
initial contacts with Oliver North about support for Contras, 202–6, 277, 286
on Oliver North, 279, 316
participation in Project Jungle Jim, 24–29
Pentagon duty of, 166
plea bargain of, 347–48
on John Poindexter, 236
POW rescue of, 65–70
on Ronald Reagan, 191–92
retirement of, 195, 198–99
secret military flight missions in Vietnam, 27–43
service and awards of, 391
meetings with the Shah of Iran, 123–25, 130, 136–37
suit brought by Eugene Hasenfus, 348
training at the Naval War College, 100–101
on Vietnam War, 41–42, 110–11
and Edwin Wilson affair, 184–93, 195–97, 378
Secord, Sandra, 9
Secord, Vernon, 9
Secord, Wahneta, 9–10
Seek Sentry, 126–28, 132
Semi-Automated Ground Environment (SAGE), 127
Shackley, Theodore (Ted), 56–59, 70–72, 78, 81–82, 89–92, 97, 185, 220
Shakespeare, William, 5, 184
Shamir, Yitzhak, 191, 230, 294, 332, 357
Sharon, Ariel, 174–79, 192, 193, 233

Sheehan, Daniel, 277
Shelton, "Wee Willy," 21–22
Sick, Gary, 164
Sikorsky, Igor, 147
Silkwood, Karen, 277
Simpson, Bill, 48
Simpson, Captain, 42
Singlaub, John, 65, 204–6, 209–11, 320, 365, 381–82
Site 85, Battle for, 75–92
Smith, Woben, 245–46
Southeast Asia Coordination (SEACOR), 58–59
Southerland, James, 237, 297–98, 311, 320
Southern Air Transport, 348, 369, 374
South Vietnamese Air Force (VNAF), 27, 29–31, 34, 42, 55
Soviet Union
    invades Afghanistan, 131–34
    backs foreign wars, 174
    Caribbean encroachment of, 199
    attempts to spread communism worldwide, 47
    influence in Iraq, 123
    and Iran, 227, 322
    and Iran Initiative, 265, 302
    and Iran-Iraq war, 234, 237, 287–88, 290–91, 325
    aids Iraq, 228
    attempts to secure Kurdish independence, 47–48
    Middle East interests of, 125
    military strategy of, 125
    aids Nicaragua, 203, 206
    U.S. attempts to limit expansion of in Persian Gulf, 121
    weaponry of, 227
Spain, 228
Spencer, Thomas, 348
Sporkin, Stanley, 239–40, 286, 327, 341
Stanford Technology Corporation (STC), 200–201
Stanford Technology Trading Group International (STTGI), 201, 206, 218, 279, 289–90, 308, 337
Starbird, Lieutenant General, 71–72
Starline International, 223
"Star Wars," 227–28, 291
Steele, Jim, 273, 276
Stewart, Jimmy, 59
Stockholm Syndrome, 313
Stokes, Louis, 345
Strategic Integrated Operations Plan (SIOP), 107
Strong, Morgan, 319
Su, Captain, 55
Sullivan, William, 104, 120, 140–41
    as ambassador to Iran, 133–35
    and military operations in Laos, 75–79, 88–89, 91
Sultan, Prince, 167–68
Supreme War Council, 288
Swasey, J.R., 54–56, 153
Swiss Air, 374
Symington, Stuart, 61
Syria
    and American hostages in Lebanon, 280, 285, 297, 312

and Iran Initiative, 319
and Israeli invasion of Lebanon, 176
terrorist activities of, 297
and Yom Kippur War, 113

T–6G (Texan), 17–18
Tadayon, General, 121, 124, 126, 128–29, 131, 136, 272
Taft, Will, IV, 188–90, 192–93
Taiwan, 262
Tambs, Lewis, 272
Tannenberg, Battle of, 113
Taylor, Maxwell, 111
Tehran, Covert mission to, 1–5, 28, 254–69, 271, 277–78, 315–17, 319–20, 344, 387–89
Teicher, Howard, 2–5, 263, 326–27, 340
Temple, Tom, 30
Terrorism
    against Saudi Arabia, 301
    threats against Oliver North, 344
    threats to Israel, 175
    in Iran, 134–36, 217, 239
    by Iranians, 314
    in Lebanon, 177–79
    by Libya, 270
    in Middle East, 192
    by Syria, 297
Tet Offensive, 78, 81–82, 89, 91, 103
Texas, 222
Texas National Guard, 160
Thailand, 56, 58, 61, 67
Thatcher, Margaret, 297
Thieu, Nguyen Van, 103–5, 107–8
Tho, Le Duc, 103, 109
Thompson, Paul, 237, 239, 330
Thornburgh, Richard, 350
Three Mile Island, 277
Tillman, Arnie, 48
Toodle, Lyn, 2, 262–63, 267
Toufanian, General, 120, 127
Tower, John, 337
Tower Commission, 262, 282, 296, 337, 340, 346, 354
Train, Harry, 102, 105
Trible, Paul, 343, 345
Truman, Harry S., 12, 14, 47, 325, 330
Tudeh, 134–36
Turkey, 222, 355
Turner, Stansfield, 53, 158–59

Udall, Morris, 214
Udall Corporation, 214
Udall Research Corporation, 249, 338
Under Fire (Oliver North), 347
United Nations
    and Arab-Israeli peace, 191
    and Israeli policy in occupied territories, 183
    and multinational peacekeeping force in Lebanon, 177–79
United States
    arms for hostages, 3, 220, 224, 226–28, 230–33, 290–91, 293, 296–303
    covert support for the Contras, 203–19, 233, 235–37, 243, 246–52

overthrows Ngo Dinh Diem, 47
energy crisis in, 113
foreign military sales by, 142–47, 185–88, 193–95, 201, 207, 209, 239, 256
covert mission to Iran of, 1–5, 28, 254–69, 271, 277–78, 315–17, 319–20, 344
Iranian arms embargo of, 218, 239
Iranian dissidents in, 137
Iranian MAAG operations of, 119–38
sale of F–14s to Iran, 126
helps Iran repel Kurdish insurgency, 47–53
relations with Israel under Ariel Sharon, 174–79
Oman Access Accords, 174
invasion of Panama, 50
political problems of, 358
sale of AWACS to Saudi Arabia, 166–74, 183–84, 189, 192–93
secret missions to Vietnam, 27–43
University of Oklahoma, 22–24
U.S. News and World Report, 338
U.S./Oman Access Accords, 174

Van Atta, Dale, 303
Vance, Cyrus, 148
Vandenburg, Sandy, 120
Vaught, Jim, 149–52, 155–59, 161–62
Viet Cong, 27, 48, 55, 216
    "civic action" initiatives by, 49
    destruction of, 103
    and Ho Chi Minh Trail, 57
    and Operation Farmgate, 29–30, 35, 37–39, 41
    weapons of, 33
Vietnam
    aircraft runways in, 33–34, 38–39
    military life in, 39–40, 55
    secret missions to, 27–43
    See also North Vietnamese Army; South Vietnamese Airforce; Viet Cong; Vietnam War
Vietnamization, 103
Vietnam War
    bombing of Hanoi, 58
    U.S. commanders in, 96–97, 105–8, 110–11
    U.S. command structure during, 58–59
    fall of Saigon, 117
    mining of Haiphong Harbor, 101, 103, 203
    overthrow of Ngo Dinh Diem, 47
    Commando Club bombing operation, 74
    end to U.S. ground combat role, 102
    cease fire in, 103–4, 109
    Christmas bombings of, 102–10
    CIA involvement in, 53–92
    "civic action" initiatives in, 49
    Dr Pepper strategy of U.S. commanders in, 62
    escalation of, 51, 53
    Iron Triangle offensive, 58
    media coverage of, 42, 108, 110, 183–84
    U.S. military planning in, 40–42
    U.S. Navy in, 58
    POWs in, 109
    protests against, 54, 97
    rescue of POWs in, 65–70
    Soviet influence on U.S. strategy in, 104, 106–7

stalemate in, 103
U.S. strategy in, 70–71
Tet offensive of, 78, 81–82, 89, 91, 103
U.S. troops withdrawn from, 109
Vinh, Colonel, 55
Von Marbod, Eric, 188
Vorys, James, 11
Vuy, "Flash," 31

Waite, Terry, 310–11, 313–14
Walsh, Lawrence, 336–38, 342, 350–51, 357
War and Multigenerational Ethnic Conflicts, 50
Washburn, Evan, 82–83, 85–88
*Washington Post*, 191, 195, 288
Watergate, 101, 105, 112, 117, 183, 189, 240,
    326, 328–29, 343
Weaponry
    of the Contras, 207, 209
    used in Iran against Kurdish insurgents, 49–50
    use of in Vietnam, 37
    *See also* individual countries
Weinberger, Caspar, 165, 175–76, 188–90, 191,
    193, 195, 198, 220, 233
    indictment of, 350

and Iran Initiative, 232, 234, 328
and U.S. policy in Lebanon, 178
and sale of AWACS to Saudia Arabia, 170, 173
Weir, Benjamin, 224, 228, 309–10
West, Bing, 170, 175
West Germany, 228
Westinghouse, 127, 200
Westmoreland, William, 111
West Point, 12–16, 22, 26, 39, 52
White Revolution in Iran, 121
Whitman, Walt, 24
Wilson, Charles, 194–95
Wilson, Edwin, 199, 207, 209, 273, 326, 329,
    331, 334, 335–36, 338–39, 344
    relationship with Richard Secord, 184–93,
    195–97, 378
Wilson, Joe, 97
Wilson, Woodrow, 354
Wright, Jim, 329

Yom Kippur War, 112–13

Zahedi, Ardeshir, 141
Zucker, Willard (Bill), 200, 209, 249, 331, 339
Zumwalt, Elmo, 112